Inuit Morality Play

Inuit Morality Play

The Emotional Education

of a Three-Year-Old

Jean L. Briggs

Yale University Press

New Haven and London

Published with assistance from the Mary Cady Tew Memorial Fund.

Printed in the United States of America.

Library of Congress Cataloging-in-Publication Data
Briggs, Jean L., 1929–
Inuit morality play : the emotional education of a three-year-old / Jean L. Briggs.
p.   cm.
Includes bibliographical references (p.   ).
ISBN 0-300-07237-6 (alk. paper)
1. Inuit children—Psychology.   2. Inuit Children—Attitudes.   3. Inuit—social life and customs.   4. Socialization—Northwest Territories—Baffin Island.   5. Social skills in children—Northwest Territories—Baffin Island.   6. Baffin Island (N.W.T.)—social life and customs.   I. Title.
E99.E7B744   1998
971.9′50049712—dc21   97-32605
                                                                      CIP

A catalogue record for this book is available from the British Library.

The paper in this book meets the guidelines for permanence and durability of the Committee on Production Guidelines for Book Longevity of the Council on Library Resources.

10   9   8   7   6   5   4   3   2   1

For Don Handelman
who begat this book

and for Chubby Maata
who is *the book*

Contents

Acknowledgments

It is difficult to set boundaries around the influences that help to shape an observational study of individual lives and the way those lives interact. At one level, a book like this one is a product of a lifetime of experience, multifaceted and tangled, a lifetime during which the author-to-be has grown both sensitivities and blindnesses through incorporating and transforming messages of all shapes and sizes in encounters of all sorts—just like the protagonist of her book. Thus the net of gratitude is spread wide. I first and most profoundly appreciate those who have been, wittingly or not, my educators: the families, teachers, students, colleagues, and friends who have inhabited and helped to create the emotional-cognitive-moral world I live in and contributed to shaping my own perspectives on that world.

I am fortunate in having been provided with five highly nurturant environments. Four of these are universities: Tromsø and Bergen in Norway, the Hebrew University of Jerusalem, and most fundamentally, my home university, the Memorial University of Newfoundland. All of these places are populated by scholars good to think with and friends good to be with. (There's a good deal of overlap between these two categories.) In addition, Memorial and its Institute of Social and Economic Research generously funded by far the largest part of the fieldwork and data processing I did for thirty years, gave me the time in which to do that work, administered funds that originated with the Izaak Walton Killam Foundation and the Social Science Research Council of Canada, and in every way smoothed my path. The fifth environment is the Interdisciplinary Colloquium on Psychoanalysis and Anthropology, a group of culturally aware psycho-analysts and psychologists, and anthropologists who study psychological ques-tions, which meets annually for four days of discussion under the aegis of the American Psychoanalytic Association. Since 1971, I have attended almost every year, have presented my data on Inuit emotional structure and childrearing three times, and have benefited greatly from all the discussions.

I have been equally fortunate in the "bad" experiences that have come my way: experiences of standing on peripheries—not least, the trial of being ostracized while living with an Inuit family—which honed my powers of observation and ultimately produced *Never in Anger*.

The book is a child of *Never in Anger*, the offspring of more than three decades of experiencing and puzzling about Inuit emotional life and socializa-tion. So my Utkuhikhalingmiut family in Chantrey Inlet and my associates in Qipisa—the list headed by a little girl I call Chubby Maata—are among my most valued teachers. My Utkuhikhalingmiut mother and father and the mothers and fathers of Qipisa all gave me an enduring admiration for the sensitivity and wisdom of Inuit parenting, and Chubby Maata made it abun-dantly clear that these qualities are not the exclusive property of parents; her perspicacity, imagination, and charm did much to reconcile me to the unavoid-able vicissitudes of childhood everywhere. I am grateful to her and I love her for being herself and for admitting me—however ambivalently—into her world, and I am grateful to her parents for tolerating my presence, which was not always easy for them.

The inside experience and insights of two other Inuit friends, Minnie Aodla Freeman and Rachel Qitsualik Tinsley, have gone a long way toward filling the lacunae in my outsider's understanding of the meanings of events and words. To them, too, *quyannamik atsualuk*.

In my western worlds, the following individuals deserve special mention for seeding, fertilizing, watering, and helping to shape the bonsai that is my view of Chubby Maata's three-year-old life. I list them in chronological order.

Hanne Haavind's stimulating insights into the meanings of my dramatic socialization data during a series of seminars I gave in Tromsø in 1976 left a lasting impression, which bore me forward long after I returned to Canada.

I learned from Don Handelman in Jerusalem during every meeting of the course we taught together in 1980–1981 on the anthropology of play and in particular my Inuit dramas, and every time we walked home together afterward across the Valley of the Cross; but one suggestion is especially memorable because it opened to me a whole new way of working: "Why don't you take one sequence of dramas, played in the course of one evening, and see whether you can find cumulative messages in that sequence?"

Six years later, Jan-Petter Blom concluded my series of seminars in Bergen and set me on another productive course by contradicting me: "You do have a theory. You just said, 'Inuit culture is a mosaic of dilemmas.'"

Later in the same year, when, struggling to find a way to present those dilemmas, I wildly proposed writing the book entirely about one drama, Elliot Mishler remarked, "It does sound as though one drama were a microcosm of Inuit society."

Robert Paine said, "Just keep writing. If it doesn't work, try something else." I followed that excellent advice for ten years.

An invitation to present my ideas about "the collectivity and the individual" at a meeting of the Society for Psychological Anthropology in 1989 forced me to think through those ideas in a more general and organized way; and Peggy Miller's appreciation encouraged me to develop them.

Stuart Pierson, historian and renaissance man, upon reading the first draft of the Introduction, endeavored to inoculate me against dead words that ended in "-ion" and upstart words like "focus," and shared with me his passion for Fowler and his respect for the English language.

Don Handelman, faithful friend and supporter, two decades after the first seed germinated, bolstered sagging determination by confessing to a certain impatience: "I don't believe you *will* finish."

And when the book was *almost* finished in 1996, the informal discussion of the manuscript in a study group consisting of Nancy Chodorow, Hanne Haavind, Arlie Hochschild, and Barrie Thorne, which was taped for my benefit, gave me the final spurt of energy and inspiration that enabled me to prove Don's not-unreasonable prediction wrong.

Don Handelman and Sharon Roseman took precious time from their own scholarly activities to render detailed, thoughtful, and challenging commentaries on the entire book. I am in their debt—all the more so because a stubborn desire that Chubby Maata should see the light of day in my lifetime made it impossible for me to incorporate many of their suggestions. I have stored their observations and criticisms for future thought and use.

I am also indebted to Terrence Murphy, Memorial University's dean of arts, and to Gladys Topkis, acquisitions editor at Yale University Press, for their unflagging support of this book. They opened, and kept open, Chubby Maata's passage through the mazes of publication, patiently enduring interminable queries along the way. My nephew Jeff Briggs, with more patience and good humor, drafted and redrafted the diagrams of dwellings to meet the specifications of his perfectionist aunt, and Charles Conway and Gary McManus of the Cartographic Laboratory of Memorial University's Department of Geography devoted the same care to the maps.

Temporally the last but in volume not the least gratitude goes to the Yale University Press editors who groomed the copy. Gladys Topkis, behind the scenes and beyond duty, and Brenda Kolb, manuscript editor, combed my prose meticulously, sensitively, and with grace, smoothing and clarifying while treading lightly on idiosyncrasies. I learned a lot from their editing, and I take full responsibility for the bumps that I insisted on reinserting.

People

All names except for my own are pseudonyms. Everybody in the camp had both Inuit and Qallunaaq (Euro-Canadian) names—often more than one of each—and both kinds were in common use, although some people were called more frequently by Inuit names, others by Qallunaaq names. In assigning pseudonyms I have followed the practice of the camp in this respect. I have chosen Qallunaaq names that were in common use in the eastern Arctic and have given them their Inuktitut shapes: Maata, Liila, Jaani, and so on. My own name also appears in its Inuktitut form: Yiini.[1] I have attached the epithet "Chubby" to Maata's name because she was often called by a descriptive nickname, and this one suits her appearance.

Ages given for children and teenagers are approximate because the data were gathered over a six-month period.

Because most of the multiple kinship relationships among the characters are not essential to the discussions in this book, because suppressing some pieces of the mosaic helps to conceal identities, and because the drama centers on Chubby Maata, individuals are identified more or less from her perspective. I say "more or less" because

Chubby Maata may have been unaware of some of the facts presented below. Moreover, like other Qipisamiut, Chubby Maata used kin terms for almost everybody, but many of these terms were "name terms" (see Chapter 4, n. 3). I judge that it would unnecessarily strain the understanding of readers to present those terms and explain those relationships here, but I do render the terms faithfully, with explanatory endnotes, when they appear in direct speech. Note also that the name "Ukaliq" is shared among several children.

For the same purpose of protecting identities, I refrain from listing all Qipisamiut and organizing them into households.

Aalami: Maata's husband
Aana: Jaani's mother; Chubby Maata's paternal grandmother
Aatami: a neighbor, age four and a half; Nivi's son
Aimu: possibly one of Chubby Maata's names
Aironi: an adult brother of Liila
Aita: Chubby Maata's not-quite-year-old sister, adopted by Arnaqjuaq
Arnaqjuaq: Liila's mother; Chubby Maata's maternal grandmother
Chubby Maata: three-year-old daughter of Jaani and Liila
Iqaluk: Jaani's father; Chubby Maata's paternal grandfather
Jaani: Chubby Maata's father
Jakupi: a man from Pangnirtung, who visited Qipisa with the game officer
Juda: Liila's ten-year-old brother
Juupi: an adult brother of Liila
Kaati: Chubby Maata's cousin and friend, age three and a half, who was
    adopted by Arnaqjuaq
Lia: a name wrongly or playfully claimed by Chubby Maata
Liila: Chubby Maata's mother
Liitia: a young Pangnirtung woman not living in the camp
Liuna: Liila's fourteen-year-old sister
Luisa: Liila's nineteen-year-old sister
Luki: a two-year-old boy not living in the camp
Luukasi: Jaani's two-year-old brother
Maata: a neighbor of Chubby Maata; adopted daughter of Natsiq
Malvina: Chubby Maata (her other English name)
Matiiusi: Jaani's sixteen-year-old brother
Miali: a neighbor; Nivi's daughter, age eight and a half
Miika: a neighbor; Rota's daughter, age four and a half
Mitaqtuq: Liila's father and Chubby Maata's maternal grandfather

Natsiq: father, adoptive father, grandfather, or great-grandfather of almost everybody else in camp except Iqaluk's household

Nivi: a neighbor; daughter of Natsiq

Papi: Chubby Maata's puppy

Paulusi: a neighbor; Saali's uncle

Piita: a man from Pangnirtung visiting in Qipisa

Pitaruusi: Liila's sixteen-year-old brother

Rosi: Chubby Maata's four-year-old sister

Rota: a neighbor; adopted daughter of Natsiq

Ruupi: Jaani's fifteen-year-old sister

Saali: a neighbor; Rota's son, age three

Simioni: Chubby Maata's cousin, age one, who is visiting in Qipisa with his parents

Taina: possibly one of Chubby Maata's names

Tiimi: a neighbor

Tuuma: an adult brother of Jaani

Ukaliq: a name shared by Natsiq's deceased wife, Jaani's seven-year-old sister, Miika, Miali, and Chubby Maata

Yiini: the anthropologist

Inuit Morality Play

The Canadian Arctic

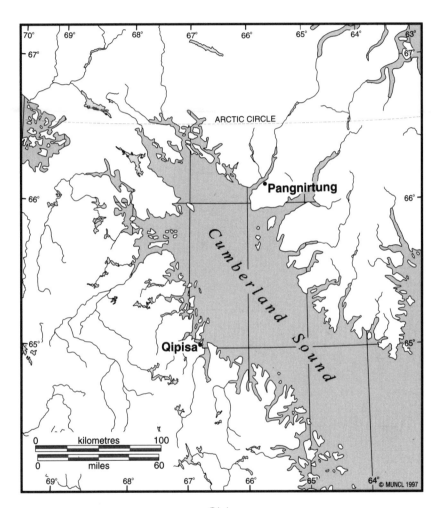

Qipisa

Introduction: Individuals
in Culture

This book is a story about six months in the life of one little girl, an Inuit child—I call her Chubby Maata—who, when I knew her, was growing up in a small hunting camp in the eastern Canadian Arctic. The book is also about Chubby Maata's society, an account of the motives, wishes, loves, and fears that drove the people who lived in that camp and, I am sure, the many others like it.[1]

Anthropologists who are interested in both the textures of individual lives and the contours of societies often experience a tension between these two concerns. One way they try to force the horns of the dilemma closer together is by inserting the definite article before the word "individual." The expression "*the* individual" directs attention to what individuals have in common and creates a homogeneous and infinitely reproducible individual to insert into society. Such a strategy reduces to a manageable quantity the amount of complex diversity that anthropologists and readers have to deal with and makes it possible to generalize about behavior within, and sometimes across, cultures—very reassuring to authors and readers in search of order.

The trouble is that when all the rich detail of individual lives, the essence of individuality, is left out, our ability to understand these lives is greatly reduced. The notion that meaning inheres in culture and that people receive it passively, as dough receives the cookie cutter, is rapidly being replaced by the idea that culture consists of ingredients, potentials, which people actively select, interpret, and use in various ways as opportunities, capabilities, and experience allow. But it is not *the* individual that creates meanings; it is individuals who do so. And to understand what a life means to the person living it, we must be able to observe the processes through which the person conceives and creates the life: its purposes and goals, dangers and desires, fears and loves. What motivates a person, cognitively and emotionally, to retain and build on *this* or *that* experience out of all those that she or he participates in, while ignoring or forgetting others? What imbues these special experiences with meaning? How are motives created? I argue that the formative experiences and the emotions they give rise to strongly influence not only the shapes of motives, wishes, and fears but also how they operate in everyday life.

But how are we to reconcile our interest in these individual activities with our uneasiness about diversity and detail? How are we to go about studying the processes by which meaning is created? Do we risk losing our grip on generalization if we attend to individual*s*? Or can bringing individuals clearly before our minds contribute to our understanding of how culture operates in persons and how persons operate with culture, each creating the other?

In this book I address these questions by following as best I can in the mindsteps of three-year-old Chubby Maata as she tries, by guess and by gorry and with remarkable acumen, to make sense of her world and to become an effective actor in that world. My aim is to demonstrate how much can be learned, both about individuals and about society, by attending to the very personal process of creating meaning. In writing this book, I have discovered that the more I follow this little girl, the more I see; and paradoxically, the more detailed my analysis of *one* event, enacted on *one* occasion with *one* child, the broader and richer becomes my vision, not only of the workings of that one child's psyche but also of the psychodynamic underpinnings of Inuit culture and the potentials for interrelationship among various bits and pieces of that culture. To the extent that the processes of Inuit psychology and culture resemble what we find elsewhere in the world, I also learn something about psychology and culture in general—how they actively reconstitute themselves and each other in the tangle of experience.

QIPISA AND ITS CHILDREN

I won't go into detail here on the social structure and values governing Inuit society; volumes have been written on those subjects. Childrearing practices in various parts of the Inuit area have also been described, and the accounts, though differing in detail, have much in common (for example, Briggs 1970, 1974, 1975, 1990; Chance 1966; Honigmann and Honigmann 1959, 1965, 1970; Freeman 1978; Hughes 1974).[2] Nevertheless, a brief introduction to Chubby Maata's camp is in order.

Qipisa was the only year-round camp on Baffin Island during the years when I visited it, and the nearest community, the town of Pangnirtung, was about a hundred miles away, across Cumberland Sound. The Qipisa people, who numbered about sixty, were seminomadic. They moved frequently in spring and summer, hunting seal in some places, hunting caribou and picking berries in others. In all these temporary camps, they lived in homemade canvas tents, traditional for many years in their part of the Arctic; but in the winter camp, which they occupied more or less from late August until sometime in April, the old-style winter tents—long, Quonset-shaped structures with wooden frames and double walls of canvas stuffed with an insulating layer of heather and heated with seal-oil lamps—were gradually giving way to flimsy one- or two-room houses of plywood, heated by fuel oil brought in from Pangnirtung by snowmobile or outboard-motor-driven canoe.

The people of Qipisa were not poor by their standards. Game was usually plentiful, and they had a considerable cash income from selling sealskins and carvings, mostly of whalebone, and from government subsidies of one sort and another. Putting together all these sources of income and sharing resources to varying degrees, they kept themselves quite well supplied with the store goods needed for camp life: fuel, ammunition, guns and motors, clothing, food and tobacco, even such luxuries as shortwave radios and tape recorders. Twice or more during the year they were physically cut off from Pangnirtung—during freeze-up in the fall and breakup in the spring, and occasionally during the winter, if winds, crosscurrents, and unexpected thaws broke up the ice—but such conditions rarely continued for more than a few weeks. While they lasted, they caused inconvenience and feelings of deprivation, especially if supplies of flour and tobacco were exhausted, but there was never a danger of starvation or of freezing to death in unheated houses; the camp had daily radio contact with Pangnirtung, and in cases of real need, the government always came to the rescue, flying in food and fuel by helicopter or plane.

Under normal circumstances, small groups of Qipisa men traveled across to Pangnirtung whenever they ran short of supplies and had the wherewithal to buy more, and Pangnirtung men also came to Qipisa to hunt and visit. Usually once a year, in August, when the sound was clear of ice and the sea calm, the women and children of Qipisa would accompany their men to visit relatives and friends in Pangnirtung. Women also went to Pangnirtung or were flown to Iqaluit to give birth; planes were sent to evacuate camp members who became seriously ill; couples went to Pangnirtung, sooner or later, to marry; and once each winter a plane carrying a government official, a nurse, and the Anglican missionary would visit Qipisa to make sure that all was well. So the people of Qipisa rarely felt really isolated. At the same time, in most respects life in the camp proceeded quite independently of Pangnirtung. The elements of foreign culture, material and otherwise, that had been incorporated were of the people's own choosing. The Qipisamiut were Anglican; the camp "leader" led religious services on Sundays and sometimes prayer meetings on Wednesday evenings, which were attended by almost everyone.[3] A few of the older children of Qipisa had attended school briefly during periods when their families lived in Pangnirtung, but when living in Qipisa they were under no pressure to go to school, and they did not go. Except for the odd phrase said in playful imitation, no English was spoken in the camp, and as far as I could see, the children were brought up entirely by Inuit methods.

Almost all the children of Qipisa during the years I visited there were well loved and tenderly nurtured. Most of the Inuit I knew, in Qipisa and elsewhere, loved babies and small children and gave them a great deal of sensitive care and attention, nursing or feeding them when they were hungry, putting them gently to sleep when they were tired, comforting them when they were unhappy, holding and cuddling them a great deal of the time when they were awake, chanting to them over and over again special affectionate refrains that wove strong bonds between child and caretaker, and always including them in the company and activities of others, both children and adults.[4] I heard older women in Qipisa tell young mothers that they should not leave a baby or small child alone when it was awake. Parents now and then expressed momentary annoyance when a child was obstreperous or disobedient, but they rarely showed anger. To be angry with a child was demeaning; it demonstrated one's own childishness, and one older woman told me that, as an educational device, scolding was likely to backfire and cause a child to rebel. When anger was expressed toward a child, the community strongly disapproved.

So the children of Qipisa were growing up in a very small and warm world. To an outsider from an immense and complexly structured society, accustomed to strangers, to formal organizations, to the machinations of overwhelming powers whose intricate operations are dimly or not at all perceived, it must seem, from a social point of view, a simple and a safe world. But I think that to adult Inuit it was neither simple nor safe; it was full of hidden dangers. Socialization was in part a matter of becoming sensitive to these dangers, and interactions of the sort this book describes were an important mechanism in this process, creating, channeling, and maintaining a sense of danger in social life.

TO CAUSE THOUGHT

A central idea of Inuit education was to "cause (or cause to increase) thought": *isummaksaiyuq*. According to Stairs (1992:122), Inuit in northern Baffin Island use the word *isummaksaiyuq* (in Stairs's orthography, *isumaqsayuq*) to distinguish traditional learning from the "formal" education introduced by Euro-Canadians, which they call *ilisayuq* (or *ilisaiyuq*). Stairs says, speaking in general terms, that when Inuit raised their children in their own ways, the children developed values through their relationships with other persons and with the environment. A way of stimulating children to think and to value that Stairs does not discuss was to present them with emotionally powerful problems that the children could not ignore. Often this was done by asking a question that was potentially dangerous for the child being questioned and dramatizing the consequences of various answers: "Why don't you kill your baby brother?" "Why don't you die so I can have your nice new shirt?" "Your mother's going to die—look, she's cut her finger—do you want to come live with me?" In this way, adults created, or raised to consciousness, issues that the children must have seen as having grave consequences for their lives.

These questions and others equally potent were asked frequently and repetitively in interactions between adults and all small children—especially children between the ages of about two and four. The adult questioners quite consistently perceived themselves, and were perceived by other adults, to be good-humored, benign, and playful. Indeed, the questions could not have been asked and the ensuing dramas could not have been enacted if this had not been done in a mode that could be viewed as "playful," because these initiatives violated the rules of moderation, restraint, and nonintrusiveness that governed "serious" behavior.[5] But the children did not know this at first. The questioning began in infancy, long before the baby understood speech, and continued until the child's responses became unremarkable—a point that will be clarified presently. A large proportion of the interaction between adults and small children consisted of this questioning. The adults' motives were both playful and serious; questioners were simultaneously and to varying degrees teaching and testing, challenging and teasing. The interrogations also frequently served adults as a means of expressing, reliving, and perhaps relieving their own concerns and problems.

Questioning of this sort was an essential ingredient in the Inuit educational process. The questions—always thought- and emotion-provoking for the children—tended to focus on transitions or crises that a child was known to be going through: weaning; adoption; the birth of a sibling; the transition from being a baby, securely attached to its mother's back or lap, to being a child who comes and goes with his or her peers. And if the child was not aware of a transition or crisis, the questions might create one or call the child's attention to it: "Are you a baby?" "Who's your daddy?" "Do you love your baby brother?" When children learned to disentangle the playful from the serious in a particular interaction and could no longer be drawn into the trap that an adult was setting, interrogation on that subject would cease. As one Alaskan Inuk said (in English), "When children begin to respond like adults, it's not fun any more (to question them)."

In a sense, this education was a trial by fire. For uninitiated children who were not yet able to understand either the motives of their adult interlocutors or the playful aspect of the questions, the challenge might be severe and the tease a torment. Moreover, from time to time, when adult players shaped a drama to embody their own concerns, they might lose sight of the child's situation or even exploit it to their own ends. In such instances, a game might backfire. But in most cases, the ground was not really shaking under the child's feet. Since the adult players were neither angry nor afraid, they were perfectly in control of the situation, and I think children tended to perceive the safety as well as the danger. Though they might protest, burst into momentary tears, or look watchful, I never saw them develop a terror of those who offered to adopt them or suggested that they die. Indeed, I will argue in Chapter 5 and demonstrate in Chapter 6 that these interactions in various ways enhanced the children's safety and protected them from defeat, even while they elicited their fears. But I don't want to anticipate too much. Here my aim is to orient, not to persuade; to spark interest; and to calm (if possible) any ethnocentric tendencies toward shock and horror. The dramas, in interaction with other everyday experiences, had the potential to create both strengths and vulnerabilities, as I think is true of all childrearing practices everywhere.[6]

Dramas that developed around the core question grew spontaneously out of the surrounding, ongoing interaction and faded back into it. Because the dramas were informal and highly personalized, intimately related to the immediate concerns of both adult and child and responsive to the child's reactions, the plot might vary. At the same time, it is a striking fact that this mode of socialization and the questions themselves were highly uniform across Inuit time and space—from Alaska to Greenland, among groups that had not been in contact for generations or centuries. One can still hear the questions in modern Inuit communities, and I have known cases in which Inuit women married to non-Inuit men and bringing up their children in the south have used these techniques to teach various lessons. The durability of the behavior clearly indicates its emotional power and its importance to Inuit ways of being.

It should not be assumed, however, that the questions and the dramas fit into the social fabric in exactly the same way under all social circumstances. A plot or a "right answer" might change even though the provocative question remains the same. Moreover, in complex communities, where different values and different styles of communication interact, the possibilities for misunderstanding are vastly increased. One person may not hear the celebration in a hostile-sounding remark; another may not hear the criticism in an admiring question. Hence, dramas enacted with children may not serve as messages among adults quite as readily as they used to, and some young mothers, who are not attuned to the deeper levels, are beginning to disapprove of these subtle means of socialization.

In two communities I have found women who did not recognize this genre of behavior and were shocked by it. Two women, one elderly, one young, lived in a Labrador coastal village, and the third, a grandmother, came from a city in West Greenland. How representative these women are I don't know, but it is worth noting that both Labrador and West Greenland were settled relatively early by Europeans, and both areas were under strong Moravian influence.

In view of the prominence and ubiquity of this behavior, it is curious that, as far as I know, no student of Inuit society has written about it before. I, too, failed to see its importance when I wrote *Never in Anger* (1970), although several instances of it crept into that book almost without my being aware of it (see, for example, pp. 114–115, 148–150, and 169–173). I may have been infected by my own world's tendency to see spontaneous, unorganized behavior as trivial, especially if it looks playful. The fact that Inuit do not label the interactions in question may also have contributed to my blindness. It certainly contributed to the difficulties I have had in talking about the events.

THE PROBLEM OF GENRE

As I have worked on the emotionally charged interactions described in this book, I have been increasingly plagued by the problem of what to call them. When I first discovered that the events were worth attending to, it was the often gamelike and playful quality of their style that was most salient for me. As contrasted with other interactions, which might be seen as "serious," interrogations and dramas were characterized by exaggeration (both in tone of voice and in verbal content) and by pretense; and often they were built around frequently repeated and therefore ritualistic-sounding key phrases or questions, the meanings and consequences of which were acted out, dramatized. So I called them "games" and "play." My choice was supported by the fact that when I asked adults what they were doing when they interacted with children in these ways, they often answered, "Just pretending (*pingnguaqtunga*)," "Pretend-talking (*uqangnguaqtunga*)," or "Joking (*mitaqtunga*)."

But the lines between serious interactions and playful ones were fuzzy, partly because the play always contained serious aspects or layers—intentions, motives, consequences—and partly because interactions based on a key phrase or question sometimes did not have other characteristics of games or dramas: the question might be asked in a conversational voice, not an exaggerated one; or the implications of the question might not be dramatized. Moreover, I had the impression that the same question or remark tended to slide back and forth on a continuum between playful and serious, occupying different positions at different moments in one encounter or on different occasions or, indeed, containing both elements in varying proportions at one and the same time. Sometimes it was as hard for me as for Chubby Maata to determine what was meant.[7]

Thus, in order to avoid incorporating into my labels assumptions about playfulness and seriousness, I began calling the events, more neutrally, "dramas" and sometimes "interrogations." Neither label suited all events, however. Interactions didn't always develop into dramas; sometimes they began and ended as interrogations. On the other hand, questions were not always asked. I cannot find for the behavior a single term that applies to all instances; no choice does justice to the richness of the data.

Another difficulty with classifying these interactions is that they had multiple functions. In this book I examine their use in the socialization of children, but because they were motivated in part by concerns arising from relationships among the adult players, there were messages in them also for adults, and they were forces in the adult realm, too.[8]

Inuit themselves do not label the dramas "socialization behavior"; and when adults describe for non-Inuit audiences how they were taught as children, they never mention these interactions (see, for example, Muckpah 1979; Anoee 1979; editors of *Ajurnarmat* 1979; Freeman 1978; Hughes 1974; Washburne 1940). They say, rather, that their parents, grandparents, and others "talked" to them, told them moral stories, exercised them in practical skills. Similarly, when Inuit respond to open-ended inquiries about how they bring up their own children, they never mention questioning or the dramatizing of issues. Nevertheless, when a young man once persistently interrogated me about my reasons for coming to Qipisa, his mother said to me, dictating my lines in playful mode, "Say to him, 'You are treating me like a child.'" And when I recount dramatic interactions that I have witnessed, Inuit usually respond with accounts of other dramas in which they themselves have engaged. Then they are quite clear about the lessons they intended to convey.

But why, one may ask, do I try to apply one label to all of the interactions anyway? Since no rubric is applied to them in Inuktitut, why consider them a "genre" of behavior? The answer is that they do have a coherence. One kind of evidence for this is the fact just mentioned: when I give examples, Inuit say, "Oh, *I* do that!" and then spontaneously offer other instances. The behavior constitutes a "covert category" (Whorf 1956), a category that people *act* in terms of while unable to define it in words. Adults cannot initiate such behavior by saying, "Let's play," as they would initiate a game of ball or string figures or throwing stones at tin cans. The behavior is marked, set off from everyday serious acts in two ways: first, the consequences of the questions and the actions in the dramas are not what they would be if the behavior were serious (*pivik-*); and, second, as I have said, certain kinds of action—loud, aggressive, intrusive—that would be prohibited in serious mode are allowed in the context of this other genre. It is these differences that actors have in mind when they say, on being pressed, "I was only playing."[9]

I suspect there may be a lesson for us in this classification difficulty, a lesson certainly about Inuit ways of thinking and perhaps about our own as well. Inuit do not suffer from the Platonic constraints that, as Dewey (1965) reminds us, often plague our thinking, forcing it into neatly bounded ideal types and dragging our behavior after it by the coattails. Darwin, says Dewey, pointed us in the direction of liberation by showing us that all living "categories"—we may include human behavior and ideas—are constantly changing. We have proved resistant to liberation. Inuit use categories, too, of course, in a rough and ready way when it is convenient; at the same time, they are much more comfortable than we are with metamorphosis, and they are less addicted to boundaries (Briggs 1992a; Fienup-Riordan 1988). Indeed, Phyllis Morrow, in a marvelously insightful paper, tells us that Yupik Eskimos consider meaning "essentially indeterminate" and "verbalization . . . potentially dangerous and misguided." Consequently, they "tend to treat practice . . . as variable and by nature non-definitive" (1990:145).[10] If Inuit ways of thinking resemble those of their Yupik cousins—there is evidence that they do—it is to be expected that social phenomena will have continually shifting qualities and uses, and no names. This does not prevent loose collections of practices from having tacit and functional coherence. Perhaps it is partly because there is no label that people do not spontaneously mention "dramas" and "interrogations" among their socialization experiences and practices. But I think the shiftiness, the elusiveness, of the genre contributes substantially to its power. "What are you doing?" "Just playing." A perfect cover for subversive manipulation.

In this book I shall call a particular encounter an "interrogation," a "drama," a "game," or "play," depending on what feature strikes me as most salient. Variety of designation points up the fluidity of the events, but each label implies others, insofar as they apply to the incident in hand.

METHOD, PREMISES, EVIDENCE

This book has been bubbling on a back burner like Mrs. Beeton's pot-au-feu for the past twelve years, and in that time many ideas have dropped into it. I am not sure that I would dignify these ideas by dubbing them "theory"; no, they wear the more modest dress of "assumptions" and "insights," picked up here and there along the way and dropped helter-skelter into the soup. In this section I want to retrace my steps as much as I can, to lay on the table the underlying ideas and approaches that have shaped this book and to share something of the way that I came by these ideas.

Modes of Analysis

I began my investigation of Inuit dramas in a relatively conventional way by defining areas of social behavior that interested me, looking for dramas that seemed to bear on this behavior, and then examining those dramas—removed from most aspects of their immediate contexts—to see what messages they might contain and how those messages might influence behavior in the area in question.[11] In this manner, I looked at how Inuit created and transmitted values, managed conflict, and learned to cope with an environment fraught with dangerous uncertainties (see, for example, Briggs 1979b, 1982, 1983, 1991a).

Years of observing and taking part in interactions with Inuit in various parts of Alaska and Canada had given me a sense of what behaviors and attitudes were socially important, frequently repeated, and widely understood in their worlds, and I drew on this knowledge in identifying the messages in the dramas. The same background knowledge, supplemented by hypotheses about the psychodynamics involved (hypotheses derived from sources that I will describe below), allowed me to interrelate messages across dramas and to create "plots"—composite messages, often tangled and contradictory, that I thought would influence action in the domain under study.

An example of such a plot, which draws on several dramas played with many children, is as follows. I have mentioned that in some dramas children were asked whether they loved or wished to kill their new baby siblings, and ways of killing the baby were demonstrated. In other dramas they were cross-examined on their own lovability: "Are you lovable? Are you *really?* No, you're not, you're no good; aaaaq!" (The tone was one of disgust.) In still others it was suggested that they might lose their parents: mother might die ("Look, she's cut her finger"), or father might fail to return from a trip ("And who are you going to live with then?"). It seemed to me highly likely that the first kind of drama would make children aware of any jealousy they might feel toward a newborn sibling—or would help to create it if they did not feel it—and this awareness, combined with the knowledge that they were supposed to love and nurture those babies, would exacerbate any doubts about their lovability engendered by the second kind of drama, while the third might make them wonder who would rescue an unlovable child in the event of a parent's death or defection.

This analytic procedure, which I call the "noncontextual mode," resulted in certain images of the fears, wishes, and motives underlying Inuit social phenomena—images that were complex and untidy enough to seem realistic to me and that were recognizable to Inuit who heard or read my ideas. So it seemed to me that my approach taught me a good deal about the psychic motors that drove Inuit behavior in the areas I was investigating and also carried me some distance toward understanding what the dramas accomplished in Inuit society and how they worked.

However, the more I wrote, the more I noticed that I was saying the same things all the time—using the same data, making the same arguments—and I began to wonder whether I was in a rut, able to see only one dynamic. Fortunately, I expressed these thoughts to Don Handelman.[12] He suggested that perhaps not I but Inuit culture itself was in a kind of rut. That is, all the domains that I was looking at—values, conflict, uncertainty—were connected, so the dramas I was analyzing really did contain messages or lessons that were relevant to all of them. Following this line of thinking, I began to see potentials for illuminating more of Inuit culture.

At the same time, Handelman pointed me further into the realm of the individual. It happened that the dramas were usually, if not always, sharply directed to one child at a time. It also happened that they often occurred in sequences, one spontaneously leading into the next, sometimes five or six in succession, as precipitating circumstances changed. An adult asked a question. The child made a certain response, trying to solve the problem posed. Adults responded by dramatizing the consequences of the child's attempted solution or by asking new questions, which made the child think about what the consequences might be. The child responded again, and again the adults countered with new problems, and so on. Or the surrounding situation might change in some way: new actors might enter and old ones leave; somebody might change position or cut a finger. The slightest occurrence could be picked up and utilized as an ingredient in the drama.

Handelman suggested that I look at these naturally occurring sequences to see if I could find in them cumulative messages or plots, as I had previously found, or created, plots by drawing individual messages out of the separate dramas that I considered relevant to my subject. My very first experiment (which appears here as Chapter 2) showed me the fruitfulness of this new line of inquiry, and thus was born the idea of looking in detail at all the dramas that I saw played with one child during the seven-month period of a field trip.

This second analytic procedure, which I call the "natural history mode," provided me with material enough to write many pages on one instance of one drama enacted with one child, where previously I had written seven pages on four dramas (1979b) or two pages on three (1994), assuming that all Inuit (or at least Qipisa) children experienced the same dramas in the same ways. At the same time, I found another sort of insight opening to me, a vision broader and, I think, deeper than the one I had previously had of the ways in which the Inuit I knew—and, I think, many others, as well—psychologically constituted and experienced their culture. I hope that this book, written in the natural history mode, will illustrate the value of looking in depth at one small event in the life of one small child.

Psychodynamics and Culture

Because my work has sometimes been seen as having a psychoanalytic cast, I would like to say, first of all, that I did not set out from and do not stand on a psychoanalytic or any other platform, nor do I use any set of theoretical tenets systematically. When I first set out to study Inuit life, I wanted to find that humans varied profoundly with regard to the emotions they felt, the motives on which they acted, and the ways in which those emotions and motives interacted. Of course, my radical hopes were disappointed; Inuit speculating on what someone's behavior might mean or generalizing about human motives often sounded very familiar indeed. Nevertheless, my relativist bias left in its wake a strong preference for letting my interpretations emerge from the data.

At the same time, however, I share the dominant view that "raw data" is a contradiction in terms, that data are always to some extent "cooked" in the very process of observation. As Rudolf Arnheim put it (1969), perceiving is conceiving. I apply this assumption to my own interpretations as much as to Chubby Maata's. Among the ideas that inform my observation are some that I have drawn (more or less) from psychoanalytic theory, combined with experience of personal analysis and introspection. I expect to find, among Inuit as among ourselves, that at the deepest level all action and all motives derive from emotions—hungers, fears, angers, attachments; that emotions are shaped by powerful experiences, which are culturally and individually variable; that motives are by no means all conscious and many meanings cannot be articulated at will—though some may be consciously recognized when pointed out, even when they cannot be called to mind spontaneously;[13] and, finally, that motives rarely if ever come singly but instead are multiple, "overdetermined," and very often contradictory.

Although here I use English terms for emotions as a sort of shorthand, I want to make it clear that I do not believe in the universality of specific emotion concepts and experiences. Far from it. I think there is evidence for fundamental differences across cultures in the conceptualization and experience of phenomena cognate with what *we* call "emotion." Views about the cross-cultural variability of emotions and emotional experience—indeed, the appropriateness of the concept of "emotion" itself on a worldwide scale—and the universality (or not) of psychological structures are widely discussed these days in anthropology, psychology, and in some cases linguistics and philosophy, too. I hope that Chubby Maata will contribute to these discussions in her own way, but I leave it to readers to determine how she does so.[14]

Particularly useful in my attempts to interpret Chubby Maata's experience are psychoanalytically oriented scholars who have made fine-grained studies of normal child development in the United States and Britain. The work of Margaret S. Mahler and her colleagues (1975) on the "separation and individuation" of children vis-à-vis their primary caretakers; D. W. Winnicott's ideas (1971) about the uses of "transitional objects" and play in the separation process; Melanie Klein's observations, developed also by Winnicott (1965), concerning the difficulties of managing ambivalent feelings toward a loved and needed parent; Anna Freud's ideas (1966) about "defense mechanisms"; and Selma H. Fraiberg's vivid examples (1959) of the difficult business of developing a conscience, which are based on Anna Freud's ideas, all illuminate my observations in the Inuit world, though, again, I have used these authors only occasionally, when some piece of their thinking seems to me to cast light on something Chubby Maata has done.

I see culture as a "bag of ingredients" actively used by individuals in creating and maintaining their social-cultural worlds. Untidiness seems to me to be implicit, even essential, in this view of culture. Why, then, do my analyses repeatedly create higher orders of coherence out of apparent chaos and contradiction? I want to stress that I am not a functionalist. I do not believe that the bits and pieces of culture are *necessarily* interrelated in mutually supportive and logically coherent ways. Even less do I believe that each piece exists *because* it has a positive function within an overarching system. I do, however, think that both actions and ideas *do* things in the world, and so they are linked with other—most often with many other—actions and ideas, both causally and consequentially. In other words, they do have functions, which may be both constructive and destructive of socially approved goals and individual aims in different contexts, or even in the same context at the same time. Our job as observers and analysts of culture and of individuals as thinking-feeling beings is to find out what events, what images and beliefs, what thoughts, feelings, and motives are cognitively-emotionally connected; if possible, how the links were created; and how the connections—the meanings—operate to do things for individuals or groups.

I do not expect to find a totalizing system in any cultural world. I don't even expect to find a "total" culture—a point that I will return to after we have watched Chubby Maata in operation. I do expect to find webs of connection woven by each individual, cumulatively over a lifetime, out of the materials available: cultural, physical, biological, and so on. The constructions of any one individual are no more likely to add up to a coherent whole than are all the bits and pieces of culture. Values, beliefs, attitudes, rules may be quite contradictory, and any one of these may be supported by contradictory emotions and motives. Choices are never free, of course; they are weighted by associations created in emotionally charged experiences both past and present. Some of these resonances can be complex indeed and also hard to undo. Nevertheless, we can expect constructions to shift over a person's lifetime, as the individual's understandings, goals, fears, and wishes change.

In this book, I try to call attention to important experiential-emotional links that may go unperceived by a casual analyst because on the surface the phenomena involved seem contradictory or unrelated, but I make no claim that Inuit culture "works" perfectly or that contradictions support each other under all circumstances. I hold that the degree and kinds of connection that individuals perceive among cultural ingredients at any point in time, and the degree and kinds of similarity and difference between individual designs, are open questions, to be investigated in each case that we want to understand.[15]

To see society through the variegated lenses of individual perceptions is very Eskimo. Morrow, using "named categories of spiritual beings" as an example, argues that it is a philosophical tenet of Alaskan Yupik "that one's experience may differ from that of others," so "variable accounts [of the supernatural and many other things] are not particularly disturbing" (1990:152). Among Inuit, too, one finds this acceptance of personal truths, all considered equally valid when supported by personal experience. It is quite possible that my lenses have been tinted by the Inuit I have studied. At the same time, it is clear that this view of culture and the role of individuals within it, which I have arrived at by my route, is similar to the postmodern views that other anthropologists to right and left of me are arriving at these days by their routes; I suspect there has been some osmosis from those quarters, too. How a Zeitgeist manages to infiltrate the world of someone who is so thoroughly immersed in her own data that she rarely reads is a marvel—a rather disconcerting marvel to one who cherishes individuality of perspective and insight. At the same time, the fact that it does so shows us once again by what devious devices culture works. The more we strain away, the more cultural to the core we reveal ourselves to be.

The Nature of Knowing and Problems of Evidence

I am often heartened when Inuit agree with my generalizations about the psychodynamics of Inuit interpersonal relations—particularly since my conclusions are by no means based entirely on what they have told me. To limit myself to what Inuit say—or even to what they verbally concur with—would eliminate consideration of the possibility that people might be unwilling or unable to verbalize some of their feelings and motives, and, as I have said, I think the evidence is overwhelming that in all cultures people create associations among ideas and emotions in modes of thought that are not verbally articulated or perhaps even susceptible of articulation.

I assume that any person "knows" in a variety of modes—that is, experiences different kinds of awareness; that awareness constitutes a continuum and so may exist in different degrees; and that awareness fluctuates, so that a person may be distinctly aware of a motive, an emotion, a wish in one mode or at one moment in time and less aware, or not aware at all, in a different mode or at another moment. In the sense that I intend, any vibration of the psyche that influences action constitutes awareness of some sort. I may have a gut awareness of trouble brewing in the offing long before I am mentally aware of unease. Or I may be aware that someone is afraid of me without being able to articulate *how* I know. In both cases I may act on my awareness, becoming more alert, more wary, or more reassuring without realizing that I have done so. Infants, of course, are aware of many things before they can use language. We know they are because they respond to those things by smiling, crying, reaching out, turning away. So I assume that only small fragments of our mental-emotional processes are expressed in words and that these fragments shift continually. At the same time, the unsaid parts of these processes influence action just as the verbally explicit fragments do.

When I speak of "different kinds of awareness," I have in mind both the paths along which information may be conveyed—visual, auditory, kinesthetic, and so on—and the ways of organizing, storing, and expressing knowledge: words strung together in a line; images joined into a mosaic by the different logic of dreams and associations; the ability to recognize words or faces when we hear or see them or, more difficult, to recall them in their absence; the awareness of word-meaning that enables one to read a foreign language versus that which enables one to translate that language; and so on. Different cultures or eras may train for different kinds of awareness and ways of thinking. Arnheim (1969) describes in some detail the characteristics of "visual thinking" and argues that it involves ways of perceiving that are destroyed or inhibited by the emphasis that contemporary Western cultures place on verbal thinking. Presumably, then, visual thinking cannot be expressed in words. Nevertheless, for a person capable of "drawing on the right side of the brain" (Edwards 1979), it is a way of perceiving and of coming to conclusions about the world.

If one accepts this view of the nature of knowing, then it is not fruitful to ask whether Inuit know what they are teaching or whether they are aware of what the drama is about. The situation is clearly far too complex to allow us to sort events tidily into two boxes, those of which we are aware and those of which we are unaware. I would ask, rather, what aspects of an event we have what kinds of awareness of, and under what circumstances.

Complicating matters still further, we know that sometimes—indeed most of the time, I would suggest—the knowledge that we articulate to ourselves and others does not correspond fully to the awarenesses that we have on other levels. We lie to ourselves and to others; we rationalize and forget; and so in our culture, when we want to discover someone's motivations, we tend to give as much, or more, weight to actions and their consequences as to words. Whether we are conscious of it or not, we also pay a good deal of attention to the adumbrative or less controlled aspects of speech—slips of the tongue (S. Freud 1951), tones of voice—and to unspoken communications contained in settings, body language, and so on (Goffman 1959; Hall 1959, 1969).

Now, how does all this relate to Chubby Maata? When I talk about that little girl, I am often asked, How do you know? How do you know what she was thinking and feeling? And how do you know the ways in which her experiences at the age of three influence her later life?

The straight answer is, I *don't* know. Part of the problem is that I lack the requisite data: I wasn't with Chubby Maata every minute of the day and night; I couldn't see, hear, smell, taste, and touch all that happened to her. More fundamentally, I am not Chubby Maata. I did not have her accumulated store of thoughts and feelings with which to meet events, react to them, create them, and build on them. And not only did I not have Chubby Maata's thoughts and feelings, I had a great many of my own, which certainly interfered with my perceiving hers accurately.

Equally fundamental difficulties arise from the "fact"—it is an assumption—that the potential meanings of any incident are many, for Chubby

Maata as for me. I think she probably experienced several emotions at once, or in rapid succession, on any one occasion and interpreted these feelings in multiple and perhaps contradictory ways. I also think that she continually revised her understandings as her circumstances changed and her experiences accumulated and as she learned to read more accurately the obliquities that lay under simple-sounding questions. I think Chubby Maata herself was continually guessing, as I guess, about the implications of what she saw and heard.

I argue that Chubby Maata perceived as problems—often dangerous ones—the interrogations and dramas she participated in; that the need to locate and counter or neutralize the perils she saw in those interactions acted as a magnet, drawing her attention to all available clues; and that the search for clues alerted her to the emotionally charged phrases and questions, the dramatic tones of voice and gestures that she repeatedly met in those encounters. These words and acts, I suggest, became the nuclei of Chubby Maata's investigations into meaning. Any event that occurred in the penumbra of the focal events became a clue to the significance of the key phrase, tone, or gesture and helped her to weave larger plots out of originally isolated questions and to see every issue as multifaceted.

Chubby Maata also gives *us* clues to how she perceived what was happening to her, and if we pay close attention to those bits of evidence, assume that everything derives its meaning in one way or another from associated experiences, and bear in mind some of the alternative hypotheses available to her, it will be possible to make guesses about her interpretations that are not blind but culturally informed.

In order to follow in Chubby Maata's steps, I observed dramas and interrogations line by line in a fine-grained way, attending not only to the verbal dimension of messages but also to other aspects: voice tones, laughter, silences; facial expressions, gestures, postures.[16] I listened to how adults phrased their messages, to Chubby Maata's attempted responses, and to the countermoves of the adult players. I noted the contexts that elicited particular dramas or questions and what were the right and wrong ways of playing. I watched the dramas that Chubby Maata herself created, the questions she asked, the remarks she made, the details of her actions, and how her adult audiences responded to all these. I observed Chubby Maata's strategies: whom she identified with, what she imitated, and how she transformed the dramas played with her when she herself created new dramas. And in all this, I tried to see what drew and repelled her, what puzzled and plagued her, and what plots developed. It is possible to find plots in the development of single themes in the context of a single sequence of interactions; in the interrelationships among themes within the single sequence; in the development of the same theme on different occasions; and so on. By observing closely Chubby Maata's reactions in the multifarious situations of the dramas and interrogations, we can watch her weaving a world for herself out of these complicated ingredients and can see something of the texture of that world.

Other evidence of motivations, intents, and consequences comes from direct explanatory statements made by Inuit. Sometimes I heard actors in these interactions interpreting troubling aspects of the drama to the children they were playing with: "Do you wrongly imagine [your grandfather] doesn't love you [when he pretends to strike you]?"; "*Now* he's beginning to just smile." At other times someone explained matters to me: "[When we tell the puppy to bite the little boy's penis off], we aren't trying to make [him] afraid, we're celebrating his maleness"; "We tell children their genitals are bad in order to make them feel a little bit careful"; "I [pretend to reject my niece] so that she'll know I love her"; "They're trying to let her know she's not quite perfect—it's dangerous for children to think they're perfect."

Since I assume that people do not and cannot articulate all their motives, I also use indirect evidence derived from contexts that I judge to be germane on the basis of assumptions derived from my own culture about psychological process: events that have occurred just prior to the incident in question; the nature of the emotional relationship between the players; problematic events in the lives of the players which seem to be reenacted in a given drama; remarks made by players on some other subject which, to my ear, resonate with events enacted or questions asked within the drama; and so on.[17]

When hypothesizing about possible *consequences* of interactions, I often work backward, using my general knowledge of Inuit ways of thinking and behaving, together with the postulate that ultimately it is emotions that motivate reason and action. Thus, when I want to explain a bit of adult behavior or reasoning, I ask myself what kind of emotionally powerful experience could have made that behavior or thinking seem natural and right to the adult in question. Finally, where possible, I take note of Inuit reactions to my interpretations.

I want to make it clear that I do not assume that on any given occasion children perceive all the lessons an interaction potentially contains. They will understand whatever their experience allows them to, and that understanding will change continually as experiences accumulate and become associated with one another. But all interrogations and all dramas urge children toward some interpretations and away from others. Karen Freeman, an insightful psychologist, has suggested to me that these interactions resemble our guessing or hiding games in which the person who is It, the guesser, is helped by being told, "Warm—cold—warmer—colder—hot—hot—hot!" (personal communication 1994). Often, there may not be a single, narrowly right answer, but, as I have said, a play will be repeated with variations until a child's responses are no longer noteworthy.

THE STORY LINE

One of the reasons this book has been so long on the fire is that every fragment of data, when closely inspected, explodes with potential meanings, with themes, implications, and connections. Also dragging at my heels for too long was, I confess, a foolish notion of "totality." I wanted (changing the metaphor) to weave a complete tapestry of Chubby Maata's world as she experienced it when she was three. That was a fruitful folly, however, because it was in the attempt to accomplish it that I realized most profoundly that cultures, even seen from a distance, don't *have* totalities, and even less do individuals incorporate total understandings of the cultural materials available to them. So I present here a cloth full of holes, the very sort of cloth that Chubby Maata herself was weaving. My threads may not have been hers in every case—but they could have been. They are culturally possible, and I think that is the best any of us can claim for our understandings. However imperfect my conclusions, I believe the analysis demonstrates the usefulness of examining cultural and personal *processes.*

When I looked over my records of the unsettling interrogations and dramas in which Chubby Maata was protagonist, I found that even those that appeared simplest contained hints—or more than hints—of many themes or issues. In choosing which of them to attend to, I had to leave others aside. I was guided, as I think Chubby Maata was, by the phrases and questions that occurred over and over again and by plots containing emotionally powerful issues that seemed to develop around those words. Each chapter describes encounters, sometimes extended, in which Chubby Maata had to face one or several issues and find ways to deal with them. I present these in an order that makes sense to me in terms of a logical chronology of development, each issue laying the conceptual groundwork for others. In one instance—described in Chapter 6—the presentation of issues to Chubby Maata was sequential over time, but of course, in other instances, the issues were presented simultaneously, and the echoes among them must have been complex.

I start gradually and work into greater complexity. Chapter 1 is a narrative introduction to Chubby Maata and her world, which I hope shows her as a person, a very delightful little person, as she moves through her days among the people who surround her.

Chapter 2 is an account of one extended interaction among Chubby Maata, her mother, her sister, and her mother's sister. I focus on the theme of Chubby Maata's "babyness." As we shall see, the drama gradually dislodges her from her baby stance even while it celebrates babyness. The analysis also illustrates how playful and serious threads in a drama work together to shape Chubby Maata's understanding.

Chapter 3 carries the same theme further, showing us how babyness comes under discussion in a variety of contexts, from which more than one moral may be drawn. Being a baby is no simple matter. The chapter also shows us how a plot may grow and shift, developing denser and more complex texture as it is acted out in a variety of contexts.

Chapter 4 introduces the larger world of Qipisa, into which a neighbor tempts Chubby Maata to move as she leaves babyhood. The issues concern belonging, possession, and attachment. Where is Chubby Maata's home? What is hers? And how can she hold onto it? The interaction that we work with here—really a series of several dramas, interrogations, and games that grow, spontaneously, one out of the other—demonstrates how a plot can build throughout apparently disparate fragments of interaction to create a more complicated plot structure of interrelated themes.

If one is to grow up, one must learn not only where one's base is and how to hold onto it but also how to behave responsibly toward associates in the larger society. Chapter 5 deals with these issues. Whom should Chubby Maata like? How should liking be expressed? And how should our little girl like herself? Indeed, what is "liking" all about? In this chapter we see tensions and ambiguities, values and antivalues, working together to create a moral person.

Finally, in Chapter 6 we see dramatic discussions over time concerning one relationship, which is problematic not only for Chubby Maata but for her mother as well. The relationship is between Chubby Maata and Yiini, the anthropologist, who is at the same time outside and inside Chubby Maata's world. We watch Chubby Maata's mother teaching her how to feel about and behave toward me, and then we watch Chubby Maata constructing her own dramas—learning to play—in her efforts to negotiate a relationship with this scary and attractive person. In the play that she initiates, we see that she has made giant steps along the road to growing up.

Chapter 1 Chubby Maata's World

Chubby Maata was not quite three when we first met. Although it was some years ago, a vivid impression of that day still remains.[1] I had visited Qipisa before, and it had been agreed before I left on the previous occasion that my return would be acceptable, but nobody—least of all I—had known when I would come. Nor did I know ahead of time how I would travel or with whom I would stay—that is, who would make himself responsible for helping me with transportation, food supply, and lodging. Such matters are difficult to arrange in advance. So my first move on arriving in Pangnirtung was to look for someone who was planning a trip to Qipisa. It turned out that Aironi, a Qipisa man who was at that time living in Pangnirtung, was going to Qipisa to see his family and to do some caribou hunting. Another Qipisa man who had been visiting in Pangnirtung was returning with him, and Aironi offered to squeeze me into the modest amount of space remaining among the oil drums and sacks of flour in his outboard canoe.

It was a gray autumn day, the breeze cut with a wintry edge, and our tiny open craft seemed very fragile as we headed out into the open waters of Cumberland Sound, past the formidable cliffs of Nasauyaq, which mark the entrance to Pangnirtung Fjord. The bluffs of the south coast, low and undistinguished in comparison to the spectacular mountains of the north coast, are invisible from the north side of the sound, and I wondered, as I had before, by what signs Aironi guided the canoe accurately across that empty expanse of water exactly to the entrance of the fjord he wanted. But guide it he did, and then for more hours he threaded our way, first through a maze of barren, smooth-scraped skerries and ledges, then in and out of inlets narrowly cut between black cliffs that echoed the wingbeats and startled croaks of the ravens who seemed to be the only inhabitants.

I remembered with some amusement that when I first saw this landscape I had played with the fantasy that the concept of Hell had originated here. It had taken me a long time to realize that those cliffs sheltered a softer, greener world of great beauty and life. There, caribou graze in hidden places, and eider ducks nest around sharp-edged pools in the granite, from which their haunting cries of "anguuuu putuuuu"—as one Qipisa man rendered them—carry far across the fjords until they are turned back by the cliffs.[2] But that world is visible from the water only to the experienced imagination, and in that icy wind I was more occupied with my fingers and toes. My untrained eye and memory recognized none of the rock shapes we passed, but I was not so foolish as to admit that fact to Aironi, who was expertly steering our way through the labyrinth. He would have reminded me of my inadequacy till kingdom come—or till I learned—as he continued to remind me of a time, a few years earlier, when I had fallen through rotten ice into the middle of the sound. "Yiini!" He used to call my attention, amusement in the loudness of his voice, his eyes sharp to watch my reaction. "Hai?" "Do you remember?" "What?" "You fell in."

Finally, signs of human presence appeared—an oil drum, a ledge black and sticky with ancient seal fat—clues to the proximity of Qipisa. When we rounded the last bluff, I recognized most of the men and boys who met the boats at the gravel slip: our boat and one other, which had traveled most of the time out of our sight and sound, at such a distance that I was not aware that we were accompanied. I also recognized the group of women and girls, though not the small children of both sexes, who stood watching high above us, atop the ledges at the edge of the camp. They had all heard the boats in the distance and had come to see who the travelers might be. Some of the children had probably been sent as scouts by their mothers, who waited at home to hear who had come and what game they had brought.

The camp itself looked a bit different from the last time I had seen it. Of the eight *qammat,* the winter tents of wood and canvas, that I had known on my first visit, only two remained. In addition to these tents, I saw four small, plywood houses scattered on the slope in the pocket between the two bluffs that sheltered the campsite. Six dwellings housing thirty-five people (sometimes more, sometimes fewer); two narrow, stony beaches where boats could be pulled up; a small, swampy pond used for target practice and, when it was frozen, for sliding and other games; a small waterhole in the side of one of the bluffs, which caught seepage; and several huge middens—this was the camp as I experienced it. The middens—the accumulated detritus of more than thirty years of living—were for me the most salient feature of Qipisa, because in summer, on the rare occasions when the camp members passed a night or two there en route to more savory places, it was difficult for me to find a spot clear of feces and tin cans on which to pitch my tent. The Qipisa people, too, expressed revulsion toward the summer face of the camp and preferred to live elsewhere until clean snow came to cover the sticky mess.

On the day of my arrival, snow had not yet fallen, and the camp was at its ugliest; the sky was as gray and the air as chill as it had been in Pangnirtung. As I stood uncertainly on the shore, very cold and very hungry after the day-long trip and wondering where to turn, I was considerably relieved when Chubby Maata's father, Jaani, came forward from the cluster of men and invited me to his house.

I thought at the time that it was probably his prior acquaintance with me and his Inuit courtesy that motivated him, and of course this may have been so; but I later learned that Jaani, who had had some experience of life in Arctic towns, had appointed himself—I think without ratification—mediator between the Qipisa people and all Qallunaat who had dealings with them.

I was not the first Qallunaaq whom Chubby Maata had encountered at close range. Nevertheless, she was far from being at ease. She and her sister Rosi were playing when their father and I came into the house. Tall as an Inuit man, bulky in my traveling clothes, I must have loomed in the tiny room; my baggage certainly filled it. The two children did what most other small Inuit children I have met do at the sight of me: they froze and retreated to their mother's side. Rosi, who was just about to turn four and was not a baby any more, stood close by her mother's side with a stiff face and watchful eyes, but Chubby Maata's enormous black eyes first stared, then vanished, as she clung to her mother's thigh, cried out, and was raised to safety in Liila's arms. Liila offered me her hand in the pressureless grasp of Inuit everywhere—almost not a grasp at all. Her voice as she spoke to Chubby Maata held a familiar mixture of tenderness and amusement. It was the voice of an Inuit parent reassuring a small child who doesn't know that no real danger threatens. "Because you're afraid (*kappia-*)?" she asked, and she offered Chubby Maata her dry breast.[3]

Chubby Maata's terror was relieved for the moment, but it was some time before either she or her sister approached me, smiled, or spoke to me. During the six days I lived in their house, while I waited for Jaani, Liila, and their mothers to build me a qammaq of my own, both Chubby Maata and Rosi maintained a discreet distance from me. That was difficult to do in that tiny kitchen-living room, as my duffel bags and I sat very prominently in the middle of the floor. But if the children passed from one end of the room to the other, they made a wide berth around me and my baggage; otherwise they either ignored my presence or watched me cautiously from the bedroom door at the far end of the living room.

Chubby Maata, just short of three years old, was still her mother's baby, as well as baby to her father and to her mother's parents, who lived in the closest house, a few yards away. She *was* a darling child, with huge, dark eyes in a round face, and, when she was not frightened, a shining baby beam and a bounce that said, "Here I am! Notice and love me!" I was charmed, as were, I'm sure, her other admirers. She was cuddled and snuggled, undressed at night and put to bed with a bottle of milk, dressed again in the morning, and helped to lower and raise her trousers when she wanted to sit on the toilet can.

The center of Chubby Maata's world at this time consisted, in her words, of "our house"—or just "ours"—and "Kaati's house." Kaati, who was the same age as Chubby Maata, was her cousin and friend. She lived with her grandparents, who were also Chubby Maata's grandparents. She was the daughter of Liila's brother Aironi, the man who had brought me from Pangnirtung, but Aironi's and Liila's mother, Arnaqjuaq, had adopted Kaati when the child was born. Arnaqjuaq said she did it to ease the creaks and crochets of old age, but the atmosphere of her household was by no means subdued and elderly; it was the biggest, liveliest, and noisiest in the camp. Five of the eight living children of Arnaqjuaq and her husband, Mitaqtuq, were still unmarried and living at home, and they were joined not only by Kaati but, two years later, by another adopted child: Chubby Maata's baby sister Aita, who, when I arrived, was just about six months old.

Chubby Maata spent most of her time within the invisible boundaries that enclosed these two houses. Most often, when her mother was at home, Chubby Maata was at home too, but sometimes she played with Kaati or with her sister Rosi outdoors, never more than a few feet from home, or she ran to visit Kaati at

CHUBBY MAATA'S HOUSE

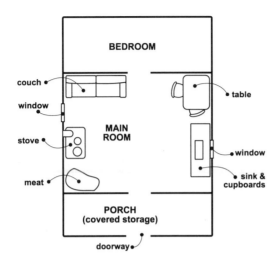

YIINI'S QAMMAQ

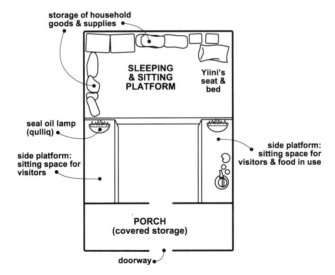

her home a few yards farther away down the slope. As I sat writing in my small qammaq next door to Chubby Maata's house, I heard her chirpy little voice calling, "Kaati! Come!" or, "Mother! Mother!" And Liila's reply from the edge of camp, as she set off up the bluff to fetch water: "I'm coming back." Chubby Maata's echo: "You're coming back, yes?" Liila: "Yes." Sometimes I heard: "Let the door be opened—let the door be opened—let the door be opened," the original summons quickly turning into a cheerful chant if the response was not immediate (Chubby Maata was too short to reach the handle of her door). Sometimes, even when I didn't hear her, I knew she was there because I heard her grandfather, Mitaqtuq, crooning in the voice he used only to her: "Aaaiiit!" He sounded as though he were suffering, but it was affection he was expressing. "Aaaiiit! *Don't* come to visit!" He meant the opposite, of course: his intent was welcoming; he must have seen her on her way to his house to find Kaati.

Chubby Maata was never alone for more time than it took her to cross from her house to Kaati's or to return, and even then, someone somewhere in the camp was pretty sure to see her and to take note of where she was going. Often that someone was her mother's father, Mitaqtuq. Mitaqtuq didn't like to hunt and had retired from that activity as soon as his sons were old enough to do it for him. Instead, he did odd jobs of repair and maintenance around the house, indoors and out; kept his wife, Arnaqjuaq, company; and, because Arnaqjuaq was afraid of wind, he sat up all night in windstorms to make sure that the roof didn't blow off or, in summer, that the tent didn't blow away. More than once I had reason to be grateful to him, when he rescued *my* tent or qammaq while I slept. He liked to joke, too, and I was not so grateful for that, since many of the jokes were at my expense. On the rare occasions when Mitaqtuq did go hunting or to Pangnirtung—usually because Arnaqjuaq had gibed him into it with jocular aspersions on his masculinity—I breathed relief, but other women, including Arnaqjuaq, said they missed him; the camp was quiet without him.

One of Mitaqtuq's major roles was that of Observer. Coming and going—or just standing—around the camp, Mitaqtuq saw everything that happened outdoors. He also popped in and out of other people's houses, paying short calls, drinking a cup of tea and leaving again, in a way that seemed to me more characteristic of children than of other men his age. This too annoyed me, as I was included in his surveillance, but his purposes were often benign. He checked my kerosene supply and refilled my can, noticed that I was running out of meat and told me to fetch more from his house. Among other things, he watched the children, and if he saw a small one heading toward danger—the fjord, the pond, the bluffs at the edge of camp, or, in the days of dogs, a loose dog—he called a warning, either to the child or to its careless caretaker. In this way he protected Chubby Maata, unbeknown to her.

Liila too had a sharp ear for her little daughter's voice, distinguished her cry of distress from any other child's, and leapt to investigate and, if necessary, to rescue. So Chubby Maata lived in a charmed circle of loving protection. She was very often in her mother's company, even when she was not distressed. She played beside her mother at home and accompanied her when she went visiting. She did have other caretakers and companions: sometimes her father, one of her mother's teenage sisters, or her ten-year-old uncle Juda took her visiting; her father or her aunts occasionally helped her dress or undress, braided her hair, or put her to bed at night. But whenever she was tired or sick or afraid, whenever she wanted to be comforted or rescued, it was her mother, home, and milk she cried for. These were not three separate comforts but all aspects of the same one. "Mother!" she would urge. "Let's go home! Let's go home, mother!" "What for? What are we two going to do there?" Chubby Maata mouthed a word silently. "What? You're going to have a bottle?" When Chubby Maata widened her eyes in affirmation, Liila's "eeee (oh)" was quietly amused.

When Chubby Maata wanted to be comforted or rescued, succor was usually forthcoming, though not always immediately. If Liila was busy with a task she didn't want to interrupt, if she was enjoying a conversation or some other activity, or if she judged Chubby Maata's demand to be inappropriate, she might ignore her daughter's whines, try to distract her attention, or expostulate sharply, "You've just drunk tea!" or "You'll have it at home!" Once in a while, she might even explicitly say, "No!" Sometimes someone else in the audience might try to distract, comfort, or caution the little girl, but if her whines became importunate, she usually got what she wanted in the end, even if the milk bottle was thrust at her with ungracious abruptness or accompanied by a disapproving protest: "Unaaaaluk (that bad one)!"

Chubby Maata didn't seem to feel injured by these signs of maternal impatience; she accepted the bottle, climbed up on the couch and sucked with absorption, gazing without seeing into the distance or up at the ceiling. Occasionally, she sucked herself to sleep, and when her eyes had closed, her mother or father would pick her up with tender (*niviuq-*) sounds, carry her into the bedroom, lay her gently on the bed, and cover her up.

Perhaps the most important clue I had to the shape of Chubby Maata's world was her visiting behavior. In October, when she was not yet three, Chubby Maata rarely went anywhere except to Kaati's house without an attendant caretaker. She did visit Kaati's house alone, drawn, I think, by the warmth with which she was treated there—a warmth expressed in the special tones and phrases (*niviuq-, aqaq-*) with which Qipisa parents and grandparents assured their small children and grandchildren that they were loved. This tone told Chubby Maata that she was welcome and that her solitary visit was appropriate. Chubby Maata's paternal grandparents, Iqaluk and Aana, lived only a few steps farther away, but Chubby Maata was not at home in their house. They, too, expressed affection to her, but they *niviuq*-ed and *aqaq*-ed her much less, and so it seemed to me that Chubby Maata was not quite so special, not quite so much of a darling to them. She feared Iqaluk "because," said Aana, "she doesn't understand that he is her father's father." Chubby Maata never came and went alone to that house.

It must have been clear to Chubby Maata that Liila, too, considered her daughter's visits to Kaati's house appropriate. Liila often sent her there when she was restless, to distract her from some undesirable activity, or to get her out of the way when Liila wanted to concentrate uninterrupted on some job such as scraping sealskins or sewing. In addition to Kaati, there was certain to be a grandparent, an aunt, or an uncle there—often several—who would make sure that the children came to no harm and that their conduct remained within acceptable bounds. In Kaati's house, Chubby Maata's baby bounce and beam— behavior that her elders called *qaqa*- and that meant to them that the child wanted to be *niviuq*-ed—the freedom with which she talked, ran about, and asked for tea when others were drinking it showed that she did not feel *ilira-:* she did not fear or expect criticism or unkindness. When she visited the other households in the camp with her caretakers, she behaved with much more restraint. There she sat on the caretaker's lap or stood quietly by the caretaker's side or between her knees and said very little. If she was asked a question, she usually answered with silent gestures rather than with words: widened eyes for "yes" and a wrinkled nose for "no." And if she made bold to ask for tea, she whispered the request in her caretaker's ear. Gone was the confident baby bounce, replaced by self-conscious diffidence, a sign that she did feel *ilira-* in that house.

Chubby Maata's sister Rosi and the other children who were a bit older than Chubby Maata did not so often accompany adults and young people (*inusut-tut*) on their visits. Though they might follow adults occasionally, most often they ran in packs of from three to a dozen children of both sexes—bands with outlines that shifted slightly from day to day but that seemed to my eye to be based roughly on age. Made bolder by numbers, these bands of children visited all the houses of the camp. At least, the children called it "visiting (*pulaaq-*)"; more than one adult said to me, "Children don't visit."

Just as it was easy to see whether small children, visiting with their caretakers, were inside home territory or not, so it was easy to make that judgment when the older children visited in bands. If they happened to be visiting the home of a sister, a brother, or a grandparent with whom they felt comfortable, they came all the way into the house, sat down on the side platforms (see the diagrams on page 27), helped themselves to tea from the kettle and to pieces of bannock from the loaf beside the kettle, and chattered and laughed freely among themselves and with their "hostess," just as if they were at home. The home of Chubby Maata's paternal grandparents was a center of this sort for a number of grandchildren between the ages of four and eight—grandchildren who did not share Chubby Maata's discomfort in that house. Aana, looking at these children as they made themselves at home around her, remarked to me: "Children don't feel ilira- any more when they visit. When we were children we used to feel *very* ilira- when we visited. We stood just inside the door of the house. We didn't say anything and we didn't eat anything."

Aana seemed to welcome the visits of her grandchildren; she never told them not to eat or asked them questions that made them feel *ilira-*. But when they became too noisy, she might remark, "It's confusing (*uimanaq*)!" Then she would urge them: "Go out and play! You are children. Children play." The children often—but not always—heeded these exhortations and departed, with no evident dampening of spirits. Unlike Aana, I had the impression that when children of any age were not on home territory, they were still very *ilira-*. They stood, as Aana said she had done in her own childhood, just inside the door of the house, watching, silent and impassive, responding monosyllabically or with a silent gesture to any question or comment that might be addressed to them. After a minute or two, one would whisper to another, "Let's go out," and out they would dart, often pursued by unheeded cries of "Shut the door!"

Sometimes the children would find something to do outdoors for a while. There might be an adult engaged in some activity that was interesting to watch: building a porch, repairing a snowmobile, loading a sled. The comings and goings of the men were always the most interesting activities of all. Sometimes the children organized expeditions of their own: to make tea on a campfire up on one of the bluffs, to explore for birds' nests, or, in winter, to fetch ice from a frozen stream at the edge of camp to offer to various householders in hope of eliciting a small gratitude present—which they often got. As Arnaqjuaq once said to me, "I give them a little something because it makes them *so* happy." Sometimes, too, a game would start: tag or follow-the-leader or, especially in the dusk or after dark, hide-and-seek around the edges of the houses, behind oil drums and boulders, sleds and snowmobiles. Pulling toy sleds across the frozen pond or sliding were favorite activities, but more exciting than these was playing *tunraq:* pretending to be a frightening spirit creature and chasing other children, who fled, shouting and laughing in a thrilling mixture of delight and fear.

Often, when the children left a house where they had been visiting or when an activity lost its hold on them, I would hear them consulting: "Where shall we go now?" "Let's go to Aatami's." Or: "Let's slide." "Yes!" And off they would run. Often, too, I heard the older children try to shake off the younger ones who had attached themselves to their number, especially the ones just next to themselves in age. The fifteen- and sixteen-year-olds mooed at the twelve- and thirteen-year-olds in discontented tones: "Always following (*malik-*)!" "Don't follow!"[4] The twelve- and thirteen-year-olds mooed at the eight- and ten-year-olds in similar vein, and they in turn at the four- to six-year-olds. The unwanted children were sometimes hard to shake; their faces became stony and their ears deaf. But sometimes they made a sulky-faced retreat and went off in another direction.

When she was three and even when she was three and a half, Chubby Maata was still very much on the periphery of the group life of children. Once in a while I saw her and perhaps Kaati in company with a few other children of their age and older—but not often, and never for very long. Caretakers were never far away from the three-year-olds. And traveling in the shadow of a caretaker, Chubby Maata was protected from much of the callousness of child-to-child interactions, the mooed rejections—"Don't follow!"—and threats of exclusion: "*I'm* going to Pangnirtung tomorrow but my father says *you're* not going."

Nonetheless, Chubby Maata already had considerable experience with the miseries of being excluded, being left behind (*qimaktau-*) when she wanted to follow. Sometimes it was a sympathetic adult who left her, with reassurances of return or promises of happy events to anticipate: "When I come back we two will eat clams." But her sister Rosi was not sympathetic when she said to Chubby Maata, "*You* can't come up on the bed" or "*You* can't play dolls." And her fourteen-year-old aunt Liuna was not sympathetic when she refused to take Chubby Maata to visit the new baby in four-year-old Aatami's house.

On that poignant occasion, Liuna had offered to take Chubby Maata's sister Rosi to see the baby, but when Chubby Maata began to pull on her socks so that she could come too, Liuna's face closed rejectingly and she mooed, "It's not the time (or place)[5] for visiting." Chubby Maata wept and protested, and Liila and her nineteen-year-old sister Luisa both took her side and urged their younger sister Liuna to let her follow. Nevertheless, Liuna, seeming not to hear them, silently departed with Rosi. Chubby Maata shrieked and sobbed, "Let me follow!" But now that the others had gone, Liila and Luisa abruptly changed their tone and said to Chubby Maata in dramatically frightened voices: "Because a tunraq would get you![6] There's a tunraq out there!" Chubby Maata, who was beginning to be suspicious of this familiar threat, was not convinced. "There is no tunraq!" she cried. "Aaaaaahai! Yes, indeed, there is! Out there!" insisted Liila and Luisa.

Chubby Maata stopped shrieking and instead began to weep and whine: "Amaamak ([I want to] suck)!" She went and found her bottle, took it to her mother to be filled with milk, climbed up on the couch, and gradually sucked herself to sleep. As her eyes closed, her body slipped toward Liila, who sat beside her on the couch. She leaned against her mother's shoulder and her hand sought Liila's arm. Liila gave no sign that she noticed, but when Chubby Maata was asleep, she picked her up and, as she carried her to bed, said tenderly, *niviuq*-ing, "Aaakuluk (little sweetheart)!" On this occasion, I think Liila herself was partly responsible for Chubby Maata's disappointment. Just before Rosi and Liuna went out to visit the baby, Chubby Maata had been lying across Liila's lap while her mother talked to her in a soft voice of happy anticipation: " . . . You'll see the new baby. . . . It doesn't have any muscles at all . . . "

My own role in Chubby Maata's world changed rapidly in the first few weeks after I arrived in the camp. While I lived in her house, Chubby Maata continued to be uneasy in my presence. She stayed close to her mother when I was in the vicinity, and if I opened a can of fruit to share with the family, she refused to take her spoonful from my hand; her mother had to serve her. Now and again her mother or father might ask her in a gently amused tone, "Are you afraid (*kappia*-) of Yiini?" And when, with widened eyes, she silently affirmed that she was, they would say with matter-of-fact assurance, "She's not frightening." But Chubby Maata was clearly not convinced.

She began to relax only after I moved into the new qammaq that her parents and grandmother had built for me next door, and she discovered that visitors to that qammaq were always served tea, with milk and sugar, and fried bannock—a delicacy that I had introduced from the central Arctic[7]—with butter and jam. Such treats were rare except when a man of the household had just returned from a trading trip to Pangnirtung, and even then it could happen that after a day or two the butter, jam, and milk would be moved to the back of the food platform or the inside of the cupboard, for the use of household members only.

Since I had been defined as in the care of Jaani and Liila and, by extension, under the wing of Arnaqjuaq and Mitaqtuq, I belonged most closely to Chubby Maata's part of the camp. One or another of my protectors visited me frequently, and when it was Jaani or Liila who came, Chubby Maata very often came with them. She stood quietly between the sheltering knees of her parent and whispered in her caretaker's ear her wish for tea and bannock if refreshment wasn't immediately forthcoming. This was the manner of a child who stood on uncertain ground—but it was short-lived in her relationship with me.

Bannock and jam were not the only icebreakers. Equally effective was "school." Not long after I had settled in, Matiiusi, a boy of sixteen who had had a little schooling in Pangnirtung, suggested that I provide the same for all children between the ages of four and twenty. I was dismayed. Although I have a good deal more liking for camp-educated Inuit children than I have for the children of my own world, I doubted that I was capable of enduring the presence of multiple children of varying ages for any length of time on a regular basis if I had to take responsibility for their behavior, let alone teach them anything. How in the world does one teach English and arithmetic, anyway? I had no idea and no desire to find out. I wanted to sit quietly on the sidelines, visiting and perhaps babysitting occasionally; distribute bannock and aspirin, fruit, cigarettes, and ammunition; and take note of what I saw and heard, as I had done in former days. But that was no longer sufficient. The new spirit of the times had given Qipisa people new ideas about what to ask of me and had made me feel uncomfortable about my old-fashioned notions of how to do fieldwork. Perhaps I wasn't giving them enough. Perhaps I did need to justify my presence in new ways. Matiiusi was insistent and even suggested—falsely, it turned out—that he would teach the little ones while I taught the older ones. So I agreed, albeit with reluctance and trepidation.

Fortunately, I quickly discovered that the enterprise required much less stamina than I had imagined and that the fringe benefits were considerable. The actual population of scholars quickly leveled off at ten: the three boys and seven girls who were between the ages of three and ten. Matiiusi, having done the job of precipitating the school into motion, vanished into the morning mists. After some chaotic sessions, in which it proved impossible to keep the littler ones quiet enough so that the older ones could concentrate on the English words I was trying to teach them, the eight-year-old wisely suggested that we divide into two classes. So we did. The five children who were between the ages of six and ten came in the early afternoon for as long as they chose to remain, which was usually an hour or two; and the five little ones, who were all in the neighborhood of three and four, came in the late morning for as long as *they* chose, which was rarely more than half an hour.

The educational benefits of this school were, of course, negligible for the children. The older children learned to say, recognize, and write the letters of the English alphabet and the English names of most of the objects in my qammaq. They added and subtracted on their fingers (they already knew numbers), and they drew pictures. The three- and four-year-olds drew pictures, too, and learned a few words.

I, in contrast, learned a lot. The children almost immediately lost their fear (*kappia-*, *ilira-*) of me, chattering and laughing and playing as freely in my qammaq as they did at home—in fact, perhaps more freely, since I consistently tried to prevent them from feeling *ilira-* and didn't chide them for being noisy and confusing (*uimanaq*), as other adults did. I criticized only if the children were aggressive toward one another, and I tried never to embarrass or confound them.[8] Indeed, when I later had some difficulty moderating the lively games that they played in close proximity to my two precariously perched seal-oil lamps, several women told me that my problems arose from the fact that I did not try to make the children fear (*ilira-*) me. "You should scold them," they said. "Tell them, 'Settle down, be quiet!'" Even the older children told each other and the little ones, looking to me for confirmation, "If you're noisy, we'll stop (school for the day)—isn't that true, Yiini?" But I didn't want the children to be quiet; I wanted to listen to their conversation, look at what they were drawing, and glimpse the world for a moment through their eyes.

Chubby Maata was the youngest of the scholars and the least inclined to school. She soon stopped attending, although her sister Rosi and her friend Kaati both came regularly. Nonetheless, when she visited me after she had dropped out and when I visited in her house, she seemed to feel as much ease with me as the other schoolchildren felt.[9] In fact, both Chubby Maata and Rosi relaxed before Kaati did, and proud they were of it, too. On the second day of school there were six children, all eight years old or younger, sitting and drawing on my sleeping platform when Kaati was brought in by Luisa, the sister—sociologically speaking—who took primary care of her. Kaati didn't want to stay at all. She blinked her eyes rejectingly and turned away toward Luisa. Luisa took her out. A little later Kaati came back by herself, and the other children asked her if she had come because she wanted to participate (*pi-qatau-*). She did briefly sit and draw with the others, but then she got up and went out. As she left, Chubby Maata, to my amusement, said to her, "Because you're afraid (*kappia-*)?" I didn't see her answer, which was silent, but it must have been "yes," because Rosi said, "*I'm* not afraid (*kappia-*); you're the only one." I saw no answer to that charge, either.[10]

There may have been some bravado in Chubby Maata's question and Rosi's assertion—a desire to convince *themselves* that they were not afraid. Nonetheless, staying to visit me the next day, after the third session of school, Rosi ventured to test her courage and the safety of my conduct. She made faces at me, distorting her eyes and mouth as people do when they play "evil spirit," and ordered me to do the same. (Was she showing me that *she* was the frightening monster? Trying to make me fear *her?* Testing herself to see whether she could endure the sight of *my* distorted face? Proving that she could control my actions?) She pronounced openly and vigorously a desire—which of course I gratified—for tea: "One has an urgent wish for tea!" And she sat down beside me—close beside me, not at the far end of the platform, squeezed in precariously behind the seal-oil lamp, as her sister had done two weeks earlier on her first visit to my qammaq in the company of other children. She questioned me on my food tastes: Did I like sugar? Jam? Butter? (Was she telling me that *she* liked sugar in her tea, and jam and butter on her bannock?) She asked whether there were houses in my country, and whether the houses had glass windows. A window got broken in Pangnirtung, she said. (I wondered whether a child had broken it and, if so, whether the child had been scolded.) To my amazement, Rosi even let me touch her head after a while, in an affectionate gesture.

I am not sure that Chubby Maata was present on this occasion, but she was certainly present on other similar ones, so perhaps Rosi's courage infected Chubby Maata, too. More important, perhaps, Chubby Maata saw that Rosi's experiments in approaching me had no dangerous consequences. In any case, two days after I recorded that Rosi had gotten over her fear of unkindness (*ilira-*), I recorded that Chubby Maata was over hers. It was not long before I began to hear Chubby Maata's voice outside her house, saying to one or more small playfellows, "Yiinimun (shall we go to Yiini's)?" And in a minute my porch door would creak and slam, my inner door would creak open, and two or three small persons would appear in the entrance. Solemn or smiling, their gaze was always intent. Sometimes they would declare that they wanted to draw, sometimes they would just look, but increasingly often they would come and settle themselves without invitation on the sleeping platform and tell me the latest news: "Saali's household has a new puppy. Tauki (the puppy's mother) is sca-a-ary (*iqsi-*)!" "I hurt my finger. Look, Yiini." A minute scratch would be held out for my inspection. Finally came the request for tea, often amusingly subdued or subtle; they knew they shouldn't ask. "Tea," someone would whisper. "One feels like drinking tea." Or, more indirectly, "Isn't there any tea?" Actually, it wasn't the tea that interested them so much as the accompanying bannock, which was not mentioned. If I said, as I occasionally did, that there was no hot tea, one of the children—sometimes it was Chubby Maata—might lay her hand on the side of the kettle to see whether I was telling the truth.

Sometimes the smallest children—most often it was Chubby Maata or Rosi—would themselves experiment with untruth. "I've come to fetch!" one of them would announce, standing expectantly in the doorway. "To fetch what?" I would ask. "Bannock." (Or jam or milk.) "Who says?" It was my turn to check veracity. "My mother." "Eee (oh)." Booty in hand, the messenger would beam an extravagant "thank-you (*quyannamik*)!" and run home.

Often they really had been sent by their mothers, but not always. If not, the bearer of the booty would probably encounter interrogation at home, too. "Where did you get that?" "From Yiini." And later, when Liila and Chubby Maata were visiting me, Liila would ask me: "Did Chubby Maata fetch milk from you this morning?" "Yes." "Eee." Liila's face as she looked at Chubby Maata would be amused and her voice warmly *aqaq*-ing as she queried: "Because you're a baby? Heee? Because you're a baby?" Chubby Maata's eyes would widen in affirmation. "Ait!" Liila usually made this exclamation in a loud, sharp, almost suffering tone, a tone of intense affection, accompanied by a sharp nod of the head toward Chubby Maata, and Chubby Maata would beam her brilliant baby beam and bounce self-consciously between her mother's knees.

A great deal of the communication between Chubby Maata and adults took the form of playful-sounding interrogations, and a great deal, too, made use of special dramatic voices. These facts were especially striking when I compared them with Liila's interactions with her other daughter, Rosi, who was only fourteen months older. Although Liila did speak to Rosi once in a while in a *niviuq*-ing voice of intense affection, and although Rosi had by no means entirely outgrown interrogations, playful and otherwise, nevertheless there was a significant dimension in her relationship with her mother that was lacking in Chubby Maata's case.

Liila often treated Rosi as a companion, giving and receiving information in a matter-of-fact, sociable way. She played cards with her elder daughter occasionally and helped her, as requested—and once in a while when her help was not wanted—with her projects: sewing doll clothes, frying a morsel of fish for herself. Chubby Maata did not undertake such projects. She received relatively little information and was asked relatively few questions in a matter-of-fact mode, but she received a great deal of *aqaq*-ing and *niviuq*-ing. And while Chubby Maata often used her baby beam and bounce to elicit affection or bannock and jam or a bottle from others—from her parents, maternal grandparents, teenage playfellows and caretakers, and, later, from me—Rosi never did this. If Rosi had once had a self-conscious shining beam, she had lost it.

It was the playful interrogations and the associated dramas in Chubby Maata's life that interested me most, however. These were the interactions that played so significant a role in the education of Inuit children and the operation of Inuit society. As next-door neighbor after my qammaq was built, visiting and being visited daily by Chubby Maata and the other members of her household, seeing Chubby Maata also on her visits to the other households in the camp, I had hundreds of opportunities to see and record the encounters that engaged Chubby Maata during the six months of my stay in the camp. On the same field trip and on others, both earlier and later, in Qipisa and elsewhere, I recorded many similar interactions with children, from shortly after birth until well into adolescence—not to mention the dramas that were enacted with me and the much less elaborated joking and playful behavior that adults engage in with one another. Although I don't explicitly draw on this other material here, it informs my interpretations of Chubby Maata's experiences.

Let's look now at the dramas and interrogations in which Chubby Maata was protagonist and try to figure out what she might have learned from them about her world and her place in it. I begin with a drama about babyness. Though the incident I describe was by no means the first drama that I saw enacted with Chubby Maata, the focal question—"Because you're a baby?"—caught my ear very early, while I was still living in her house. The theme of babyness was much in the forefront of Chubby Maata's interactions with her caretakers during those first weeks.

Chapter 2 "Because You're a Baby"

"Because you're a baby"—sometimes "Are you a baby?"—is a phrase or question that was often addressed to Chubby Maata.[1] The tone—tender, *aqaq*-ing—did not sound like a scolding. Nor did it sound like a matter-of-fact statement or request for information. What was being communicated, we—like Chubby Maata—will gradually discover.

The development of any particular interaction depended partly on the circumstances that elicited it, partly on Chubby Maata's responses, and partly on concurrent events that were incorporated when they sparked the imaginations of the participants and fed their purposes.

The example I've chosen to begin with is one of the longer sequences in my notes and therefore perhaps capable of sparking *our* imaginations in a variety of directions. It took place just before Chubby Maata's third birthday—a fact that would be quite meaningless from the point of view of Qipisamiut but that may interest readers who want to make comparisons with child development in other cultural contexts.

THE DRAMA DESCRIBED

Episode 1 (November 26)

Liila, Rosi, and Chubby Maata came into my qammaq to visit. Liila sat down on the side platform where I kept my food supplies, the usual spot for visitors who didn't want to intrude on my sleeping platform. Rosi sat down between Liila's knees, where Chubby Maata was accustomed to sit. (Between the caretaker's knees was the spot usually occupied by children of Chubby Maata's age—a position, with feet firmly grounded and back resting against the caretaker's chest, that they seemed to prefer to the lap.)

Chubby Maata wasn't at all happy with her sister's occupation of her territory, and she expressed her displeasure with the wordless whine that one often hears from Inuit children who are annoyed, even ones much older than Chubby Maata. In this case it had no apparent effect, either on Rosi or on Liila. Liila kneaded her gum between her teeth, pulled one end out in long, sagging threads and put it back to be kneaded again, all the while looking off into space. Rosi's expression, too, was blank.

Chubby Maata, however, was not so easily discouraged. "Remove her!" she demanded, addressing her mother. Liila continued to chew her gum, her face as blank as before. She seemed to hear nothing. Chubby Maata insisted: "Remove that one!" The object of the demand was slightly more explicit this time, but still there was no response. Once again she insisted, and this time she was perfectly explicit: "Remove Rosi!" Clearly it wasn't from failure to understand her wish that her mother ignored it.

What to do now? Chubby Maata, having reached a dead end in that direction, took the gum from Liila's mouth, put it in her own mouth, and began to chew it—not at all an unusual thing for a little girl to do, but in doing it, she made some gesture (I don't know what it was) that made her mother laugh. "Do this," Liila said, smiling at Chubby Maata, and in rapid succession she clapped her hands, slapped her knees, crossed her arms, and held her nose with one hand and her ear with the other. Chubby Maata imitated one gesture after the other, her face a funny mixture of brilliant beam and concentration and her arms a tangle. Rosi began to imitate too, with just as much enjoyment and no more success, and the laughter of all three wove them together.

Suddenly Chubby Maata said to her mother, "Shall I sit *here*?" She pointed to a spot beside Liila, not the coveted spot between her knees. Liila, still playing with gestures, said, "Do it squatting on the floor." Qipisamiut didn't sit in squatting position unless they were working at something on the floor, but they did play at squat-kicking with arms akimbo, a kind of acrobatic that looked to me like a Cossack dance. Chubby Maata didn't respond to her mother's playful suggestion, so Liila simply said, "Yes," and Chubby Maata sat down beside her.

I watched all this with amusement, leaning back comfortably against my sleeping bag with my hands behind my head. Chubby Maata, now established beside her mother, looked at me, put her hands behind her head, and said in a pleased tone, "Yiini." Liila and I laughed.

At this point, Liila's younger sister, Luisa, who was nineteen, came in, and Liila said to Chubby Maata, "Imitate Yiini." The word she used, *Yiiningnguarit,* means "Pretend Yiini." Chubby Maata immediately repeated her imitation, but this time, instead of saying "Yiini," she said, "Tiini," as a younger child might do. There were still many words that Chubby Maata herself mispronounced, but "Yiini" wasn't one of them.

Luisa nevertheless asked, "*T*iini?"—questioning, as Inuit do when their intent is to make a person think again about the correctness of something she or he has said. Or perhaps Luisa wondered whether she had misheard Chubby Maata. But Chubby Maata confirmed that she had intended to say what she said. "*T*iini," she repeated. Luisa questioned again several times: "*T*iini?" And each time Chubby Maata confidently confirmed: "*T*iini." Luisa couldn't be mishearing now.

Finally, Rosi, seeming impatient with her little sister's mispronunciation, said in an emphatic, how-can-you-be-so-silly voice: "*Y*iini!" It was clearly *her* intention to correct. But Chubby Maata replied in her innocent voice, "*T*iini?"

Now it was Liila who intervened. Her tone caressed Chubby Maata and dramatized her affection for her; it was a playful version of the *niviuq*-ing voice that Qipisa parents and grandparents often used when speaking to babies and small children in order to teach them that they were loved. What she said was: "Say 'ungaa' (make the cry of a baby) because you're a baby." When Liila said "ungaa," her voice was the voice of a tiny baby crying. And Chubby Maata's voice, when she echoed "ungaa," was a small replica of her mother's. Liila hugged her daughter extravagantly and exclaimed in the same intense, playful *niviuq*-ing voice, "That darling little one (*unakuluk*)!"—her arms and voice and words all part of the hug.

Then, still in the same playful voice, palatalized and nasalized, a chant that rose at the end of each word, Liila dictated for Chubby Maata to repeat: "Anaanak (mother)!" "Ataatak (father)!" "Amaamak (suck)!" "Uququu (game food)!" It was baby talk she was dictating to her baby, and her voice as much as the words assured Chubby Maata that she *was* a baby. Chubby Maata's voice again echoed her mother's exactly, and she repeated: "Anaanak!" "Ataatak!" "Amaamak!" But when she said "ququu," she added another syllable—"ququu-ququu!"—saying the word this time not only like a mother talking to her baby but also as the baby herself might say it. And Liila enveloped her in another extravagant hug. They repeated the same litany several times, a celebration of babyness.

But suddenly a rude interruption: somebody (it was Luisa) pushed Chubby Maata's bottom lightly with her boot sole. The spell was broken. Chubby Maata turned, looking annoyed, and asked, "Who's hurting (*anniq-*) me?" There was no answer.

Liila said to Chubby Maata, "Say 'ungaa.'" Again the voice of the tiny baby crying, echoed by Chubby Maata when she replied, "Ungaa." And again her mother hugged her. She didn't succeed in restoring the celebration, though, because Luisa's push had given Rosi an idea. Now it was she, smiling broadly, who attacked Chubby Maata from behind, and this time Chubby Maata had no doubt as to who the aggressor was.

Liila explained, "Because you're a baby she's attacking (*ugiat-*) you." We laughed. What she said was true, and possibly in more ways than one. People did express intense affection toward babies in aggressive ways that were called *ugiat-*, but Rosi might have had her own reasons for being inspired by Luisa's gentle kick. Perhaps that was one of the reasons why we all found Liila's benign explanation comical. The children's laughter might have expressed relief, too, because the explanation made the attack safe; it made it playful. And so it turned into a wrestling bout between Rosi and Chubby Maata, a bout filled with laughter—until Rosi exercised a little too much strength. "A'aaa (ouch)!" exclaimed Chubby Maata.

"Say 'ungaa,'" said Liila. "Cry (*qia-*) and I'll rescue you." This time Chubby Maata didn't reply immediately, but after a minute she did say "ungaa," and then Liila, laughing, pushed Rosi away from her sister. Rosi returned, however, and the two girls began again to wrestle and to laugh—until once, when Chubby Maata attacked Rosi, Rosi ran, still laughing, to hide behind Luisa, who was standing near the door.

Liila held out her hands to Rosi, affectionately beckoning her to come. But when Rosi trustfully came toward her, Liila's arms shot out, not to embrace but to imprison. Holding Rosi down, she said to Chubby Maata, "Hurt (*anniq-*) her; make her angry (*ningngassaari-*); hold your hand on her head so she can't get up."

Chubby Maata was quite willing to follow these instructions, and she also had ideas of her own as to how the game might be elaborated: "Shall I pull her hair?" She clutched a handful of hair, but Rosi protested with a cry, and Liila said, "No, just hold your hand on her head so she can't get up." Chubby Maata did so, but Rosi wrenched herself free and escaped back to Luisa.

Liila, with an amused look, commented to everybody and nobody, "She's really attacking (*ugiat-*)!" And indeed, the children were beginning to look angry; the muscles of their faces were taut, and they exerted considerable force as each strained against the other, trying to upset, and perhaps even to damage, her opponent. The earnestness of the two small creatures—perhaps, too, the imminent risk to life and limb, which was no *real* risk—was comical, and Liila, Luisa, and I broke into laughter. But at the same time, when the girls began to flail at each other, Liila took the precaution of holding her hand between them. She didn't really want to lose a daughter.

And then—did Liila hear a sound outside or only pretend to?—she cautioned, "Be good, please; someone's coming in." The children stopped fighting and one of them asked, "Who is it?" Liila lowered her voice to an intense whisper, resonant with memories of bugaboos, and said, "Visitors from another camp (*niurruat*)!" The effect was magical, as Liila had every reason to think it might be. "Visitors from other camps" were a formidable presence in the worlds of Qipisa three- and four-year-olds and indeed caused some apprehension among their elders as well. So the children stood still within their mother's protective circle and waited.

For a few minutes no one came in. Then footsteps were heard in the porch, and the door was pulled open to reveal—not *niurruat* but two very familiar boys. One was the girls' ten-year-old uncle, Juda, the youngest brother of Liila and Luisa; the other was sixteen-year-old Matiiusi, a brother of the girls' father, Jaani. Juda was in and out of Liila's house all the time; he was a frequent playfellow of both girls, and occasionally, as I've said, he also took care of Chubby Maata, accompanying her on her visits from house to house. When Matiiusi was not out hunting with one of his two married brothers, he too was a frequent visitor in their houses, and the girls played with him readily.

This time, however, when the boys came in, Rosi whispered in Liila's ear, "Let's go to Kaati's." And Chubby Maata whispered in her other ear, "Let's go home." Liila made no response at all to Rosi's plea and pretended not to have heard Chubby Maata's. She made her repeat it several times: "Hai?" "Hai (what did you say)?"

Chubby Maata did repeat her request several times, each time a little more distinctly, and finally Liila said—in a matter-of-fact tone that didn't belong to play—"Say 'ungaa' and we'll go home." Chubby Maata didn't respond at once, but when she did, her voice was matter-of-fact like her mother's, and immediately afterward she claimed fulfillment of the bargain. "All right now!" she said in an insistent voice, "Let's go home!"

Liila didn't seem to be listening. She replied in an abstracted voice, "After a while (*uatsiaru*)." It was the standard way of putting someone off. Then suddenly she changed the subject—or so it seemed. Speaking again to Chubby Maata, she asked, "Shall Yiini and Luisa come and visit?" Chubby Maata wrinkled her nose to say no, and Liila chuckled. I joined in, repeating the question, as Inuit often do: "Chubby Maata! You don't want me to visit?" "Yes," replied Chubby Maata: she did not want me to visit. Liila said in a tone of amused surprise, "She agrees!" Then, speaking to Chubby Maata, she asked in the same amused tone, "Because you still don't like her?" Chubby Maata, opening her eyes wide and raising her brows to say yes, confirmed that her mother had understood her motive; and again Liila and I chuckled.[2]

Finally, Liila and the children left, Liila saying, "All right now! Let's go home." They were the same words that Chubby Maata had used to no avail a few minutes earlier. Luisa and Juda followed them out, and Liila and Luisa mooed rejectingly at their brother, making it clear to him that his presence was not wanted. He followed anyway, and Matiiusi, after a minute, followed too.

THE DRAMA ANALYZED: INTENTIONS, MOTIVES, UNDERSTANDINGS

On the most obvious level, this is a spontaneous, warm, playful exchange between an affectionate mother and her much-loved three-year-old daughter, with some participation by the mother's four-year-old daughter and sister. There is nothing special about it; exchanges like this happen frequently when Liila and her children are out visiting, or at home when Liila is not busy.

The more closely one looks at the interaction, however, the more one sees. It is actually a densely textured drama, which can show us quite a lot about the fabric of Chubby Maata's three-year-old life, its psychologically meaningful issues, and the way those issues are created and structured—largely unconsciously, I think, as an unintended by-product of fun.[3]

The issue in the forefront of the drama, of course, concerns Chubby Maata's babyness. From my point of view as a fascinated observer, the play is mainly about that babyness. Liila is playing *with* Chubby Maata's babyness. She repeatedly tells Chubby Maata to make the cry of a baby—"Say 'ungaa' "—and the action of the drama develops out of these cries. A look at how the action develops can tell us something about the dimensions of babyness that Liila perceives and that Chubby Maata is learning to perceive, together with the rewards and costs of being a baby. It can also give us clues about what Chubby Maata already understands and what she still doesn't know about these matters.

Moreover, when we look at how the drama develops, we see that the action moves back and forth between two modes of interaction: playful and serious. Sometimes the actors are all playing, sometimes they're all serious, sometimes some are playing while others are serious, and sometimes it's very hard to tell whether intentions and perceptions are playful or serious or both at the same time or something in between these analytically but not always actually distinct poles. Sometimes definitions of the situation seem to occur retroactively. A look at how these transitions and discrepancies occur and how the actors use them may tell us something important about the ways in which Chubby Maata is acquiring social awareness of herself and of others: the ways that she learns who she is, the meanings that her actions have for others, and the meanings that others' actions have for her.[4]

Let's look, then, at how the theme of babyness develops throughout the drama. How does Liila—who controls the development of the drama from start to finish—play with Chubby Maata's babyness, and what may be the consequences of the play?

Celebration

The first thing that happens when Liila and her two daughters come into my qammaq is that Rosi silently establishes herself between her mother's knees in the baby position, a position that is usually occupied by Chubby Maata. Chubby Maata protests several times, applying obliquely to her mother and avoiding direct confrontation with her sister, but framing her demand with increasing explicitness and in the imperative—a manner of speaking that her mother would perceive as babyish. Liila seems not to hear her, and Rosi follows suit. In other words, Chubby Maata's serious, bad-tempered, and babyish demand to be treated as a privileged baby who has a right to dyadic physical intimacy with her mother is not respected, is invalidated, by her mother. Of course, we have no evidence that Chubby Maata herself is thinking in terms of categories like "baby" and "right"; she is simply, for all we know, asking to occupy her usual position.

When Chubby Maata finds herself defeated, she drops her demand, perhaps distracts herself from it, by taking the gum from her mother's mouth and chewing it. This action too is an ordinary one, for which many models existed in the behavior of older Inuit. Mothers often shared morsels of the food they were chewing with children of Chubby Maata's age and even older ones, sometimes at their own initiative, sometimes in response to a demand on the part of the child; adolescents and young parents also passed gum from mouth to mouth.

At the same time, however, Chubby Maata's action on this occasion might have for her a number of "baby" meanings of which she is not aware. For one thing, mouth-to-mouth food sharing could remind her of how her mother passed prechewed food from her own mouth to Chubby Maata's when Chubby Maata was a smaller baby. And since the sharing of food is very early represented to children as an expression of affection, Chubby Maata could be assuring herself of her mother's continued love, which Liila's "rejecting" behavior might have caused her to doubt. She could be taking part of her mother, or something that is her mother's, and incorporating it, thereby reestablishing symbolically the intimate relationship with her mother. At the same time, she could be expressing some resentment as she chews on her mother's possession; she could even be substituting removal of the gum for removal of her sister. In other words, she could be, all at once, eliminating the unwanted separateness between herself and her mother, conquering or consuming her mother, taking revenge on her sister, and comforting herself—as older Inuit did all the time, and as she herself clearly did on other occasions when she was upset—by giving herself food and drink in a manner reminiscent of a mother feeding her small baby. And, surely not least, she is getting her mother's attention.

It's also possible that Chubby Maata is *playing* when she takes the gum from her mother. The gesture that made Liila laugh might have been deliberately intended to be funny. The sharing of gum was often elaborated into a game with small children, a game in which a caretaker—the mother or an older child, boy or girl—held one end of the gum in his or her mouth and the small child held the other, and both gobbled as fast as they could, each trying to get as much gum as possible into his or her mouth before their mouths touched.

In any case, Liila sees the potential for play in her daughter's action, perhaps partly because of playful associations with gum sharing and partly because Chubby Maata's gesture amuses her. Both adults and children often built games out of fortuitous everyday occurrences that were not intended to be communicative. In this case, Liila picks up, supports, and elaborates Chubby Maata's deflection of her original goal. She responds to her daughter's gesture by showing her other gestures to imitate, and Chubby Maata follows her mother's lead and imitates them. The interaction has now clearly assumed a playful form, and it is a form of play—imitation—that is often seen in exchanges between babies and adults. In creating this form of play, Liila seems to be recognizing, consciously or not, Chubby Maata's babyness; perhaps she has perceived Chubby Maata's motivations in taking the gum as those of a baby. Perhaps she is deliberately eliciting Chubby Maata's charming baby incompetence, a sight that is likely to make her feel tenderly maternal and protective, as well as tenderly superior and amused—all delightful feelings for her.[5] In tripping up Chubby Maata and laughing with and at her, she is also incidentally calling attention to her daughter's babyness, demonstrating it both to Chubby Maata and to the audience.

Imitation, however, is not exclusively a baby activity. Older children independently use the imitation skills that they have learned as babies, not only in fun but also in acquiring finely tuned coordination and all the subsistence techniques that they will need as adults. So although Chubby Maata, in following her mother's directions to imitate, acts in a way that adults perceive as babylike, her play is a kind of baby behavior that merges gradually into the autonomous behavior of older children and adults. Rosi joins the game, and this time Chubby Maata doesn't object to Rosi's participation in her relationship with her mother. Though Rosi may perceive herself to be entering into Chubby Maata's baby relationship with her mother, as she entered it earlier by usurping Chubby Maata's place between Liila's knees, Chubby Maata doesn't seem to perceive Rosi now as interfering with her special babyness. I don't think she sees herself as in any way special—as different from Rosi—at this moment. She is just unself-consciously following her mother's lead, learning and having fun doing so. It might also be relevant that while there was room for only one person between Liila's knees, there is room for two in *this* game.

But after the imitation game has gone on for some time, Chubby Maata suddenly reverts to her original concern: where shall she sit? She asks a serious question—returns to the serious mode of interaction—but this time she *consults* her mother, in the manner of a more mature child, recognizing Liila's authority instead of demanding something from her and resisting that authority. The tone is good-humored, and she asks for the position of an older child (beside her mother) instead of that of the baby (between her mother's legs). She is no longer, for the moment, a baby. The play seems to have temporarily aged her, as though the act of imitating an adult's actions had somehow suggested adultness to her. Perhaps practicing new skills, however ineptly, made her feel that she was growing up. Or perhaps it's only that *playing* (with an adult?) has detached her, for the moment, from her serious baby concerns—even though Liila has defined her as a baby in this play.

In any case, Liila is now willing to respond to Chubby Maata's wish, but at first she tries to keep the interaction in the play mode ("Do it squatting on the floor"), and she tries to keep just a little farther away than Chubby Maata would like. Is Liila trying to keep her daughter from reverting to serious babyness? Is she "telling" Chubby Maata to treat as a game her serious wish to be near her mother? But then she acquiesces to Chubby Maata's request. Chubby Maata, after quite a detour, has achieved a compromise solution to her initial problem—or, more likely, I think, she has outgrown, for the moment, her original wish. She sits.

Now what happens? Chubby Maata, seeing that I have put my hands behind my head as I watch, begins an imitation game of her own. In this game she is being "adult"—though she may have no such category—in two ways. First, she is consciously imitating a person who happens to be an adult, and, second, she is, probably unwittingly, imitating the adult role of initiating imitation games, which her mother has just demonstrated.[6] But her mother and I, the adult imitated, respond with laughter, laughter that probably contains a variety of ingredients, all deriving from our perception of Chubby Maata as a baby: amusement at the incongruity of a baby's pretending to be an adult; perhaps a bit of embarrassment at seeing the Outsider suddenly reflected in miniature; affection for the baby who has unwittingly created such a charming incongruity and who is so innocently enjoying her performance; and surprise and appreciation because she is so observant.

Chubby Maata, of course, may simply see the laughter as an expression of warm approval of her (adult) imitation. On the other hand—or at the same time—it may return her to darling-baby status in her own eyes. In a moment, when Luisa comes in, Liila gives her daughter an additional clue to her baby status. Resuming the role of initiator and director of action, she tells Chubby Maata to repeat her imitation of Yiini. Only very small children (and anthropologists) were given instructions in playful mode. Older children ignored playful directions when they were attempted, so people stopped playing with them in this way. But Chubby Maata may not see this clue to her mother's view of her. When she obeys her mother's instruction, she may simply be demonstrating unself-consciously that she *is* a baby—a message that the adults receive but she doesn't.

On the other hand, there is something different about Chubby Maata's imitation this time. She elaborates it in a way that sounds very much as though she were not unself-consciously being a baby but, instead, deliberately playing the role of a baby. She uses baby talk—or what seems to the adults to be baby talk—even though, as we have seen, she knows how to pronounce my name correctly. And if she *is* using baby talk, then it seems likely that, in one way or another, a message about babyness as an identity (not necessarily her own) has reached her.

Of course, she may *not* be playing the role of a baby. She may not yet have a consolidated, multifaceted concept of babyness. She may not even perceive herself to be using baby speech; she may instead be playing with sounds, with words, as she has heard older children, including her sister Rosi, do on occasion. Nonetheless, it is clear that Chubby Maata progresses from directed imitation of a person's *action* (when Liila demonstrates gestures to imitate) to self-initiated imitation of action and perhaps also of a person (when Chubby Maata says she is doing or being "Yiini") to directed imitation of a *person* combined with a self-initiated pretense of some sort (when Liila says, "Pretend Yiini," and Chubby Maata replies, "Tiini"). At the very least, I think, this shows us that Chubby Maata sometimes knows how to pretend and that she is moving in the direction of being able to play *roles*—if she hasn't already arrived at that point.

It seems to me just possible that when Chubby Maata says "Tiini" she is already playing not one role but two: both Yiini (the person imitated) and baby (the imitator). A highly sophisticated achievement, if so, and one that moves her a giant step away from *being* a baby. Earlier in this series of interactions Chubby Maata *was* a baby unself-consciously: first in serious mode, while trying to get rid of Rosi, then in playful mode, while imitating her mother's gestures and mine. If now she is *playing* at being a baby—even playing at one aspect of being a baby, baby speech—she must be becoming aware of the dimensions of babyness as they are perceived by other people. She is also learning that behavior can be put on and off at will, a knowledge that will eventually help her direct herself to stop behaving like a baby, being a baby.[7] But I'm getting far ahead of the story.

Here, Chubby Maata is merely saying "Tiini," pretending either that this is the correct pronunciation or that she is unable to say "Yiini" correctly. Alas for her sophistication! Luisa gets the message that Chubby Maata is a baby, all right, but not that she is playing. Perhaps this is one of the first times that Chubby Maata has pretended something. Luisa responds in serious mode, treating Chubby Maata as an unself-conscious baby. "Tiini?" she repeats, perhaps checking whether she has heard correctly or playing the adult role of correcting through questioning. One begins to suspect at this point that children may often experience some difficulty in getting their definitions of situations accepted. Compare Chubby Maata's inability to remove Rosi with the ease with which her mother and I "undo" through laughter the little girl's pretense of being Yiini. In any case, Chubby Maata insists that she *meant* to say "*T*iini," and Luisa continues to misunderstand her intention, now making it quite clear that her own intention is to correct Chubby Maata's pronunciation; she can't have simply misheard every time. A deadlock has been created, which neither Chubby Maata nor Luisa can break. It's probable that neither girl realizes that she is talking past the other, that they perceive the situation differently, the one playfully, the other seriously. Moreover, Chubby Maata may lack the skill to communicate her playful intention in alternative ways that Luisa might better understand.

Eventually, Rosi tries to help Luisa correct Chubby Maata. Now it is she, imitating Luisa, who adopts the adult role of correcting the baby who can't pronounce properly. But in one important respect she fails to follow her model: she makes her correction as a statement, not as a question. Consequently, Chubby Maata, who seems to know that statements and questions should alternate, is forced into the position of having to say "Tiini?" interrogatively, thus implying, "Did you mean to say '*T*iini'?" Of course, it is possible that in saying this, she is deliberately trying to correct Rosi, trying to get her as well as Luisa to accept her playful pronunciation—or her baby role, if that is what she is pretending—but I have no evidence that she has yet acquired this adult technique of correcting through questioning, any more than Rosi has.[8] It seems to me more likely that in Chubby Maata's mind question simply follows statement, in this case producing a tangle in which meaning becomes buried under form.

It is Liila who straightens matters out again, and again she does it by commenting on Chubby Maata's babyness, this time not in laughter but in words: "Make the cry of a baby—say 'ungaa'—because you are a baby." I think it likely that Liila views Chubby Maata as being self-consciously cute, showing off to get attention (Qipisa people call it *qaqa*-); and she, like other Qipisa adults, defines this behavior as that of a baby. So in saying what she does, she may simply be recognizing Chubby Maata's real babyness again and making it a basis for play, as she did when she invited her daughter to imitate her gestures. Perhaps, too, Liila, unlike Luisa and Rosi, at some level recognizes Chubby Maata's own playful intention, perceives or imagines that Chubby Maata is playing baby, and is responding to that by continuing the playfulness and the baby flavor of the interaction. In addition, of course, in labeling Chubby Maata a baby and teaching her baby speech, she interprets Chubby Maata's behavior and enables Chubby Maata to share that interpretation.

Chubby Maata follows her mother's lead and says "ungaa" in her mother's own playful voice. And Liila, hugging and *niviuq*-ing her—telling her what a darling little one she is—goes on in the same affectionately playful voice to dictate other words for Chubby Maata to imitate. The first three of these— "mother," "father," and "breast" or "suck" or "baby bottle" (the word in its baby-talk form, without suffixes, has all these meanings)—exist in or are derived from adult vocabulary, but they are among the first words that babies utter, and they continue for at least three years to be prominent in baby vocabulary, as they represent important infantile concerns. The other word— *ququuu*—which, as far as I know, is pure baby talk and is not derived from an adult word, I heard said far more often by adults speaking to babies than by babies themselves. It refers to game animals or to food derived from animals and represents interests that adults try to teach babies to have, interests in hunting and in eating: important adult concerns.

Ququuu is also the basis of another game which tries to create, in children younger than Chubby Maata, a fear of moving, biting objects. In this game the *ququuu* object is a bit of fur or any other tiny, fuzzy thing that can be made to move in the hands of a tormentor, who moves it toward the baby—sometimes first tying it to a piece of string so that it seems to move of its own accord—and says in a soft tone, which is a cross between saccharine-persuasive and threatening-warning: "Uquuuquuu—it bites!" Children withdraw, slap at the fuzz, cry out, and cling to the caretaker—who may at the same time be the tormentor. For this or other reasons, children grow up to have an ambivalent or multivalent relationship to animals, large and small: fearing and being repelled by them, loving and pitying them, even as they kill them. The fear becomes a strong motive for killing and helps to overcome the affection and the pity, while the warmer feelings help to moderate or inhibit the urge to kill.[9]

This analysis takes us well beyond the scope of "Are you a baby?" but it gives us some inkling of what feelings may be aroused in Chubby Maata when her mother says "ququuu." It suggests that when Chubby Maata says "ququququu" she may be playing, among other things, with fear.

In any case, when Chubby Maata says "ququququu," she again imitates her mother's words and voice, and once again, as when she changed "Yiini" into "Tiini," she clearly shows us that she knows she is playing. Moreover, it again looks very much as though she were consciously playing baby when she expands her mother's "ququuu" into "ququququu" every time she repeats it. It looks as though she had discovered that reduplication is characteristic of baby talk. It is even remotely possible that Chubby Maata, in repeating her mother's words playfully, perceives herself to be both grown-up and baby, as I suggested might be the case when she was pretending to be Yiini and saying "Tiini." She is grown-up in that she is repeating accurately the words of a grown-up. It is interesting that she does not play with words that are based on real adult words, whereas she repeats as a baby might, or as an adult might say to a baby on occasion, the word that is said only to babies. This may be another clue that she recognizes baby talk as baby talk.

Of course, the alternative possibility, that Chubby Maata is playing with sounds, can't be ruled out. But whatever she is doing, she has certainly hit on a way of making the word more charming and lovable, more babylike, to her mother's ear; indeed, Liila hugs her extravagantly every time Chubby Maata says it, just as she does whenever Chubby Maata says "ungaa." Moreover, Liila dictates "uququu" in the same tone of voice in which she dictates "ungaa." So if Chubby Maata doesn't today associate with babyness the word she has invented, she may do so tomorrow. In the meantime, her *mother* is playing baby with *her* and teaching her how to play the role.

The Fate of Babyness I

Now, what has happened so far? It seems that the action of the game has moved Chubby Maata through various identities from the point of view of others and—less articulately—from her own point of view, too. She begins by being an *unself-conscious baby* who feels threatened by a loss of privilege that others would label a baby's privilege. Then she is a *child,* who can relinquish that privilege for the moment. Having achieved this more mature stance and gotten it accepted by her mother, she imitates an *adult,* but this time she has gone too far; her mother and I, by laughing, return her to baby status—*darling baby* status, the quintessence of desirable babyness. Chubby Maata responds to our action by *playing an adult* as a baby would do, or performing something that looks very like this to at least one and maybe two of the observers: her mother and the anthropologist. Her aunt and sister, in failing to see Chubby Maata's playfulness, return her to the status of an *ordinary unself-conscious baby* who lacks understanding. Her mother, however, sees in Chubby Maata's play not an ordinary baby but her *darling self-conscious* baby and initiates a rhapsodic celebration of babyness with Chubby Maata alone, which elevates conscious playful babyness to the center of their very rewarding relationship.

Liila's role as orchestrator of this progress is interesting, too. First she ignores her baby; then she recognizes and activates her babyness (when she dictates gestures and trips her up); then she "returns" her to babyness and marks the status vividly (by laughing at the imitation of Yiini); then she labels babyness, links Chubby Maata's behavior to that status ("Say 'ungaa' because you're a baby")—and celebrates it.

A most important caveat implicit in her actions, however, is that serious baby behavior is unacceptable; it is the playful baby who is celebrated. Chubby Maata, who began this series of interactions in serious mode, has been maneuvered into operating, more and more consciously, in play mode. It is playfulness that gets her what she wants—and we will see later what other consequences it may have.

Vulnerability

But now a most unexpected jolt interrupts the happy, intimate, and playful celebration that is absorbing mother and daughter. Luisa "attacks" Chubby Maata secretly, lightly pushing her from behind with her boot sole. Chubby Maata is jarred out of playfulness into annoyance and out of the dyadic relationship into an awareness of the presence of others—but she receives no answer to her serious question about who is causing the disturbance, just as she received no response to her serious demand that Rosi be removed from her place between Liila's knees. There is a difference, however: whereas Liila did not encourage reestablishment of the *serious* dyadic relationship between herself and Chubby Maata, now she does try to reestablish the baby-*game* between the two of them by telling Chubby Maata again to "say 'ungaa,'" to cry like a baby.

Liila might have succeeded in healing the break in the play if Rosi hadn't taken a cue from Luisa (as she had also done when she corrected her sister's pronunciation). Now Rosi playfully attacks Chubby Maata from behind, and this time it's clear who is perpetrating the attack. Rosi's imitation of her model is not perfect; she has not yet learned to conceal her aggression, as adult players often do. Liila develops the opportunity that Rosi gives her. Instead of rewarding Chubby Maata's baby cry with an exuberant hug, as she did after Luisa's attack, Liila alerts her daughter to one of the unpleasant consequences of being a baby. She tells her that it is because she is a baby that she is attacked. She also implies, by using the word *ugiat-*, that Rosi's aggression is motivated by affection, but I'm not sure that Chubby Maata has the experience necessary to understand the affectionate connotations of the word, as her mother does. Chubby Maata has heard the word used primarily by people who are warning her, in alarmed voices, not to hurt some smaller person. (Occasionally, in later months, Chubby Maata will be warned not to *ugiat- me* when she is stroking my face or playing with my nose, but we are not yet on such comfortable terms.)[10] So her attention may focus on the fear of injuring, which her mother has tried to instill in her by such warnings, rather than on the affectionate motives that adults call upon to explain their own, always very mild, physical aggression toward babies. If it is fear of injury that comes to her mind, then what Chubby Maata is likely to understand from Liila's explanation on this occasion is that babies are in danger of being attacked. So! It is not only a nice, warm experience to be a baby; it can also be dangerous, or at least disagreeable.

To be sure, when Liila makes the association between being a baby and being *ugiat*-ed, the laughter of all the adults present could tell Chubby Maata that, after all, the attack is not to be feared, that it might even be enjoyable; and the fact that the children laugh with the adults assures us that, at the moment, they are not overly alarmed by the dangers of *ugiat*-ing and being *ugiat*-ed. At the same time, if Chubby Maata doesn't enjoy the attack, the ground is laid for her to think, "I could avoid this unpleasantness by not being a baby."

The attack turns into wrestling, and for a while the wrestling continues to be fun. But then Rosi gets a little too rough—which is just what mothers fear when they warn against *ugiat*-ing—and Chubby Maata utters a cry of pain. The playful mood is in danger of being broken again, as it was when Luisa pushed Chubby Maata, and again Liila tries to restore play by telling Chubby Maata to "say 'ungaa,' cry (*qia-*) and I'll rescue you." Play mother's darling baby (or demonstrate playfully that you are that baby?), and all will be well. So here we have another positive side of babyness: babies are rescued. At the same time, Liila for the first time associates *ungaa,* the charming and lovable cry of the tiny baby, with *qia-*, a word for crying that has mainly negative connotations. Chubby Maata has frequently heard her mother say sharply, both to her and to Rosi, "Don't cry (*qiangngillutit*)!" or "Stop crying (*qiaguirit*)!"

Clearly, the messages about babyness are getting more complex. First, Luisa—or, rather, some unidentified outsider, for unknown reasons—has disturbed the happy dyadic idyll of babyhood, which Chubby Maata and Liila have been enacting. Happy baby relationships are fragile. Second, babies are in danger of being hurt (because they're loved). On the other hand, babies can also be rescued because they're charming and lovable. But wait a minute: is *ungaa* such a charming cry? Mother has just equated it with *qia-*.

This time it takes Chubby Maata a little while to respond to her mother's invitation to say "ungaa." Has she caught the association between *ungaa* and *qia-*, or perhaps a glimmer of the other complexities that the messages contain?

Perhaps she is only strongly engaged in wrestling, or simply doesn't know what she wants at this moment. We can't know. But after hesitating briefly, she does say "ungaa." Knowingly or unknowingly, she announces her babyness, she plays baby, and Liila gestures in the direction of carrying out her promise to restore the mother-baby dyad against the world by playfully taking sides with her baby against her older child. It is not a very vigorous gesture, and the two children resume their play together—wrestling-play that cannot be specifically characterized as babylike and that does not involve any role-play. Liila neither participates nor intervenes.

Soon, however, the play approaches *Rosi's* limits of tolerance. She seeks protection, taking her cue from Liila, who has just seemed to demonstrate that allies are legitimate. The ally she chooses, however, is not her mother, who has shown herself to be on Chubby Maata's side; it is her aunt, who has already twice served as her model in this series of games. This time the playful mood is not broken, as it was when Chubby Maata said, "Who's hurting me?" and "Ouch!" But now Rosi makes a mistake. Her mother offers protection to *her,* and she believes in the offer; she slips momentarily into serious mode, and that is her undoing. When she trustingly approaches her mother, Liila captures her for the benefit of Chubby Maata and tells Chubby Maata to "hurt (Rosi), make her angry" by holding her captive.

In this betrayal, there is a message for Rosi about babyness: she, the elder child, can't expect to have a protective, dyadic, world-excluding relationship with her mother; mother will take the side of the baby and allow the elder to experience helplessness in face of the alliance between the other two. Liila is, playfully and certainly unwittingly, demonstrating the real displacement of the elder child by the younger, the baby.

But there is also a message, a subtler one, for the baby. Is she really being rescued because she's a charming baby? Indeed, is she really being rescued at all?

First of all, there may be more to saying "ungaa" than meets the ear. To be sure, until now in this series of interactions, saying "ungaa" has been part of a celebration of babyhood, rewarded in itself as a symbolic expression of baby-ness. The soil in which the seeds of self-awareness are being planted has been one of pure warmth. Now, however, the direction to "say 'ungaa'" is presented as a means to an end, a condition that Chubby Maata must fulfill in order to achieve the goal of being rescued, of maintaining her alliance with her mother. Babyness is still being rewarded, but now we begin to glimpse the saying of *ungaa* from another angle. It begins to sound less as though Chubby Maata is being invited to *play* baby or demonstrate her babyness for the enjoyment of herself and others, and more as though she is having to "prove" that she's a baby by making a public declaration of babyness in order to obtain what she wants. Are the first steps being taken toward the perception of babyness as a price to be paid for protection? The notion of reward is being made verbally explicit, and the underside of reward is cost.

And is that protection really something that a baby can count on, or is it a mirage? Remember that at the beginning of this series of interactions, when Chubby Maata seriously tried to displace Rosi, Liila did not take sides and did not intervene. Had she done so then, she would have been supporting Chubby Maata's bad temper and interfering in a problem that concerned just the two children. To put it in an Inuit way, she would have been making Chubby Maata feel "strong" vis-à-vis her sister and encouraging her to take advantage of that strength. Children should learn to fear (*ilira-*) other people a little so that they won't impose on them. Alliances can be dangerous in serious life.[11] By initially taking sides in play, however, Liila is able to create a situation in which both children can experience helplessness and a certain amount of discomfort—that is, exactly the situation in which they can learn to fear each other a little. When the going gets rough, she stops taking sides and lets the wrestling take its own course for a while. And when it appears to be getting out of control, the manner of her stopping it is evenhanded. So Chubby Maata is not quite as "rescued" as she may have imagined she would be.

Both Chubby Maata and Rosi, unbeknown to them, are betrayed in another way, too, which will help to complicate their ideas about babyness and show them its costs. When Rosi first attacked Chubby Maata playfully, Liila defined her attack as "ugiat-," underlining its affectionate connotations by saying, "She does it because you're a baby." Adults always perceived playful *ugiat-* behavior as affectionately motivated, and in theory, babies were always *ugiat*-ed playfully and thus affectionately. In serious mode, however, the word *ugiat-* means to kill without weapons, and, as I have said, mothers tended to fear that, since small children have no judgment, when they *ugiat-* they will inadvertently cross the flexible and, to them, imperceptible line that divides play from serious behavior and will injure the person that they are *ugiat*-ing. Liila uses the word in this sense—without the connotation of affection—when she remarks with amusement that Chubby Maata, wrestling with Rosi, is "really ugiat-ing." Serious *ugiat*-ing was behavior that Qipisa people strongly disapproved of and considered *silait-*: mindless, lacking in understanding—in other words, "babyish" in a negative way.

On the face of it, then, it looks as though Liila were encouraging exactly the behavior that she fears and disapproves of when she instructs Chubby Maata to "make Rosi angry," thereby setting up, I think deliberately, a situation that is certain to escalate the wrestling into the serious mode. But there is more to this than one might think. We have seen that even when Liila defines *ugiat*-ing as affectionately motivated, Chubby Maata may find it uncomfortable to be its object. We have also seen that Liila has taken advantage of Rosi's innocently playful attack on Chubby Maata to create a drama through which the children can discover for themselves the serious side of *ugiat*-ing, the danger of uncontrolled aggression. Equally important, Liila has maneuvered the children into the position of making fools of themselves. Whereas when Rosi first attacks her sister, Liila "tells" Chubby Maata that it is *darling* little babies who are playfully *ugiat*-ed, her manner of stopping the game—her amused remark ("She's *really* attacking!"), followed by laughter—communicates clearly that it is *silly* little babies, those who lack control and understanding, who seriously *ugiat*-. Liila does not, on this occasion, use the word "silait-" to characterize Chubby Maata's behavior, but she has done so on many other occasions when the children were attacking each other.

Again Liila has complicated the picture of babyness. In distinguishing between serious *ugiat*-ing—that is, uncontrolled, angry behavior—and playful *ugiat*-ing, which is controlled and affectionate, Liila implicitly differentiates between a mindless, *silait*- baby, who engages in serious *ugiat*-ing and a charming, -*kuluk* baby, who is the object of playful *ugiat*-ing. We shall see later that the situation is even more complex than this. Not only can babies be both *silait*- and -*kuluk*; *silait*- behavior may itself be -*kuluk*. But I anticipate. Here, Liila simply discourages serious *ugiat*-ing and encourages the playful sort. I judge that the children understand the encouragement, because when Liila explains Rosi's attack as playful, affectionate *ugiat*-ing, the children laugh together with the adults, and I hear it as happy laughter. When the wrestling begins to turn serious, on the other hand, only the adults laugh, and they seem to be expressing amusement at the children's expense. It is harder in this case to know what messages, if any, the children are picking up. Nevertheless, another sentence has been written on the wall in preparation for a shift in the values attached to being a baby.[12]

The play is not quite over. When Liila stops the wrestling game, the children, now set back into the serious world in "equal opposition" to their mother, try, each separately, to recapture Liila's attention and create another mother-child alliance in serious mode. One addresses mother's left ear, the other her right. Both girls, in trying to get their mother to go where *they* want to go instead of taking off on their own, are behaving in a way characteristic of babies and small children, and as usual, Liila turns a deaf ear—two deaf ears—to their serious demands for alliance. Instead, she creates another game and again directs it to Chubby Maata, who has made the more babyish of the two requests: "Let's go home." Liila, by pretending not to hear what Chubby Maata says, forces her to make her serious baby demand public, to expose her babyness to an audience. Here, because of the opposition between mother and daughter—Liila's resistance to Chubby Maata's insistence—Liila's intention of making Chubby Maata *announce* to an *audience* that she is a baby is clear. It doesn't sound this time as though Liila were encouraging Chubby Maata to *play* baby; she dictates no play tones of voice but merely asks Chubby Maata to repeat her serious wish more loudly.

On more than one occasion when Liila has by similar means forced Chubby Maata to announce her wish to go home, she has also maneuvered her daughter into admitting her baby reason for wanting to go: to have a bottle. This time, too, when Chubby Maata has finally made her wish audible, Liila publicly defines it as a baby wish by telling her to "say 'ungaa'" as a condition for having her wish granted. Again, as when Rosi first attacked her sister, Liila "tells" Chubby Maata that babies can be rescued, that their wishes can be granted—as long as they make their babyness public. And again there is a delay before Chubby Maata responds to the instruction to say "ungaa." When she does say it, she immediately claims the promised reward: "OK, let's go!" But her mother's side of the bargain is not immediately fulfilled. Liila doesn't exactly "betray" her baby daughter, as she did Rosi, when Rosi believed that her mother's affectionate gesture was serious, but she does procrastinate, and she doesn't pay the same kind of extravagantly loving attention to Chubby Maata's baby performance that she paid at first, when they were playing their baby-talk game. This time, although Liila dictates the baby role to Chubby Maata, the interaction doesn't fully turn into play. Not only does Liila not dictate "ungaa" in the playful voice that she first used, but Chubby Maata does not respond in that voice, as she did on the earlier occasion, and Liila does not fulfill her promise in playful mode, as she did when she grabbed Rosi and held her down. Instead she responds in serious mode: "Wait awhile."

Liila's partial but incomplete reversion to the play form suggests more clearly than before that throughout this series of interactions, Liila, in playing with her daughter's babyness, is accomplishing serious as well as playful ends. At this moment, Chubby Maata seems to perceive that her mother is not fully playing: she expects fulfillment of a serious contract—if I say "ungaa," I'll get to go home—and she herself doesn't revert fully to play form, saying "ungaa" in a matter-of-fact voice.

But are serious and playful ends really distinct? When Liila says "Say 'ungaa' because you're a baby," she is teaching Chubby Maata to perform what she really is, so "Say 'ungaa'" can mean several things, separately or all at the same time: play baby so we can enjoy your babyness together; play baby so you can discover that you are one; playing baby is better than seriously being a baby; play baby so I can see whether you are one—and if you are one we can laugh at you. I think we are beginning to see how slippery these meanings are, how easily they metamorphose, one into the other, and to what dilemmas they might lead. Chubby Maata herself may not see clearly yet, but the fact that she already senses danger of some sort in self-exposure is evident in the subdued nature of her reply to her mother's questions. Here is no bounciness, no baby beam, but a whisper—a sure sign that she feels *ilira-*, afraid of criticism.

And now, instead of taking Chubby Maata home, as promised, Liila sets out to explore yet another dimension of her daughter's babyness, taking her point of departure from the serious negotiation that is in progress concerning going home. She asks Chubby Maata, "Shall Yiini and Luisa come and visit?" Chubby Maata, wrinkling her nose, indicates that she doesn't want them to. Here again, as often before in this sequence of interactions, the play is one-sided: one actor is playing—in part—and the other isn't playing at all and, moreover, doesn't know that the other *is*. First Liila and then Liila and I are testing her, both in fun and seriously, to see what she thinks of her aunt and of me—and whether she will speak her thought. Chubby Maata, by answering her mother as she does, shows that she is unaware of being tested. She still doesn't know that people shouldn't reject others—and that if people do feel rejecting, they certainly shouldn't say so. In a word, she doesn't know that the social world legitimately contains others besides mothers and babies. Thus her answer demonstrates to the adults that she is still a baby.

Liila's laugh could serve as a clue to Chubby Maata that her inhospitable answer is inappropriate, but when I push her to see whether she will stick to her guns, Chubby Maata confirms that she doesn't want me to visit. Her mother's amused comment, "She agrees!" publicly recognizes and defines Chubby Maata's action, just as her earlier remark, "She's really ugiat-ing," did. And her probing question, "Because you still don't like her?" defines a reason for Chubby Maata's rejection of me, thereby either confirming Chubby Maata in a reason that she, Chubby Maata, is already aware of and exposing it publicly, or suggesting a new possibility to her—probably the former, since she says "suli (still)," which shows that her remark is part of an ongoing "discussion" concerning Chubby Maata's feelings about Yiini.[13] Chubby Maata accepts the reason her mother offers her and says yes, she doesn't like me. Liila and I again, through our laughter, give Chubby Maata a clue to the fact that there is something inappropriate in her answer, but we don't tell her what it is, so the negative evaluation of her behavior and the reasons for it probably remain too subtle for Chubby Maata to pick up at this moment.

Instead, the game is brought to an end in a way that should make it easy for Chubby Maata to overlook any lessons it might contain for her. She gets what she wants, and moreover, when her young uncle Juda starts to follow them, Liila and Luisa in serious mode express toward him exactly the same rejecting sentiments that Chubby Maata had expressed toward Luisa and me. Liila is doing what she had just laughed at her daughter for doing. And neither Luisa nor Juda seems to take the seriously toned rejections seriously; they follow anyway.

Nothing is clear; nothing is resolved.

The Fate of Babyness II

But have we really come back to the beginning? There is a logic to the way in which ideas about babyness are developed in this series of interactions—a logic that corresponds to the outgrowing of babyness, even though, at the same time, Chubby Maata's essential babyness continues to be socially recognized throughout. We have seen that in the first half of the sequence there are two parallel developments in Chubby Maata's identities. First, Chubby Maata moves from being a (serious—annoyed and annoying) baby through being a (playful) child to being a (pretend) adult—before she returns to being a baby (this time quintessentially adorable and playful), a baby whose adorableness is celebrated by and with her mother. Second, Chubby Maata moves from being an unselfconscious baby, happily playing in a baby *mode,* toward being a self-conscious baby, who can observe babyness and consciously play a baby *role.* The movement from baby through child to adult happens to be—is it only coincidental?—a microcosm of the process of growing up, whereas the movement from being an unself-conscious baby to a self-conscious one represents progress in acquiring techniques for growing up.

A third line of development has to do not with the baby identity itself but with the ways in which that identity is evaluated—the places that babies occupy in human society. In the first half of the sequence, Chubby Maata moves from being an annoying baby standing on the periphery of her social world to being an adorable one, cuddled at its center. This third development does not lead directly to growing up, and it runs into trouble in the second part of the sequence.

In this second half, spurred by Luisa's kick, the plot thickens, and identities become more complex. The quintessentially adorable baby, whose dyadic baby relationship with her mother has just been celebrated, begins to become aware of an outside world that interferes with that relationship, a more complex world that contains the potential for hostility as well as affection—and more complicated still, it contains the possibility that affection may be expressed painfully. The dark underbelly of babyness begins to be exposed. Not only may it be somewhat dangerous to be a baby because one is vulnerable to attack and alliances suddenly disintegrate, but it may also turn out that when one thinks one is being charming (*-kuluk,* saying "ungaa"), one is instead being perceived as mindless (*silait-, qia-, ugiat-*). The adorable baby in the arms of her enchanted mother has become a mindless baby in the eyes of a larger and less enamored world. Again it is the growing-up process in a nutshell. It is also a return to the position that Chubby Maata occupied at the beginning of the sequence—but with a difference.

What happens to the development of Chubby Maata's consciousness of babyness after Luisa jolts her out of celebration? Three times—the first three times that Chubby Maata feels injured—Liila reminds her daughter that she is a baby, but after that, babyness seems to go underground. Perhaps Chubby Maata temporarily forgets about it in the heat of wrestling. In any case, it's clear that she is now unaware that her mother is playing with her. The little girl recognizes play when she and her mother are playing companionably together but not when she is her mother's toy.[14] Now again, as at the outset when she tried to remove Rosi, Chubby Maata is behaving in a babyish way without seeming to realize it. But we have not really gone back to the beginning. The seeds of self-consciousness have been, and are continuing to be, sown as Liila, in various contexts, repeats "Say 'ungaa' " and "Because you're a baby." A situation has been created in which Chubby Maata's budding knowledge of the dimensions of babyness and how people regard them can begin to give her a sense of the advantages and disadvantages of that identity—a sense that may influence her behavior. Though Chubby Maata catches only a glimmer of it at the moment, a motive is provided for growing up.

To put it differently, the sequence of dramas I have described allows us to see that at this particular moment in her life Chubby Maata is learning several separate things all at the same time: that there is an *identity* that people recognize as that of a baby, an identity that is constituted by *actions* that people label as those of a baby; that she can *play* at being a baby; that she is *herself* a baby in the eyes of other people; and that being a baby has *consequences,* both positive and negative, for the way people treat her. And what Liila is doing, with varying degrees of consciousness, as she plays with her daughter is to help her to become more aware of all these facts of her three-year-old life. The play provides both techniques and motives for growing up, as well as provoking Chubby Maata to think about goals.

THE DRAMA ANALYZED: HOW PLAY WORKS

How does play work to accomplish these ends? Does it make a difference that the goals are achieved through the medium of play? Let's look at the play from a little distance, beginning with its absence or disruption. Where does serious behavior occur in this sequence? What does it signify and what follows from it?

The interaction begins with serious behavior as Chubby Maata voices a wish that her mother apparently disapproves of. Liila ignores the expression, and the interaction between mother and daughter is deadlocked until Chubby Maata accidentally or deliberately unlocks it by initiating play with the help of Liila. So seriousness here represents undesirable behavior and is unsuccessful as a mode of interaction, whereas the reverse is true of play.

Play—in this case mutual—between Chubby Maata and Liila continues until Luisa, followed by Rosi, misunderstands it, whereupon it breaks down; Luisa and Rosi make serious efforts to correct Chubby Maata, and another deadlock occurs. Again the channels are cleared and successful communication between Chubby Maata and Liila is reestablished by the initiation of mutual play, this time by Liila alone ("Say 'ungaa'"), and again the play continues until it is interrupted by another misunderstanding expressed in serious mode. This time it is Chubby Maata who misunderstands Luisa's playful gesture, a gentle kick on the bottom. Chubby Maata makes a serious exclamation ("Who's hurting me?"), and for the third time, Liila reestablishes good communication—not necessarily between Luisa and Chubby Maata but between herself and Chubby Maata—by reinitiating play (again with "Say 'ungaa'"). In both of these last two instances, what Liila's playful *ungaa* does is to "explain" the breakdown that has resulted in serious behavior. It breaks the deadlock by explicitly recognizing Chubby Maata's babyness and explains the difficulty as being in a sense the result of that babyness—casting perhaps a faint shadow on Chubby Maata's horizon? Looked at from another point of view, these ruptures in the play provide opportunities for Liila to redirect the play, to use it to call attention to Chubby Maata's babyness and demonstrate the operation of that identity in Chubby Maata's social life.

We have already seen that matters become more complex in the second half of the sequence with regard to identities. The same is true with regard to the nature and uses of seriousness and play. Nonetheless, the initial exchange between Chubby Maata and Liila at the next transition from playfulness to seriousness looks familiar. Once again, serious behavior signals trouble. As the wrestling escalates, Chubby Maata again breaks out of play mode because she feels injured, and Liila again suggests a playful solution, which is signaled by "Say 'ungaa.'" But this time, making Chubby Maata's babyness focal and explicit does not explain the breakdown of play and thereby reestablish clear communication between Liila and Chubby Maata. Instead, the declaration of babyness is presented as a condition to be fulfilled before Liila can repair the troubled situation, so this time Chubby Maata has to make a decision: does she or does she not want Liila to rescue her? And the decision is not a simple one. *Ungaa,* the immediately rewarded cry of the adorable (-*kuluk*) baby, is suddenly associated with *qia-,* the disapproved behavior of a mindless (*silait-*) baby. There are now more serious undertones, a first hint of a point that will become clear only much later: charming, lovable behavior (*qaqa-*) is mindless (*silait-*).

Moreover, though mutual play is reestablished as before when Chubby Maata says "ungaa," it is a subtly different play. This time, in addition to the mutuality between Chubby Maata and her mother, there is mutual play between the children; in fact, Liila, unbeknown to Chubby Maata, is preparing to withdraw from the game at this overt level, leaving it entirely to the children. In a moment she will retire to a level of play of which Chubby Maata is unaware, a play in which Chubby Maata is the Object, not the Companion. Liila is tricking her into serious behavior, which she disapproves of, as she disapproved of Chubby Maata's first serious behavior—her attempt to remove Rosi. As I said earlier, Liila is testing both children to see whether they can be seduced into serious aggression, and she is playfully creating a situation in which the girls, if they do exceed the limits of play, will experience the uncomfortable consequences of seriousness. So again she is discouraging serious behavior—serious *baby* behavior. She does it, not by involving herself in that behavior and in its resolution—for example, by seriously contributing to the attack (which would terrify Chubby Maata)—or by legislating against it or seriously suggesting how to deal with it (which would deprive the children of the opportunity to actively participate in the solution of a problem), but by disengaging herself and letting the children explore for themselves the possibilities and consequences of the behavior: physical discomfort, criticism from others (expressed as amusement), and disintegration of the cherished mother-baby dyad. These are experiences that the children could not be given in serious mode, because in that mode physical aggression between people is unthinkable and encouraging it would be condemned as "mindless" (*silait-*). Instead, Liila encourages the development of "mind" (*isuma*) in the children by tricking them into displaying their lack of it. Similarly, she facilitates Chubby Maata's discovery that she's a baby by manipulating her into displaying her babyness—her adorable babyness in the first half of the sequence and then her mindless babyness in the second half.

This time Liila, playing over the heads of the children, so to speak, is not clearing the lines of communication between herself and Chubby Maata when she says "Say 'ungaa.'" This time, when she calls Chubby Maata's attention to her babyness, she is pulling her daughter by the nose. When Qipisa people play with children in this complicated way, which is part test, part experiment, part seduction, part dramatization of the plots of their own lives, clarity for the children is not an immediate aim of the adult players. In such situations, when the ground is a quagmire underfoot, children may seek simple truth in serious messages, and adults may resort to seriousness to restore reason to the interaction—or end it.

That is what Liila does now, in order to keep her play and the children's increasingly unplayful aggression from running out of control. Holding her hand between the flailing children (an unambiguously serious gesture), she addresses serious-sounding words, first to the audience, "She's *really* ugiat-ing," and then to the children, "Please behave well (*pitsialaurisi*)." The first remark exposes Liila's detachment from the children's aggression. It shows us how far she has removed herself from their play, which is no longer play; but one can hear at the same time that it is the author of the game who is speaking, observing with amusement the game she has successfully created. In other words, at the children's level Liila is not playing, and at her own adult level she both is and isn't playing.

In the case of the second remark, "Pitsialaurisi," Liila's use of -*lau(q)*- (please) is a clue—to me and possibly to the children—that she is speaking in serious mode. When she is playing, she uses the imperative forms -*rit* and -*ruk*: *ungaalirit* (say "ungaa"), *qialirit* (cry), *anniruk* (hurt her).[15] She may or may not, however, be telling the truth when she says she hears someone coming in. I didn't hear anybody, and neither did the children. They are not sure how to interpret her warning. There are several possibilities. One is that she is serious and telling the truth; the second is that she is serious and lying. The children may suspect the untruth when they ask, "Who?" The third possibility—which I quote from Liila's explanation on other similar occasions and which the children are not yet wise enough to suspect—is that she is "pretend-talking (*uqangnguaq-*) because the children don't understand, they are unenlightened (*qauyimangngit-, silait-*)." In other words, she is only pretending to be serious; she is still playing. Or, perhaps more accurately, there is still a large measure of play in what she says. This last hypothesis is confirmed (for adult listeners) when she answers the children's question by saying "visitors from another camp"—a bugaboo commonly used in dramas concocted to modify the behavior of children who are being obstreperous. But the children don't know this, so Liila's pretense of seriousness and the children's doubt about whether or not Liila is telling the truth have put a stumbling block in the way of communication, distracted them from their activity, and ended Liila's game, as she intended it should.

When interaction begins again, it is in serious mode, as it was at the outset when Chubby Maata was trying to remove Rosi. As before, Chubby Maata—and this time also Rosi—is trying to persuade Liila to accommodate a seriously expressed wish: to leave. And again Liila turns the interaction into play, which forces (the word is appropriate here for the first time) Chubby Maata to expose her babyness. If Chubby Maata wants to achieve her expressed goal, she will have to do as Liila asks and say "ungaa."

The points at which communication overtly breaks down because serious and playful modes become tangled are still giving Liila opportunities to make Chubby Maata state that she is a baby, but this time Liila is engineering, not repairing, the breakdown: "Hai? Hai?" And her playfulness is not clear to Chubby Maata. As was the case when she warned the children about "visitors," there is room for uncertainty about whether she is serious or playing when she tells Chubby Maata to say "ungaa." Both the context—saying "ungaa" as a means of achieving a serious goal—and Liila's tone of voice give the request a serious flavor, a flavor that was hinted at earlier when Liila made saying "ungaa" the condition of a rescue that she playfully designed and that Chubby Maata seriously believed in. Here too, even more than last time, Chubby Maata takes seriously the condition her mother sets, says "ungaa"—after some hesitation that makes me wonder whether she is trying to decipher her mother's meaning—and immediately claims the reward.

Liila, however, bypasses this serious confrontation by starting another game that Chubby Maata doesn't recognize as a game: "Shall Yiini and Luisa come and visit?" Indeed, this time, though Liila laughs at her for taking it seriously, Chubby Maata doesn't seem to even suspect hidden levels of meaning. And this time Liila does not explicitly point out Chubby Maata's babyness, does not try to bring her daughter's consciousness into line with her own. She allows the play to end in serious mode: "All right, let's go home." And they leave.

The educational principle of "causing someone to think" (*isummaksaiyuq*) seems most applicable to what is going on here. It's clear that throughout this sequence of interactions Chubby Maata's mind is being exercised on the subject of babyness. Liila's contribution is to draw her daughter's attention to babyness by activating and labeling it—that is, by suggesting to her, always playfully, that she perform it. And, to repeat, it is the moments when communication breaks down—the moments when seriousness intrudes into play or, in the last case ("Let's go home!"), when a serious communication is blocked by a playful response—that provide Liila with her opportunities to interpret Chubby Maata's behavior and to call her attention to babyness as an identity.

In the first half of the sequence we find rather simple dichotomies between playfulness and seriousness, which are created simply because one person understands another's act in the "wrong" mode. Once it is Luisa who misunderstands, but usually it is Chubby Maata. And always it is Liila who interprets the situation, returns it to the safe sphere of play, and so reestablishes a clear, simple, and secure life, with mother and baby at its core.

In the second half of the sequence something different happens. Simple dichotomies disappear and are replaced by multileveled communications, part play, part serious. And it is Liila, no longer clarifier but obfuscator, who creates these ambiguities by pretending to be serious when she is not and pretending to play when she does not. Or both at the same time. Chubby Maata, of course, misunderstands more than ever, while we, watching bug-eyed from a safe distance, can see that life is no longer made clear and simple but on the contrary is very complex, that the dyad of mother and baby is being undermined, and that Chubby Maata is being left to her own interpretive resources.

Once again this small sequence of interactions appears to be a microcosm, this time of the tangled and treacherous nature of communication in adult society. Chubby Maata is learning several lessons about playfulness and seriousness that will be of use to her all her life. I think she has already learned that it is possible to act in more than one mode, and she is beginning to learn that truth and reason are not the exclusive property of one mode or the other. Either mode can clarify or obscure truths expressed in the other, and each mode can serve as a foil for the other. That is, when communicative trouble looms on one plane, it can be dealt with by switching into the other—although play often works better than seriousness. At the same time, and somewhat contradictorily, Chubby Maata is learning that no communication can ever be trusted to be what it seems to be. It is always necessary to be alert to the possibility of hidden meanings: seriousness under playfulness, playfulness under seriousness, the two intricately enmeshed.

As to the lessons about babyness that Chubby Maata is learning, it's clear that the playfulness of the medium both simplifies and complicates the learning process. Some of Chubby Maata's performances of babyness are initiated by her mother and others by herself, and they take various forms, but all of them dramatize babyness in clear and simple images. Chubby Maata seems to recognize, create, and communicate the positive images of the -*kuluk* baby quite well already, though she may not be fully, articulately aware of what she is doing; but she appears to have only the faintest, glimmering awareness of the existence of the *silait*- baby. Nevertheless, all the performances alike, both the conscious or semi-conscious ones in the first half of the sequence and the probably unconscious ones in the second half,[16] give Chubby Maata the opportunity to discover, to explore, and even to create ("Tiini," "uquququu") the various dimensions of babyness and the consequences of being a baby. They make her *live* babyness richly and with increasing awareness. And, for the moment, by and large with joy. At the same time, they give her practice in experimenting with new behaviors in a milieu that is fun and, in an important sense, safe. When Liila playfully says "Say 'ungaa,'" she is not—as far as Chubby Maata can see—threatening her babyness. In fact, she is enjoying it; she presents herself as Chubby Maata's playfellow and ally, so Chubby Maata has no need to oppose her and to resist the lessons that she subtly presents. Indeed, Chubby Maata is maximally open to those lessons, because she is in a happy and relaxed mood, not in crisis.

In *performing* babyness, Chubby Maata is willfully, actively, putting on baby behavior. And of course what is willfully put on can also be willfully taken off, so Chubby Maata, in learning to play the role of baby, is unwittingly learning how to take distance from babyness. At the same time, in performing babyness, Chubby Maata will also discover—indeed, she may already suspect—that she is displaying it; she is performing what she is, and audiences will confirm her understanding, in hugs and words and in laughter that contains many meanings, evaluations both wanted and unwanted. We have seen that the fuzziness of the boundary between playing baby and really being a baby disrupted Chubby Maata's play when Luisa mistook her playful mispronunciation for real baby incompetence. It is because she is playing at being what she really is that the boundary is problematic, and it is because it is problematic that it is educational. It is the identity between playful and serious selves that makes it possible for the play to serve as an announcement of self, for the audience reaction to create awareness of self, and for negative audience reactions to someday strike home and bring about a change.

Chapter 3 *"Are* You a Baby?"

It should already be clear that the innocent and loving little question "Because you're a baby?" and the associated instruction "Say 'ungaa'" work in a variety of ways to mature Chubby Maata and mold her into a person who thinks and feels in Inuit ways. Still, we have only scratched the surface of how this question and the associated dramas work.

Chubby Maata hears "Because you're a baby," "Say 'ungaa,'" and "Are you a baby?" not just once in a while but several times a day during this period of her life. Many of the interactions built around these phrases are short and fragmentary, relatively few develop into full-fledged dramas, and it's often difficult to sense to what extent the intent of the adult speaker is playful. But in spite of these variations in performance, I hear the words, and I'm sure Chubby Maata does, as a refrain, each occurrence resonating with others, tugging at her attention, provoking a response from her, and in this way working in her to organize around the nucleus of the refrain a multifaceted web of important meanings.

Each occurrence of the refrain is highly charged, first of all, by the adults who use it, for whom babyness has powerful meanings, as we shall see. It is charged for Chubby Maata, too, because her parents communicate their strength of feeling—if not precisely their own feelings—to her; because they make of the encounters experiences sometimes delightful and sometimes uncomfortable for her; and not least because, often individually and certainly collectively, the incidents present her with problems. I have already suggested what some of these might be. A look at other occasions on which Chubby Maata hears the "baby" refrain may enable us to fill in the contour a bit and see what cumulative meanings and puzzles these interactions may generate for her.

First, however, let's look at some of the meanings that being a baby has for Chubby Maata's parents. Jaani and Liila show us aspects of these meanings both in the way they talk about babies in general and in the way they interact with their own baby, Chubby Maata. Though the complex understandings and feelings of Liila and Jaani are not reflected in any clear and simple way in the puzzles that confront Chubby Maata, they certainly help to create those puzzles, as Chubby Maata interprets the ways in which her parents treat her through the filter of her own motives and understandings.

We saw in Episode 1 that Liila is, perhaps partly deliberately and partly without conscious intent, encouraging Chubby Maata to grow out of being a baby. Chubby Maata's seriously phrased baby requests seem to annoy her. On the other hand, she delights in the *playful* babyness of her daughter and repeatedly confirms in word and action that a baby is a good thing to be. Other "baby" interactions show us that Jaani's feelings, too, have more than one face.

Chubby Maata, seen through the eyes of the adults around her, has two salient qualities. On one hand, she is *-kuluk*, a *babykuluk*, a charming wee baby; on the other hand, she is *silait-*, unaware, lacking in understanding. Her *-kuluk* behavior is enjoyed, even cherished, while her *silait-* behavior is both exploited and implicitly criticized, as it was when Liila made use of Chubby Maata's innocence to organize a game in which her little daughter was made to act foolishly, attacking (*ugiat*-ing) Rosi. When Chubby Maata began to aggress against her sister in an uncontrolled fashion, Liila's amused remark, her laughter, and the fact that she brought the game to an end all suggest that she considered Chubby Maata's behavior to be that of a *silly* baby; she appeared to be establishing an opposition between charming, lovable (*-kuluk*) baby behavior, which is encouraged, and undesirable, foolish (*silait-*, though she didn't label it) baby behavior, which should be extinguished. These two qualities, *-kuluk* and *silait-*, seem to provide an organizing principle that explains why some of Chubby Maata's experiences of babyness are happy while others are uncomfortable for her.

There is, however, an exception to the dichotomous "rule" that governs Chubby Maata's experiences in Episode 1, and this may alert us to the oversimplified nature of this analysis. The exception, of course, is that both *-kuluk* and *silait-* qualities are responsible for Chubby Maata's being *ugiat*-ed, attacked.

The *ugiat*-ing scenario is not clearly spelled out in Episode 1, because the *ugiat*-er herself is a small child, nearly as *silait-* as her sister in this context and merely a stooge in the game of her mother, who only wants to make a "simple" point or two. Adults say they *ugiat-* because they are overcome by affection for the charming baby, but I suspect they may have other motives, too, not so available for discussion. For one thing, I think they may be intensifying their affection for the baby by hurting it a little.[1] One mother told me explicitly that "hurt babies are more lovable"; the baby's distress elicits nurturant feelings. And I would not be surprised if the baby's uncertainty about what motivates the adult's rough treatment—the movement of the small face from tears to laughter and back again—added spice to the enjoyment: the same spice that flavors a game being played over a child's head. That kind of enjoyment, at the child's expense, owes its existence to the small one's being *silait-*, not understanding what is going on. So the events of Episode 1 suggest the possibility that, for Liila, *-kuluk* and *silait-* are not altogether distinct qualities. In other interactions built around the phrases "Are you a baby?" and "Because you're a baby," the complexity of the dialogue between these two characteristics takes shape more fully.

Occasionally, when Liila or Jaani says to Chubby Maata, "Are you a baby?" or "Because you're a baby," I can see no special and immediate reason for it; they seem to be simply appreciating her presence. Much more often, however, they are commenting on some baby action: she may be sucking a bottle of milk, beaming her baby beam, or asking questions one after another without pause. In almost all these cases, her parents are *aqaq*-ing her when they ask her if she is a baby; they are telling her in tender voices that they love her baby self, and sometimes, as in the first half of Episode 1, the interaction seems to be a pure celebration of babyness. Sometimes, however, though the tone is the tender tone of "*-kuluk,*" my darling little baby, it is not "*-kuluk*" that is said but "*silait-,*" my foolish little baby.

Thus, for the adults in Chubby Maata's world, *-kuluk* and *silait-* are not always in opposition. Jaani expressed this vividly one day. He and Chubby Maata were cuddled together on my sleeping platform in a private world created by the caress in his voice as he cooed almost soundlessly: "Are you a baby? Say 'ungaa.'" "When you leave," he said to me after a while, "you'll think of her all the time because she's so very silait-." Surprised, I asked, "Does one miss (*unga-*) silait- babies?" "Yes, of course," his raised brows signaled. He seemed equally surprised that I didn't take the obvious fact for granted.

I suggested in Chapter 2 that the sight of Chubby Maata's physical helplessness, her incompetence in performing the complicated physical manipulations dictated by her mother, might make Liila feel maternally protective, as well as tenderly superior and amused. Social, mental, and emotional incompetence—being *silait-*, not understanding the exigencies and impossibilities of life and the social rules that govern it—made small children lovable to adult Inuit in these same ways and in a number of other ways, too.

Inuit parents, both Qipisamiut and the Utkuhikhalingmiut of the central Arctic,[2] have remarked to me that babies are lovable in the sense of being pitiable (to be *nallik*-ed) because they don't understand that what they are crying for sometimes isn't available and that they are loved (*nallik*-ed) even when they can't be given what they want. But the helpless dependence of small children can elicit not only the mature, nurturant love called *nallik*- but also a dependent, needy attachment, which reciprocates that of the child. Qipisamiut and Utkuhikhalingmiut alike call this dependent love *unga-*, and I think it likely that the name is semantically related to the baby's cry, which, as we know, is heard as "ungaa." *Unga*- is considered to be quintessentially the love of small children for their parents, but one old father told me that he still *unga*-ed his middle-aged daughter deeply because he had brought her up alone and she had clung to him, *unga*-ed him, very much when she was little. And I wonder whether another root of this adult attachment is identification with the child's neediness. I once heard two tired young mothers explicitly identify in fantasy with the babies they held on their laps: "Who would you like to be today?" "I'd like to be my baby." "Me too."[3]

Silait-ness, lack of understanding, is lovable in yet another way, too; it is the source of the *qaqa*-ing behavior that parents and grandparents, aunts, uncles, and older siblings find so charming (-*kuluk*): bouncing and beaming, playfully or familiarly calling attention to oneself, coming to be cuddled when invited—in general, all the behavior signifying the happy certainty that one is the center of the universe, unconditionally loved and able to count on being treated tenderly (*niviuq*-ed, *aqaq*-ed) and given what one wants. Several young mothers, asking me which of their small children I liked best, told me that their own favorites were the children who *qaqa*-ed: who responded readily to their mother's affectionate overtures and made overtures of their own.

Mutually responsive courtship between caretaker and child is certainly a source of happiness to both of them, as it weaves a protective cocoon of affection and appreciation around both, making each feel noticed by the other and counteracting any tendency to feel rejected. But expecting to be the center of the world is just as unrealistic, as *silait-*, as not seeing that one's family loves one even when they can't provide everything one wants; and I would guess that because this expectation is doomed, it is pitiable (it is to be *nallik*-ed) in the eyes of adults, just as the feeling of being *un*loved is pitiable. So *qaqa*-ing may contribute in more than one way to the lovableness of small children who are *silait-*, and the lovableness of *silait-* behavior is in turn composed of many strands, of which *qaqa*-ing is only one.[4]

It is clear that the *silait-* behavior of a baby creates strong bonds between the baby and other family members. At the same time it can be annoying, and it gradually becomes inappropriate. Behavior that is charming or touching in a three-year-old—crying, demanding, asking to be the center of attention, however playfully and beamingly—is not so appealing in an older child; it interferes with other immediate wishes and needs of the parents as well as with their long-term goals for the child. When an older child is criticized as *silait-*, the tone is not tender but is strongly disapproving. When children outgrow *silait-* behavior, then, they earn approval, and the parents avoid the disapproval of *their* elders, who will blame them if their child goes awry; but all the family members together sacrifice the rhapsodic intensity of the daily expression of affection, which gives them such pleasure. So I wonder whether Jaani and Liila—though they never suggest this to Chubby Maata—may not feel, in some recess of the heart, that when she gives up baby behavior she will be just a little less lovable. When Jaani says that one misses *silait-* babies, he implies that one does not miss older children. And an Utkuhikhalingmiut parent once told me that the most intense bonds of both *nallik-* and *unga-* were those between parents and their youngest children.

A baby, then, is not a simple thing to Chubby Maata's parents. They want Chubby Maata to grow up even as they want her to stay just as she is, and these complicated feelings are reflected in complex actions.

Babyness is not a simple thing to Chubby Maata, either. She, too, is moving forward and holding back at the same time. But the problems that she faces are not those of her parents. She cannot see her own charm through the prism of her parents' eyes. That glass was created by experiences that are not hers. Nevertheless, the way her parents treat her must have some effects on how she perceives her situation. Let's see, then, what other interactions can tell us about Chubby Maata's own view of babyness and the problems that she currently has with her baby status.

One important thing we will discover is that Chubby Maata does have a concept of babyness with which she sometimes operates—something that wasn't clear in Episode 1. She considers being a baby a legitimate status for her to occupy, and, as we have already seen, she still very much enjoys being a baby. She delights in the intimacy with her mother, so full of extravagantly expressed affection: the *niviuq*-ing, the *aqaq*-ing, and the shared play, as well as the sweet flow of milk, sugared tea, bannock and jam, all available on demand. Her mother's presence, the warm comfort and safety of her mother's touch, is still a bulwark for her, too, when she is afraid, unhappy, or tired, and, as we saw in Episode 1, she still demands that presence unashamedly, even when she is not upset.

Chubby Maata is a *qaqa*-ing child, a very lovable child. She invites affectionate attention and is quite sure that, in the natural order of things, being a sweet little (-*kuluk*) baby is enough to evoke her parents' tenderness and the care (or the rights) that go with it.[5] She demonstrated this view delightfully one day.

Episode 2 (Excerpt, November 29)

Three days after Episode 1, Liila stopped in to visit me briefly with Chubby Maata.[6] Now Chubby Maata wanted to go home. Several times she said to her mother, "Let's go home," but Liila, who was absorbed in trimming my seal-oil lamps, paid no attention. I asked Chubby Maata, "Because you're going to do what?" Chubby Maata replied, "Because I'm going to suck a bottle—at our house." I questioned further: "Because you're a baby?" Chubby Maata raised her brows, then beamed her shining baby smile, clapped her hands and, turning to her mother, said, "I *am* a babykuluk, *aren't* I?" Liila smiled: "Mmmm." "Come, then," Chubby Maata urged. "Let's go home!" Her mother got up and they left.

Chubby Maata has interpreted my question, "Because you're a baby?" as recognition of her -*kuluk* identity—subject only to her mother's confirmation. The question elicits and intensifies her enjoyment and her sense of legitimacy. Clearly, she understands the phrase (it's a single word in Inuktitut) when it celebrates her babyness, and for her, as for three-year-old Saali (see note 5), being a baby is reason enough for her to have what she wants.

Liila often confirms the legitimacy of Chubby Maata's baby self-image by granting her daughter's wishes. On the other hand, in Episode 1, we saw her resist two of Chubby Maata's baby demands: to stand between her knees and to go home. She also pointed out to Chubby Maata that being a baby makes her vulnerable to the physical discomfort of being *ugiat*-ed, attacked.

What Chubby Maata understood on that occasion about the mysteries of *ugiat*-ing was not clear, and what she understood of the subtler hazards of being a baby—being criticized, laughed at, exploited, and betrayed—was even less clear. But at two moments in the second half of Episode 1, we did see Chubby Maata hesitate before saying "ungaa"—behavior that gave us cause to wonder whether she glimpsed something ominous under the surface of the tender refrain. Other occurrences of the refrain give us more evidence that she does sometimes see more than tenderness in it. It occasionally happens that Chubby Maata rejects the suggestion that she might be a baby. Let's look at two of these instances and see whether we can guess what is going on inside her small self when she does so.

Episode 3 (October 7)

Jaani came into my qammaq carrying his four-month-old daughter, Aita, who, you may remember, lived next door with her grandparents. A minute later Liila came in with Chubby Maata. Chubby Maata made a sudden gesture in the direction of Aita's face, which startled the baby and made her cry. I don't think Chubby Maata slapped her, but the effect was the same. When Aita burst into tears, Chubby Maata immediately returned to her and started to snuff (*kunik-*) and hug her,[7] but her attempted reparation was defeated by Liila, who snatched Aita out of Jaani's arms, held her above Chubby Maata's reach, and looked down at her three-year-old with an expressionless face.

Chubby Maata, unable now to snuff and hug Aita, stroked her leg and licked her boot sole instead. Jaani drew Chubby Maata between his legs, put his arms around her, and, in a tender, *niviuq*-ing tone, asked her, "Because you're a baby, too (*babyummigaviit*)?" Chubby Maata wrinkled her nose, "No," but Jaani contradicted her: "Yes, you're a babykuluk." He continued, "Because you're a baby, jump." He was telling her to raise herself off the ground, holding onto his hands—a game of physical skill or strength. She did so. Liila took Aita out, and almost immediately Jaani followed with Chubby Maata.

Episode 4 (Excerpt, October 29)

Jaani and Chubby Maata came into my qammaq.[8] Jaani sat down on the sleeping platform; Chubby Maata sat between his legs, with his arms around her. Pointing to one of my seal-oil lamps (a *qulliq*), Chubby Maata asked her father, "What's that?" She knew full well what the answer was. Jaani said: "A qulliq. Because you're charmingly lacking in understanding (*silait* . . . *kuluk* . . .)?"[9] His voice was affectionate, *niviuq*-ing. I didn't see her response, if indeed she made one.

Jaani then asked, "Are you a baby?" Chubby Maata wrinkled her nose. Jaani's arms were still around her, and his voice was tender. "Say 'ungaa,'" he said. Chubby Maata wrinkled her nose.

In neither of Episodes 3 and 4 is Chubby Maata's babyness being celebrated. In both cases, she has just done something that her interlocutor considers inappropriate for a child at her stage of development.[10] In the first instance, she has approached too vigorously the baby sister who lives next door—she has *ugiat*-ed her, with what mixture of feelings we can't know. Perhaps she was only making a friendly overture, but her mother and Aita herself clearly feel that she has gone too far. Liila signals her disapproval by lifting Aita out of reach and holding her there, foiling Chubby Maata's attempt to make amends. She implies that Chubby Maata is *silait*-; she can't be trusted to stay within safe limits.

The tone in which Jaani asks his question makes it sound more like a sympathetic interpretation of Chubby Maata's behavior than like a criticism. Nevertheless, Chubby Maata rejects the baby label—or Jaani's use of it in explaining her behavior. Her mother's action and the stony face that accompanied it must have contained a powerful message, and Jaani's question has related that message to her babyness. The fact that Jaani has asked her a *question* following her mother's action may also suggest to her that she is being criticized. As we shall see, though not all questions are criticisms, a great many criticisms—or tricky tests that, depending on the answer, could lead to critical judgments—are phrased as questions, and Chubby Maata may already be acquiring sensitivity to this fact. Her sensitivity is by no means mature, however. We saw in Episode 2 that Chubby Maata saw no criticism in the question I asked her about her baby identity. And when Jaani goes on to tell her that she's a -*kuluk* baby, she is easily reassured and willingly plays the baby game of "jumping" with him.[11]

On the second occasion (Episode 4), Chubby Maata asks her father a question to which she knows the answer. I think that at this point she is initiating her own game with Jaani, engaging him in talk; she often did that with her mother and later with me, too. But Jaani either doesn't perceive her game or doesn't want to play it with her just now. In asking his little daughter whether she is *silait-* and *-kuluk,* he asks her to consider whether her question is foolish (*silait-*), albeit charming (*-kuluk*). But Chubby Maata denies being charmingly foolish, and when Jaani asks her whether she is a baby, she denies that, too.

It may be that her denial is part of her game with her father; children of her age often do give the wrong answer, with a mischievous smile, to "playful" adult questions. But this time there is no smile, so I think it likely that the "silait-" in the question has alerted Chubby Maata to the presence of a worm in the apple: she associates being *silait-* as well as being *-kuluk* with babyness, and she doesn't want to be *silait-*, even if she is *-kuluk* at the same time. Her priorities are beginning to be those of an older, "aware" (*qauyima-, silatuu-*) child.

It appears, then, that the foundations for a complex concept of babyness have been laid. Babies are both *-kuluk* and *silait-*. I think we can assume, however, that the tangled connections between these two qualities, which are present in the minds of her parents, are not present in Chubby Maata's mind. Chubby Maata doesn't have her parents' reasons for finding *silait-* behavior *-kuluk* and *-kuluk* behavior *silait-*. She may see some of the *silait-* in the *-kuluk* soon. The analysis of Episode 1 has suggested that she may already, occasionally and dimly, suspect that when she thinks she is being *-kuluk*, others see her as *silait-*. That, surely, is a first step to the more sophisticated perception that being *-kuluk* is *silait-*, but she won't see the reverse, the *-kuluk* in the *silait-*, until she is much older. I think it's likely that once upon a time, perhaps not very long ago, she heard the loving tone of the *silait-* comments more clearly than the words themselves and read them as *-kuluk;* she certainly hears tone as dominant over words when her grandfather croons at her, "*Don't* visit!"[12] But at this moment in her life, I see no evidence that she is confused by her father's tender voice when he calls her *silait-*. She has—in this context—already learned to respond to the word, not exclusively to the tone. For Chubby Maata, right now, *-kuluk* is good and *silait-* is bad—as they are, at least on the surface, presented to her in Episode 1 and are repeatedly presented, every day, in many other interactions. The problem that she faces at this point is not whether she does or doesn't want to be *-kuluk* (she does) nor whether she does or doesn't want to be *silait-* (she doesn't). The problem is whether she does or doesn't want to be a baby—a person who has both *-kuluk* and *silait-* qualities, one who has experiences that are sometimes rewarding and sometimes uncomfortable.

The dilemma takes root in this untidy situation of inconsistent experience. Liila and Jaani water it by directing Chubby Maata's attention to it, keeping it salient, and providing her with ingredients with which to think about babyness. By these means, they grow it into a larger dilemma. In Episode 1 we saw that

Liila labeled Chubby Maata a baby and that she verbally pointed out and also dramatized, with Chubby Maata as the protagonist, consequences, both agreeable and not so agreeable, of being a baby. In other "baby" interactions, we find other ways in which Liila prods Chubby Maata into thinking about babyness.

Episode 5 (Excerpt, October 29)

Two hours before Episode 4, Liila and Chubby Maata were visiting in my qammaq.[13] Liila, reciting words for Chubby Maata to imitate, dictated, " . . . baby—not baby—baby—not baby . . . " Instead of repeating the words, Chubby Maata smiled her broad baby smile at her mother, a *qaqa*-ing smile. Liila said something in a tender *niviuq*-ing voice about Chubby Maata's being a sweet little (-*kuluk*) baby and then said, "Say 'ungaa.'" Chubby Maata complied in a more or less matter-of-fact voice, not imitating the sound of a cry, but with her baby smile. Liila *aqaq*-ed and snuffed her. Chubby Maata interrupted her by pointing to the skylight and asking in a conversational voice, "What's that out there?" Her mother, also in a conversational voice, replied, "Sila." (The word means weather, outdoors, the world.) Chubby Maata went on to ask other questions on other subjects.

Episode 6 (Excerpt, December 30)

Liila and her sister Luisa were drinking tea with me when Chubby Maata was heard outside.[14] Liila called to tell her daughter where she was, and Chubby Maata came in all by herself, in great good humor. Opening the door, she announced her arrival in a ringing tone: "Toilet paper!" Then, seeing the cups, she immediately demanded, "Tea!" Her tone was the playful, bouncy, *qaqa*-ing one that said, "I know I'm loved." Liila poured tea for her and spoke tenderly to her. Then, as Chubby Maata was drinking her tea, Liila, still in the tender *niviuq*-ing voice, asked her, "Are you a baby?" Chubby Maata must have wrinkled her nose, because Liila, continuing in the same tone, asked: "In what horrid little (ways) are you behaving, then (*suyuruluuvitli*)?" Chubby Maata beamed her baby beam and didn't answer.

Episode 7 (October 1)

Liila and Chubby Maata were at home, and Jaani's older brother Tuuma and I were visiting. Liila asked Chubby Maata, "Are you a baby?" (I don't know in what context the question was posed.) Chubby Maata wrinkled her nose: "No." Liila asked for confirmation: "You're *not* a baby?" Chubby Maata raised her brows silently, meaning, "That's right." Tuuma asked her: "Because you feel shy (*kangngu*-)?" I didn't see Chubby Maata's reply, if she made one. Liila said, tenderly, "You *are* a sweet little (-*kuluk*) baby, though."

A little later, when Chubby Maata asked for a bottle of milk, her mother said:

"What did you just say? If you're not a baby, you don't drink from bottles." And she gave her the bottle.

Episode 8 (December 21)

Liila wanted both Chubby Maata and Rosi to go to bed. The lure of a seaweed-gathering expedition the next day failed to persuade them; the girls paid no attention. Then Liila asked Chubby Maata, "Have you stopped being a baby?" Chubby Maata wrinkled her nose. Liila said, "Yes, you have stopped being a baby; *babies* go to bed." Chubby Maata paid no attention, and a few minutes later, Liila's young sister Liuna picked both girls up bodily, undressed them, and put them to bed. Neither protested, and Chubby Maata fell asleep at once.[15]

On all four of these occasions (Episodes 5–8)—and of course on many more—Chubby Maata is faced with the question of whether she is or isn't a baby, and this fundamental puzzle is developed in different ways in each case, often generating or laying the seeds for other puzzles along the way.

The first instance (Episode 5) is the simplest, when taken by itself. Prior to this excerpt, mother and daughter had been playing "who are you (*kina-uvit*)?"[16] and some other games in which Chubby Maata's responses were sometimes babylike and sometimes more mature. Now Liila playfully and implicitly suggests to Chubby Maata two identities: that of a baby and, more vaguely, that of a nonbaby. She doesn't specify whether she is commenting on Chubby Maata's present behavior—sometimes babyish, sometimes not—or pointing to a transition that is in store for her. Indeed, she doesn't explicitly refer to Chubby Maata at all. Nevertheless, Chubby Maata seems to take personally the references to babyness. Instead of responding enthusiastically to this particular dictation, she merely smiles her radiant baby smile and says nothing. She avoids the unfamiliar "not-baby"—which her mother has not defined—by retreating into the safe realm of *babykuluk,* and her mother readily affirms the success of her performance: she is indeed a *babykuluk.*

But wait. Chubby Maata's defense in an awkward moment is certainly a baby's defense; however, she doesn't perform her baby role fully. She takes distance not only by refraining from repeating her mother's dictation but also by saying "ungaa" in an ordinary, matter-of-fact voice and by changing—at least apparently—the subject: "What's that out there?" She ends the baby game for the moment; she is not really interested in playing it. She "tells" her mother that she is both baby and nonbaby, and her mother follows her lead; she responds to Chubby Maata's sweet baby actions with warm confirmation of her darling babyness and replies matter-of-factly to her more "grown-up" overtures.

There are two questions in this game, then, which Chubby Maata appears to respond to. First, what is Chubby Maata? Baby? Not-baby? And, second, what is a not-baby? Chubby Maata seems to answer the first by acting out "both"; and she avoids dealing with the second—unless she is skirting around its edges when she asks her broad vague question about "what's out there" in the world beyond the familiar qammaq that encloses her, her mother, and me.

The second example, Episode 6, looks on the surface as simple as the first, but it's really a good deal more complicated. As in Episode 5, Liila hints at the possibility that Chubby Maata might be something other than a baby, but the formulation is different in several ways: the possibilities are distinct alternatives and not options that might be simultaneously available; they are phrased as questions, which are explicitly applicable to Chubby Maata; and the choice requires Chubby Maata to examine, categorize, and take responsibility for her behavior. Most interestingly, the nonbaby alternative is presented through the medium of a critical word that is said in an affectionate voice. The formulations in Episodes 5 and 6 have one important thing in common: ambiguity. And it is up to Chubby Maata to fill in the gaps and sort things out as best she can.

Let's see what is taking place. First of all, Chubby Maata has not entered the qammaq in the timid (*ilira-*) and unobtrusive manner of an older child or of a small child who is afraid of how she will be treated. She has announced her presence and her wish for tea in the bold and confident way of a child who knows that she is a darling. Liila, tenderly *aqaq*-ing, confirms Chubby Maata in her certainty; but then, clearly commenting on her little daughter's behavior, she asks her whether she is a baby.

What kind of commentary is this? Here we are face to face again with the problem of Liila's evaluation of baby behavior, the problem of -*kuluk* and *silait-*. On one hand, Chubby Maata's presence and her *silait-* behavior—her shining eyes, her bounce, her certainty that she is loved—warm the qammaq and are charming. On the other hand, calling attention to oneself and demanding to be given something are not behaviors that Liila wants to encourage in the long run. Her question, then, could contain a tangled variety of feelings and thoughts: affectionate appreciation of her daughter's baby charms; a suggestion that Chubby Maata be aware that her behavior is perceived as belonging to a baby; and Liila's own awareness that Chubby Maata will, and should, change.

Chubby Maata responds to her mother's question by denying that she is a baby. In so doing, she may be continuing in the mode in which she entered—

shocking her audience with the unexpected, pulling them by the nose, playing with them to hold their attention, saying the opposite of what she means. In her playful mood, she may also be experimenting a little with nonbabyness, shocking herself as well as her audience. But again, or in addition, she may also sense a note of criticism in her mother's question. She may remember that Liila, before giving in to her requests that tea be served to her in my qammaq, has sometimes protested: "You just drank tea"; "You'll have some at home"; or "Who invited you to drink tea here?" We have just seen that Chubby Maata is beginning to acquire a sensitivity to questions, an intuition that they may contain more than they appear to. Moreover, this particular question—are you a baby?—may already contain echoes not only of moments of celebration but also of other occasions when it has been associated with attributions of mindlessness (*silait-*), as it is in Episodes 3 and 4. If this is the case, Chubby Maata may wish to deny that she *is* that criticizable creature: a baby.

The possibility may occur to Liila that Chubby Maata doesn't mean what she says, because Liila's own modes of communication include both denial and "backwards" messages. On the other hand, it is possible that she thinks Chubby Maata is still incapable of using these modes.[17] In any case, this time Liila takes—or seems to take—Chubby Maata's "no (I am not a baby)" at face value. She holds her to what she has said and challenges her to explain herself, thereby launching her daughter on the wide seas of ignorance. Is she, after all, a baby? If not, how can she account for her behavior? Is baby behavior horrid? Or not? And what are the alternatives?

Liila is pressing her daughter to think again about her denial of babyness. For her, the question "Suyuruluuvitli?"—in what horrid little (ways) are you behaving, then?—probably means, "Do you wrongly imagine that your behavior is not babyish?" But Liila may attach more than one value to this second question, too. On one hand, she may be saying, "How could you possibly be anything but a sweet little baby?" She could be telling Chubby Maata that because she *is,* after all, a sweet little baby, she, Liila, accepts her baby ways. On other occasions she does suggest that babies are exempt from responsibility for what they do.[18] On the other hand—or in addition—she may very well intend to urge that Chubby Maata consider the appropriateness of her behavior.

There is ambiguity in what Liila says, carried both in the word that she has used and in the apparent contrast between the word—which has a negative flavor—and the warmly affectionate tone in which it is said. The ambiguity is appropriate if her motivations are, as I imagine, untidily complex. But that ambiguity is compounded for Chubby Maata by the experience—and the lacunae in the experience—that she has available to draw on in trying to make sense of her mother's utterance. Her problems of interpretation are considerable, even though she may not yet be wise enough to see all the possibilities in what her mother has asked.

What might Chubby Maata understand? Our most immediate clue is her broad baby smile, but that is open to more than one interpretation. It is possible that she doesn't hear any contradiction between the tone and the word of Liila's second question: "In what horrid little (ways) are you behaving, then?" From the earliest months of her life she has heard and understood intense affection expressed backward: "Don't smile!" "Don't come to visit!" "Big bad child, bad child . . ."—these last words chanted by an adoring mother to her beaming baby, who is swaying from foot to foot holding onto her hands. In all these cases, the tone carries the substance of the message, and I suspect that when the negativeness of the words begins to be heard, the effect is not to counter but to intensify the affection heard in the tone. If the new experience resonates with these others, then Chubby Maata may hear -*ruluk* (horrid little . . .) as a strong form of -*kuluk* (darling little . . .).[19] In this event, she beams because she hears in her mother's tone—and perhaps in her word, understood backward— nothing except welcome confirmation of her sweet babyness. She is pleased to have her playful rejection of baby status contradicted and to be assured that she is indeed a *babykuluk.*

But we have already seen that words and tones of voice fit together rather untidily, not only in the backward expression of affection but also sometimes in criticisms ("Are you *silait-?*" said caressingly), and that although Chubby Maata often ignores the words or perhaps reverses them to match and intensify the tone when adults *niviuq-* and *aqaq-* her, she is beginning to pay attention to some of the critical words that may be hidden behind a *niviuq*-ing tone. In other words, she is beginning to "hear" not only the *niviuq*-ing and *aqaq*-ing intentions but also the critical ones. It may be especially easy for her to hear criticism in "Suyuruluuvitli?" not only because it is a question but also because she has heard the same question uttered in a different tone of voice, as an expression of displeased surprise: "What on earth are you doing?"

And how might Chubby Maata explain to herself any sour note that she hears in the question? One possibility is that she is taken aback at her mother's rejection of the experiment, playful or otherwise, that she has made in denying her babyness. She thinks, "Oops! I said the wrong thing!"[20] Another possibility is that she fails to explain the sourness, she is at a loss—or even trapped: since Liila is interpreting her daughter's nonbaby performance as babyish, Chubby

Maata can't know whether she is or is not a baby; she doesn't know whether her mother is criticizing or appreciating her babyness or both; and she doesn't know whether her mother likes or dislikes nonbabies. She smiles her baby smile because, taken aback, at a loss, or trapped, she wants to avoid answering the question and she wants reassurance. She hears in Liila's tender voice that she is speaking to her *babykuluk,* and she knows that her smile has never failed to elicit love for that *babykuluk,* so it is safe (or at least well worth trying) to appeal for affection under the shelter of that identity—even if its foundations are beginning to shake a little. In any case, she is brought up short by her mother's questions and is made to focus on her babyness, to react, to feel, perhaps to think—the more so as Liila does not respond tenderly when Chubby Maata beams.

The third and fourth interactions (Episodes 7 and 8) taken together are complicated in a different way, and I see in them a number of potential puzzles and dilemmas for Chubby Maata.

In Episode 7, Liila again—and more clearly—suggests two possible identities to Chubby Maata, and because Chubby Maata rejects the first before the second is presented, they sound distinctly like alternatives: to be or not to be a baby. Again Liila frames the options as questions and explicitly applies the questions to her daughter: is Chubby Maata a baby or is she not? As in Episode 6, Liila points out to her daughter that there is a discrepancy between her babyish behavior and her claim that she is not a baby. And, as before, she leaves the nonbaby alternative undefined except by the absence of baby behavior, thus honing Chubby Maata's alertness to look and listen and discover from clues around her what the substance of nonbabyness might be.

As in Episode 6, Chubby Maata rejects the familiar alternative. Whether she is feeling boldly experimental, playful, or for some reason uncomfortable with her babyness, I can't guess this time. Her audience gives two different responses to her twice-repeated assertion that she is not a baby. Her uncle follows her lead, accepts her rejection of babyness, and elaborates on it, suggesting to her a reason—shyness—why she might have said what she said. In explaining her behavior, he simultaneously gives her a hint that "baby" might not be such a desirable identity. *He* seems to think it is not.

One might expect Liila to take advantage of her daughter's decision that, for the moment, she is not a baby and to use Tuuma as an ally in the enterprise of growing Chubby Maata up. She might agree that, indeed, being a baby was something to feel shy about. But no, nothing of the sort. She contradicts her daughter and "undoes" Tuuma's work, assuring Chubby Maata, as usual, that she is a sweet little (-*kuluk*) baby, the sweet little baby that she enjoys cuddling and playing with.

However, there is another surprise in store. A little later, when Chubby Maata asks for a bottle of milk, a demand that is out of keeping with her claim that she is not a baby, Liila points out the discrepancy: "What did you just say?" Ignoring her own recent assertion that Chubby Maata *is* a baby, no matter what *she,* Chubby Maata, says, Liila suddenly gives weight to her daughter's assertion and points out its consequences: "If you're not a baby, you don't drink from bottles." And then she gives her the bottle, as if to say again, "But you *are* a baby."

As an educational ploy, this seems a little odd in several ways. First, Liila reverses her own position—that Chubby Maata is a baby. Then she points out to her daughter a *dis*advantage of growing up, since bottles are one of the great pleasures and comforts of Chubby Maata's three-year-old life and are not to be readily relinquished. And finally, in providing the bottle, she reverts to the position that Chubby Maata *is* a baby and gratifies her baby wish.

I suspect that Liila at that moment did not feel like preparing a bottle. On the other hand—or at the same time—she may, in some secret place, have felt a little injured at her darling baby's rejection of babyness. In any case, she had to overcome some reluctance before she could produce the bottle. It seemed to me at the time that her unsettling observation—"If you're not a baby, you don't drink . . . "—was partly motivated by irritation. The remark, however, is of a type that is very familiar to Chubby Maata. It calls her to account for her words and points out connections between words and actions and between identities and actions that Chubby Maata may never have thought of before. If she *has* made these links, her mother's remark may remind her of them. Babyness and nonbabyness have consequences. One should be prepared to demonstrate that one is what one says one is. Chubby Maata doesn't have to pay the price of nonbabyness right now, since her mother—at least on this occasion—is willing to accommodate her changes of heart and, more, is accommodating her *own* wish that Chubby Maata be a baby. But Chubby Maata has been made more self-aware (or potentially so), and a "responsible" mode of thinking has been suggested to her.

Perhaps Chubby Maata is also becoming aware that words in the mouth of mother shift, and actions with them. We see another of these shifts in Episode 8. Here Liila seems to be trying to build on Chubby Maata's own liking for her baby role. Her goal is different, so her argument runs in the opposite direction, but, as before, she points out to Chubby Maata a connection between identity and action. In both cases, moreover, the consequence of the identity is something that Chubby Maata doesn't want at the moment when her mother speaks. It is formulated as a price that she has or will have to pay for the identity she has chosen. In the one instance, it is nonbabyness that has disadvantages; in the other case, it is babyness.

There are good things about growing out of babyness. Chubby Maata is proud of being able to reach up high toward the lintel of my door. Sometimes she wants to run with Rosi and the other children around the camp. She was grieved and angry when Liuna took Rosi to visit the new baby in Aatami's house, while *she* was told that spirits (tunrait) would get her if she went because she was so small. And one day, when her father took Rosi fishing with him on his snowmobile, all bundled up in fur traveling clothes, I'm sure that Chubby Maata heard the voice of happy anticipation with which her mother celebrated Rosi's departure and the excited welcome she gave Rosi when they came home: "We missed (*unga*-ed) you! Did you cry? Did you pee in your pants? Were you cold? Did you see fish? You did? Were they alive? Did you have tea? Was it fun?"

One avoids bad things, too, by giving up babyness. In Episode 1, Liila tells Chubby Maata that Rosi is *ugiat*-ing her because she is a baby. In other dramas, her uncle implies that babies should feel shy about being babies; and her mother tells her that babies go to bed when they don't want to. On the other hand, she will lose her bottle—and if she's *not* a baby, how on earth *is* her (horrid? or dear?) little behavior to be defined? The world is getting very complicated indeed.

Among them, Episodes 5–8 raise several questions that Chubby Maata will sooner or later have to deal with. Is she or isn't she a baby at this moment? Does she or doesn't she want to be a baby at this moment? Does her mother want her to be a baby or not? Is she pushing her toward nonbabyness or confirming her in babyness? Or both? What is it to be a nonbaby? Does she or doesn't she have to pay a price for becoming a nonbaby? (She got the bottle, remember, even though she claimed to be a nonbaby.)

Yes, indeed, the world is complicated. And mother does not provide solutions. On the contrary, she increases the complexity of the situation. She does point out some of the consequences of being and not being a baby, but the picture she paints is not consistently or simplistically weighted on one side: all black on the baby side, all gold on the other, or vice versa. And she does not tell Chubby Maata either to move or to stay. The cards are stacked, to be sure, but

Chubby Maata cannot know that. As far as she can see, she is free to make her own decisions and many of her own discoveries, weighing the far-from-simple variables—the benefits and the costs—as well as she can. Her mother and uncle have modeled for her a "responsible" mode of thinking, and the correlations that they suggest will probably rattle her baby complacency a little. In these interactions, as in many others, that is their contribution to her growth.

Chapter 4 "Want to Come Live with Me?"

One might continue indefinitely to find new problems for Chubby Maata or new variants of old problems in interactions that treat of babyness, partly because every instance of the interaction grows spontaneously out of naturally occurring incidents in everyday life, each of which gives rise to, or is embedded in, its own appropriate motivations; and partly because Chubby Maata's experiences and hence understandings are continually accumulating and shifting: new resonances develop, old ones fade. Every time a game is played, a drama enacted, an interrogation conducted, it will be slightly different, and if Chubby Maata perceives that difference, it will cast new light for her on earlier versions, which she has assimilated into her experience of the world. In addition, as Chubby Maata grows and her life changes, new concerns will develop and old ones fade. Even the transient preoccupations of a morning or an afternoon will serve as lenses through which some of the potential messages will appear sharp and clear while others will be fuzzy or altogether invisible.

The same is true of any interrogation or drama and indeed any social encounter at any period in a person's life. It is impossible, then, to present a total picture of the meanings inherent in any drama or question, no matter how stably repetitive are the key phrases, the tones of voice, and the gestures. It is impossible even to conjure all the meanings that might lie in any particular interaction for even one of the players, let alone all of them, and for the audience, too. The best I can hope for is to provide a glimpse of some of the important themes in Chubby Maata's three-year-old life and some of the patterns they form.

The episodes in Chapters 2 and 3 have shown us something of what Chubby Maata is learning about the dimensions of her identity and role as a baby who is a central figure in a world populated by loving kin. They have also shown us that Chubby Maata is beginning to move out of the central position. She is becoming a child, someone who must negotiate and take responsibility for relationships in a larger world and at the same time figure out where she belongs in this expanded environment. We turn now to dramas and interrogations that teach her some of these lessons. Analyzing their structure, we also learn more about how tissues of meaning are woven and continually rewoven.

The first episode I want to look at is really a series of dramas, which grow into and out of each other. All these dramas draw in people who are not in Chubby Maata's most intimate circle, and the first one tries to draw Chubby Maata *out* of that circle: "Want to come live with me?" In order to make sense of the sequence, we need to know who is out there and what is the flavor of the relations among the households. Who are these other people to one another and to Chubby Maata?

THE ADULT WORLD OF QIPISA

Beyond the cluster of dwellings in the middle of the camp that constituted the core of Chubby Maata's world—the houses of her parents and of her mother's parents, together with my qammaq, which stood close by her parents' house—there were several other dwellings.[1] In a large qammaq on one side of Chubby Maata's cluster lived her father's parents, Iqaluk and Aana, with several unmarried children, both biological and adopted, who ranged in age from sixteen to two. On the other side was a cluster consisting of two houses and another large qammaq where lived Natsiq, the patriarch of the camp, together with five of his children, almost all married, who ranged in age from nineteen to probably a bit more than thirty. Four of these "children" were biologically grandchildren who had been adopted either at birth or in early childhood. The remaining "child," and the oldest of them, was Natsiq's youngest daughter, Nivi. Of all the children he had sired, she was the one to whom he was most deeply attached, with the dependent love that is called *unga-*. He explained: "Her mother gave her to me (when she died). She was still small, and she unga-ed *me* very much."

The ties among the three households of Natsiq's orbit were various and strong, and there were also strong ties, of both adoption and marriage, between those households and that of Iqaluk and Aana, on the other side of the camp.

The people who lived in the central cluster—Liila and Jaani, and Liila's parents, Mitaqtuq and Arnaqjuaq—were also related to both Iqaluk and Natsiq. Arnaqjuaq was Natsiq's daughter and was unfailingly loyal to him; and Liila's husband, Jaani, was the son of Iqaluk and Aana. But these were the only ties between the families of the central cluster and the others. Chubby Maata's parents and maternal grandparents shared many more goods and services with each other than they did with the other families. And they were at home in each other's houses—sat at their ease, helped themselves to food, played with the children—whereas visits between them and the households outside their own cluster tended to be a little more formal if the visitor was an adult or more strained, on the child's side, if the visitor was a child.

Older teenagers came and went in most households of the camp with little appearance of restraint. The adults who had made them uneasy and afraid (*ilira-*) when they were very young were—with a few exceptions—no longer so alarming to them now that they were nearly grown. At the same time, as I have mentioned, adolescents had not yet acquired the sense of propriety and of domestic dignity that governed the behavior of their elders. Teenagers were thought to have less emotional control than adults in some respects—to be less patient, less nurturant—and adults seemed to be tolerant of their still immature social behavior and to grant them a certain license to be rough and spontaneous, especially in interaction with their peers and with children. A few adults continued to expose them in painful ways, to question and to criticize, and young people who felt themselves vulnerable to attack tended to avoid visiting the households in which they were made to feel uncomfortable.

There was one household in which almost everybody—even, to some extent, the younger members of the household itself—showed respectful restraint tinged with fear (*ilira-*). That was the house of the patriarch Natsiq, father, grandfather, or great-grandfather of almost everybody else in camp. For several years after the death of his third wife, Ukaliq, Natsiq shared his house only with the youngest of his adopted children, a teenage granddaughter named Maata, whom we shall meet in Episode 9. Maata tended Natsiq's house and kept him from being utterly lonely. To be sure, Natsiq's other children came in and out daily, but their visits—except for those of his favorite daughter, Nivi—seemed to be motivated more by feelings of consideration and concern than by pleasure in his rather austere company; they didn't stay long. Nivi seemed to feel much more at ease than the others; she was often to be found in her father's house. Nivi and Maata were very close, too. Nivi had helped to mother Maata when Maata was an adopted baby in Natsiq's household, and now, since the death of Natsiq's last wife, she was the only mother that Maata had. When Maata wasn't occupied with tasks at home, she spent a great deal of her time in Nivi's house.

The other place where the teenage Maata could often be found was in the qammaq occupied by Natsiq's other adopted children, Rota, Tiimi, and Paulusi. Like Maata, Tiimi and Paulusi were grandchildren of Natsiq and had been adopted by him. Rota was a granddaughter of Ukaliq and had been adopted by her. All four of these young people were close in age, and all of them had grown up together in Natsiq's household—in fact, in that same qammaq, which had been home to Natsiq and Ukaliq until, after her death, he built another house. Soon after Ukaliq's death, Rota and Tiimi married each other—I suspected that Natsiq had arranged the marriage in order to keep them both near him— and after the birth of their first child, Natsiq turned over the qammaq to them. His other adopted son, Paulusi, still unmarried, lived there with them and their two small children. We shall meet Rota and her three-year-old son, Saali, in the next episode, too.

Maata acquired a husband on the day I arrived in camp, but I didn't learn that until several weeks later, when I discovered that it was the canoe of her intended, Aalami, that had accompanied us at such a discreet distance on the trip across Cumberland Sound. Aalami moved in with Maata and Natsiq, so then there were three in Natsiq's house—but marriage didn't prevent Maata from spending most of her time, as usual, next door in the homes of Nivi and Rota.

There was one other important part-time resident in Natsiq's house: Rota's four-year-old daughter, Miika. Miika technically belonged to her parents, Rota and Tiimi—that is, they had not given her away in adoption to Natsiq—but she slept every night in Natsiq's bed, to keep him company. He was very lonely after Ukaliq's death and said that he slept badly if he didn't have a warm body next to him. Miika was named for Ukaliq, and Natsiq called her "my sweet little other (wife), the only one I have (*aippatuakuluga*)." He was pleased when she claimed to prefer him to her mother as a bedfellow. Maata, as the only adult woman in Natsiq's household, played the role of "mother" to Miika during the hours that Miika spent in her grandfather's home.[2]

It is Maata, newly married, who asks the question "Want to come live with me?" which we shall hear presently.

THE DRAMA DESCRIBED

Episode 9 (January 9)

One January evening, Maata[3] and I arrived at about the same moment to visit in Liila's house. Liila, Rosi, and Chubby Maata were at home, and two of Liila's brothers, Juupi, a man of twenty-seven, and ten-year-old Juda, were visiting them. Chubby Maata was playing with a little pup named Papi (Puppy), which someone in Pangnirtung had sent her as a present the last time her father had gone in to trade. Maata, almost as soon as she arrived, began to suggest to Chubby Maata that she and Papi come to live in their house. Her voice was soft, persuasive, seductive—a voice that was often used by adults in speaking to small children when they wanted a child to do something. Chubby Maata consistently wrinkled her nose: "No." After a while, Maata called Papi to her, petted him, picked him up, and turned toward the door, with Papi in her arms. Chubby Maata let out a cry, rushed to the puppy, grabbed him around his neck with such force that I feared she would choke him, and pulled him strenuously away from Maata. She was half-laughing, but the laugh sounded anxious, too, and she exerted a great deal of energy.

This drama was repeated several times during the first part of the visit, each time initiated by Maata. Once, Chubby Maata, tugging at Papi, trying hard to separate him from Maata, protested, "He's all shitty!" Maata ignored this argument; she didn't let go of Papi—but she didn't take him out of the house, either.

The last time Maata asked Chubby Maata if she and Papi would like to come and live with them, Chubby Maata said something that I didn't hear before she said no; then, after refusing, she commented, as if cheerfully surprised at herself, "Ih! I almost agreed!" Maata's ear was quick. She exclaimed, "Oh, you agree!" And this time she picked up Chubby Maata instead of Papi and started toward the door. Chubby Maata struggled and cried out in protest, and after a few minutes, Maata put her down. Chubby Maata ran first to her mother, who ignored her, and then to Juupi, who picked her up and set her on his lap. From that protected position, she looked over her shoulder, laughing with a triumphant gleam at Maata.

The next thing I noticed was that Chubby Maata had initiated a game with herself in which she ran, over and over again, from the door to Juupi and back, saying, "One, two, talee (three), GO!"[4] as she started each lap of the "race" and flinging herself across his lap every time she returned to him. Once when she returned, Juupi hit her bottom lightly, and when she cried out, protestingly, he said, in a light and innocent tone, "It wasn't me, it was Yiini." I was sitting beside Juupi on the couch, well within reach. It could indeed have been me.

Chubby Maata looked at me, her small face serious, her eyes watchful. Liila asked her, "Do you like (*piugi-*) Yiini?" Chubby Maata wrinkled her nose, looking at her mother, not at me. Liila, her voice amused, asked, "Why on earth don't you?" Chubby Maata put her head down on the seat of the couch and hid her face in both hands. But she was not to escape that way. Maata, her eyes fixed observantly on Chubby Maata, took up the interrogation: "Who, then? Who do you like?" Everyone was watching Chubby Maata. She didn't answer. Maata persisted: "Do you like *me?*" Chubby Maata, with a great burst of energy, resumed her game of "One, two, talee, GO!" but that didn't save her, either. It was Juupi's turn: "Do you like *me?*" This time Chubby Maata raised her brows: "Yes." Would that answer satisfy? No. Juupi inquired further in a soft and confidential voice, "Just me alone, yes?" Chubby Maata responded again with "One, two, talee, GO!" Poor Chubby Maata. Both Maata and Juupi pressed her for an answer, but the only response they got was the same refrain and a great deal of energetic running.

At this point, two new visitors came in: Maata's adoptive sister Rota and Rota's son, Saali, who was just a few weeks older than Chubby Maata. As the visitors stood by the door, hesitating politely for a moment before coming in and sitting down, Liila exclaimed to Chubby Maata: "Look, your darling little mother's brother[5] is wearing your shirt! He's trying to steal it! Look at him!" Chubby Maata ignored her mother's remarks, as did Rota and Saali, and Liila did not pursue the subject.

Rota came into the room and sat down on the couch, while Saali stood between her legs in the usual position of the visiting three-year-old, leaning against her while he watched the activities in the room. In a few moments he turned around to his mother and demanded a suck: "Amaamak!" But Rota said, "Go run wildly (*uimak-*) with Chubby Maata, instead."

Saali did run with Chubby Maata for a few minutes, from the couch to the door, back and forth, back and forth: "One, two, talee, GO!" until Rota said to him, "Pretend to be an evil spirit (tunraq)." Saali immediately hunched his shoulders, bowed his arms like an ape, closed his eyes tight, and so transformed into a miniature monster, began to stalk Chubby Maata and Rosi, rolling from leg to leg like the proverbial sailor just come ashore. The two little girls cried,

"Iq!"—an expression of alarm, sometimes of delighted alarm—and, watching Saali over their shoulders as they ran, they fled to the far end of the room, where they huddled together, holding each other tightly and laughing. Saali stopped in the middle of the room, and when the girls had relaxed, he began again to stalk them, and again they ran, holding onto each other, watching him and laughing from a distance. Rota, her eyes amused, showed Saali how to stick out his tongue as well as screwing his eyes shut: "Do this." He imitated her gesture, and the adults laughed.

The evil spirit game was repeated a number of times. I don't remember how it came to an end—perhaps the children just lost interest—but when it did, Saali returned to stand in front of his mother. As he stood there, facing her this time, Chubby Maata came up behind him, grabbed him in her arms, pulled his hair, and said happily, "I'm ugiat-ing!" Saali protested with a wordless cry, and Liila said to Chubby Maata, "Don't do that!" Chubby Maata stopped attacking Saali, but when she had withdrawn, he again asked his mother for a suck, this time in a plaintive voice, and this time she gave him what he asked for. He stood leaning his face against her bared breast, sucking contentedly, his mother's arm lightly around his back.

But suddenly, as Saali stood there sucking, Juupi, who was sitting on the couch beside Rota, said to him: "Shall I nurse? Shall I kiss it?" And he pushed his head in between Saali and his mother and made as if to snuff the soft skin of the breast. Saali bit his mother's nipple in a mighty effort to hang onto it, while Rota laughed in pain, "A'aaa!" and protested to Juupi, "He bit it! Don't do that!" Juupi accordingly switched his tactics, said to Saali, "Shall I tickle your mother?" and proceeded to do so. Rota hastily withdrew from the couch to the floor, and Saali, still sucking, went with her.

At this point, one of the other women, Maata or Liila, suggested to Chubby Maata that she turn in circles, and Chubby Maata innocently followed the suggestion, but after she had turned herself around a number of times, the two women, pretending excitement, exclaimed, "Look at that thing up there!" Chubby Maata was an easy victim. When she raised her eyes, dizziness came upon her, she fell to the floor, and the adults laughed. The game appealed to Chubby Maata. She got up and repeated the performance several times, and all the other children present—Rosi, Saali, even ten-year-old Juda—followed suit, Saali in spite of his mother's admonition not to do so. Finally, Chubby Maata fell hard, cried, and came to fetch her bottle from Liila. Standing near her mother, her face still tearful, she sucked comfort. No more dramas were enacted that evening.

THE DRAMA ANALYZED: INTENTIONS, MOTIVES, UNDERSTANDINGS

"Want to Come Live with Me?"

This winter evening's entertainment is more complexly structured than the simple "Because You're a Baby" drama (Episode 1) that I analyzed in Chapter 2. Whereas it was possible to analyze that drama as though it dealt primarily with one problem of Chubby Maata's life, her babyness, this second series of interactions cannot be treated in that way. This time one drama leads to a second, the second to a third, and so on. And each one has something different—though perhaps related—to say. Let's analyze it in the same way as the first, line by line, and see what we find.

Maata, on entering Liila's house to pay an evening visit, sees that Chubby Maata is playing with her puppy and almost immediately inquires whether the two of them would like to come and live at her house. This is by no means the first time that Chubby Maata has been asked this question; it is a question that people outside the intimate family circle often ask small children.[6] Maata in particular was fond of addressing it to both Chubby Maata and Miika. Occasionally she would add, "You'll be my baby," so I wondered whether her liking for this drama was related to the fact that she was newly married and was looking forward to having children of her own. The drama might also have resonated both with her own history of adoption and, in the case of Miika, with that little girl's ambiguous semiadopted status in Maata's home. As I have mentioned, adults often do dramatize their own life situations and concerns, as well as those of the children they play with, in the games they initiate.[7]

Maata is a frequent visitor to Chubby Maata's house. She is several years younger than Liila—indeed, she is just about the age of Liila's younger sister Luisa—but the three of them, Maata, Luisa, and Liila, and Maata's adoptive sister, Rota, who is about Liila's age, were all teenagers together before Liila and Rota were married, and Maata feels free in Liila's house to sit at her ease, chat with her peers, and play with the children and other young visitors.

On this occasion, when she issues her invitation to Chubby Maata, her voice is soft and seductive. It is a voice often used with this and many other questions and suggestions that Chubby Maata has heard; it belongs to the repertoire of voices that adults regularly use with small children to dramatize the emotional content of their words.[8] The "saccharine-persuasive" voice, as I have labeled it, is used, as the name suggests, when an adult wants a child to do something.

Ordinarily, Chubby Maata plays readily with Maata; she does not withdraw timidly to her mother's side, feeling *ilira-,* when Maata visits. But she is not easily tempted to give up her own home and go to live with Maata. She consistently refuses the invitation. Maata, however, is not readily discouraged. She switches to a more forceful tactic. Instead of affectionately offering a home to Chubby Maata directly and giving her a (deceptively) open choice of whether to accept it or not, Maata cuddles Chubby Maata's beloved Papi and pretends to start home with him. Now Chubby Maata must either give up mother and home in order to follow Papi, who is being removed against her will, or exert a force greater than Maata's to keep the puppy—and herself—at home. Which does she love more: Papi or her mother? Her mother or Maata? And how strong are these loves? What will she do to protect them? What *can* she do to protect them?

Maata intends, I think, to test the limits of Chubby Maata's attachments to home, to Papi, perhaps to Maata herself—to test whether she knows what is hers and how determined she is to keep those possessions. And, in testing, she may create or heighten Chubby Maata's emotional awareness that she has a home and wants to stay there and that she has a puppy and wants to keep him.

Maata is surely also testing—it's one of the usual motives for playing these games—to see whether Chubby Maata will take her questions and actions seriously.[9] And Chubby Maata does indeed seem to half-know that Maata is playing—but only half. Her laughter when she tries to pull Papi away is strained. She doesn't trust Maata to put Papi down of her own accord, nor does she rely on the effectiveness of a direct verbal request. She tries a manipulative ploy that she has heard adults use when they want *her* to avoid some object or place—"It's all shitty!"—and at the same time she counters physical force with physical force. Neither tactic works. Maata doesn't take her warning seriously; she overrules Chubby Maata's attempted construction of the situation by ignoring it. Moreover, she is physically stronger than Chubby Maata and chooses to exercise that strength. She holds onto Papi. Chubby Maata has succeeded only in demonstrating her own childishness.

But is Maata the only person Chubby Maata doesn't trust in this situation? At one revealing moment, she gives us a hint that she is, after all, tempted by Maata's offer or seduced by her voice. "Ih! I almost agreed!" she exclaims, standing guard over her feelings. Perhaps some of the force with which she pulls Papi away is directed against herself.

Maata hears Chubby Maata's self-observation and immediately seizes her advantage: "Oh, you *agree!*" Attributing the decision to Chubby Maata, pretending that she is only carrying out Chubby Maata's will, Maata swings the little girl into her arms and heads for the door. Chubby Maata, alarmed at this development, struggles, protests, and succeeds in regaining her freedom. For the moment, she has extricated herself from her predicament—autonomously, as far as she knows—but she seems to doubt whether she can do it again. Does she realize that she got herself into the predicament in the first place through her own feelings and her own words? Perhaps she only fears that Maata may prove physically stronger than she in the end. In the tug of war over Papi, Maata has already demonstrated that her strength will make any struggle a close one.

In any case, Chubby Maata looks for a protector to save her in case of further attacks—from Maata and perhaps also from her own mixed feelings. Her mother is her first line of defense, but Liila does not seem inclined to help her, to reward her for having chosen her own home over Maata's. When her daughter runs to her, she ignores her. Perhaps she wants to see what Chubby Maata will do next and whether she can solve her own problem. She may want Chubby Maata to experience weakness.[10] At the same time, she may wish to signal that the problem is not a "real" one requiring protective intervention. Perhaps, too, she is curious to find out how determined Chubby Maata will be, in the absence of maternal succor, to retain what is hers—whether, indeed, she will recognize what is hers without her mother's acknowledgment.

Chubby Maata's uncle Juupi is more supportive. He picks her up and sets her on his lap, giving her the protection that enables her to feel that she has won the battle—a protection that may even enable her to recognize that Maata was only playing. She laughs, in a manner that seems to say, "Ha ha! You can't catch me!" Danger can be fun when one feels safe.

Chubby Maata *has* won this particular battle; Maata stops playing this game for the moment. Nevertheless, it seems to have left a powerful impression. When Chubby Maata begins to run back and forth, back and forth, between her protector and the door, saying, "One, two, talee, GO!" each time she leaves Juupi and flinging herself across his lap every time she returns, it looks very much like a reenactment of Maata's drama, but this time under Chubby Maata's own control. It is she who decides to run to the door and she who decides to return, and her protector is always there, waiting for her—albeit passively and in silence. She is Maata and Chubby Maata, aggressor and victim. She can act out Maata's wish to take her home and her own wish to be persuaded by her friend (or her involuntary response to the dangerous seduction of Maata's voice) and yet be sure—this time—of winning against both aggressors, outer and inner. She may also be acting out escape from this difficult situation, without having to really escape because Juupi is there to protect her when she comes back. Finally, the very energy exerted in the rerunning of the drama must help to relieve the tension caused by the original performance[11]—tension created by the experience of being attacked and of feeling conflicted in a way that gave every sign of having dangerous consequences.

"Who Do You Like?"

Chubby Maata has shown no signs of tiring of her game when Juupi suddenly, rudely, interrupts it by hitting her lightly on the bottom. Is it just an affectionate tap? Or does Juupi intend it to have the effect that it does have? Chubby Maata cries out: the wordless cry of protest that is characteristic of Inuit children, both small and not-so-small; we heard it from Rosi in Episode 1, when Chubby Maata asked if she should pull her hair. Juupi protests his innocence: "It wasn't me, it was Yiini."[12] Is he testing to see whether Chubby Maata can distinguish truth from fiction? I *could* have hit her; I was sitting well within reach of her bottom when she was lying across Juupi's lap. There might also be a message for Yiini in that touch: a naughty desire to get *my* relationship with Chubby Maata into turbulent waters? A vicarious pat on *my* behind? Juupi was one of several young men who descended on me regularly and en masse in the evenings for the purpose of playing explicit and persistent sexual games, dramas that I enjoyed not at all but didn't know how to avoid.[13]

Chubby Maata looks at me intently. Is she trying to judge the truth of Juupi's accusation? Trying to imagine why I might have hit her? Or is it that she believes Juupi's charge and is just displeased with me? She must be puzzled. Ordinarily, I was good to her: I welcomed her frequent visits to my qammaq and gave her all the tea with milk and bannock and jam that she asked for—which was considerable—and she seemed to be making "good progress" (my view) in overcoming her early fear of me.[14] Often, when she came to visit me with her mother or other companions, she chattered in the friendliest manner and initiated spontaneous little games with me. I loved her, and I'm sure she felt it.

Liila was not so happy about her small daughter's familiar ways with me, and she did not approve of my encouraging them. Once, when Chubby Maata began a conversation with me, I heard Liila say, irritably but under her breath, "Yiini, as usual (*Yiiningaasit*)!" In any case, on this occasion, when Chubby Maata turns to look at me solemnly, Liila asks her, "Do you like Yiini (*Yiini piugiviuk*)?" Chubby Maata, with an air of embarrassment, avoids my eyes and wrinkles her nose in denial. Liila could have scored an easy victory at this point, confirming that Chubby Maata was right to dislike me and should be a little careful of me; one never knew what I might do. But she does no such thing. Instead, she asks, "Why on earth *don't* you like her?" Her amused voice says clearly, "What a strange notion, not to like Yiini."

Chubby Maata is nonplused. Is it so strange to dislike someone who has hit her? But *had* I hit her? I had never hit her before. Does she or doesn't she—should she or shouldn't she—like me? The problem is too hard for her; there is something in it that she doesn't understand, perhaps a hidden message that she can't find. She puts her head down on the couch and hides her face in her hands.

Her inquisitors are relentless. Now it is Maata who takes up the attack: "If not Yiini, then who *do* you like?" The open-ended question is even harder than the other. Having begun to perceive that the obvious and natural answer does not always satisfy the questioner, Chubby Maata is becoming cautious. She needs a clue to an appropriate response and none is forthcoming. She doesn't venture out on the unfamiliar ground; she is silent. But Maata is as persistent in her pursuit of this question as she was in pursuit of her first one. She tries a different tack: "Do you like *me?*" Oh, dear. Maata, like Yiini, is often a good companion, warm and friendly, but today she is being troublesome—and besides, if Chubby Maata says she likes her, perhaps Maata may try again to take her home with her. Does Chubby Maata like her or doesn't she? And whatever her feelings may be, what is it safe to *say?*

This time, instead of hiding her head, Chubby Maata tries to regain control of the situation, as she did the first time Maata tormented her: "One, two, talee, GO!" As before, the great burst of energy with which Chubby Maata shoots toward the door expresses and relieves her discomfort, and again, as before, the race may represent to her a much-needed escape. Moreover, if her anxieties about Maata's intentions have been rearoused by the new question, the race may still enact the conflict of deciding on a home and may again represent an attempt to master that situation. But the new question may be giving the original dilemma an additional dimension or underlining one that was before only dimly visible in the background. If Chubby Maata says she likes someone, is she giving that person permission to possess her and take her away? In order to be safe, does she have to control only the behavior of others or her own feelings as well? She has already received a hint that the latter may be the case in Maata's vigorous response to her slip: "I almost agreed!" So the race with herself may have shifted meanings slightly, in accordance with a new perspective or a new emphasis. And whatever else is going on in her mind, Chubby Maata may hope that her loud exclamation and the activity that follows it may distract the attention of the adults and make them stop questioning her; certainly it expresses the wish that they stop.

Alas, the game that gave her a sense of control the last time she played it is not so successful this time. The questioning continues. But perhaps she has gained something nevertheless? At least now it is her friend and protector, Juupi, who asks the question, "Do you like *me?*" The answer seems easier this time; after all, he *is* her friend and protector. Chubby Maata ventures to say yes, she does like him. Oops! She is undone again. He does not accept the natural answer but continues in a saccharine, seductive voice: "Just me alone, yes?" This time Chubby Maata recognizes the betrayal. Juupi has trapped her, and she responds again with "One, two, talee, GO!" Let me out of here! Both Maata and Juupi press her for an answer, but now Chubby Maata is aware that she has no idea what answer will satisfy—and probably no idea, either, whom she does or doesn't like at this moment. Her "One, two, talee, GO!" now seems to be only a release for confused feelings, a desperate perseveration of a strategy that once worked to give her mastery over a difficult situation and other confused feelings, and an equally desperate attempt to distract her tormentors and make them stop.

"Saali Stole Your Shirt"

The question of whom Chubby Maata likes is not resolved, but Chubby Maata is saved for the moment by the fortuitous arrival of two new visitors: Saali and his mother, Rota. Eyes shift to them—though not altogether away from Chubby Maata. When the visitors appear in the doorway, Liila draws her daughter's attention to Saali's shirt. She may be trying to distract Chubby Maata from her noisy game or merely taking advantage of a new situation to start a new drama. The topic that she introduces is a familiar one in the repertoire of dramas in which she engages Chubby Maata, but it may have been suggested to her at this moment by the first drama, in which Maata tried to "steal" Chubby Maata from her, and Papi from Chubby Maata.

The shirt had probably been a Christmas present to Saali from Chubby Maata. It was the custom for everyone in the camp to give a present to everyone else, and on Christmas Eve sacks upon sacks of used clothing were pulled out from under beds and from storage bins, and suitable items were chosen for distribution. But Liila doesn't remind Chubby Maata of this fact; instead, she pretends that Saali has stolen the shirt. It's another test: will Chubby Maata recognize the truth? Liila's voice is excited, but this time Chubby Maata doesn't take the bait. Either she is wise enough to know that her mother is lying or the question of who owns the shirt doesn't exercise her. Who possesses *her* and *Papi*—those are the problems of ownership that occupy her at this moment. Liila, seeing no sign of concern in Chubby Maata's manner, drops the subject, and Chubby Maata continues to run energetically back and forth from the door to the couch, where Juupi is still sitting.

Three-year-old Saali, standing between his mother's legs, watches Chubby Maata and the others for a few minutes, and then, perhaps in need of a little reassurance—he is, after all, on "foreign" soil, and Chubby Maata's activity is certainly not calming—he turns to his mother and demands that she nurse him: "Amaamak!" But Rota is not willing to gratify his baby wish; she tells him, in effect, to go and be a child—to run with his peer instead of retreating into the soft comfort of his mother's body. At the same time, she condemns that childish activity, labeling it wild, mindless, confusing, meaningless. *Uimak-*, the word she uses, is disparaging. It is usually said as a prohibition: "*Don't* uimak-!" To an adult ear, it doesn't sound as though Rota considers the child a more attractive creature than the baby, and, oddly, the behavior that she is recommending to her son is the very antithesis of the reticence (*ilira-*) expected of a well-behaved visitor. On the other hand, it effectively distracts him from his baby wish.

Saali does not appear to have any negative associations to his mother's instruction. Showing no sign of being offended, he joins Chubby Maata in her race, and in the enjoyment of its vigor, he seems to lose any feelings of unease (*ilira-*) that might have afflicted him when he entered the room. And of course he also ceases to behave with the decorum that those uncomfortable feelings engender.

"Play 'Evil Spirit'"

But now Rota has an idea that will at once escalate and "civilize" the fun by giving social form to the idiosyncratic wildness of the two running children. "Play that you are an evil spirit (tunraq)," she suggests to Saali. Playing tunraq was a favorite entertainment of children of all ages. Titillated by the fear aroused by the distorted face and body and the strange manner of locomotion adopted by the tunraq, children would run, screaming with delight, to a safe distance or a secure hiding place, from which they could laugh at—and with—the tunraq, who thoroughly enjoyed the dramatic effect of his or her performance. Adults, too—hearing the excited laughter of the children as they fled—

stopped and turned and smiled, sometimes even opened doors and looked out to see the tunraq.

But it is the fear of real tunrait that gives spice to these performances, and that fear is a much heavier matter. Few, if any, Qipisa people of any age were altogether free of it, and many children, even teenage girls, were nearly paralyzed by it after dark. Teenage boys kept their fear under closer control,[15] but children—even ten-year-old Juda—going from house to house in the evening, regularly asked an adult to watch them to make sure that they arrived safely at their destination. And girls, going out to urinate, to fetch meat or water, or to visit after daylight had faded, traveled in pairs or groups and expressed astonishment at anyone—like the anthropologist—who didn't share the fear. "It must be very convenient," said one girl wistfully, seeing me set out alone at dusk toward the waterhole on the edge of camp. But at the same time, I had the impression that it was considered a little "mindless" (*silait-*) not to be afraid of a presence that was so palpably real.

Saali's performance probably evokes the real tunraq in a scary way only for Chubby Maata and Rosi, the youngest of his spectators. These two small girls flee the miniature monster with gratifying cries of alarm and excited laughter and huddle together at a distance, poised to run again as soon as he comes too close. The others, however, may have another mixture of feelings. For one thing, Saali is so small a monster that, for an adult, he is a comical contradiction in terms. Only a child nearer his size could identify *him,* in a threatening way, with the invisible shapes that skulk in the darkness, scratching on lit windows and ever ready to grab the back of one's jacket as one runs. But he himself clearly imagines that he's big and scary when he swells himself up into monstrous form. More, he enjoys being big and scary: his eyes gleam with delight. And to see both his "misunderstanding" of his nature and his pleasure in his phantom self must amuse the adults mightily.

There is another contradiction, too, in the children's game. I have pointed out that Rota, in suggesting to Saali that he play tunraq, is at one and the same time escalating the excitement, the wildness, of the children's play and "civilizing" it, in the sense that she is turning Chubby Maata's personal game, which she perceives as lacking in shape and meaning, into a socially patterned form of *silait-* behavior, which does have meaning for her; and I think that the adult viewers of the small monster are probably enjoying both the impropriety of the game and its propriety, its antisocialness and its socialness. It is not right to aggress against people and frighten them, nor is it right to escalate excitement.

Souls can fly out of people who are excited.[16] On the other hand, the aggression of the pretend-tunraq is controlled (Rota pulls the strings); it is standardized—one might even say ritualized—in form; and it is far too small to really frighten adults. Unwittingly, small Saali may be showing the adults their own monsters—their own aggressive feelings and their own fears—allowing them to vicariously make those monsters stalk the floor with clawed fingers and, at the same time, allowing them to reassure themselves, because the bugaboos are all so insignificantly tiny The children who run and squeal certainly see the same monsters but on a different scale and so are not so easily reassured. Nevertheless, they are not seriously frightened either. Serious fear would elicit not squeals but cries, not laughter but tears or frozen silence.

Perhaps the game loses its vividness with repetition; in any case, it comes to an end, and the monster shrinks back into a baby, who needs the presence of his mother. (Had he perhaps frightened *himself* just a bit?) Now it's Chubby Maata's turn to attack. Is it revenge? Or just the fizz of aggression in the air? Perhaps both—compounded by the turbulence of the feelings so recently roused in her. She comes up behind him, grabs him, pulls his hair, and says "happily," "I'm attacking (*ugiat-*)!" This time she herself civilizes her extravagant behavior by giving it a socially acceptable label. She may or may not know that *ugiat*-ing is properly done as an expression of affection; she does know that adults—occasionally even children—get away with aggression against children when they call it *ugiat*-ing and do it with good humor.[17] But her understanding of the situation is not accepted. Saali cries out in protest, and Liila tells Chubby Maata to desist. Chubby Maata obeys. But now Saali really does need comfort, and he asks for it—and receives it—in the form in which it is most commonly offered, the form of mother's milk.

"Shall I Nurse?"

Alas for Saali's infant peace, the dyadic intimacy of a loved baby with his mother; Juupi sends it crashing. First, he asks Saali if Saali will allow *him* to be the baby: "Shall *I* nurse?" He is pretending to compete with Saali as one baby with another, on equal terms. Then, suddenly, he is not a baby but a grown man—"Shall I kiss (*kunik-*) it?"—and is competing on very unequal terms. Not only is Juupi a socially powerful adult competing with a socially weak baby, he also has much greater physical strength and can easily usurp Saali's possession, as he demonstrates by acting out his suggestions.

Juupi's motivations for this interference are probably mixed, and so too are the messages sent in Saali's direction. First, it is clear that, at age twenty-seven and a still unmarried man, Juupi has a young man's sexual interest in Rota's breast. I imagine he also thinks—as Liila does of Chubby Maata—that it is beginning to be time for Saali to give up nursing. His game doesn't take the form of "Wouldn't you like to nurse from *another* woman?"—a game that is played with younger children; it is "Let *me* do it instead of you."

At the same time, Juupi may also at some level retain a baby's interest in the breast. I have already mentioned adult identification with babies. Inuit men as well as women often felt strongly attached to their mothers in a dependent (*unga-*) way throughout their lives, and the love of men for their wives tended to acquire some of the same character. It was common to see a married man, of any age, lying relaxed in his wife's lap while she groomed his head or face. He might have done the same for her at other times, but I saw less of this. In addition, for adults and babies alike, being fed typically carried powerful messages of affection, of being nurtured, cared for, *nallik*-ed. Two incidents that I observed spoke with exceptional clarity of this dependent relationship and its association with mother's milk. On the first occasion, a middle-aged man was lying in his wife's lap while she searched his dark hair and plucked out the telltale gray of age, which was said to itch. As she worked, he picked up his little son's bottle of milk, which lay discarded beside him, and sucked. There was no evidence that he was doing anything unusual. On the other occasion, a young man curled around his baby's back as they lay on the sleeping platform while his wife, Liitia, who was curled around the other side of the baby, nursed the child to sleep. Son and father fell asleep together, and when Liitia rose, she looked down at the two of them and remarked in a disgruntled voice, "My two sons."

When Juupi, then, says to Saali, "Shall *I* nurse?" the potential messages for Saali are complex. What Juupi may intend to convey is "See how silly I (and therefore you) look, nursing in this babyish way." He is not the only person who is beginning to send Saali this message in one form or another. But feelings born out of his own concerns may shift that message subtly or add to it another: "I want the breast—and I want to torment Rota—and therefore you can't have it."

Saali doesn't have the experience that would enable him to pick up Juupi's meanings very accurately, but his own concerns, resonating with Juupi's, may help him to sense some of the vibrations or to feel possessive strains that in part resemble Juupi's.

What are Saali's concerns? For Saali, as for other children of his age, milk sucked from a bottle or, better, from mother's breast spells comfort. And the contented and peaceful way in which he leans against Rota while he sucks tells us that the milk he imbibes is part of a special and very important relationship with his mother: a baby relationship—and perhaps soon, or even now, a bit more than that.

I have no evidence that Saali at this moment has "Oedipal" feelings—a little boy's fantasy of taking his father's place—but I think it probable that he may object to his father's interfering with *his* place;[18] and I wonder whether the two forms of possession, linked, as we have seen, in adults, are not similarly linked in three-year-olds. This question was raised for me by another Qipisa boy, Luki, who was a little younger than Saali and who, like Saali, was still nursing. Luki's father had playfully pulled his wife onto his lap and was holding her there. Luki, catching sight of them, let out an angry shriek, ran over, and tugged strenuously at his mother's skirt. Luki's mother, like Rota, took her son's side. She laughed at Luki with affectionate amusement, got off her husband's lap, and picked up her child (Briggs 1975:174). Although I think that Luki at that moment was jealous not so much of his father's mature, husbandly role as of an interloper's interference with his own baby role, the links between baby and adult roles seem presaged in the little boy's behavior. Indeed, it is hard to know how the elements of baby and adult are distributed in this scene.

Whatever the exact nature of Saali's emotional involvement with mother, milk, and breast at the moment when Juupi interferes, the message that he is most likely to pick up is that he is in danger of losing something valuable. Juupi's sudden, competitive head thrust may heighten Saali's awareness of what he values. More, it may intensify the value itself, both because it is clearly something that Juupi wants, too, and because Juupi is threatening to take that valued something away from him. Juupi is demonstrating for Saali—just as Luisa's kick in Episode 1 did for Chubby Maata—that the outer world of Other People exists and has the power to disrupt Saali's private enjoyment of babyness within the protective circle of his mother's arm. This, together with Juupi's competitiveness, Saali can hardly help but see. And the interference stimulates him to defend what he values, impulsively and vigorously—just as Maata's aggressive invitation alerted Chubby Maata to danger.

The "models" that Juupi, wittingly or unwittingly, is providing for Saali may be harder for the little boy to see. I have already suggested that Juupi may be showing Saali how silly it looks for a big boy to nurse. At the same time—although perhaps both he and Saali are unaware of it—he may be teaching Saali that the breast, and the closeness to a nurturant body, are not really lost when one stops nursing. The baby relationship can be replaced by an adult sexual one. Nursing and kissing are linked, and Juupi, consciously or not, demonstrates this clearly and shows Saali how to relate as an adult man to an adult woman. Moreover, because he himself is gleefully enjoying that relationship, he makes the appropriate "feeling-tone" potentially available to Saali, too. Saali may not be far from a childlike appreciation of sex, either; his four-year-old sister, Miika, like other four-year-olds of both sexes, is already very aware of sex and takes a gleaming delight in talking about it.

But now Rota defends herself against Juupi's playacting and its painful consequences—"He bit it! Don't do that!"—and Juupi, perhaps titillated by her cry, perhaps taking it as an invitation, continues his "attack" on Rota, more aggressively and more sexually. And again, he asks Saali's "permission": "Shall I tickle your mother?"

If Saali had perceived Juupi's questions as threats to Rota, he might have been impelled to protect his mother, and perhaps on some other occasion he will be so motivated, but at this moment, he perceives the questions as threats only to himself. Most concerned to protect his milk supply, he demonstrates clearly to his audience how much of a baby he still is. Rota is left to defend herself—and him. In protecting herself, in telling Juupi not to interfere and then removing herself from his vicinity, Rota incidentally protects her son. And so, despite the size and force of his competitor, Saali wins—just as Chubby Maata won against Maata with Juupi's "help."

Finale: "Turn in Circles"

At this point, one of the other two young women, Maata or Liila, suggests to Chubby Maata that she turn in circles. Their intent is to bring her to grief— playfully, of course. They hope she will make a comical fool of herself, be charmingly *silait-*. Their intent may also be to protect Rota—though perhaps they are only seeking new and more vivid diversion in the wild and mindless spirit of the preceding events. Whatever the intent, the effect of protection is achieved, because now all attention is directed to the new game, and Juupi does stop tickling Rota.

Chubby Maata's performance is indeed comically *silait-*, and so is her enjoyment of the performance. All the other children join in the mindless fun—in Saali's case, despite his mother's warning. Rota, though she didn't explain it to Saali, has foreseen exactly what will happen: after a few minutes of riotous fun in which the children probably enjoy both the odd bodily sensations and the laughter of the adults—which they fail to interpret as being at their expense— somebody falls too hard, and the game ends in tears. As it turns out, it is not

Saali who is the victim after all but Chubby Maata, the child whose *silait-* lack of foresight allowed the game to start in the first place. She cries and seeks comfort in her baby bottle of milk and in her mother's near, though passive, presence. So ends the sequence of dramas for this evening.

THE DRAMA ANALYZED: THEMES AND PLOTS

Structures in the Dramas

It is clear that dramas grow spontaneously out of ongoing social activities and are woven into these activities in ways that seem fitting to the players, especially the adult players—one drama following the next with an emotional-cognitive logic (indeed, more than one) that is sometimes obvious, sometimes not. I have suggested that adult actors may have a variety of reasons for initiating a particular drama with a particular child at a particular moment. Some of these reasons have to do with aspects of the child's behavior or with an event in the child's life that makes the topic appropriate; others have to do with events in the adult's own life. Adults are testing, experimenting with, and seducing the child, dramatizing the plots of their own lives and expressing their own feelings and wishes all at once. So, at one level, the logic of any drama concerns the motives of the adult actors. Any one adult may have several motives, simultaneously or sequentially, in the same interaction, as well as in different instances of the same drama; moreover, the motives of each actor may differ from those of others.

Idiosyncrasy is, of course, not allowed free sway; there are disagreements about how dramas should be enacted, ideas about rightness and wrongness. I saw this one day when Maata was playing "Want to come live with me?" with four-year-old Miika. Thinking, I judge, about her own future motherhood, Maata suggested to the little girl that she come and be Maata's baby. An old lady in the audience thereupon said to the child, "You'll carry Maata's baby on your back, won't you?" Maata's personal motives had led her astray from the plot acceptable to the old lady, who then corrected her. The logic here is provided by a sense of the social fittingness of certain responses or questions as opposed to others, the social or cultural appropriateness of certain sequences of events, certain outcomes, as distinct from others.

I do not mean to imply that the two levels are regularly distinct; social rules give shape to personal lives and create goals and motives, while goals and motives in turn shape rules and give meaning to them. Sometimes a question seems to be motivated by a person's perception of a rule—"Are you a baby? Babies don't do that"—while actually the rule is evoked only to support a personal goal: getting Chubby Maata to go to bed or not *ugiat-* Aita. At other times a question sounds as though it grows out of a personal concern—"Want to come live with me?" or "Do you like Yiini?"—while at the same time it inculcates socially proper attitudes and behavior: knowing where one belongs and how to be circumspect. The web of rules is untidy, often vague, and full of holes, open to various constructions and to contrary pulls. It is mainly when rules collide or are not followed that we become aware of how actively individuals perceive, construe, and organize their lives. And it is when rules collide— with each other or with personal wishes—that we can see that more than one logic exists.[19]

Each of these levels of logic—the one expressing and making sense of events in personal lives, the other following and validating social rules—contributes something to the structure and coherence of individual dramas. Both levels also contribute to the structure of the sequences in which the dramas are played. It is the interweaving of these levels of logic, together with the child's understanding or lack of understanding of the associated messages, that creates the plots of the dramas and the lessons for the child.

The tendency of both rules and personal concerns to combine into themes and plots further complicates the project of understanding the matter before us, because themes and plots, being large and abstract constructions, tend to recede out of the awareness of actors. I am reminded of a Charles Addams cartoon in which a party of pith-helmeted explorers stand consulting one another in the middle of an enormous footprint on the desert sands. One says to the other, "Well, I don't see any point in looking any farther. It was probably just one of those wild rumors" (Addams 1954:39). Themes and plots are like that footprint: too big to be visible. Nevertheless, if we can find them, they can illuminate the structures of these interactions.

One can find quite a few themes in long dramatic sequences like Episodes 1 and 9, and several plots, too, as the themes develop and combine. The dramas are like Inuit sculptures, which, when turned and held at different angles, may represent human, animal, or spirit entities, depending on one's point of view. Some sequences cohere more tightly than others. We saw that, looked at from one point of view, the interactions in Episode 1 spelled out in microcosm the process of Chubby Maata's growth from adorable baby to criticizable baby, and from baby to child. Episode 9 does not give us the same neat progression. The dramas that compose the sequence are more disparate than those of Episode 1; there is no single refrain that links the whole and presses us to search for a cumulative meaning to that whole. Nevertheless, there are themes that recur in various forms throughout the sequence, and each recurrence of a theme adds elements to the plot concerning that theme. Moreover, each drama seems to grow naturally out of the previous drama. So again it may make sense to look at the sequence as a whole.

Of course, though I speak of "wholes," I do not mean that any theme as developed in a dramatic sequence or interrogation has one complete structure. I argue throughout that Chubby Maata "hears" different messages as her experience grows and anxieties come in and out of focus. Perhaps the image of a kaleidoscope works better here than that of a sculpture: when experience shakes the tube, all the bits that make up a theme fall into a different pattern or plot. The same thing applies to combinations of themes.

Hence, there can be no "total" number of themes in a drama or sequence of dramas. Like Chubby Maata, an analyst looking at the same sequence on different occasions may perceive different themes, depending on what is momentarily foremost in her or his mind. And, of course, the perspectives of each actor and of each member of the audience concerning salient themes also differ from one another, depending on their concerns and on the accumulated experiences that they utilize in making their interpretations.

Belonging, Possession, and Attachment

I have already talked about some of the probable motives of the actors in the sequence, motives in which personal concerns and rules are all entwined. Now I want to stand back a little farther, look at a theme, and see what plots concerning that theme are created over the course of the sequence, what lessons may be contained in it, and how these are communicated.

For me, just now, the most striking theme in Episode 9 concerns issues of belonging, possession, and attachment.[20] Where Episode 1 asks Chubby Maata to consider the question of her own identity, defined as her position in the life cycle, Episode 9 raises questions about her relationships with other people in her community. To whom does she belong? To whom does she *want* to belong? Who are her friends and allies? Whom does she like, and whom *should* she like? Whom can she trust? And closely related to these questions: What does she own? And can she keep her possessions?

The dramas enacted with Saali in the second half of the sequence point him toward questions on the same subjects. In the first scene, the plot concerning attachment seems simple. Maata tells Chubby Maata through tone of voice and words that she loves her and her puppy and would like them to come and live in her house. She asks Chubby Maata if she would *like* to come, but when Chubby

Maata refuses, Maata escalates her offer and turns the invitation into a threat by starting—still with tender mien—to execute the plan, first against Papi and then, when Chubby Maata hesitates, against Chubby Maata. Chubby Maata has to exert increasing energy to make her point of view prevail, and she has to find an ally, but in the end she is allowed to win, and she can laugh at Maata's threat.

But is Chubby Maata's situation really so simple? She is confronted with two questions in this first scene, both of them potentially dangerous. The first in order of presentation is: How do I feel about going to live with Maata and her family? The second is: Regardless of how I feel, can I control the situation? Can I prevent her from taking me to live with her? In whose hands is the initiative?

I have the impression that, notwithstanding the slip—"Ih! I almost agreed!" which tells us that Chubby Maata is keeping guard over mixed feelings—it is the second question that presses most on her in this scene. When she catches her slip, her tone is cheerful, as if she doesn't perceive her own feelings to be problematic. But the energy with which she pulls herself and Papi away from Maata, her cries, and her attempt to alienate Maata from Papi—"She's all shitty!"—all betray a good deal of anxiety. It is *Maata's* intentions that are problematic.

We have seen that, in vividly dramatizing the consequences that would follow on Chubby Maata's acceptance of her invitation, Maata has turned that invitation into a threat. The dramatization certainly makes the threat seem very real, and if Chubby Maata is sufficiently aware of events in the world about her, she may find evidence there, too, to support her anxiety.[21] Remember that Chubby Maata's younger sister, Aita, and her playfellow Kaati, both of whom are much loved, as she is herself, are living with adoptive parents. Chubby Maata may already know this. She is often present when games that comment on their adoption are played with them.[22]

Maata is testing Chubby Maata to see if she understands enough to resist her invitation consistently. At the same time, in picking up first Papi and then Chubby Maata, she is structuring the situation in such a way that it is likely to elicit and strengthen exactly those feelings that will produce the negative answer. This is very helpful of her: Chubby Maata doesn't have to think much about what to do; her reactions are, by and large, immediate, spontaneous, and strong.

Nevertheless, she *is* confronted with a dilemma created by the juxtaposition of forceful action with a tender voice. The one arouses her resistance while the other—we can assume from "Ih! I almost agreed!"—seduces her. Perhaps the tone recalls other times when people using it have offered her things that she wants: comfort, closeness, food, a bottle. Or perhaps it reminds her specifically that she likes Maata and has had good times with her. We have seen that Chubby Maata very much enjoys being the center of affectionate attention, and her enjoyment of affection is not confined to her relationships with her parents. Liila and Jaani are very important to her, it is true, but she also enjoys being cuddled and *aqaq*-ed—or played with in a simpler sense—by her maternal grandparents, Arnaqjuaq and Mitaqtuq, by aunts and uncles, by Maata, and by me. She responds affectionately to many of the people who offer affection. So, by any of several routes, Maata's inviting voice brings Chubby Maata potentially face to face with the first of the dangerous questions I mentioned: How does she feel about Maata's offer? And about Maata?

The fact that soon after Maata stops her game Chubby Maata begins one of her own, which symbolically and with great energy recapitulates the game of the older girl, strongly suggests that the questions raised by Maata have not been resolved for Chubby Maata. The dangers are still there. It is a highly charged moment, a moment when loving and being loved by one object, Maata, has become associated with the possibility of losing other loved objects: home, mother, puppy. And now, at the very moment when Chubby Maata is working to gain control of these threats, a second interrogation begins, echoing the first in various ways and elaborating its theme in such a way that the perils associated with attachment proliferate.

In the first scene of the sequence, the message from Chubby Maata's point of view seems to be: "Maata loves me and is trying to possess me—and if I give any sign at all of acceding to her wish, my puppy or my home is lost." The second scene—the interrogation about whom Chubby Maata likes (*piugi*-s)—brings the little girl's feelings about Maata under closer scrutiny and makes them problematic. Instead of being elicited spontaneously and in the right direction through dramatic action, they are called up verbally to be analyzed by Chubby Maata herself, and clues to right answers are extremely subtle or altogether lacking. Chubby Maata is pressed to label the feelings and to take responsibility for them publicly, while Maata still looms dangerously on the horizon, ready to pounce if Chubby Maata gives her a chance.

If Chubby Maata says she likes Maata, will Maata pounce? Might such an admission be similar to almost agreeing to go and live with her? That possibility might incline Chubby Maata to say she doesn't like Maata, but when, just previously, she had said she didn't like Yiini, her mother was amused—a sure sign that Liila considered the answer *silait*-. We shall see later that Chubby

Maata is frequently subjected to powerful interrogations concerning her likes and dislikes for the people around her and that there are no easy answers. In the present case, too, it is clear that all her attempts to find acceptable answers to the question fail—under circumstances in which it seems to her extremely important to find a right answer, because she has already, in scene one and on other occasions, experienced hairbreadth escapes in consequence of a wrong answer.

In other words, whereas scene one might dispose Chubby Maata to a spontaneous gut resistance to being loved by Maata and to loving her in return, scene two, the second interrogation, forces her to take conscious possession of her reactions and at the same time calls those reactions into question without suggesting any easy alternative responses and without spelling out what might happen if she says the wrong thing. Both the answers and their consequences are left to Chubby Maata's imagination—an imagination tutored both by the vivid drama in scene one and by past experiences.

Another thing that scene two does is to expand the number of relationships in which Chubby Maata has to define her position and make public her feelings of attachment or the reverse. Now it is not just Maata but also Yiini, Juupi—even Liila when she participates in the questioning—who threaten her. Indeed, it is potentially anybody or everybody, as Maata's open-ended question—"Who, then? Who do you like?"—hints. What will *they* do to her if she says she likes them—or, for that matter, if she says she doesn't? What if she likes *one* and not others? Difficult problems indeed for a three-year-old, especially while doubts, engendered by scene one, concerning her ability to control others' behavior are still alive. No wonder she races back and forth with a "One, two, talee, GO!" She is running between the frying pan and the fire.[23]

Yet another way in which later events build in an unsettling way on the first scene concerns the matter of alliances. In that first scene, Chubby Maata tries briefly and unsuccessfully to enlist her mother as an ally against Maata, but her failure does not defeat her; she simply tries somebody else and without much trouble finds (she imagines) a secure protector in Juupi. We have seen that she is sufficiently confident of his support to be able to laugh at the danger she was in.

The alliance is of short duration, however. When Juupi hits Chubby Maata, he undoes her feeling of being protected, even though he denies having been the aggressor. At the end of scene one, it must have seemed to Chubby Maata that if her resistance were sufficiently single-minded and vigorous and that if she had an ally, she could keep what she valued, provided only that she knew what that was. But a few moments later—just before she is interrogated about whom she values—her alliance begins to come apart at the seams, and she is left alone facing a phalanx of adults who unanimously attack her, verbally if not physically. When she is struck on the bottom, she has two choices as to how to interpret the situation: either she can perceive her former protector as well-meaning but more ineffectual than she had imagined, or, in spite of Juupi's protestations of innocence, she can suspect, on the basis of past experience with similar dramas, that he is the real aggressor. At the same time, she is given reason to doubt the simple benevolence of another important person in her world: Yiini—"mother" and playfellow.

As the story line develops, then, other people besides Maata begin to appear complex and unpredictable. Nobody can be trusted consistently to support and not to attack. The problems inherent in attachment to people are proliferating, and the waters of understanding are becoming increasingly muddy as simple, superficial solutions disintegrate. By the time Rota and Saali come in, a number of questions have been raised concerning Chubby Maata's relationships with the other people in her world, people outside her immediate family; and with regard to all these relationships, it must be less clear to Chubby Maata than at the close of scene one what the dangers are, what the right answers are, and what will be the consequences of a wrong answer. The possibilities opening to imagination are broad indeed.

But there is still more to the problem. So far, I have treated scene one as though it were about *people,* pure and simple, but in fact Papi plays quite a sizable role in the drama. What is the nature of that role?

First of all, Maata involves Papi as though the puppy were part of a unit that includes both dog and child. She says, "You-and-Papi," and the assumption is that where Papi goes, Chubby Maata will follow. The same threat is extended to both, and the same fate will be experienced by both. Papi is a person, too. And conversely, Chubby Maata is a possession.

To the extent that Chubby Maata perceives an identity or sympathy between herself and Papi, the dramatized removal of her pet must help to make vivid the danger of her own removal. At the same time, Papi is also her possession, one that could be separated from her, and to the extent that she perceives this, Maata's treatment of Papi adds another dimension to Chubby Maata's dilemma and to the lessons that she learns. Now she will perceive herself as having *two* possessions, Papi and her home, both of which can be lost, and she has to choose between them. In either case, Papi, an actor in the drama as innocent as herself, helps to enliven and develop two lessons that we have already seen in this drama: first, Chubby Maata and her possessions are attractive to others, and, second, what others want, they'll try to take, regardless of the owner's

wishes, if it isn't given voluntarily. In other words, people are viewed as possessions. Consequently, there are three dangers: *being* desirable; *having* desirable
things; and, as we shall see even more vividly later, not appreciating what one
has. All these situations can bring about the loss of what one values.[24]

The lessons about possession are not cumulative in this sequence of dramas,
separately from those concerning attachment. Indeed, when possession—the
matter of Saali's shirt—comes up for discussion in a context divorced from
problems of attachment, Chubby Maata pays no attention at all. This doesn't
necessarily mean that problems concerning the possession of objects are meaningless for Chubby Maata except when they are tangled up with problems
concerning affection. Other dramas show that Chubby Maata is sensitive to
issues of property, quite apart from the question of who owns *her.* But they also
show that she is beginning to be wise when her mother playfully tests her
knowledge of who owns what.[25] She is no longer easily fooled, as she once was.
So it is possible that when her mother "warns" her that Saali has stolen her shirt,
she recognizes in Liila's tone of voice or in the form of her remark a clue to the fact
that she is being given false information. In addition, or alternatively, she may at
this moment be so absorbed in the other problems that are being presented to
her that she has no emotional space left over for shirts—the more so as the latter
issue is not acted out on this occasion in a way that compels her attention.

Later in the sequence another drama concerning possession occurs, and in a
form that once more meshes possession thoroughly with attachment to people.
This time the contested object is a breast, and Saali is the child protagonist-
victim, but if Chubby Maata is watching, and if she has eyes to see, she may find
the plot in some respects familiar. Juupi echoes Maata in pretending to value for
himself and to "take away" for his own use something that a child also values—
something that is attached to a whole complex of values surrounding self,
mother, and home, so that the theft threatens the child with the disruption, the
loss, of his entire familiar, safe world. This time, too, the attacker asks the child's
permission for the invasion, but at the same time he overrides the child's
resistance with his greater physical force; the child "wins" only by his own
vigorous effort and with the help of an adult ally.

There are also differences, of course, between the first possession drama and
the last. Chubby Maata is threatened with losing both her puppy and her
home, whereas Saali is threatened with the loss not of his home but of the
breast. He can keep the possessor of the breast.

But Chubby Maata is not likely to perceive such hair-splitting differences.
She is much more likely to see similarities between her situation and Saali's. In

the first place, she, like Saali, is being weaned, so she herself is sometimes the protagonist in dramas like the one that Juupi enacts with Saali, dramas that may resonate with this one in her mind.[26] In the second place, as Episode 2 has shown us, "home" for Chubby Maata is still imbued with baby meanings, and the special dyadic baby relationship with her mother continues to be very important to her. One of her refrains, whispered to Liila when they are out visiting, is "Let's go home to have a bottle." So loss of the breast, separation from her mother's body, may seem to her to be not very different from loss of home. The same may be true for Saali. He, too, may still be young enough so that the breast embodies mother and mother embodies home.[27] Both children, then, are likely to feel at the end of this sequence that their secure but babyishly unthinking attachment to mother has been called into question by the intrusion of the larger world and that the larger world is somewhat menacing.

In the long run, one of the lessons of dramas like this will be that the two extremes of attachment are both inappropriate. On one hand, it is dangerous to respond indiscriminately to all offers of affection. Such a response might cause one to lose the most important and legitimate source of love and nurturance: one's home. Chubby Maata and Saali are learning to recognize who it is that takes care of them, whom they belong to, and they are learning to respond with powerful and unquestioning devotion. In dramas like these, which test a child's progress in this domain, the key adults in the child's life are likely to take a back seat at the performance, to offer no support but instead to watch with absorption to see whether the child will reward their affection and their care by clinging to them or by stating clearly and firmly her or his allegiance, while other adults in various indirect but forceful ways push the child toward deciding in favor of home.

At the same time, the children are learning that exclusive relationships are also inappropriate or even dangerous. In this sequence, Juupi is the carrier of this lesson. He conveys it to Chubby Maata when he disturbs their alliance by surreptitiously hitting her, and again when he asks her if she likes him alone; and he communicates it to Saali when he intrudes between the little boy and his mother. But neither the moral logic of the prohibitions nor their full dimensions are spelled out in this series of dramas. To discover these things, the children will have to draw on other experiences, both playful and serious.

Wildness and Decorum

The sequence has not yet ended, however. On the surface, the last scene, turning in circles, seems a mere epiphenomenon following weighty issues concerning mothers, milk, and sex. But we should not dismiss it too soon. I think we have already begun to see that incidents of "wild" behavior—ugiat-ing and uimak-ing—have something to teach both Chubby Maata and us.

The first time we saw Chubby Maata and her sister incited and seduced into wildness was in the second half of Episode 1. There, Rosi was tricked into a position vulnerable to Chubby Maata's attack (ugiat-), and the ugiat-ing, escalating into serious reciprocal aggression, allowed both children to experience the uncomfortable consequences of uncontrolled behavior.[28] In Episode 9, adults twice incite wild activity: first, when Rota suggests to Saali that he uimak- and play tunraq; then when someone invites Chubby Maata to turn in circles. As in Episode 1, the grown-ups seem to be playing with fire. They let children experience the fun of unreason but also its danger: physical injury. And in each instance, when the children really or symbolically fall down, the blaze is extinguished, the play ended, and the children return—one might say retreat—to serious life with an enhanced appreciation for the serious values of home, mother, and milk. In Episode 1 we hear this in "Let's go home" or "Let's go to Kaati's." In Episode 9, first Saali and then Chubby Maata retreat to the fount of peace and safety: mother's breast and bottle. The moral certainly is that safety is found not in attack but in retreat.[29]

So the children are learning something about the comforts of civilization and the perils of social wilderness.[30] They may, however, also be learning that it is fun to test the limits of safety—in playful mode. And here, adult agendas will encourage them. I have suggested that Saali's tiny tunraq may have spoken to adult fears of monsters, internal and external, and that the adults may have enjoyed Saali's performance because it allowed them to both express and control those concerns. Is this another reason that silait- children are charming? Perhaps the same is true of turning in circles. The parallel between adult anxiety and child's play is less clear here; nevertheless, Juupi has just been playing fire with Rota in a dizzying way and has brought her low, literally—to the floor. When one of the other women tricks Chubby Maata into dizziness, it not only ends the attack on Rota, it moves socially disruptive behavior from the adult sphere to that of children, where the adults can watch it from outside, vicariously enjoy it, laugh at it from a superior height, control it, and bring it to grief. From the adult point of view, disorder is again reduced to an insignificant, childish thing—a puppet whose strings the adults pull in play—while the children discover its serious perils safely, and everybody, in different ways, has fun.[31]

Chapter 5 "Who Do You Like?"

Before adding another dimension to the picture of Chubby Maata's world, we should pause to take stock. We have been watching the gradual expansion and complication of that world—Chubby Maata's transition from baby to child and the proliferation of her relationships with other people. We have traced some of the strands of the emotional web in which those relationships are embedded, glimpsed dangers hiding in attachment, and guessed at the ambivalences and doubts, wishes and fears, born of the conflicting and ambiguous experiences. These feelings and perceptions are becoming ingredients in a moral plot: informing the rules that govern relationships and motivating (both supporting and subverting) their performance.

But we and Chubby Maata still have much to learn about this plot. What feelings *should* Chubby Maata have for her associates, and how should she treat these people? What can she expect of them in turn, if she treats them well or if she treats them badly? Not least, how should she evaluate herself in relation to the others? What is *her* worth in her world? And how do the emotional vibrations of the plot activate morality? Dramas concerning "liking" (*piugi-*) can help us to address these questions.[1]

In Episode 1 and other dramas that deal with babyness, we watched Chubby Maata begin to become aware that others perceive her as a baby and that being seen as a baby has certain consequences, both pleasant and unpleasant. In these dramas, Chubby Maata's attention is drawn primarily to her own qualities, and these attributes are characterized sharply and simply in baby terms: she is -*kuluk,* a darling little thing, and she is *silait-*. The social relationship that is in sharpest focus is the affectionate one-to-one tie with her mother, but at the same time Chubby Maata is "told" that others love her, too. And in interrogations like the one that follows, it is suggested to her that it is right, sensible— even safe—for her to respond to affection with affection.

Episode 10 (October 1)

Chubby Maata, at home, was sitting cozily on her mother's lap. Her father's brother Tuuma and her mother's sister Luisa were watching. Liila asked her daughter, "Do you consider your father good?" Chubby Maata wrinkled her nose: "No." "Do you consider your mother's mother good?" "No." "Your mother's father?" "No." One by one Liila listed Chubby Maata's relatives, then Yiini, and finally Liila herself. Chubby Maata rejected all of them, one by one. Liila asked her, "Are you the only good one? . . . Have you no nurturant-loving feelings? Why do you not consider ———— good? Because he doesn't nurturantly love you? Who most of all considers you good?" (Unfortunately, I failed to record both Chubby Maata's responses to these last questions and how the interaction ended.)

In other words, everybody is good, including Chubby Maata, and everybody— to some degree—loves Chubby Maata; therefore she should love everybody. In this interaction, Liila is pointing Chubby Maata in the direction of an interdependent, reciprocally nurturant ideology and suggesting socially appropriate reasons for liking others. In one case, she seems to be pointing out an appropriate reason for *dis*liking: response to someone else's dislike. Here, however, as often before, we must suspect that Liila is suggesting the opposite of what she says: she is asking Chubby Maata to question her impressions, to consider the possibility that ———— *does* nurturantly love her and therefore should be considered good (liked), like everybody else. Liila is outlawing dislike. Her questions sketch for Chubby Maata a clear outline of the rules for ideal social life in her society and suggest to her the motives that ideally underlie that conduct. More, they smooth the way for her to feel safe in following the rules— safe enough to *feel* these ideal motives.

The fact that Liila does not condemn Chubby Maata for disliking others—

does not tell her she is bad but rather asks her if she is "the only *good* one"—and the fact that this exchange takes place not in a coercive, punitive context but in the relaxed context of cozy conversation tell Chubby Maata that she is appreciated and has no reason to be alienated from society, to resist being socialized. Liila reassures her explicitly, too, by drawing her attention to the fact that people like her and in this way motivates her to feel benign in turn. Her strategy keeps Chubby Maata oriented toward society, accessible both to being sanctioned and to being appreciative of other people.

So far so good; the lesson is simple and straightforwardly presented. The problem is that it represents an unrealistically sunny view of social life, which, among Inuit as in other societies, is full of pushes and pulls, currents and countercurrents and undercurrents, rules that contradict each other, and feelings that are not consonant with behavioral dictates. Chubby Maata, as she moves out into the larger world of her camp, will have to learn about darker matters in order to interpret other people's behavior, to respond appropriately, and, when necessary, to protect herself. She will have to learn how to recognize the plots of everyday life: what people's goals are in any interaction, what their strategies are, what feelings and wishes motivate these strategies, what the reactions to *her* behavior are likely to be, and what are the probable consequences of all this. Most important, she must acquire feelings and sensitivities that will help her to make intuitive sense of the darker plots, cognitively and emotionally, and motivate her to respond appropriately.

It is not surprising, then, that changes in the simple, sunny picture are presaged in the second half of Episode 1 and that in Episode 9 we saw Chubby Maata's world become considerably more complex.[2] In the latter drama, when Chubby Maata is asked whom she likes (*piugi-*), the context is not warmly reassuring but threatening. Although she is still given no reason to doubt that she is loved, one of the perilous side effects of that state is in high relief, and, from Chubby Maata's point of view, the threat is serious—not a momentarily uncomfortable physical assault, as in Episode 1, but the danger of being forcibly carried away to live in someone else's house, the danger of losing the tie with mother.

The instruction to respond to affection with appreciation underlies Episode 9 as much as Episode 10, but in the first instance the point is far from explicit. It is one of the darker plots that is in clearest view in that drama. I have argued that, instead of encouraging widespread "liking," it motivates Chubby Maata to cling to home and mother while making her wary about being loved too much by people outside her immediate family and suspicious of other people's intentions and of their power over her.[3] Can such unideal emotions create a moral person, one who profoundly appreciates social values and is strongly inclined to support them? Let us look in greater detail at some of the other situations in which Chubby Maata is presented with the problem of "liking" and try to figure out what she may learn.

Episode 11 (Excerpt, March 3)

Chubby Maata's grandmother Arnaqjuaq was visiting in Rota's house. Chubby Maata came in by herself and went directly over to Arnaqjuaq, who was sitting on one of the side platforms in the inner half of the qammaq.[4] Rota, in an amused voice, commented to the world at large, "She's unstoppable, she goes straight to her goal (katsungait-), as usual." Then she added, this time speaking to Chubby Maata, "I'm going to shoot your father." Chubby Maata looked at Rota with a blank face. Rota, with an amused smile, asked, "Do you like (piugi-) him?" Chubby Maata wrinkled her nose. Rota double-checked: "You don't like him?" Chubby Maata raised her brows, confirming that she didn't like him, whereupon Rota turned to Saali, who was standing near her, and exclaimed in mock surprise: "You don't like him! Saali! Here's an adoptive father for you![5] She doesn't like her father!" Saali seemed to ignore these remarks. Chubby Maata's face was watchful. No further games were played with her while I visited. Instead, the focus of play shifted, first to Saali, then to me.[6]

How does Rota's drama compare with Maata's in Episode 9?

Both dramas threaten Chubby Maata with the loss of a parent, and we saw in Chapter 3 that father and daughter—like mother and daughter—have a close and comfortable relationship, one that Chubby Maata would miss if it were lost. But this time the loss will come about not because she is too much loved but because of her social failings, her baby silait- qualities.

Chubby Maata's first "crime" is to put herself forward in an inappropriate way; perhaps another is to single out one person in the room—a person who is not her mother—for attention. Visitors of all ages who are not closely associated with the household should stand just inside the door unless invited to come in and sit down.

The feeling that motivates such proper behavior is ilira-, a mixture of respect and the fear of being scolded or treated unkindly. A person who does not feel ilira- is not, and cannot be, socialized.[7] Chubby Maata, in approaching her grandmother, demonstrates that she does not feel ilira-, either toward her or toward Rota, mistress of the house; and I think that Rota is trying to create a situation that will change that state of affairs. She may have been particularly sensitive to Chubby Maata's forwardness because, as a visitor, she herself was always reticent, never casually familiar like others of her age. Indeed, Rota gave me the impression that she felt much more *ilira-* than most people did.[8]

In any case, in threatening to injure Chubby Maata's father, I think Rota intends to make Chubby Maata wonder about Rota's power over her world. But Chubby Maata's face is not easy to read, and Rota, watching her, may be curious to know whether Chubby Maata is too much of a baby to feel appropriately protective (*nallik-*)—though the word is not used in this drama—toward her father. So Rota's second attack is aimed more directly at Chubby Maata: "Do you like him?" And when Chubby Maata gives the wrong answer, Rota tells her what the consequences will be. This time she doesn't say she will hurt Jaani; she says she will take him away from Chubby Maata and give him to Saali. Chubby Maata has, in a sense, "released" him. So Rota makes Chubby Maata responsible for both her father's fate and her own. But at the same time, both threats represent Rota as stronger than either Chubby Maata or Jaani, a loving parent whose strength Chubby Maata, in her weakness, might naturally be inclined to rely on.

Rota's attacks, then, have several prongs and can prick Chubby Maata at several points. They may make Chubby Maata aware that her father is vulnerable to injury and that she is vulnerable to losing him, and they represent these awful fates as being, at one and the same time, in the hands of Rota and a matter of Chubby Maata's own responsibility. If Chubby Maata combines these messages, she might hear, "If you don't appreciate (*piugi-*) and want to protect your father, he will be too weak to defend either himself or you from me, so both of you stand alone and vulnerable to injury."

There is an echo in all this of Maata's threat to remove Chubby Maata from her home, which had the potential to awaken Chubby Maata to appreciation of home, make her a little uneasy about both Maata's strength and her own responsibility for her fate, and cause her to doubt Juupi's ability to protect her. She stood alone on that occasion, too.

Both Maata and Rota are strengthening Chubby Maata's budding awareness of kinship and teaching her its social importance, but their dramas differ in one important respect. Whereas Maata's threat to steal Chubby Maata has the potential only to intensify the little girl's dependence (*unga-*) on her mother, Rota's threat to shoot or steal Jaani may strengthen not only *unga-* feelings but also *nallik-*, protective concern—a much more mature kind of attachment than the babyish (though also useful) *unga-*.

Episodes 9 and 11 show us that the "liking" (*piugi*-ing) behavior of a Qipisa adult did not always reflect simple, warm, ingenuous feelings, natural responses to the affection and interest of others. Of course, liking sometimes did have this dimension, too. But it was more than this. It was at once a social obligation, a danger, and an emotional necessity, built up in part out of a variety of anxieties. Chubby Maata is being shown two related sanctions against liking that is inappropriate: insufficient or too exclusive or misdirected. The first threat is the possibility that a loved one may be attacked; the second is the possibility that Chubby Maata may be separated from a loved one and find herself alone and unsupported. Both of these threats may intensify Chubby Maata's need to bond with *some* others, to *piugi*- them; but is *general* liking fostered? We find a partial answer in the next two episodes, which concern Chubby Maata's relationship with a kinsman she really does not care for.

Episode 12 (December 1)

Jaani's fifteen-year-old sister, Ruupi, brought Chubby Maata and Saali's almost-five-year-old sister, Miika, to visit her parents, Chubby Maata's paternal grandparents. Miika, who was unusually independent in her comings and goings (and who was not closely related to the old couple) left almost immediately by herself. Then Chubby Maata's grandmother Aana said to her, "Do you still not want to kiss (*kunik*-) your horrid little old father?" She was referring not to Jaani but to Chubby Maata's grandfather Iqaluk, who was sitting beside her on the sleeping platform. The kin term was the term of endearment that Chubby Maata had been taught to use for her grandfather.[9] Chubby Maata's face was blank. Aana asked her, "Are you beginning to like (*piugi*-) him?" Chubby Maata wrinkled her nose: "No."

Iqaluk said, in the throaty timbre that was used to dramatize mild threat when speaking to a child, "Let me pull your braids!" And he reached out a hand toward Chubby Maata's head. Chubby Maata's face remained blank. She didn't move.

Aana asked her, "Do you want to kiss your horrid little old father?" I didn't see any change in Chubby Maata's blank face, but Aana said, "She agrees!" Iqaluk then called her to him: "Come!" She came and turned her cheek to him. He snuffed it lightly, and Aana commented, laughing, on Chubby Maata's having turned her *cheek*. (The gesture was a distancing one; the nose or the front of the face were more usual spots at which to aim snuffs.) Iqaluk said, "I'll no longer pull your braids."

That was the end of the interaction, but when Ruupi took Chubby Maata out a few minutes later, Aana remarked with a smile on how big Chubby Maata was growing.

Episode 13 (March 4)

Three months later, two hunters from Pangnirtung, who were being housed overnight by Aana and Iqaluk, were sitting on the sleeping platform of the qammaq and talking with their hosts (mostly the hostess) when the door opened and Ruupi came in with Chubby Maata. The girls stood close to the door, showing that they felt uneasy in the presence of the visitors. Chubby Maata's wide eyes and still, serious face gave clear sign of her *ilira*- feelings. She stood motionless, watching the people on the sleeping platform.

Aana identified Chubby Maata for the visitors: "That's Jaani's youngest daughter." (She didn't mention Chubby Maata's baby sister, Aita, who, as we know, had been adopted by her other grandparents.)

One of the men said to Chubby Maata, "Have you never seen me before?" The question sounded like a comment on her *ilira*- behavior and was perhaps an attempt to remind her that she had indeed seen him not many weeks before and so need not fear him, as small children fear strangers. But Chubby Maata raised her brows. Either she didn't recognize him or she wasn't going to admit that she did.

Aana said quietly to her visitor—or perhaps to anyone who would hear, including Chubby Maata: "She lacks awareness (she is *silait*-). She thinks her father is not Iqaluk's son."

At this, Iqaluk immediately said to Chubby Maata in a loud, mock-hostile voice, "Your father's no good (*piungngit*-)!" Chubby Maata looked at Iqaluk without changing expression. No more attention was paid to her, and I think she and Ruupi left quite soon thereafter.

A clear moral of these two episodes is that one ought to like and respond warmly to one's grandfather. Not to do so is tantamount to rejecting the kinship connection and gives the offended person a strong motive for reciprocating. A close look at the ways in which Iqaluk formulates this message may give us more evidence of the emotional and social "logic" of liking that Chubby Maata is learning.

In Episode 12, Iqaluk, with mock hostility, threatens to attack Chubby Maata, in revenge for her rejection of him. It is an easily understood tit for tat: if you don't like me, I won't like you—or a milder version: if you treat me discourteously, I'll treat you discourteously. In either case, Iqaluk directly and simply brings to the surface the unstated underside of the benign reciprocity that Liila advocates in Episode 10.

The message of Episode 13, however, is more like that of Episode 11. Iqaluk "revenges" himself not against his offending granddaughter but against her innocent father. Like Rota, he draws Jaani into the attack, and perhaps for one of the same reasons: a wish to awaken Chubby Maata to an awareness of kinship. Telling her that *she* is bad only communicates disapproval of her attitude toward him, a disapproval that may not concern her very much—or that may drive her farther from her grandfather—since she says she doesn't like him, and since she isn't dependent on him in any way.[10] On the other hand, if Iqaluk says her *father* is bad, he implicitly asserts that there is a link between Chubby Maata and Jaani, which should make Chubby Maata feel threatened and protective (*nallik-*) on Jaani's behalf. He also affirms, as Rota did, that Chubby Maata's attitude—in this case, rejecting a kinsman who is *un*important to her—has consequences for how kin who *are* important to her are treated. If Chubby Maata does not confirm the kinship between her father and Iqaluk, Iqaluk will repudiate him. "When *you* reject, *I* reject," says Iqaluk, in effect. So, her father, like herself, appears vulnerable to sanction, and perhaps, as suggested in Rota's drama, he lacks the strength to protect his daughter. If Chubby Maata identifies at all with her father, doubts about whether she is protected may be intensified, as she experiences vicariously what it feels like to be cast off, to stand alone—an experience that, as I have argued, has the potential to awaken in Chubby Maata both concern for her own status and appreciation of her kin ties. Altogether, in this episode, as in Episode 11, directing the attack against Jaani multiplies and ramifies the lessons for his daughter, drawing her far more thoroughly into the social network than mere disapproval would have done. Only, in this episode, the lesson that one should *piugi-* is extended even to kin one doesn't care for. Perhaps even further. Aana's criticism about Chubby Maata's treatment of her grandfather may be just the tip of the iceberg. If, as I think, Aana's intention is, at least in part, to explain to the visitor why Chubby Maata rejected *his* friendly overture, her remark is a comment not only on Chubby Maata's failure to recognize her kin but also on her inability to respond to everyone with even-handed friendliness. The latter criticism is certainly the message of her other grandmother in the interrogation that follows.

Episode 14 (November 28)

Chubby Maata's nine-year-old cousin, Miali, came into my qammaq, back-packing Chubby Maata's baby sister, Aita, in her parka. Chubby Maata's grand-mother Arnaqjuaq followed her, both to see if her little adopted daughter was crying and to rest for a minute from scraping sealskins. Arnaqjuaq was in turn followed by Rosi and Chubby Maata, both girls snowsuited and red-cheeked from cold.

I playfully touched Rosi's cheek and sharply withdrew my hand, pretending to be burnt by the red cold: "A'aaa (ouch)!" My gesture was meant to be friendly, an attempt to encourage Rosi, too, to be friendly and not *ilira-*. Rosi smiled but didn't speak—a minimally friendly response, as I read it. I turned to Chubby Maata: "You too?" I touched her cheek in the same way and said, "A'aaa!" Chubby Maata looked at me. She didn't move away from my touch, but she didn't smile, either. I read that as a less than minimally friendly reaction, but less *ilira-* (or *kappia-*) than the response she might have made a few weeks earlier.

Arnaqjuaq bent down and said to Chubby Maata, "Do you like (*piugi-*) her?" Chubby Maata wrinkled her nose: "No." Arnaqjuaq double-checked: "Do you dislike her?" Chubby Maata raised her brows, confirming that she did. Arnaqjuaq persisted, "Do you dislike *me?*" Chubby Maata wrinkled her nose, and Arnaqjuaq laughed: "How little understanding she has (she is *silait-*)! Do you dislike Aita?" Chubby Maata wrinkled her nose. Arnaqjuaq laughed again and repeated, "Silait-!"

I asked Chubby Maata, "Am I the only one (you don't like)?" I didn't see her answer, but Arnaqjuaq said to me, "She's silait- (she has no understanding). Sometimes she likes (*piusaq-*), and sometimes she can't like at all!"

Now we have returned full circle to the sunny plot sketched by Liila in Episode 10. Arnaqjuaq, however, is far more explicitly critical of Chubby Maata than Liila was, and, surprisingly, she is just as amused by her granddaughter's socially appropriate positive answers as she is by the inappropriate ones. She labels Chubby Maata *silait-*, lacking in understanding, not when Chubby Maata says she *dis*likes me but when she says she *likes* her grandmother and baby sister. And at the end Arnaqjuaq explains to me that it is Chubby Maata's inconsistency of attitude that she finds amusing and babyish. Remember that in Episode 9 Juupi, too, cross-examined Chubby Maata when she said she liked him, and he tried to trick her into making the inappropriate statement that she liked him alone. Liking, too, can be wrongly done.

Little by little, the moral schema full of sweetness and light that Liila sketched in Episode 10 is being developed into a much more complicated play, one laced with sinister possibilities. This richer morality play will show Chubby Maata a less savory side of human nature: self-interested, vengeful, hostile, greedy, possessive. And it will teach Chubby Maata to make her way warily in a world that contains shadow as well as sun.

At the same time, I have been arguing, the antisocial suspicions and fears that

the shadowy aspects give rise to are not necessarily antisocial in their consequences. Under some circumstances, they may indeed make it impossible to
behave morally, and when things go wrong in the social world, we may expect
to find these tensions active in the breakdown. However, we have seen that
under other circumstances, the same tensions, far from subverting the ideal
social rule, have the potential to motivate the warm appreciation and nurturance that that rule calls for. We'll come back to these points later. But if we are to
understand how the plot works in practice, we must still add two essential
ingredients that have not been in high relief in the interactions we have so far
looked at. The first of these is the affectionate ambience of all these encounters,
without which they might have quite different effects.

Often the warmth in a drama or interrogation can be hard for a small child to
find, especially when she is left to her own devices to figure out what actions and
questions mean. We have seen that Chubby Maata is frequently helped only by
hints that her responses are *silait-* and by further questions and dramatizations
that illustrate or point out to her the implications of her inappropriate responses. The assumption is that what she doesn't understand on one occasion
she may pick up at another time. When the exercise becomes too severe, too
distressing, however, adults do sometimes offer explanations—or, more often,
ask questions—that help Chubby Maata to find the benign intents under the
threatening behavior and to become aware of the reasons *she* is unable to feel
loving. Episode 15 is an intervention of this sort.

Episode 15 (January 27)

This drama was played out in the home of Chubby Maata's great-grandfather, Natsiq. Natsiq was the Anglican religious leader of the camp. Services
were held in his home, and it was his custom, after all services, to walk around
the room and shake hands with all who had attended, big and small. On this
occasion, Chubby Maata was standing beside her father. When Natsiq approached them, he put his arms around Jaani's neck and, looking at Chubby
Maata over his shoulder, pretended to prevent her from approaching her father.
Once he even swatted in her direction as she approached, whereupon Chubby
Maata started to cry.

At sight of Chubby Maata's tears, Natsiq immediately took his arms away
from Jaani and smiled at Chubby Maata. Liila put her arms around her daughter, pulled her into her lap, and said to her in a low voice: "Does he worry
(*pingigaq-*) you? Do you dislike (*piugingngit-*) him? Does he like (*piugi-*) you?
Does he love (*nalligi-*) you?" I couldn't see Chubby Maata's face. Jaani was
smiling at her, sitting beside wife and daughter on a bench against the wall.

On the surface, Episode 15, like Episodes 9 and 11, is about the competitiveness of *piugi*-ing. Both Natsiq and Chubby Maata value (*piugi-*) Chubby Maata's father, but Natsiq, being stronger, can and will take Jaani away from Chubby Maata. Here is another familiar plot, presented in a particularly forceful form. Natsiq, great-grandfather to Chubby Maata and grandfather or father to the majority of her elders, is the most symbolically powerful person in the camp, the one most likely to cause *ilira-* feelings in almost everybody, and Chubby Maata certainly knows this by contagion. Further, in this interaction, unlike the one initiated by Rota, the danger is expressed not verbally but dramatically, and the object of the threat, Jaani, is present and playing "stooge," not resisting Natsiq's possessive overture. Finally, Natsiq, unlike Maata and Rota, doesn't make the slightest pretense of consulting Chubby Maata's wishes. Much less does he make his action dependent on Chubby Maata's rejection of the object he values: her father. On the contrary. He rejects *her*, brushing her off with a swat. Chubby Maata clearly understands Natsiq's threatening message, and I imagine that such strongly dramatized versions of the plot help to inform and infuse with emotion Chubby Maata's understanding of the less dramatic and more verbal versions presented to her in episodes like 11.

What Chubby Maata does not understand is that Natsiq's game with her— the notice he pays her—is friendly. Liila is at some pains to point out this aspect of the message to her distressed little daughter. Her questions suggest to Chubby Maata that Natsiq loves (*nalligi-*) not only Jaani but also her, Chubby Maata. In calling Chubby Maata's attention to Natsiq's warmth and sympathetically interpreting Chubby Maata's own troubling feelings, Liila reassures her daughter. She also exposes to view an element of the *piugi-* plot that is in very small print indeed in the other dramas we've looked at. It is the moral of Episode 10: if people love you, they won't really do anything to hurt you, no matter what they *seem* to say. The *route* to being well thought of—namely, thinking well of others—is made explicit in other dramas like Episode 12.

Now, let's leave for a while the lessons that Chubby Maata is learning about how to treat other people and consider the other side of the coin, the second missing ingredient in the picture: how do other people evaluate Chubby Maata's own qualities? And how, consequently, should she view herself? We have seen that in interactions that celebrate her babyness, Chubby Maata is -*kuluk*, wrapped in warm and uncritical approbation. We have also heard her called *silait-*: unaware of "adult" realities and the rules of social life. And we know that she is beginning to *hear* these criticisms, beginning to pick them out from the affectionate tones in which they are usually uttered. Chubby Maata is emerging from the Garden of Eden, coming to realize that she is a person of mixed qualities, not quite perfect. But only when this realization acquires emotional force will she be capable of participating in the moral plot. Dramas like the following contribute materially to this development.

Episode 16 (October 10)

Late in the evening, Chubby Maata's grandmother Arnaqjuaq brought her little adopted daughter Aita, Chubby Maata's baby sister, to visit Liila because Aita was wide awake and cranky. Liila, tender as always with the baby she had given up, held Aita on her lap and fed her bits of prechewed bread. Meanwhile, Chubby Maata, sitting beside her mother, played with a band of cardboard that had once been the envelope of a package of cigarettes. She was trying to cut a strip from it which could be "burst" with a satisfying *pop* by clapping it on her knee. Children and young people often entertained themselves and each other in this way, but Chubby Maata was not yet capable of managing the scissors effectively. Liila ignored all of Chubby Maata's requests for help.

Aita was crying, and Arnaqjuaq remarked that the baby was angry (*ningngat-*). Her own voice was warm, sympathetic, and amused, and she used the tender form, -*kuluk,* which we have often seen addressed to Chubby Maata. Seeking a cause for the tears, the two women decided that Aita was displeased because the bread she was sucking on was not a bottle of milk. No one else was present. Jaani had left for Pangnirtung in the morning and would be gone for several days; Chubby Maata's sister Rosi was already asleep.

Suddenly, Arnaqjuaq—without any cause that was evident to me—began chanting to Chubby Maata: "Your father is VERY BAAAD (*piungngitTUUQ*)." Her eyes were smiling, but her voice was vigorous and emphatic, the tone rhythmical, a chant. Chubby Maata did not smile in response. I saw no change of expression in her profile, and her body was perfectly still. She was watching her grandmother.

After a while, Arnaqjuaq changed the words of her chant, but her tone remained the same, and her eyes were still smiling: "Your father is VERY BAAAD. Your mother is VERY BAAAD. My dear little mother's sister is VERY BAAAD.[11] Isn't that so? You are bad, aren't you? Your father is bad, isn't that so? I've heard that my dear little mother's sister is bad, yes indeed! Your mother is VERY BAAAD," and so on. The stream of words was unremitting and inexorable.

At some point during Arnaqjuaq's speech, Chubby Maata covered her face with her band of cardboard. Arnaqjuaq said, imperatively, "Look at me!"

Chubby Maata didn't move, but Liila removed the wrapper from her daughter's face and began to watch her with an amused smile, while Arnaqjuaq continued to rain "BAAADS" on Chubby Maata.

Chubby Maata sat motionless for a while and then suddenly leaned over and snuffed Aita, who was still sitting on Liila's lap. The kiss didn't seem particularly rough to me, but Arnaqjuaq said in a cautionary tone, "Don't bite her." And then to Liila: "She's trying to bite; she's beginning to attack (*ugiat*-) the baby."

Chubby Maata replied, "My father cut his finger—isn't that so?" She turned to her mother for confirmation and said something else about her father which I didn't understand. Her tone, to my surprise, was conversational, as though she were conveying perfectly ordinary information to her grandmother.

Her mother ignored her, and Arnaqjuaq said rejectingly, "Never mind (*quyana*)!" She resumed her chant: "Your father is BAAAD." Then, all at once, she began a new theme: "Your genitals are bad. Aaq! They stink!" She came over to Chubby Maata, who was sitting with knees raised, and poked a finger between the little girl's legs. "Are you aware of your horrid little (-*ruluk*) genitals? THERE they are!" And she pretended to pull down Chubby Maata's trousers from behind.

Chubby Maata burst into loud tears, but they lasted only a short minute and stopped as abruptly as they had begun. The two women laughed, and Arnaqjuaq said to Liila, "She took it seriously (*pivik*-)!" Her voice and eyes were amused. Then, in a different tone, she said to Chubby Maata, "(Did you cry) because you felt shy (*kangngu*-)?" I don't think Chubby Maata answered.

Arnaqjuaq resumed her chant about the badness of father and mother, but with less force and intensity. Chubby Maata made no further response, and after a few more repetitions, her grandmother stopped.

Chubby Maata began to tease Aita with the cardboard band, repeatedly brushing it against Aita's fingers while Aita tried in vain to catch hold of it and whimpered, I judged, in frustration. Liila commented, "She's angry (*ningngat*-); she wants to boss." At this, Chubby Maata began a chant of her own, directed at Aita: "She cries easily . . . " The tune of the chant was the "*nya*-nya nya-*nya*-nya" chant of scorn with which children in my own world taunt their fellows.[12] Chubby Maata was saying the equivalent of "*cry*baby, *cry*baby . . . "

Eventually Arnaqjuaq got up to carry Aita home to bed, but before she took the baby from Liila, Liila held Aita toward Chubby Maata and said, in a tender, persuasive tone, "Give her a little kiss." And Chubby Maata snuffed her.

Aita, however, was still cranky. Arnaqjuaq remarked as they left, "She wants very much to be the boss." Her tone was warm and accepting.

Though we have seen Chubby Maata's behavior criticized before, this is the first drama in which it is suggested to her that *she,* or some part of her, is bad. What might Arnaqjuaq's purposes be, and what the effects on Chubby Maata? Let's follow the thread of the interaction.

It is possible that Arnaqjuaq, frustrated by her inability to calm her cranky baby, is casting about for distraction and entertainment—for herself, since she has had no success with Aita. She does not seem to be irritated, but if she is so, entertainment with a slightly aggressive flavor may appeal to her. In any case, she lights on Chubby Maata, who is quietly occupied in the vicinity of her mother.

Arnaqjuaq begins by telling Chubby Maata that her father is bad, but her smiling eyes signal that she doesn't really mean it.[13] There are a number of things that she may mean. For one thing, we already know that in playful interactions people often say the opposite of what they mean. So Arnaqjuaq could simply be telling Chubby Maata that her father is good or trying to provoke Chubby Maata into defending her father against attack—raising to consciousness Chubby Maata's own awareness that her father is good and worth protecting. This is a familiar strategy; we've seen it in other dramas, most directly in Episode 13. In addition, playing a game about father when he is away on a trip can help to keep his memory fresh and his presence strong in his absence.

But when Arnaqjuaq gets no obvious rise out of Chubby Maata, she escalates the attack, aiming it first at Chubby Maata's mother and then directly at the little girl herself. Moreover, in another move that is familiar to us, she asks Chubby Maata for *her* opinion: "Aren't you?" "Isn't that so?" In this way, she forces Chubby Maata to examine her virtue and take an active part in the criticism. Given the pattern of saying the opposite of what one means, the push of these questions toward a positive answer could suggest to Chubby Maata that a *negative* reply is expected. But if a clue is there, Chubby Maata doesn't pick it up. Finally, Arnaqjuaq introduces a wider and more solid base for her criticism, exposing Chubby Maata to a judgmental audience that could conceivably include everybody: "I've heard . . . yes, indeed: eeelaaq!" Her phrase and tone are insistent, overriding protest and admitting of no doubt. Chubby Maata is alone again, attacked from without by a united phalanx of critical people and perhaps from within, too, by a germinating conscience. And when Chubby Maata, overwhelmed, tries to escape by covering her face, her elders bring her back to the spotlight and compel her to face them, openly and without protection.

Yet, in a sense, Chubby Maata is not alone. She is not the only person singled out for critical comment; she is in company with others whom she loves—an association that could have a variety of effects, depending on the issues that exercise her at the moment. For one thing, Arnaqjuaq's attack on the parents whom Chubby Maata depends on could resonate with other dramas in which Chubby Maata is deprived of, or betrayed by, supporters. If Chubby Maata senses that her parents, too, are weak in face of criticism, association with them could paradoxically intensify her feeling of aloneness and vulnerability and increase the force of the attack, as I argued in interpreting Episode 13. Clearly, her parents can't protect her. And indeed they are not protecting her; her father is absent, and her mother is in league with her grandmother. On the other hand, if Chubby Maata identifies with the "badness" of her parents, the force of the attack may be diluted; Chubby Maata may be reassured by the fact that she is not the only bad one. Moreover, identification with her mother may dispose Chubby Maata to notice that Liila is not upset by Arnaqjuaq's attack against *her*, so the way is open for Chubby Maata to conclude that she is not in danger either. Finally, if the attack makes Chubby Maata feel protective toward her beleaguered parents, it gives her a reason for feeling good about herself as well. And if she can see goodness in herself, that may help to fortify her against any feelings of badness that the attack on her elicits.[14]

It is hard to know which of these possible dynamics are salient for Chubby Maata, but she does try to counter accusations of badness with assertions of goodness. She tries distracting tactics, which are at the same time claims to virtue. And what happens? First, Chubby Maata kisses the baby, a nurturant gesture that should earn approval—and that also enables her to hide her face again. She may be trying only to return life to a comfortable, affectionate track. But perhaps her gesture is a little too rough: made awkward by her discomfiture or by hostility toward the baby, who is getting all the tender attention while she gets the critical blast. Perhaps she is angry at her attackers, too. However the kiss is motivated, her elders perceive it as rough (*ugiat*-ing). Women often expect small children to snuff babies too hard; they warn them against *ugiat*-ing. So Chubby Maata is criticized again instead of being approved.

She tries once more. This time she says something that could be heard as concern for her much maligned father: "He is hurt." Her remark could be interpreted in a number of ways. The words, together with the mature voice in which they are uttered, suggest that Chubby Maata may be saying, "I am adult; I don't injure people; I don't bite them; I am concerned for them." Is she trying to deflect criticism concerning her own act of aggression? The remark could also elicit sympathy for Jaani, which would turn attention away from *his* "badness," or it may merely express anxiety about Jaani's safety, since he is under attack. Or, in displaced fashion, Chubby Maata may be expressing anxiety about her own safety and trying to enlist her mother's support: "Isn't that so?" Still another possibility is that Chubby Maata's conversational tone signals that she has withdrawn from her grandmother's attack. She is no longer personally involved. Neither aggressor nor victim, she offers her father as a victim in substitution for herself.

All or several of these motives in combination, and not necessarily conscious, might contribute to explaining Chubby Maata's remark about her father's finger. But her move, however motivated, succeeds neither in deflecting her grandmother nor in eliciting her mother's support. On the contrary. Both women push Chubby Maata back into the role of child, Liila by ignoring her daughter's observation and Arnaqjuaq by rejecting it: "Quyana (never mind)!" She devalues both Chubby Maata's information and any nurturant concern that may have been contained in the little girl's remark. Instead, Arnaqjuaq intensifies her attack by focusing it more sharply—by focusing it on Chubby Maata's genitals, no doubt to the horror of some non-Inuit readers.

It is true that Chubby Maata is upset at this moment, but we would do well to remember that Arnaqjuaq and Liila both love Chubby Maata dearly and would not for the world injure her or cause her unbearable humiliation.[15] But precisely because Chubby Maata is so -*kuluk,* so warmly and widely delighted in, there is a danger that she may see herself in too rosy a light. Episode 2 gives us a bit of evidence of such innocence: "I *am* a babykuluk (a darling little baby), *aren't* I?" This unrealistic glow needs to be dimmed a little, in order both to make Chubby Maata educable, open to sanction, and to inoculate her against serious disillusionment later.[16] Arnaqjuaq's intention is certainly not to convince Chubby Maata that she is BAAAD, but it may be that she wants to cast a little doubt into Chubby Maata's mind about whether she is *wholly* good. At the same time, and in part contradictorily, she probably also wants to make Chubby Maata aware that genitals are of special value, something to be celebrated—that people therefore "want" them and (a familiar theme) might try to take what they value. Chubby Maata should be careful to protect herself.[17]

Arnaqjuaq has already given Chubby Maata one clue to the benignity of her intentions: she is smiling, not maliciously but warmly. And when Chubby Maata cries, Arnaqjuaq offers two or three more clues. The amused laughter directed at Chubby Maata, especially when combined with the explanation "She took it seriously," could be a sign to her that she is in no real danger; Arnaqjuaq does not mean what she says. And the question "Because you feel shy?" could not only reassure Chubby Maata that her distress is understandable, appropriate, and therefore not alarming; it could also guide her in the direction in which she should grow: Arnaqjuaq takes her granddaughter's tears as a sign that Chubby Maata has begun to feel what she *should* feel about her genitals—shyness (*kangngu-*). Of course, we can't know what Chubby Maata makes of her grandmother's benign messages at this moment, but we will see presently, in Episodes 18 and 19 (the first occurring in November, the other in December), that although Chubby Maata has begun to entertain the possibility that she is not perfect, she still has a healthy measure of confidence in her goodness. But I am running ahead. Let's return, in a roundabout way, to the analysis of the data before us.

It seems to me possible that, in mentioning Jaani's finger, Chubby Maata herself gave Arnaqjuaq the opportunity to bring up the subject of genitals. In another drama, the mention of a cut finger led immediately to the subject of a cut penis. Let's look at that case to see what it tells us about the meanings that Arnaqjuaq's threat might have for Chubby Maata.

Episode 17 (March 4)

Chubby Maata came into the house where Liila and other women were cleaning a polar bear hide, and Liila held up a bandaged finger to show it to her daughter: "Look, I cut my finger." Maata, working by Liila's side, said to Chubby Maata: "You're not going to have a mother any more. Shall I be your mother?" Chubby Maata wrinkled her nose: "No." Liila said to Chubby Maata, untruthfully, "Your little mother (Rota) cut it."[18] Chubby Maata was silent. Rota said to her, "I'm going to cut your father's nasty old penis off!" Again, Chubby Maata was silent. Arnaqjuaq smiled an amused smile. Rota repeated her threat two more times, but got no response from Chubby Maata other than a look. She dropped the subject.

By and large, this drama has a familiar sound, but it also contains a new element: the association between finger and penis, which is elaborated into a story of injury, even death. The finger can be cut and the mother can die; the penis can be cut off—and the father die? In Episode 11, Rota did threaten to do away with Jaani. Moreover, Chubby Maata has certainly observed other dramas in which a little boy is threatened with the loss of his penis.[19] She would not have to leap very far to imagine that she herself had had a penis once, which was cut off, and that bodily injury can lead to death.[20]

I think it is not far-fetched, then, to imagine that when Chubby Maata remarks on her father's cut finger, ominous associations are close at hand, easily available to both Chubby Maata and her grandmother—suggesting to Arnaqjuaq the topic of Chubby Maata's genitals and, for Chubby Maata, lending force to her grandmother's attack. A force probably unmitigated as yet by any inkling that Arnaqjuaq may, among other things, be celebrating Chubby Maata's femaleness.

In any case, in having provoked Chubby Maata to tears of "shyness" (*kangngu-*), Arnaqjuaq has achieved her (probable) purpose. Chubby Maata has withdrawn to a degree, too; she no longer responds to her grandmother's goading. There is no longer any point in carrying on the attack.

What follows is Chubby Maata's attack on Aita, unambiguously hostile this time but still remarkably well modulated—perhaps better modulated from her elders' point of view than was the kiss Chubby Maata offered earlier. She "plays" with Aita, frustrating her, blocking the baby's attempts to achieve her goal. Are there echoes in this of the torments that Chubby Maata herself has just suffered in the blocking of her self-defensive efforts? Liila and Arnaqjuaq do not criticize Chubby Maata this time or worry that she might hurt the baby. Instead, Liila echoes Arnaqjuaq's opening observation about *Aita's* state of feeling: "She's angry; she wants to boss." Chubby Maata takes this as permission to taunt Aita with the chant that her mother and also older children use to criticize her own outbursts of angry tears: "She cries easily." No one criticizes Chubby Maata this time, either, but before Aita is taken home, Liila asks Chubby Maata to restore peaceful relations with her with an *affectionate* kiss. Implied in the request is the recognition that Chubby Maata is capable of warm and loving gestures, and so, perhaps, the kiss restores peaceful relations also with Chubby Maata. When all is said and done, Aita is the one whose behavior is antisocial—and the adults don't seem at all upset by that behavior. There is peace and acceptance on *all* fronts.

What have we learned, then, about the lessons in self-evaluation that Chubby Maata is receiving? Clearly, some of them are hard and challenging. It is unpleasant to be shaken out of the innocent delusions of babyhood, and mother and grandmother are severe taskmistresses; they present a united front and won't countenance withdrawal or distraction until the drama has caused pain—a sign that some message has been received with emotional force. At the same time, the women give Chubby Maata many signs that she is loved, that the attack is good-humored and not seriously meant, and that they have no wish to destroy her. Some of these signals Chubby Maata is not yet able to detect, but others she surely can. She is in fact not destroyed; she is able to make experimental countermoves and also to respond at the end with the loving gesture that her mother affectionately requests from her. What Chubby Maata is most likely to learn from dramas like this one is not to dislike herself or even her genitals but to be modest and cautious, aware that she is beheld by others and that she can be judged by them, sometimes critically; that criticism can have a good deal of force behind it (injury and death are suggested); and that she, like other people, may be vulnerable to sanction, being—perhaps (for the doubt is sown)—a little imperfect.

THE CONSTRUCTION OF MORALITY: PLOT AND PERSON, TENSIONS AND AMBIGUITIES

Bit by bit, Chubby Maata is being led through the motions of a morality play and given compelling reasons to act her part in that social drama. Let's first draw together the main outlines of the scenario and then review what the dramas have told us about what makes it work.

We have seen that Chubby Maata should be in no doubt about where her emotional center is; she should know and cling to home; at the same time, she should like everybody, nurturantly and inclusively—but not too much. The message is that if Chubby Maata maintains a "good" relationship with everybody, is always concerned for the welfare of others, and never admits to feeling—ideally, never *feels*—hostile, she will be rewarded by reciprocal care and affection and will never have to fear. On the other hand, failure to appreciate (*piugi-*) others and treat them well can lead to catastrophe—loss, deprivation, rejection, and other vengeful forms of retaliation—all events that are extremely disagreeable, even dangerous, to Chubby Maata, to the person she repudiates, or both.

At one level, it is a strong sense of reciprocity, one might even say a talionic code, that Chubby Maata is learning: if you are good (*piu-*) and if you like (*piugi-*) others, people will like (*piugi-*) you in turn and will be good (*piu-*) to you. On the other hand, if you are not liked, you will be made to suffer in retribution.

We know, however, that this superficially simple and symmetrical plot is enriched, perhaps even fundamentally altered, by potent tensions. It is not entirely safe to like and be liked, because people will compete for the possession of valued objects, including you, and you stand to lose important life supports in that competition. So you may be in danger whether you are loving and lovable or unloving and unlovable. Furthermore, if you are in danger, either because you are not-good (*piungngit-*) and don't consider others good or because you are too good, too much loved, it will be difficult to find trustworthy support; you may find yourself standing alone. Weak and vulnerable to separation from people you love, perhaps susceptible to injury, too, you stand little chance of winning in a confrontation of strength against strength. Nevertheless, weak or not, you are ultimately responsible for what happens to you. Safe or not, the decision to love, appreciate, and care for other people is yours.

There may be other ways to combine the messages in the dramas about liking that Chubby Maata participates in, but I think this is one moral plot that she is very likely to perceive. It is a complicated plot, as the elements strain against each other. The dynamics that drive it must necessarily be complex, too—unless one assumes that extrinsic motives like fear of punishment and a desire to be approved of are all that's required to hold people in line, regardless of how zig-zaggy that line is. But we know that Chubby Maata is developing much subtler sensitivities and motives than these, ones that are intrinsically appropriate to the plot. She is learning to appreciate strongly the people on whom she depends and to feel personally responsible for their fate as well as her own. She is acquiring a sturdy sense of her own worth (mixed with the merest soupçon of doubt) and an ability to resist intrusion; yet an awareness that she is weak will make her ready to appeal and accommodate, rather than combat, when she wants to gain an end.[21] The encounters that we have looked at have taught us much about how Chubby Maata is learning all this.

First of all, there are the lessons about attachment. Chubby Maata, like other babies of adoring and attentively nurturant parents, feels a natural dependent love (*unga-*) for those parents—perhaps especially for her mother. That native attachment is intensified and her awareness of it is focused and fixed by dramas that threaten her with the loss of home and parents. And when the threats are directed against the parents instead of against herself, Chubby Maata is maneuvered into discovering in herself a more mature sort of affection, the nurturant *nallik-*, which will motivate her to protect what she cares for. In some situations, these prosocial feelings will guide her "spontaneously" into moral actions.

But what of the situations in which Chubby Maata doesn't feel *unga-* or *nallik-*? *Nallik-* enters the picture nevertheless, in two ways. Remember that when Iqaluk threatened Jaani in Episode 13, he implicitly pointed out to Chubby Maata that if she didn't treat *him* well, she would endanger someone she really did love. He was placing his granddaughter in a web of interdependencies that would make her careful also of kin she wasn't directly, emotionally, attached to. Then again, when Natsiq playfully separated Chubby Maata from her father, he probably heightened her *unga-* feelings for Jaani, but he also gave Liila the opportunity to teach her daughter a more difficult lesson: to recognize *nallik-* feelings in others and to depend on the good will of people who *nallik-* her (Episode 15).

A difficult lesson, I said, and so it is, in that protectiveness doesn't come quite so naturally to a baby as *unga-* does.[22] It is also difficult to be sure that a person who is playing aggressively is really playing and is not in earnest. Can Chubby Maata be sure that everybody is as fond of her as her close kin are? Nevertheless, the many experiences she has had of being warmly appreciated and coddled by her parents and other close kin must encourage her to believe that such benign feelings exist and help her to recognize them—or incline her to trust—when she is reassured.

In any case, Chubby Maata learns that succor comes from turning *toward* people, depending on their nurturance, not from combating them. True, the dramas are full of aggressive play on the part of both adults and children, but they do not celebrate strength. How does Chubby Maata escape danger or get what she wants? By playing with her mother (Episode 1); by appealing to Juupi (9); by accommodating her grandfather's wish (12); by crying (15). Rota, too—an adult—when attacked by Juupi (9), moves away and begs him to stop: "You're hurting me!" She doesn't fight back.[23] It is weakness that prevails. So, though verbal threats show Chubby Maata the *possibility* of retaliation, her experience never confirms that counterattack works. Remember what happened when she and Rosi *ugiat-*ed each other in Episode 1. Their reward was only pain and the humiliation of being laughed at. I argued in the analysis of that incident that experiencing the physical discomfort that attends aggression may be an effective way to learn not to engage in it. An Inuit mother from another part of the eastern Arctic once put this point to me explicitly. Explaining to me why it is not a good idea to support one's children when they are quarreling with their peers, she said, approximately, "If children are helped (*sirnaaq-*ed) when they are losing a fight, they could learn to feel strong because strong people are helping them. If they are not helped, they could learn to be careful." She meant that, left alone and undefended, children will learn to feel *ilira-* and to accommodate instead of starting fights.[24] Together with *unga-* and *nallik-, ilira-,* sensitivity to a formidable and critical audience, is the third powerful socializing emotion. We will see more of *ilira-* in Chapter 6.

But is there a contradiction between the directive to rely on the benignity of others and the experience that protectors turn traitor, as Liila did to Rosi in Episode 1 and as Juupi did to Chubby Maata in 9? I think not. It is *allies,* in a confrontation between two forces, who are untrustworthy or unavailable. If Chubby Maata is in physical danger, she will be rescued in a flash by anyone who sees or hears her; we saw Liila rescue her from Natsiq's pseudo-threat, too, when the threat upset her too much (Episode 15). But in most dramas and interrogations, Chubby Maata moves alone through the various shadow plays of socially disapproved situations that are limned for her. Paradoxically, her solitary condition keeps her oriented *toward* people in general, keeps her concerned about the opinion of everyone, as she would not be if she had supporters at her back to help her confront the enemy. Indeed, solitude may both increase Chubby Maata's sense of weakness, her awareness of the punishing potential of others, and make her realize more intensely how dependent she is on the nurturance of those others. Thus, from two directions, the force of imagined sanctions is increased. She learns, unbuffered and vulnerable, what the sanctions are—being unheeded, injured, cut off from a parent—and what they feel like. Most important, the sanction comes in a form intrinsic to the situation. If Chubby Maata accepts an invitation to live with Maata, she will be seized and carried out of her home; *ugiat-*ing hurts; turning in circles makes her dizzy; if she rejects her father, he is free for Saali to take. Like the emotions of *unga-* and *nallik-,* the sanctions are logical and meaningful in terms of the whole plot; they support not just any moral behavior but precisely the morality of which they are a part. Moreover, unlike arbitrary "punishment," which might be evaded or defended against, these sanctions, as integral parts of the interactions, are unavoidable.

Clearly, the plot has an emotional, logical coherence which Chubby Maata is learning to feel viscerally. She is also coming to be aware of herself as an actor on the social stage, learning what it means to observe and be observed, to act and to be acted upon. Standing alone is only one of the experiences that contribute to this development. Other formative experiences have to do with the manipulation of Chubby Maata's autonomy—a paradox with potent effects.

Chubby Maata encounters this paradox in a variety of shapes and contexts. For one thing, we know that the open-ended questions of the dramas and interrogations give Chubby Maata, in playful mode, an experience of autonomous decision making, an impression that her feelings and actions have material consequences. At the same time, though she doesn't yet know that the autonomy she is playfully offered is not real, she does know that it is threatened by the obviously superior power of the person who is offering her the choice: Maata, Rota, Aana, Juupi . . . I have suggested that such situations are likely to give her a somewhat uneasy sense that she has the ability to influence events, a feeling that she is responsible for the outcome of her actions, while, on the other hand, she acquires a salutary awareness that others can make disagreeable, even scary things happen if she makes an unfortunate choice. Remember the anxiety expressed in "One, two, three, GO!" The experience of being simultaneously and ambiguously subject and object, actor and acted upon, may help in other ways, too, to grow Chubby Maata into a moral person. Let's look again at Episode 10: Liila's friendly inquiry into her daughter's likes and dislikes.

From one angle, Liila, exploring Chubby Maata's mind, is treating her as an independent subject. She doesn't flatly lay down the law or contradict, put down, or close off alternatives for her daughter; she elicits Chubby Maata's own feelings and thoughts. At the same time, she is playing with Chubby Maata as an object, invading her privacy, probing with a persistence that is not permissible in serious interaction between equals. So this interaction, too, contains the potential for Chubby Maata to experience both subjection to others and active agency. Her false answers show that she does experience both. She feels intruded upon; she already knows that questions may be tests, which can suddenly turn uncomfortable. But on the other hand, she is not a passive victim; she defends herself. Whether playing or simply prevaricating, she attempts to throw her mother off the scent. And she is (as far as she knows) successful; Liila doesn't challenge Chubby Maata's evasions.

In this incident, the experience of being simultaneously subject and object furthers Chubby Maata's moral development in several ways. First of all, Liila's questions, which encourage her daughter to introspect (as an agent), to analyze her relationships and act responsibly, may move her a step along the way toward internalizing the rules and acting on them autonomously. (In this instance, to be sure, Chubby Maata uses her agency to pretend to be bad. We'll come back to this point.) At the same time, Chubby Maata, feeling invaded (as an object), may grow to dislike being questioned and, in resistance, begin to develop the reserve that protects adult autonomy, keeping people at a safe distance from one another and so contributing to the preservation of the smooth surface of social life. Remember that in Episode 16, when Chubby Maata stopped responding to her grandmother's verbal barrage, the attack stopped. Finally—and most important—the fact that Chubby Maata is *simultaneously* subject and object helps to create for her the experience of ambiguity that is essential to the maintenance of order in Inuit social life.[25] Let's look at the role of this and other ambiguities in Chubby Maata's social growth.

In Episode 10, as in many other interactions, the reason Chubby Maata is able to experience herself as both agent and object is that her mother both is and is not playing with her, manipulating her. Liila both is and is not taking her daughter's false answers seriously. She wants to know (both seriously and just from idle curiosity) whether Chubby Maata's feelings are appropriate to the moral code. She may also (seriously and idly) want to know whether Chubby Maata is capable of lying appropriately when her feelings are inappropriate. And she plays along with Chubby Maata's answers, *pretending* to believe them. This pretense is what makes it possible for Liila to pursue her investigation. It allows Chubby Maata to continue to answer—as she would not have if her mother had said, for example, "*You* don't really think that!" At the same time, intrusive, pressureful probing like this belongs as much to criticism as to play and so (like song duels)[26] can be read in more than one way. Liila's "idle" questions teach serious moral truths.

Chubby Maata is not able to unravel the complex net of her mother's motivations and intents, both serious and playful, but she is already quite capable of being suspicious that there is more to the interrogation than meets the ear. I think her response shows that she is just a little unsure whether or not her mother is taking her (false) answers seriously; whether she is granting her real autonomy or presenting her with a catechism; or whether she is criticizing or just playing with her. This uncertainty—combined with the sense of danger that we have seen generated in many other playful interactions—will increase Chubby Maata's watchfulness and will ultimately make her an acute observer of meanings, attuned to the various kinds of truth that may be embedded in communications, and thus skilled in managing her interpersonal relationships.

At the same time, the warmth of this interaction, Liila's appreciation for her daughter's goodness, keeps Chubby Maata open to learning, to ferreting out meanings and experimenting with answers. Most important, it makes her feel safe enough to *feel* the warm liking that the ideal plot calls for. Liila's strategy, then, helps to develop both Chubby Maata's ability to control her own behavior and her readiness to be controlled by others; it also helps to motivate a reserve and a sensitivity to meanings concealed in ambiguous communications, which will help Chubby Maata to avoid the disruptive emergence of the underbelly of Inuit life.

In Episode 16, Chubby Maata encounters again—and with more emotional force this time—the paradoxical experience of being both subject and object, together with the attendant tensions and ambiguities. When Arnaqjuaq tells Chubby Maata that she is BAAAD, she is not concerned with her granddaughter's likes and dislikes; she is pronouncing judgment herself. Unlike Liila's judgment, Arnaqjuaq's is not seriously meant; but, again unlike Liila's, it is not charitable. Arnaqjuaq doesn't make the assumption that Chubby Maata (and other people) are good, she calls her (and her parents) bad. When she asks for Chubby Maata's opinion, it sounds not like an intellectual exchange between equals but like a dominant person's emotional attack on a weak person. And her questions—"Isn't that so?" "Aren't you?"—are not open-ended attempts to find out what Chubby Maata thinks or feels but demands that Chubby Maata assent to Arnaqjuaq's judgments. It would appear that Arnaqjuaq is trying to enlist Chubby Maata's agreement with public opinion, to shrivel her with shame. But at the same time, her questions, like Liila's in Episode 10, push Chubby Maata toward the beginnings of an autonomous conscience: an examination of her virtue and acceptance of her own imperfection.

And again, in Arnaqjuaq's drama as in Liila's, ambiguities are important, and in several ways. It is Chubby Maata's doubt—about whether Arnaqjuaq is playing or not, about whether she and her parents are good or not, about how Arnaqjuaq is going to exercise the strength she clearly has—that gives the play its force. Arnaqjuaq's aggressive inversion of the ordinary rules of behavior gives Chubby Maata a glimpse of the perils hidden underneath surface meanings and teaches her to fear them, without actually endangering her. To the extent that Chubby Maata perceives playfulness in the inversion—"She doesn't mean it, she loves me"—she can feel safe, unrejected, unalienated. But to the extent that she feels serious truth in her grandmother's accusations—"Maybe I *am* bad"— she will see herself dangerously exposed, the more so because Arnaqjuaq's accusations are not attached to any specific wrongdoing; Chubby Maata is free to call to mind whatever misdemeanors have the potential to trouble her. Moreover, it is not only wrongdoings and their consequences that are left to Chubby Maata's imagination; Arnaqjuaq also leaves unspoken the identities of Chubby Maata's "accusers": "I've heard . . . " The fact that Chubby Maata cannot be sure from whom the dangers emanate must heighten her sense of vulnerability and her vigilance. At the same time, she is prevented from turning against individuals, as she might do if Arnaqjuaq were to identify particular people who think Chubby Maata is bad. A tendency to mark villains would contravene Inuit values and rules for interpersonal behavior.[27]

Unlikely as it seems at first glance, the lesson of the "BAAAD" drama—like that of Liila's interrogation, which represented everybody as good—is to turn toward, not away, from people. As usual, Chubby Maata is learning not merely to fear and avoid aggression but to protect others as a means of protecting herself. Arnaqjuaq's (and others') pretended attacks on Chubby Maata may drive the little girl, in her weakness, to crave support from her parents, to *unga-* them, even though—or, maybe, even *because*—they are not offering help at the moment. At the same time, Arnaqjuaq's attacks on those parents will make Chubby Maata feel the absolute *necessity* of loving nurturance, *nallik-,* the highest Inuit value.

Prosocial behavior is certainly made difficult for Chubby Maata, and I think we can see now the usefulness of that difficulty. In Chubby Maata's Qipisa— and not only there—creating moral motivation is a multidimensional project. It is necessary to define the good and create emotional attachment to it; to develop a sense of responsibility for acting on the good; to create awareness of others' power to sanction; and, not least, to engender a sense of personal vulnerability. The dramas and interrogations that we have been looking at do all this not simply by modeling moral behavior but by pretending to attack it and by creating, in the dramatization of both values and antivalues, appropriate and compelling emotions to support the approved behavior. In this process, emotional tensions, uncertainties, and ambiguities are a potent yeast, sharpening Chubby Maata's ability to anticipate and respond sensitively to perilous situations, intensifying her vulnerability to sanction, and, not least, heightening for her the value of prosocial behavior.

Some of the dangers that Chubby Maata is becoming aware of are outside her, in her relationships with other people, who are perceived as stronger than herself; other perils lie within, in her own conflicting or unknown wishes, motives, fears. I have argued that if Chubby Maata feels that she must make important decisions but is unsure about what her decision should be, and if she is also unsure whether she can make her decisions prevail, she may come to feel both responsibility for her fate and a nervous respect (*ilira-*) for the power that others have over her. Feelings of responsibility and weakness are uneasy bedfellows, and their tossings and turnings may keep Chubby Maata awake to cues in the subtle messages of others that can help her to judge how much control she actually has in a situation. Moreover, if she is pulled by her own feelings in immoral as well as moral directions *and* is afraid of a strong sanction to which she feels personally vulnerable, she will be motivated to govern her behavior carefully—more carefully than if the dangers all came from without and she was free to imagine hiding places and escape hatches. (Remember "Ih! I almost agreed!" in Episode 9.) Add to these complexities uncertainty about what the multileveled and backward-stated messages really mean, and the groundwork is laid for extremely careful—indeed, irreproachable—treatment of others. It is possible that the beginnings of such watchfulness are behind the unchanging, unrevealing expression with which Chubby Maata observed Rota during the latter's interrogations in Episode 11.

To be sure, in teaching Chubby Maata to feel emotions and have wishes that go athwart the ideal patterns of Inuit social life, the dramas perpetuate the unsavory plots of that life, too. But paradoxically, even the bad supports the good, as long as it is kept where it can do no harm, for without contrary feelings and inclinations the positive plots would have no value. The difficulties that Chubby Maata experiences invest the values and their enactment with heightened meaning: what is hard to uphold and do must be worth the effort.[28]

A miracle of socialization—and all accomplished in "play," without ever applying punishment. Were Chubby Maata's caretakers to confront her when she misbehaved, to scold her or punish her in serious mode, they would have to engage in the talion behavior that they strongly disapprove. They would set a bad example, and they would create a situation in which adult models are seriously, if temporarily, pitted against the tyro they are trying to draw into their world. In play there are no grounds for rebellion. And play, unlike serious confrontation, provides Chubby Maata with a good example, a proper example, of how both adults and children should deal with the problematic urges that the dramas arouse: express them in play. At least *pretend* to be playing. When Chubby Maata grows up, all that will be needed to control her unwanted behavior is a joke—a joke that resonates with the emotionally intense dramas she experienced as a child.

In conclusion, I want to point out one way in which such play—because it *is* play—may actually make Chubby Maata's life easier. These interactions, because they are perceived by the adult actors as "playful," model and also create for Chubby Maata, as she comes to glimpse their playfulness, a safe transitional space in which she can practice putting on and taking off good and bad behavior.[29]

To take responsibility for one's bad behavior is scary and can only be accomplished in slow stages.[30] We saw that Chubby Maata, in the "BAAAD" drama, when she was upset and not playing, called her baby sister a crybaby just after she herself had burst into tears. This looks like the simple scapegoating action of a child who is not yet ready to assume blame. But when Chubby Maata is a little less threatened, she sometimes plays at being bad; she experiments with goodness and badness, with liking and disliking, with evaluating herself and others.[31] We have seen that when Chubby Maata is catechized about how she regards her family and neighbors, she often says that she does not consider her associates good. She may at times be expressing real hostility—or *ilira*-—toward a particular person; we'll see some of this in the next chapter. In other instances, she may only be trying to sidetrack intrusive and uncomfortable questions, perhaps redirecting a little of the hostility evoked by the questioner. Yet again, and in spite of the fact that the expression of dislike is frowned on, she may be giving the questioner what she or he wants; we'll see this, too, in Chapter 6. But now let's look briefly at an interaction that Chubby Maata herself blithely initiates to help her out of a tough spot. And notice how her mother responds.

Episode 18 (November 20)

Liila, Chubby Maata, her sister Rosi, and Liila's young sister Liuna were visiting me. Chubby Maata, sitting on her mother's lap, began to play with my notes, and Liila, in a mild tone, told her to leave them alone. Chubby Maata put the slips down and began to chant, over and over in a happy-sounding singsong: "Because I'm not gooood; I'm not gooood."

Liila cooed at her little daughter, tenderly, "Because you're not a baby?" Chubby Maata raised her brows, agreeing that she was not a baby, but her mother nevertheless snuffed her warmly and in the same tender voice assured her, "You're a darling little good one."

Chubby Maata began to chant again, "I am gooood, I am not gooood, I am gooood, I am not gooood." Then, after a number of repetitions, she changed the words, and in the same happy tone chanted, "Because I don't consider my chubby grandfather good, I do consider him good, I don't consider him good, I do consider him good."[32] She was talking about her one-year-old cousin Simioni, whose family had visited the camp three weeks earlier.

Liila made tender sounds to her daughter.

This interaction gives us evidence that, one way or another, Chubby Maata is indeed on the way to learning that she is a person of mixed qualities, good and not-good, and, further, that her own actions determine how she is or should be judged. The first thing she says is "*Because* I'm not good . . ." which tells us that she is associating her badness with her mother's prohibition, perhaps explaining to herself why Liila "scolded" her. Then she says simply, "I'm not good," as though she were accepting the charge. It sounds as though she were beginning to make the transition to evaluating herself, but at the same time, she has a sharp ear tuned to what other people think. She seems to be using play to simultaneously internalize and externalize—take distance from—her mother's scolding or prohibition. She attributes "badness" to herself, but in a pretending, "I don't mean it seriously" tone of voice. And when *she* is playing, she is not upset by the idea of being bad, as she was when Arnaqjuaq, with mock seriousness, called her bad.

Liila seems more concerned about her daughter's negative self-judgment than Chubby Maata herself is. Perhaps she repents of having reproved her—an act more characteristic of me than of Liila. In any case, she hears the serious content of Chubby Maata's playful chant, and instead of supporting her daughter's maturely critical self-judgment, she gives her a moral "out," an excuse for continuing to consider herself wholly good. When she says to her, "Because you're not a baby?" she tells her, in effect, that she *is* a baby, need not take responsibility for her actions, and therefore need not consider herself bad. Babies are good, and she need not make haste to grow up.

But Chubby Maata doesn't respond by relapsing into her baby role; she doesn't take advantage of the out offered by her mother. Raising her brows, she takes the role of not-baby—which will allow her to continue to experiment with badness—while Liila protests, "You're a darling little good one," an endearment that Chubby Maata surely associates with babyness and that again negates Chubby Maata's experiment in taking responsibility for her bad actions.

Although Chubby Maata doesn't accept her mother's suggestion that she is a baby, she does seem to hear Liila's affirmation of her goodness; this time her chant begins with "I am good." Nevertheless, continuing her play, she alternates between her mother's loving view of her as good and her own (experimental) view of herself as not good. Or perhaps it is rather that she alternates between the two views that her mother has expressed in this interaction, the "not-good" view implied in the prohibition and the "good" view expressed in the reassurance. She tries both on for size, alternating between being good and not-good, a baby and not a baby, taking responsibility and not taking responsibility. In any case, the alternation of selves or judgments in Chubby Maata's playful chant sounds very much like a first step toward creating an integrated self, partly good and partly bad—a more mature self than the one who taunted Aita in the "BAAAD" drama.

But now, suddenly, the chant changes: "Because I don't consider my chubby grandfather good . . . " Could the unspoken main clause of that sentence be "I am not good"? If so, it sounds as though Chubby Maata has forgotten about the note slips that she inappropriately played with and is instead remembering the babyish quality she is most often questioned about: not considering other people good. She is entertaining a new reason for being not-good, namely, that she doesn't consider her cousin good. She is beginning to make a connection between her own worth and her perception of others—as her mother did in Episode 10, seven weeks earlier.

Chubby Maata's play ends when Liila speaks tenderly to her little daughter. Perhaps her tenderness is a response to the charming babyishness of Chubby Maata's inconsistent attitudes toward Simioni. And perhaps that inconsistency is itself partly an accommodation to Liila's obvious encouragement of Chubby Maata's babyness. In any case, Chubby Maata is again restored to the innocent and comfortable role of baby. Liila has not forced her forward, perhaps has not even encouraged her forward motions, but she has given her time and freedom to grow.

I want to end this chapter with a short and charming incident that happened two months after Episode 16. I hope it will demonstrate that, in spite of the rigors of Chubby Maata's education, life does not lie heavily upon her, and her self-esteem has not suffered great buffets at the hands of relentless socializers. She is just short of three years old.

Episode 19 (December 13)

Chubby Maata, at home this afternoon, was standing in the kitchen sink, scraping frost off the window over the sink, while fourteen-year-old Liuna, her mother's sister, stood nearby. Beaming, Chubby Maata turned to Liuna and said, "Liuna, am I just wonderfully skilled?" Liuna said, "Yes," in a neutral voice that sounded to me as though she were not very interested in the topic.

Chubby Maata, not a whit deterred, took up again her work on the window, chanting over and over, "I am just wonderfully skilled, I am just wonderfully skilled . . . "

Chapter 6 "I Like You, I Don't Like You": Anthropologist in the Oyster Shell

We have been watching Chubby Maata move, psychologically speaking, from her mother's side out into the community, guided at each step by dramas and interrogations that prepare her for the issues she will meet. I have presented the dramas in a sequence that is developmentally logical but not chronological. In fact, Chubby Maata is living at one and the same time through all the issues dramatized in these encounters. A second feature of the dramas we have looked at so far is that almost all of them have been engineered by the adults around her. And although Chubby Maata has always been an active participant, she has most often been an unwilling or unwitting one. Now, to provide us with a view of her world that has a different kind of coherence, let's follow one problem—Chubby Maata's relationship with me—from its start, on my arrival, to its finish, on my departure, and see how it grows and changes, first in the hands of her mother and then in those of Chubby Maata herself. We will see that this little child, on the saddle of three years old, is already mistress of a variety of dramatic strategies, which she uses in her progress from baby to child.

Very soon after my arrival—after her initial terror subsided—

Chubby Maata began making overtures to me in the reassuring company of other children, but most of our encounters in those early days occurred in the presence of one of her parents, most often her mother. At first, Liila tried to influence Chubby Maata in the shaping of her relationship with me, and Chubby Maata tried to make sense both of her own feelings and of her mother's messages. Later, Liila stopped intervening, and Chubby Maata began to use her interactions with me for her own purposes. (We shall see presently what those purposes were.) Chubby Maata's dramas with me, like those that the adults initiated with her, are highly revealing of the emotions, motives, and plots that moved her.

The acute phase of Chubby Maata's fear (*kappia-*) of me was soon conquered with the help of tea with milk and bannock with jam. She and I saw a lot of each other. When my qammaq was built next door to her house, Chubby Maata and her mother often visited me together, and sometimes we encountered one another in other houses, especially that of her maternal grandparents, where she spent a lot of time. Already in early October, ten days after my arrival, she began to visit me with other small children, and when, two weeks later, I was persuaded to hold "school" sessions, she was one of the five three- and four-year-olds who participated.[1]

It was not until the end of January that Chubby Maata paid me her first solo visit, but the school sessions did much to ease the fear (*kappia-*) in which children held me—there is support in numbers. Long before January, Chubby Maata began to experiment with ways of relating to me, some of them so bold and disrespectful, so un-*ilira-,* from an adult perspective that her mother and grandmother, instead of trying to reassure her that I was not someone to be frightened of, as they had done at first, began to suggest to her that I *was* scary.

The change in Chubby Maata's feelings—the rapprochement—came about neither evenly nor suddenly, and all the while, Chubby Maata was enacting with me a number of dramas and playing with me a variety of games, which not only expressed the ambivalent emotions—fear, hostility, attraction—that she was struggling with but also, I think, helped her to manage those feelings and negotiate a relationship with me.

The field in which Chubby Maata was playing was, as always, an obstacle course, occupied as it was by other persons who had goals of their own. Liila, through strategies now familiar to us, was nudging her daughter toward behavior that she found acceptable for her own combination of reasons, while I was encouraging Chubby Maata in behavior that Liila did not approve of. The relationship was the arena for a quiet, unacknowledged, three-party war. These complexities may become clearer after we've looked at a few of the engage-ments, but it may be helpful to set out on our exploration holding a map of the ways in which Liila, like other adult Qipisamiut, thought about the emotions that she wanted to manipulate in Chubby Maata's relationship with me—in particular, the fears *kappia-* and *ilira-,* and the relationship between these fears and "liking" (*piugi-*ing) or not liking (*piugingng-*). We should also know a little more about both Liila's goals and Yiini's.

Kappia- is a lowest-common-denominator concept, like the word "fear" in English. It is also a fear of being physically injured or destroyed. People were *kappia-* of angry people, who might kill, or of evil spirits, tunrait, because no one knew what *they* might do to a person. It would be impossible to "like" or "consider good," to *piugi-,* a person who aroused *kappia-* feelings.

We already know that *ilira-,* from an English speaker's perspective, is a more complicated concept, and there is still more to be said about it. *Ilira-* is in part a feeling that we would label "respect," even "awe," in face of someone's superior abilities, status, or power to sanction—and perhaps force of character, though I am not sure of that. It is also a fear of being disapproved of, criticized, scolded. I have said that *ilira-* is a socializing and a socialized fear, one that children have to *learn* to feel. A person who has not learned to feel *ilira-* is dangerous; as one man put it, "A person who doesn't feel ilira- thinks he's Somebody." He meant, "That person will try to throw his weight around." However, nobody likes to feel *ilira-*; it makes one feel constrained, anxious, inhibited. People who feel *ilira-* retreat into silence or (if children) cry; they don't want to eat or to accept proffered gifts, can't laugh and joke, may chew their fingernails or brood resentfully. Worst of all, the feeling is contagious; people who feel *ilira-* make others around them feel the same way, creating uncomfortable social situations. Contrariwise, people who cause *ilira-* feel *ilira-* themselves when they perceive that they have caused the feeling. So people don't want to be known as "one who makes others feel *ilira-*"; when they perceive that someone does feel *ilira-* of them, they hasten to reassure that person. To say that a person does not cause *ilira-* is high praise. Nevertheless, people who *never* cause *ilira-* may be consid-ered a little childish, unworthy of respect. And, as I have said, a person who never feels *ilira-* is dangerously unsocialized.[2]

To summarize the social qualities of these two fears, then: *kappia-* is a feeling that one should never cause. People who do cause it can never be liked, and, in the era before police could be appealed to, they were sometimes killed by people who feared them.[3] *Ilira-,* on the other hand, is a feeling that, paradoxically, one both should and should not cause, should and should not feel. It is both source and consequence of conscience. Properly managed *ilira-* feelings are not incompatible with liking, but proper management requires that children learn to feel *ilira-* in *anticipation* of being scolded. They must learn to fear disapproval and to avert it, so that it won't be necessary for their elders to scold them. In the ideal situation, the paradox is resolved: children avoid being scolded and so can like (*piugi-*) the *potentially* scolding adult, while adults, rarely having to act on that potential, can like their children and be liked by them. In this way, both adults and children can feel comfortable in everyday life. The surface remains unruffled.

But ideal equilibria are not easy to achieve. If children feel too much *ilira-*, they won't be able to like; and if they don't feel enough, the liking, and the sense of comfort and safety that goes with it, will get out of control and lead to undesirable demanding behavior. In extreme cases, insufficient *ilira-* of the neighbors may even weaken attachment to one's home. The tightrope is thin. And as if all this weren't complicated enough, the easiest way to produce *ilira-* in a child who does not feel it is to engender the socially disruptive *kappia-,* which comes naturally to children. If children are uneasy about the destructive power of an adult, they will be afraid of incurring that person's disapproval. Thus the two fears, the one desirable, the other undesirable, are not very far apart.[4]

Liila's project, then, is not simple. She wants to relieve Chubby Maata of the babyish, extreme, and unrealistic *kappia-* fear that I will injure or destroy her, while leaving enough doubt about my destructive potential to motivate the *ilira-* sensitivity to criticism that gives rise to respectful restraint. Liila must also encourage Chubby Maata to like (*piugi-*) me even as she fears me, because fear alone, of whatever sort, is a dangerous feeling, not conducive to smooth social relationships. But Liila doesn't want her little daughter to feel too attached to me, because if Chubby Maata feels comfortable with me, the liking will destroy the *ilira-* feelings. In that event, not only will Chubby Maata be forward and demanding, she will also miss me when I leave; she will feel *unga-*. Worst of all, perhaps, a strong bond between Chubby Maata and me would threaten Liila's maternal relationship with her daughter. Chubby Maata's affection for me is in a sense stolen from *her.*

Complex as Liila's childrearing goals are and as difficult as they must be to achieve, Yiini makes matters worse by seeing them too simply. From her self-interested point of view, the problem is only how to "cure" Chubby Maata of her "fear," so that child and anthropologist can have a cozy, relaxed friendship, satisfying to both.

Finally, of course, Chubby Maata herself has goals. If she could articulate the problems in her relationship with me, she might see the focal issues as the control of fear, hostility, and dangerous attraction, together with all the tangle of ambivalences and conflicts that those contradictory feelings entail. How can she get what she wants without opening herself to being criticized, attacked, stolen, or rejected? An outsider might also see broader and more philosophical issues at stake in our relationship—issues concerning the nature and location of goodness and badness. But more of these anon.

Clearly, the currents that Chubby Maata must navigate are anything but placid. Let's see what she does as she steers her way among whirlpools to a manageable, acceptable, even sometimes gratifying relationship with Yiini. We will look, as usual, at the lessons offered by Chubby Maata's monitors—her parents and grandparents—and at Chubby Maata's reactions to these lessons. But most interesting of all are Chubby Maata's own experiments. We will see that she uses in them ingredients that she extracts—and transforms—sometimes from games or dramas that she has participated in and sometimes from interactions that she has watched between adults and me. She also does a little inventing. Let's begin with a few of these experiments in order to get a sense of Chubby Maata's changing states of mind and at the same time see a bit of the behavior that her socializers are responding to.

THE DILEMMA OF FEAR AND ATTRACTION

I have said that Chubby Maata's first experiments in relating to me were made in the company of other small children who came to visit in my qammaq. At this time—only ten days after my arrival in camp—the children were all, to varying degrees, still *kappia-* of me. After all, I was not only an unknown person in a world where everyone was known, I was also "wrong" in many ways: wrong hair, eyes, skin, and clothes, wrong language, laugh, and way of walking; I wasn't very far from being a tunraq. But the children were also drawn to this stranger in their midst, and so they came to see me. Here is the first record I have of such a visit.

Episode 20 (October 8)

Miika—four and a half years old, and braver and more independent than some of the children twice her age—came, all by herself, to visit me for a few minutes. Just as she was about to leave, Chubby Maata and Miika's little brother, Saali—both just under three—came in, so she stayed. The three children engaged in the following activities, all except the last led by Miika.

Miika stretched herself against the door and demonstrated that she could reach to the top of the frame. (She had done that the previous day, too, when adults were present.) She said to Chubby Maata: "I can reach to here. You can't." Chubby Maata stretched and *almost* reached. Said she, "*I* can reach to *here*." Saali, the shortest of the three, stretched and said, "I can't reach it."

Then Miika crossed over from the door to my sleeping platform, which occupied the inner half of the qammaq; sat down at the far end, opposite me and near the seal-oil lamp; and invited the other children to "sit here." Saali followed his sister and sat close to her, between her and me but still keeping as much distance as possible from me. Chubby Maata was the last to sit, and though there was still ample room between Saali and me, she chose to squeeze in between Miika and the wall, perilously close to the open lamp. Miika cautioned, as an adult would have done, "Don't bump the lamp." "Ee," agreed Chubby Maata.

Miika began a game of reciting words (in Inuktitut, of course), and each word that Miika pronounced, Chubby Maata—but not Saali, whose linguistic abilities were not as advanced as those of the two girls—repeated in a rapid singsong. Miika began by naming objects she saw around her, then moved on to invisible and desirable objects and the places where they could be acquired (in Pangnirtung): toothpaste, canned food, bubble gum, chewing gum, candy, store, coffeeshop . . . Then items of clothing: jacket, parka, shoe, belt . . . And off and on, Miika, followed by the other children, glanced over at me, smiling, to see if I was listening. I was.

After a while, they stopped saying words, and Miika initiated another game of "do as I do." First the children all extended their identically booted feet in the same way; then Miika crossed her feet, and the other children followed suit. They talked about their actions a little—I didn't understand what they said— and then repeated the motions.

Next they resumed their word game and began to play with the words, stretching them and increasing the singsong quality of the chant: "maa-tuu (door)"; "quuuq-viik (toilet can)"; "baa-buu-gaa (bubble gum)" . . . Again they checked to be sure I was listening.

By this time, excitement was beginning to escalate. Now Chubby Maata took the lead, pulling hairs out of one of my caribou mattress hides and "scaring" Miika with them, holding them toward her face and giggling. All three children began to do this, giggling and teasing each other.

While this game was going on, Chubby Maata's maternal grandfather, Mitaqtuq, came in and, seeing the excitement, said reprovingly, "Don't be wild (*uimak-*); visitors are not wild." The children at once stopped teasing each other with the hairs and began to stretch themselves again, this time trying to reach the roof beam over the sleeping platform, which was higher than the top of the door: "I usually reach to here; *you* can't reach." Mitaqtuq stood silently, and in a few moments the children ran out. Mitaqtuq drank a cup of tea with me, inquired about my head cold, exchanged with me a few remarks about the bad weather, and left.

Notice that the preceding games were all played in my presence and *to* me, but I was not a participant. A month later, in school, Miika, Chubby Maata, her sister Rosi, and her playfellow Kaati initiated their first games *with* me.

Episode 21 (November 6)

The first game dramatized the ritual of greeting a Qallunaaq.[5] Each girl in turn shook hands with me and said in exaggerated, Qallunaaq-like tones: "HaaaLooo." "Haló (hello)" is not only the customary greeting used by and to Qallunaat, it is also a generic name for Qallunaat, used by adults when speaking to children. Several Qipisa adults referred to me that way. Thus: "Haló won't like you if you do that." Miika was bolder than the others, as usual: while pretending merely to shake my hand, she tickled my palm with her index finger and made me jump in surprise, to the great delight of the other children.

The second game, initiated by Rosi, consisted of hiding her pencil stub and telling me it was lost. When I agreed that it was indeed lost, she triumphantly pulled it out of its hiding place and showed me that I was wrong. All four girls played this game with me with great glee until I grew bored and deflected their attention.

Episode 22 (Excerpt, November 10)

Four days later, Chubby Maata, visiting me with her mother, announced that she was a teacher (using the word that adults use for "missionary" rather than "schoolteacher") and taught me words, reciting them in a serious voice with great clarity and distinctness so that I could repeat them after her: "qu-lliq (lamp)"; "i-quu-si-ssaq (toilet paper)," mispronounced in her baby speech; "su-kaq (sugar)"; "pani-kaq (cup)"; "i-ku-mait (matches); because they *are* matches, mother?" Liila assured her that they were.[6]

Episode 23A (November 20)

Ten days after Episode 22, I was visiting Chubby Maata and Liila. Chubby Maata, standing near Liila, who was knitting on the couch, had a small scrap of crumpled toilet paper in her hand. She started to hand the scrap to me, perhaps inviting play, and I, picking up that possibly playful overture, drew my hand back suddenly and said, "Kuinat! (disgusting, tickly)." Chubby Maata beamed her baby beam at me and held out the scrap again.[7] We repeated the sequence a number of times. Then she said, "Now you," suggesting that we change roles. I held out the scrap to her, and she drew back her hand, beaming. "Kuinat!" she said. Then after several repetitions, she suddenly said, "But I don't consider it kuinat!" She switched roles again and offered the paper to me. The game ended when the two of us, tiring of it, turned to other activities. (Chubby Maata's activities are described in Episode 25.)

Episode 23B (November 22)

Two evenings later, when I went in to visit in her home, Chubby Maata started the same game, dropping a tiny scrap of red thread into my hand. And as before, when she had had her fill of my mock fear, she ordered me to switch roles and let her be the person who was "attacked."

Little by little, Chubby Maata was learning to enjoy playing with fear—to enjoy being attacked in play, and not only by familiar kin but by me. Perhaps she was incorporating me into the circle of familiars. The learning process also involved expanding her repertoire of responses to threat. An incident that occurred in December offered her a greater challenge than usual and most charmingly demonstrated this learning.

Episode 24 (December 17)

I was sitting by the table in Chubby Maata's house. Chubby Maata was on the floor, playing with her puppy Papi, while Rosi lay on her belly on the couch beside her mother. Suddenly, Rosi put her face down on the couch and called my attention to herself: "Yiini!" In playful response, imitating her concealed face, I hid my head under the tablecloth. Immediately, both Rosi and Chubby Maata exclaimed in excited fear: "Aiyai!" Rosi scrambled upright on the couch beside Liila, and Chubby Maata also ran and stood beside her mother. Seeing that they both assumed I was pretending to be a tunraq, I made a face as I emerged from under the cloth. The girls laughed, and Liila smiled. Rosi lay down again and hid her face to initiate a repetition of the sequence, and I duly played my part. But this time, when I pulled my head out, making a face, Chubby Maata, smiling at me, said, "*Nya*-nya nya-*nya*-nya" (the taunting chant of children in my own world). "Is that how it's done?" she asked. I wrinkled my nose, "No," not understanding what she meant. Chubby Maata persisted: "Is that *not* it?" I wrinkled my nose again, which Chubby Maata interpreted as "Yes, that *is* it."[8] She repeated the chant and again asked, "Is it like that?" I raised my brows, "Yes," and wrinkled my nose, "No," in rapid succession, still not sure what she had in mind. Chubby Maata, puzzled, asked,

"Have you stopped playing evil spirit?" I said, "Eee (yes)." Chubby Maata double-checked: "Hee (what did you say)?" I repeated, "Ee." She began to play with Papi again, running back and forth to the door and chanting softly to herself or to Papi, "*Nya*-nya nya-*nya*-nya."

What these games all have in common, it seems to me, is the children's effort to meet my scariness head on, to demonstrate to themselves and to me that they don't fear me. At first (Episode 20), they don't play *with* me; they perform *to* me, showing off their prowess—physical, linguistic, social, and emotional. They are tall; they know words and can recite them; they can imitate actions with accuracy; they can even scare one other and enjoy it. The first of their games— stretching against the door frame—the children invented; they will continue to do this frequently when they visit me. But when they recite words, following Miika, and when they imitate her foot motions, they are taking into their own hands enjoyable, partly educational games that adults often play with them. (Compare the games that Liila initiated in Episode 1.) The slow, distinct way in which the children pronounce the words is also reminiscent of adults teaching *me* vocabulary; but the children turn this educational wordplay into a rhythmic chant, which is increasingly exciting. Finally, when excitement has boiled up sufficiently, they attack my mattress hide and scare each other with caribou hairs. Again they are doing to one another what adults often do to them, but this time the game they are imitating is not one they enjoy when adults initiate it. Here, the children are taking the role of adult *aggressors*. And this time it is Chubby Maata, more afraid of me than is her older, bolder cousin Miika, who takes the initiative. Heretofore, she has followed Miika's leadership, but now excitement fuels daring, and the first victim of her aggressive play is Miika. Could the older child, the leader, be a stand-in for me? We will see that when Chubby Maata becomes just a little braver or less afraid of me, she assaults me directly with her scary hairs (Episode 23B).[9]

Although the children are not playing with me in Episode 20, they dare to cross the qammaq and sit down with me on my sleeping platform, as adults do, albeit at a distance noticeably greater than that of their elders. And they trust me enough (or perhaps Miika's boldness inspires them) to risk play in my presence, counteracting whatever *kappia*- feelings they may have, indeed pretending that they do not have them—and incidentally demonstrating that they do not feel appropriately *ilira*- either. The children, symbolically growing themselves larger and more adult, seem to be fortifying themselves against their fear of me. Throughout, it is as if they are titillating themselves with fire, testing their limits, and vaunting their courage, their ability to play, their adultness in general. It is important to them that I notice, and when I do, they thoroughly enjoy their performance—until Mitaqtuq cuts them down to size and ends the ebullient charade of adulthood. By labeling their behavior *uimak-*, he tells them he sees no sense in it, and then he explicitly tells them that they are *not* behaving in adult fashion. The children respond by relinquishing (for the moment) their borrowed games and reverting to the display of "bigness" with which they began this visit—the game that they themselves invented.

Two weeks later, on her second day in school, Chubby Maata, supported by her sister Rosi, was able to declare herself superior to *kappia-* feelings, superior to her playfellow Kaati. Although Kaati came to school, she stayed only a few minutes, and when she got up to leave, Chubby Maata asked her, "Is it because you're kappia-?" And Rosi underlined the point: "*I'm* not kappia-; you're the only one (who is)."[10]

Two weeks later still (Episode 21, November 6), the children, with greater daring, are engaging *with* me, and demonstrating their superiority to *me*. Again, the games they play with me are cognate with ones that adults usually initiate with them. First they explicitly recognize my scary Qallunaaq identity and play with it in such a way as to discomfit me, make me jump and recoil. Then they demonstrate that I, the teacher, know nothing: I foolishly imagine that the pencil is lost. And Chubby Maata, visiting me with her mother (Episode 22, November 10), teaches me words, as adults—and I, in school— teach her.

In Episodes 20–22, we see two related progressions in the mastery of fear. The children move from playing *to* me as an audience to playing *with* me. Concomitantly, they move from demonstrating their adultness and their supe- riority to me *in my presence* to demonstrating these things *against* me, engaging me in their play in the role of victim, dupe, or tutee, making me the child to their adult. But when we move on to the next game (Episode 23) we see yet another progression. Here Chubby Maata is not only playing *with* me, she is doing so *reciprocally.* She begins by threatening me with the same fear, *kuinat-*, that the children played with in Episodes 20 and 21. The initiative is mine, but Chubby Maata picks up the cue readily—and then she offers me the oppor- tunity to threaten her. She no longer has to be superior to me all the time; taking turns as aggressor and victim, we are "peers." And now, when it is Chubby Maata's turn to be victim, she suddenly discovers that she is not frightened. She offers to frighten me again, but since I am not really titillated by fear either, the game has lost its point, and we both lose interest. Chubby Maata initiates the same game two days later and again offers to take turns. But, as before, the threat palls after a short while, and she never introduces the game with me again.

It may be, however, that Chubby Maata has not so much lost her fear as found more satisfying ways of expressing her inner turbulence. At the end of Episode 24, when she runs to the door and back, chanting at Papi "*nya*-nya nya-*nya*-nya," she seems to be torn between a desire to escape the evil spirit and attack it; the compromise is a playful taunt—a taunt that sounds as though Chubby Maata were practicing a new defense. Papi is the unfortunate recipient of playful aggression also in the following game, which Chubby Maata initiates immediately following the first of the two *kuinat*- exchanges with me (Episode 23A).

Episode 25 (November 20)

Chubby Maata began to play with Papi. Papi lay on his back on the couch, wanting to be scratched. Chubby Maata said, "Kiss!" and snuffed Papi hard on his teats. Then she touched Papi's penis and said, "Penis." I—less knowledgeable than Chubby Maata in matters of canine anatomy—said, "She has no penis. What are these?" and pointed to the teats. Chubby Maata said, "Breasts." I agreed.

Then Chubby Maata said, "Shall I attack (*ugiat*-) him?" I said, "No." Nevertheless, she hit Papi hard in the belly with the flat of her hand several times, before snuffing him again.

After a few minutes, Papi ended up on the floor, and Liila's ten-year-old brother, Juda, began to play with him, lying on the floor and tempting him to grab something he was holding. Liila told him to stop, because he was "fixating" Papi in his activity, making him one-track-minded (*uirit*-). Juda ignored his sister. Then his older brother Juupi intervened, kicking Papi when he approached Juda, and Liila said to Chubby Maata, "Hurt him."

Chubby Maata, in an innocent, inquiring voice, asked, "Like this?" She pulled Papi across the floor by his ear, twisted his muzzle until only the white of his eye showed, stood on his neck, and kicked his head. Juupi said in an amused voice, "She's going to choke him." Papi squealed with pain. I was breathless. Then suddenly Chubby Maata said to Papi, "Kiss," and she snuffed Papi's face again.

This game, too, turns on a theme of ambivalent behavior, affectionate and hostile, but this time the instigator is Liila, the victim is Chubby Maata's puppy, and the ambivalence is dramatically expressed in *ugiat*-ing. What might this drama tell us?

We know that both Liila and Chubby Maata have conflicted feelings about me; is it far-fetched to imagine that I am present in this event, as I was in the immediately preceding one (Episode 23A)? It seems possible that, for both mother and daughter, Papi represents me, though to different ends. And for Liila, Papi may also represent Chubby Maata, while Juda represents me. But the action begins with Chubby Maata.

Chubby Maata's treatment of Papi is an ebullient shadow play of her treatment of me—the poles of affection and aggression both drawn larger than life. Having triumphed over fear in her exchange with me, she begins with a display of affection, followed by curiosity about the physical composition of this strange animal; curiosity is followed, in turn, by a query whether *ugiat*-ing— the aggressive expression of affection—is appropriate. She doesn't take no for an answer but moves back and forth between aggression and tenderness, as she has seen adults do with babies.[11] Papi's aggressive play with Juda is not of concern to her; she is in control.

Liila, on the other hand, is threatened by Papi's play, which she defines as *uirit-*, single-minded in pursuit of a goal. She has good reason to be sensitive to *uirit-* behavior, and it is only a short step from the interaction between Papi and Juda to other situations that disturb her. Like Papi, I, too, with *uirit-* persistence, am grabbing at something that doesn't belong to me: Chubby Maata. And like Juda, I fail to respond to Liila's wish that I stop encouraging Chubby Maata's *uirit-* attention to me. (Remember Liila's annoyed murmur: "Yiini, as usual!")[12] I wonder whether, in inciting her daughter to act for her in discouraging Papi from his *uirit-* behavior, Liila is symbolically discouraging—and perhaps taking revenge on—both Chubby Maata and me.

Of course, Chubby Maata's loss of interest in *kuinat-* games does not mean that she never feared me again from this time forward. The scarier evil spirit game that I inadvertently initiated a month later (Episode 24) was a considerable challenge to Chubby Maata's developing social skills. Both her quick dash for her mother's side and her concern about how to play this game betray some uncertainty about her safety; it is less dangerous to observe than to engage fully in a drama. On the other hand, she doesn't withdraw; she sturdily stands her ground at the edge of the game, half playing, half learning how, and enjoying both my "attack" and her experimental counterattack—"*nya*-nya . . . " We heard this taunting refrain before in Chubby Maata's attack on her baby sister,

Aita, when her own sense of goodness was threatened (Episode 16). What is new this time is that she experiments with the playful use of the taunt. Several times she tests and retests: what are the rules of the game? and am I or am I not still playing? Finally, having satisfied herself that the game is over, she returns to her play with Papi, and the echoes of the game go with her: "*nya*-nya . . . "[13]

After her initial terror passed, Chubby Maata played many games with me, both when several children visited me together and when I visited Chubby Maata's household. For a long time, however, much of the fuel that energized the games and made them fun seemed to be derived from *kappia-* feelings. These feelings are visible in the thread of fear that runs in and out of the overt content of the games. Further evidence lies in the fact that at the same time that Chubby Maata was participating in and even initiating playful interactions like those I have described, she was denying—under adult interrogation—that she liked (*piugi*-d) me and wrinkling her nose at me in a most hostilely rejecting manner.

LIKING AND DISLIKING

The vicissitudes of "liking," *piugi-*, are closely related to those of *kappia-* and *ilira-*, but the relationship is not simple. Let's look at four incidents in which Chubby Maata's liking for me is under discussion and try to figure out what is going on.

Episode 26A (November 24)

One day, while I was visiting Liila's mother, Arnaqjuaq, Liila came in with Chubby Maata and Rosi. Chubby Maata approached within two feet of me and, with a playful bounce, struck a shadow blow at me with closed fist. She repeated the gesture several times, until I asked, smiling, "Because you're what?"[14]

Chubby Maata wrinkled her nose, meaning that she chose not to answer my question. Then she turned away, went over to her mother, who was now sitting on the other side of the room, and said something to her which I couldn't hear.

As Liila looked amused, I asked what Chubby Maata had said. Liila said, "She says (she did it) because she doesn't like you." Her smile was again amused.

I turned to Chubby Maata: "You don't like me?" Chubby Maata raised her brows; indeed, she didn't like me. I laughed, as did other adults in the room.

Episode 26B (November 24)

In the evening, when Liila and Jaani came to visit me, accompanied by Chubby Maata, I said to Chubby Maata, jokingly, "You still don't like me?"

Chubby Maata raised her brows, and for a moment her look was hostile, but then suddenly she broke into her bright baby beam.

At that moment her grandfather Mitaqtuq—who had heard the exchange that afternoon—came in and said to her: "Are you visiting someone you don't like? You said you didn't like her. Do you begin to like her now?"

Chubby Maata wrinkled her nose. Liila and Jaani watched her intently to see her answer, and when they saw it, they laughed. I laughed too.

Episode 26C (November 25 or 26)

A day or two later, when Liila came into my qammaq with Chubby Maata, I asked again, "Do you still not like me?" And again Chubby Maata raised her brows, agreeing that she did not; but this time she broke into a smile immediately. I saw no moment of serious hostility.

Episode 27 (December 20)

Liila came into my qammaq, carrying Chubby Maata on her back. (She later told me that Chubby Maata had injured her leg that morning while running.) Mitaqtuq, who was already visiting me, said to his granddaughter, "You're *really* a baby today." Neither Chubby Maata nor Liila made any response that I saw or heard. Mitaqtuq got up to leave shortly after the others had entered, declining my offer of tea.

As soon as he had gone, Chubby Maata said, "*I'd* like some tea." Her mother asked, "Because you've been invited to drink tea?" Chubby Maata smiled and raised her brows: "Yes." "Who invited you?" Chubby Maata pointed to me, very quickly and self-consciously, and smiled. I smiled back. Liila asked Chubby Maata, "Are you beginning to like her?" Chubby Maata, for the first time, raised her brows: "Yes." I questioned, "Really?" Chubby Maata raised her brows again. Thinking that such a friendly statement—no matter how self-interested and quite possibly untrue—should be encouraged, I said, "Let her be given tea." Liila got up and poured her daughter a cup of tea, which Chubby Maata drank.

What is happening in this series of encounters?

Chubby Maata's opening gambit when she enters her grandparents' house on November 24 and finds me there (Episode 26A) is reminiscent of the aggressive games that she has been playing with me both by herself at home and with other children in my qammaq. Approaching me—but not too closely—she playfully shadowboxes toward me. I read the gesture as a cautious overture, which keeps her safely out of reach and at the same time shows me that she is strong and can defend herself if necessary. She is attracted but still afraid, and she deals with this mixture of feelings by *pretending* to attack me.

My question throws Chubby Maata abruptly into the realm of the serious and challenges her to give a reason for her behavior, which she is not prepared to give. We have already seen some of the dangers of both liking and disliking and how discombobulated Chubby Maata can be when interrogated about her feelings for others. We shall see later that she is not yet able to cope with liking for me. As she hovers on the brink, playfully expressing both attraction and repulsion, my serious question pushes her over the edge: Chubby Maata opts for dislike. Disliking seems to be safer than liking from her point of view; yet there are pitfalls in this path, too. As we know, disliking is a socially inappropriate option, and some of the ubiquitous messages that tell her so may have already reached Chubby Maata. One possibility is that if she says out loud that she doesn't like me, I may take revenge like her grandfather Iqaluk, when he threatened to pull her braids (Episode 12 in Chapter 5). She retreats to her mother's side and gives *her* the answer to the question.

For Liila, at this moment, it is not the right answer. She is amused. Nevertheless, now that Chubby Maata has said it to her mother—tested the water, expressed her dislike—and nothing terrible has happened, she can acknowledge the feeling also to me (nonverbally) when I ask her to confirm what she has told her mother. She does *not* like me. And again the answer is greeted with amusement—general amusement this time.

Perhaps the laughter has some effect on Chubby Maata. On our next meeting, that same evening, I bring up the subject again. "Do you still dislike me?" The answer is again "Yes," and Chubby Maata's first glance is hostile; her answer is serious. But this time the hostility gives way almost immediately to a bright smile, which seems to say, "I don't really mean it," or perhaps, "But I also want you to love me." Is she becoming self-conscious about the socially inappropriate expression of dislike which generated laughter earlier that afternoon? Or does the positive side of her ambivalence feel a little less scary now that the negative has been publicly asserted without catastrophe?

Her grandfather also pushes Chubby Maata in the direction of the proprieties. Whether he caught the exchange between Chubby Maata and me as he entered or was harking back to the afternoon's encounter, I don't know. In any case, Mitaqtuq's questions point out to his little granddaughter the inconsistencies in her behavior. But Chubby Maata refuses to be pushed farther than she has already ventured; she will not change her stated position. She has relaxed only enough to express it publicly: no, she is *not* beginning to like Yiini. The answer elicits more laughter.

But the next time I test Chubby Maata, a day or two later, not even the briefest of hostile glances accompanies the wrinkle of the nose which avers that she does, oh yes she does, dislike me. The smile bursts forth instantly. It seems to me that this time Chubby Maata is *playing* her dislike. Is she moving away from playing with real feelings of hostility and fear toward pretending those feelings?[15] Taking a step toward giving up those feelings? Perhaps she is beginning to have less need for a protective wall.

Nevertheless, it is not until a month later, just before Christmas, that Chubby Maata first gives a positive answer to her mother's question about liking me (Episode 27), and she thereby introduces not only a new phase in her relationship with me but also a new phase in her mother's use of *piugi-* questions.

Whether Chubby Maata actually feels liking for me on the present occasion is irrelevant to her assertion. What she wants is tea, and the messages about consistency seem to have reached her: one can't expect to be offered tea by a person one dislikes. Her mother reconfirms that familiar point when she asks Chubby Maata, who has just demanded tea, "Are you beginning to like (Yiini)?"

At the same time, however, Chubby Maata's wish to be served tea, expressed for the first time as a confident demand, alerts Liila to the need to teach Chubby Maata restraint and the *ilira-* feelings that motivate restraint. Chubby Maata's forthright request is emphatically not *ilira-,* although the fact that Chubby Maata waits for her grandfather to leave before she speaks suggests that the seeds of *ilira-* have been sown. Liila starts a line of questioning that is designed to water those seeds—to make Chubby Maata realize that she should have waited to be offered tea. "Who invited you?" asks Liila. It works. The shyness of Chubby Maata's reply shows that Chubby Maata hears the criticism and begins to be self-conscious about her demand.

This exchange gives us a glimpse of Liila tacking to a new position in the education of Chubby Maata. While Chubby Maata *kappia*-ed me, Liila tried to teach her to *piugi-* me, but now that Chubby Maata's un-*ilira-* behavior has demonstrated that *kappia-* feelings are not troubling her very much anymore, Liila will try to inculcate *ilira-* feelings to take their place. Of course, Chubby Maata should *piugi-* me, too, for it would be antisocial if she didn't, and yet the picture is not so clear, as we already know. Presently, we shall see how Liila maneuvers her daughter toward a rather complicated position.

I am of course not furthering Liila's goals when, pleased with Chubby

Maata's more friendly behavior, I tell her mother to reward her with a cup of tea. Liila will have to work hard to counter both Chubby Maata's forwardness and my blind simplicity, as the next day's encounter will reveal.

Episode 28 (December 21)

Liila came in to visit me, accompanied by Chubby Maata and Rosi. Rosi sat down decorously beside her mother on the sleeping platform, while Chubby Maata stood in front of them. Bouncing around playfully, Chubby Maata hit Rosi's body very lightly once or twice with her fist; then—even though Rosi didn't seem to mind her strikes and Liila made no disapproving comment— Chubby Maata began to shadowbox, never breaking her rhythm but never hitting Rosi either. And as she punched, with smiling eyes and bouncy manner, she said to no one in particular, "Look at me!"

No one responded, as far as I could see, and after a few seconds, Chubby Maata deposited a few punches *on* her sister—hard punches this time, which made Rosi turn sideways and duck her head toward her mother for protection. Rosi laughed but grimaced at the same time and said in a voice raised in protest, "A'aa (ouch)!" I think Chubby Maata retreated again briefly into shadowboxing, but soon she stopped her game altogether.

Liila's response, when it came, was indirect. I think even before Chubby Maata stopped hitting Rosi, Liila began to interrogate her younger daughter: "Who are you?" Rosi answered for her sister: "Aimu." Chubby Maata echoed, "Aimu." Liila persisted: "And who else?" Rosi again replied, "Taina," and Chubby Maata echoed her. Liila gave Rosi a light push and said, "Oooo," meaning "Don't tell her!" Then she resumed her interrogation: "Who else?" "Ukaliq," said Chubby Maata—a correct answer. "Who else?" "Lia"—a wrong answer.[16] Liila inquired no further.

About this time, the outer door opened, and in an excited voice, Liila whispered to Chubby Maata, "Sit down quickly! Here!" indicating her unoccupied side. Chubby Maata hastily sat down, and all three visitors sat up, very straight and quiet, looking toward the door.

Two teenagers entered: Jaani's sister Ruupi and Liila's sister Liuna, the latter carrying the baby Aita in her parka. At the sight of them, Chubby Maata got up again and bounced around as before, though she didn't punch anyone. Liila queried, "(Are you behaving this way) because you don't ilira- Yiini?" Chubby Maata raised her brows. Liila probed, "Would you ilira- her if she scolded you?" Chubby Maata wrinkled her nose. "Because you dislike her?"[17] Chubby Maata wrinkled her nose. "Do you like her?" Chubby Maata raised her brows and continued to bounce around.

After a bit, she began to make comical—or were they evil spirit?—faces at me by pulling her lower eyelids down, a gesture she had seen adults make in fun. Her mother asked, "Shall Yiini eat your eye?" Chubby Maata hesitated for a second, as if wondering whether she should be anxious, or perhaps deciding whether and how to play; then she smiled, "plucked" her eye out with her fingers, and "handed" it to me. I took it from her in pantomime and "ate" it. We repeated this game several times. I don't remember which of us wearied of it first and stopped.

The next thing I noticed was that Chubby Maata had a heavy cardboard tube in her hand and was hitting herself over the head with it. It made a hollow sound, and people laughed. She said, "Qaqquallanga," and again people laughed. I don't know what she had intended to say, but the word she chose meant "Let me bite something (a bone, or cartilage, or wood) and break it up with my teeth." Then she hit Rosi, Ruupi, and Liila on the head with the tube, one after the other, and said, "But not Aita?"

I don't think anyone answered the query directly, but Ruupi took the tube and saying, "Do like this, instead," blew into it and made a loud sound. Chubby Maata took it and imitated her. The two of them repeated the game several times. Then Liila got up to leave, and Chubby Maata and Rosi went out with her.

That night Chubby Maata sat on my lap for the first time—when I put her there—and drank her bottle peacefully.

Now, what is all this about?

It is an ebullient Chubby Maata who comes to visit, the leg injury of the day before long forgotten. Carried by her ebullience into playfully aggressive behavior, she attacks Rosi, as we have seen her do before (Episode 1); but this time, for the most part, she only feints at her sister, as she feinted at me in her grandmother's house a month earlier (Episode 26A). She is beginning to understand that aggression should and can be playful and strictly limited, and it looks as though she is pleased with herself. Whether she is pleased with her control or with her daring in pushing the boundaries of acceptable aggression—especially in my scary presence—or both (or perhaps something else altogether) is not clear.

But self-satisfaction is not all there is to it. "Look at me!" she exclaims. She also wants to have her feat observed and approved of—or perhaps monitored. How far can she go? The direct hits that follow the shadowboxing leap the bounds of the acceptable and seem very much like tests. We will see a similar sequence later (Episode 34), in which Chubby Maata calls my attention to her act of helping herself to a piece of bannock, and when I fail to forbid her, she takes it. In the present case, however, she succeeds in eliciting negative comment, and when Rosi protests, Chubby Maata pulls in her fists again.

Liila, too, attempts to restrain Chubby Maata. She disregards Chubby Maata's achievements in controlling her antisocial hostilities and fears, and focuses instead on her lack of decorum and respect (*ilira-*) for me. She is clearly determined to motivate appropriate visiting behavior in Chubby Maata. Unlike babies, children should not call attention to themselves when they are in others' houses, should not make demands, and should not treat adult outsiders as familiars. Chubby Maata offends on all these scores; moreover, as I said earlier, I think that, in Liila's eyes, the problem goes beyond matters of decorum to her own emotional needs and those of Chubby Maata, as she perceives them. In any case, she tries by various means to grow Chubby Maata up a little.

Liila's first strategy is interesting: she asks Chubby Maata who she is. Because she does this on several occasions under similar circumstances, I judge that this is a deliberate response to Chubby Maata's behavior and perhaps an attempt to provide her daughter with another sort of monitor. Liila may be evoking Chubby Maata's name-selves, the adults who "are" Chubby Maata and who form her character, suggesting to the child that she is in a sense an adult and should behave like one. She should respect her adult selves and other adults, in this way showing herself worthy of them or simply "being" them.[18] In any case, Rosi interferes with her mother's efforts; and Chubby Maata herself, when pushed, begins to draw on names that are not hers—continuing her play? and perhaps concealing some uncertainty about the correct answers.

Liila desists from her now fruitless interrogation but is almost immediately given another opportunity to introduce a monitor for Chubby Maata—a visible one this time. The porch door opens, and she whispers excitedly to her daughter, "Sit down quickly!" Chubby Maata understands that it may be strangers or other scary (*iliranaq-* or *kappianaq-*) adults who will enter, and she obeys, imitating her mother. But when the "strangers" prove to be only familiar teenage caretakers and playfellows, she quickly gets up again and resumes her bouncy play.

Chubby Maata's play is no longer aggressive, but Liila is not yet satisfied. She points out to her daughter that her behavior is indecorous by asking Chubby Maata whether she is acting that way because she does not respect me and fear (*ilira-*) my scolding. When Chubby Maata agrees that this is the case, Liila reminds her of the possibility that I *might* scold her; but Chubby Maata, with uncustomary aplomb, denies that she would be frightened by being scolded and, under cross-examination, even asserts—as she never has before—that she likes me. This in spite of the fact that the negative form of Liila's probe— "Because you dislike her?"—nudges Chubby Maata toward agreeing that she *dis*likes me.[19] Is Chubby Maata playfully lying again in resistance to her mother's questioning, as she did in October (Episode 10), when Liila asked her who she was? Is she testing herself, pushing bravado to the limit? Or does she mean what she says?

Chubby Maata begins to play to me as audience, making comical (or are they tunraq?) faces. Liila capitalizes on that game, too, to try to subdue her daughter: "Shall Yiini eat your eye?" This question has the potential to resonate with Chubby Maata's lost *kappia*-fears, but Chubby Maata's fizzy state allows her to ride—with the merest soupçon of doubt—over her mother's hint that I might have cannibalistic tendencies. She incorporates her mother's suggestion into her play—a play reminiscent of the "kuinat!" game a month earlier, in which she had bravely allowed herself to play the victim (Episode 23).[20] I enter into the game, and Liila does not interfere.

Chubby Maata turns to other games of playful aggression, this time hitting herself as well as others and carefully excluding the baby Aita (and me), while checking with the adults to make sure that her decision to protect Aita is correct. Ruupi answers her indirectly by guiding her farther away from the dangerous borderlands of acceptable versus unacceptable attack. The tube becomes a musical instrument instead of a weapon.

If we follow the progress of Chubby Maata's aggressive behavior in this interaction, we can see the germs of several developments. Although Chubby Maata is playful throughout, in the first moments of the visit her punches push and even cross the limits of the acceptable. Then, with the exchange of "eyes" to be "eaten," the playful aggression becomes first symbolic, then both symbolic and reciprocal; and when it moves back into the realm of real hitting, the weapon is so light as to be entirely undamaging. Moreover, Chubby Maata continues to include herself among the "victims" and is explicitly concerned with the rules of play. As we have seen her do before, Chubby Maata both plays and stands aside as observer of her own play; and she defines for herself limits in which an adult standard of interaction, such as not hitting Aita (or perhaps babies in general), is visible. She doesn't hit Yiini, either, but one can't know whether that exclusion is due to knowledge of a social rule, to budding *ilira*- (not otherwise much in evidence), or even to a remnant of *kappia*-feelings. We can perhaps see a hint of such feelings in the fact that she plays with fear in her games with me, both when she makes faces and when she exchanges eyeballs.

Finally, Chubby Maata allows herself to be guided away from aggression altogether, when Ruupi redefines the play as musical.

With regard to physical aggression, Chubby Maata is certainly moving toward appropriate self-control, setting limits on her play while developing the ability to *use* play. But progress toward *ilira-* behavior is less evident. Liila makes ingenious and persistent efforts to move her daughter in that direction. Her questions point out to Chubby Maata that her behavior is un-*ilira-* and inappropriate to her adult self or selves; she hints that I might scold; and, while she avoids telling Chubby Maata that I am an unlikable person, she nudges her daughter toward understanding that there are real reasons behind her dislike of me. In addition, when opportunities arise, Liila first models proper *ilira-* behavior ("Sit down, quickly!") and then tries, rather mildly, perhaps, to reawaken Chubby Maata's old *kappia-* feelings toward me ("Shall Yiini eat your eye?"). But just as she avoids telling Chubby Maata that I am unlikable, so she stops short of labeling my behavior *kappianaq-*. From now on, it is always *ilira-* that is explicitly under discussion.[21] And Chubby Maata, on this occasion, follows her own path, more than once treating the lessons that her mother contrives to set before her as obstacles to be avoided or overcome rather than as lessons to be learned.

I think that my goals were furthered by Chubby Maata's attention to her own goals. That night, when for the first time she allowed me to hold her on my lap, I wondered whether her success that afternoon in playfully redirecting both her own aggression and mine, when she turned the monster eye-eater into a playfellow—perhaps even her daring assertion that she liked me—had given her confidence a little extra boost: the sky didn't fall in either case. Chubby Maata's increased friendliness elated me—and, unfortunately, I was thoughtless of Liila's quite legitimate aims for her daughter's social and emotional development. Chubby Maata continued from that time to seem (as my notes recorded) "perfectly at ease" with me, and Liila's unease must have increased accordingly. Nine days later, her attempt to inculcate *ilira-* feelings was more forceful, as we shall now see.

Episode 29 (December 30)

Liila and her sister Luisa were drinking tea with me in my qammaq when Chubby Maata's voice was heard outside.[22] Liila called to tell her daughter where she was, and Chubby Maata came in, all by herself, in great good humor. Opening the door, she announced her arrival in a ringing tone: "Toilet paper!" Then, seeing that my other visitors were drinking tea, she immediately asked to be served, her manner indicating a bouncy, baby confidence that tea would be forthcoming.

Liila did give her tea and spoke to her in a tender voice, *aqaq*-ing her: "Are you a baby?" Chubby Maata must have wrinkled her nose, because Liila, in the same tender tone, replied, "In what horrid little (ways) are you behaving, then?" Chubby Maata smiled the baby beam with which she often deflected awkward questions.

After some matter-of-fact, nonplayful conversation between Liila and me, which I didn't record, Chubby Maata, who had been standing beside her mother, came closer to where I sat on the sleeping platform and began to converse or play with me in a way that I read as "relaxed"; bravado seemed to have disappeared. Unfortunately, I again failed to record the details. Then Liila said to her daughter, "(Are you behaving like that) because you don't ilira-Yiini?" Chubby Maata raised her brows in agreement. Liila, in a mild version of her "warning" voice, deep and throaty, said, "She's a big bad Qallunaaq; it's her custom to scold!" Chubby Maata looked at me for a second with a serious face and wide eyes—an abrupt change from the buoyant assurance of a moment earlier. Liila continued: "Are you not ilira- of her?" This time Chubby Maata wrinkled her nose: she did feel uneasy about my scolding. Her mother persisted: "Do you like her?" Chubby Maata wrinkled her nose again, "No," and moved away to the other end of the qammaq, to the door, where Luisa sat.

That did not stop her mother. The interrogation continued: "Do you dislike her?" Chubby Maata raised her brows. "What is it about her that you dislike?" Chubby Maata didn't answer. "Is it her face?" Chubby Maata wrinkled her nose. "Her hair?" Chubby Maata wrinkled her nose. "Her fur boots?" Chubby Maata wrinkled her nose. "Everything about her?" Chubby Maata wrinkled her nose. Now Luisa joined in, and the two adults, amused but relentless, went through the entire series again. Chubby Maata wrinkled her nose at each question. Then Liila asked, "Is it because you don't resemble her?" Finally Chubby Maata raised her brows: "Yes." Liila said: "What did you say? Because she reminds you of someone else?"[23] Again Chubby Maata raised her brows. Both women seemed satisfied with this reason and stopped questioning.

Later, when they all got up to leave, Liila reminded Chubby Maata to take with her an empty eyedrops bottle, which I had offered to give her as a toy. Chubby Maata, without any apparent reluctance to approach me, came over to the sleeping platform to take it from me. Liila handed her a book that was lying on the platform and said, "Here's your book." Chubby Maata wrinkled her nose. Liila asked, "Whose is it?" "Yiini's," replied Chubby Maata. Liila handed her my glasses, saying, "Here are your glasses." Chubby Maata wrinkled her nose. "Whose are they?" "Yiini's." And so they left.

In church, an hour later, Chubby Maata was as relaxed with me as ever. She swung on my foot, beamed at me, and lay down across my leg to reach something.

In this interaction, Liila continues her efforts to motivate in Chubby Maata the decorous behavior that is proper for a visitor, and this time she temporarily succeeds in subduing her daughter. How do her strategies compare with those she used nine days earlier (Episode 28)?

Liila begins by asking Chubby Maata whether she is a baby. She uses the tender, affectionate tone that Chubby Maata has reason to associate with intimate celebrations of her babyness, and indeed, Liila's tone, her eyes, and the fact that she immediately gratifies Chubby Maata's baby wish tell us that she *is* feeling tender. Nonetheless, she is also expressing criticism, and Chubby Maata seems to catch a whiff of this; she doesn't want to claim baby status—until she is nonplused by the demand that she account for her behavior. The conversation shifts while Chubby Maata drinks her tea, but afterward Chubby Maata begins to play with me, and her mother, as on the earlier occasion, suggests to Chubby Maata the advisability of *ilira*-ing me. This time she doesn't just suggest, in hypothetical, questioning form, the *possibility* that I might scold; she asserts that I *do* scold, not occasionally but regularly. More, she dramatizes the danger, in a voice that will certainly resonate for Chubby Maata with other threats that have frightened her. It is not surprising that this time Chubby Maata is shaken from her comfortable position: she does *ilira*- me, and she doesn't *piugi*- me.

But Liila does not let the matter rest there. This time she requires Chubby Maata to think through the reasons behind her feelings—in other words, to formulate a motive for behaving properly, one that will withstand my best efforts to undermine propriety. By my consistently benign treatment of Chubby Maata, I might be able to overcome her fear of being scolded, but how can I do this if I am structurally different in broad and undefined ways and therefore unknowable and unpredictable?

For the moment, the throaty warning and the interrogation that follows it do the trick; Chubby Maata stops playing with me. But Liila does not intend that her daughter should be frightened away from accepting proffered gifts. And indeed, when she has her mother's approval, Chubby Maata is not afraid to approach me. (This was not true when she was severely afraid—*kappia-*—of me.) At the same time, Liila wants Chubby Maata to know that objects are not free for the taking: they are owned and must be given. So she tests her daughter's sense of property. This test Chubby Maata passes with flying colors.[24]

The next time Chubby Maata and I meet, she seems, as usual, to have forgotten her mother's lessons; she is as babyishly familiar and relaxed with me as before. Nevertheless, there is other evidence that she is changing.

Episode 30A (January 5)

Liila and Chubby Maata came to visit me. Liila remarked that my qammaq was cold. I said I wasn't cold. Chubby Maata, beaming her baby beam, held out her hand for mine so that she could feel whether my hand was cold. I gave her my hand. She said, with the same smile, "You're not cold." I smilingly agreed.[25]

Then Chubby Maata said to her mother in a hardly audible voice, "Tea." Liila said, "Because you're invited to drink tea?" Chubby Maata raised her brows. Liila queried: "By whom?" Chubby Maata smiled self-consciously, pointed in my direction, but looked at her mother rather than at me. Liila persisted: "By whom? Speak up." Chubby Maata mouthed the word "Yiini," still looking self-conscious and avoiding my eye. Liila repeated her question several times, each time telling Chubby Maata to speak up, but Chubby Maata didn't. I laughed. And that was the end of that topic.

A few minutes later, Liila asked Chubby Maata, "Because you don't ilira-Yiini?" Chubby Maata raised her brows, smiling. Liila, with just a hint of throaty warning in her voice, said: "She's a big bad Qallunaaq; it's her custom to scold! Do you like her?" Chubby Maata looked at me with a serious, watchful face, and then wrinkled her nose. I—shame on me, still trying to counteract Liila's lessons—said: "She's lying." Chubby Maata smiled at me but looked back at her mother, who repeated, "Do you like her?" Chubby Maata wrinkled her nose. Liila, in a slightly amused voice, asked: "Why? What is it about her?" Chubby Maata, beaming self-consciously, shrugged her shoulders exaggeratedly and glanced briefly in my direction. She paid me no further attention, and soon thereafter they left.

Episode 30B (January 8)

Three days later, when Liila and Chubby Maata visited me, Chubby Maata did not ask for tea but had a very friendly, relaxed conversation with me about cold hands, again taking my hand in hers several times for the fun of dropping it because it *was* cold. She also wanted to know who owned the bowl in which I was mixing bannock and whether it was powdered milk (as I pretended) or flour that I was pouring into it. And Liila did not interrogate Chubby Maata concerning her feelings about me.

Progress is never even, and this will be by no means the last time that Chubby Maata asks to be served tea in my qammaq or behaves in other inappropriately un-*ilira*- ways which draw her mother's criticism. I began to see the value of Liila's training when, toward the end of January, she stopped discouraging Chubby Maata from approaching me. Very soon thereafter, as we shall see, Chubby Maata began coming in, usually with her cousin and playmate Kaati, to "fetch" pieces of bannock to be carried away,[26] or to ask for tea, which again was to be served with bannock, often, at Chubby Maata's insistence, well coated with butter and jam. Nevertheless, it is clear that Chubby Maata has begun to register the message that requests to be fed in my house—at least when they are uttered in the presence of her mother—are improper. Equally clearly, she does not need to have my "difference" from her spelled out; she remembers. The foundations for appropriate *ilira*- feelings are being laid, while the terrifying *kappia*-feelings that afflicted her when I first appeared in her life have been laid to rest—or, at least, thoroughly submerged.

Now I give one more example of Liila's training, which must have vividly confirmed for Chubby Maata the truth contained in Liila's lessons and fed the negative strands in Chubby Maata's tangled feelings about me.

Episode 31 (January 17)

Liila, Chubby Maata, and Luisa were again visiting me. Chubby Maata seemed relaxed and not *ilira*-. Ignoring her mother's repeated remonstrances, she was playing with the sooty lamp-trimming stick and prodding the tidy line of flame in my seal-oil lamp, making it flare. Finally, with an abrupt gesture, I took the stick out of her hand and laid it aside. Chubby Maata looked at me with wide eyes and a solemn face. Liila leapt to take advantage: "Are you beginning to ilira- her?" Chubby Maata raised her brows. Trying to soften my action and make amends, I smiled at her and asked, "Because I did what?" Chubby Maata was silent. Luisa prompted her: "It's because she doesn't want you to trim the wick, isn't it?" Chubby Maata raised her brows. Then Luisa with a smile, speaking with exaggerated slowness and very clearly, labeled my act, "Sc-o-o-o-ld!" And Liila, to my surprise, asked, "Do you want to scold Yiini?" Chubby Maata raised her brows.

Liila, with the help of her sister, seizes the golden moment to make Chubby Maata aware that she has *ilira*-feelings and that she has them for good reason.

She also brings to Chubby Maata's awareness the little girl's wish to retaliate for the affront. In labeling that wish, Liila distills her daughter's uncomfortable state of mind into hostility against me. It is an emotion that Chubby Maata ought not to feel, but one that will have the beneficial side effect of restraining the friendly overtures that Liila deplores. And whether or not Liila intends it at this moment, she is also showing Chubby Maata—and helping to create—one of the dangers of hostility: attack (mine) invites counterattack (from Chubby Maata).

At the same time, I suspect, the wish for retaliation that Liila attributes to Chubby Maata is her own wish to scold me (*sirnaaq-*), in defense of her beloved daughter. In asking Chubby Maata if she wants to scold me, Liila herself scolds me—while avoiding the overprotective behavior that is disapproved. At some level, Chubby Maata may perceive some of this, too, and feel, on more than one count, that her antisocial but useful hostility is supported.

So we see once more the complexities of the atmosphere in which Chubby Maata is learning to regulate her relationship with me and find workable ways of living both with her own feelings and with the directions in which her mother and others—not least, Yiini—are trying to move her.

BABIES AND MOTHERS: PRACTICING THE MANAGEMENT OF AMBIVALENCE

Although throughout this book I have emphasized dramas and interrogations initiated by adults and directed at Chubby Maata, we have seen that she is by no means only a passive recipient of such interactions. Think only of "One, two, three, GO!" (Episode 9), in which she transforms and takes control of Maata's scary game of "Want to come live with me?" and "Kuinat!" (Episode 23A), in which she elaborates a playful gesture of mine into a game in which first she becomes a scary person, frightening me, and then offers to take turns with me in frightening and being frightened.[27] I think that Chubby Maata's ability to play with her feelings—to take adult behavior that is both serious and playful into her own hands and mold it to her ends—is both instrument and consequence of her attainment of appropriate emotions and social behavior.

So far in this chapter, I have focused on Chubby Maata's efforts to play her way out of the fear and associated hostility that she feels toward me. Turning me into a playfellow is one way of pulling my sting. We have also seen how Liila tries, sometimes with dramatic fear tactics, to inhibit Chubby Maata's playful excesses where I am concerned. But Chubby Maata is exercised by other issues besides fear of me and has other problems to work at. These, too, find playful expression in her interactions with me, as the two following incidents illustrate.

Episode 32 (January 10)

During the school session today, Kaati (age three and a half), Aatami (four and a half), Rosi (four and a quarter), and Chubby Maata (just over three), were showing me their "writings" and drawings, asking if they were "correct," and asking me to draw or write things for them to copy. Once Kaati, asking me to draw a cup for her to copy, accidentally addressed me as "mother (*anaanak*)," but she caught herself in midword and exclaimed, "Ih!"—letting her tongue fall out in amused surprise—"I almost called you 'mother.'"

I said, "Ee—because you consider me your mother?" Kaati said, "No . . ." (I missed the rest of what she said.) Then all four children made a game out of calling me "mother," stopping in midstream as if catching themselves in error and making the dramatic tongue gesture. They repeated the play several times, while I smiled, said "Ee!" and pretended to be amused. They stopped of their own accord.

Episode 33 (January 29)

Two and a half weeks after the preceding incident, Chubby Maata and Kaati came into my qammaq to ask for pieces of bannock. Being in short supply just then, I gave them pieces that were much smaller than usual. Kaati merely accepted her piece, but Chubby Maata said "Haaa!" in the conventional tone of playful surprise, letting her tongue fall out in the gesture that conventionally accompanies that tone. Then, as the girls were leaving, Chubby Maata looked back and screwed up her face in a playful evil spirit grimace. I laughed, and they left.

In both of these incidents, the children elaborate a conventional gesture into a playfully dramatic enactment of a problematic feeling. And each incident gives us a different glimpse of the roles I play for these children: Good Mother in the first instance, Bad—Mother or Qallunaaq or merely Purveyor—in the second: contrary roles that are determined by consuming issues in the children's three- and four-year-old lives.

When I gratify the children's wishes, I am a good mother; the children are drawn to me in my nurturing mode. But in the way they handle the accidental exposure of my "motherness" I hear echoes of "Ih! I almost agreed!" (Episode 9). They are afraid to be drawn too far. They would not want to exchange their real mothers for me.

And when I don't give the children what they want, I am out and out bad. Bad what? As we have seen, Liila has all along been identifying my scary traits—real or imaginary—as "Qallunaaq." And both Chubby Maata and Kaati resort to that label in hostility. Once, for example, during another school session, when I experienced Kaati as overly demanding and impatiently refused to draw objects for her to copy, she muttered—as if speaking to herself but with a touch of the throaty scold tone in her voice—"Cussed little Yiini, cussed little no-good Qallunaaq."[28] I wonder, however, whether the very fact that the children perceive me both as a Qallunaaq—a distant and foreign creature, on whom they are not dependent and to whom they need not feel bonded—and as Yiini, an unusually accommodating adult playfellow, makes it possible for them to experiment with situating goodness and badness in the same person and trying to control these qualities.

In Chubby Maata's world, where caretakers never seriously attack children or punish them, one of the worst things a bad mother can do is to refuse to give. The problem of how to persuade me to give—how to convert my badness into goodness—surfaced quite early in Chubby Maata's relationship with me, and the focus of the request was always tea and bannock. This concern is expressed more and more clearly as Chubby Maata loses her inhibiting *kappia-*fears, and, as we shall see, the demands grow in breadth and intensity as the date of my departure draws closer. I suspect that this escalation reflects not only Chubby Maata's feelings and those of other children but also those of the adults around her.

In late winter, the camp at large was consumed by a single-minded craving for the goodies at my disposal—partly because, for almost all families, provisions were in very short supply during ice breakup, and partly because they hoped that when I left, in late March or April, I would leave behind not only the remainder of my supplies but also my camping equipment. (They received the supplies but not the equipment.) Chubby Maata's efforts to make an ungiving adult give are not quite as polished as those of her elders—and therefore, as we shall see, the elders who hear her cut her short (Episode 38). Even so, Chubby Maata shows us that she has learned a good deal about the principles underlying give and take in her world.

More broadly, Chubby Maata seems to be using her relationship with an interstitial person, Yiini, together with the interim time, or mental space, between the retreat of her inhibiting *kappia-* feelings and the establishment of proper and equally inhibiting *ilira-* feelings to work out the complex social relations required of her, together with the emotional strengths and social skills needed to negotiate and sustain those relationships. Look at the following exchange, for instance.

Episode 34 (February 11)

Leaving my qammaq after school (on the same day when Kaati had scolded me for not providing her with pictures to copy), Chubby Maata picked up a very small fragment of bannock from a dish by the door and held it up to show me. "Can I have this bad little piece for Kaati?" she asked. "I won't take *this* one." She patted the big loaf that lay beside the fragment. I said, "School-children don't eat bannock." But Chubby Maata persisted: "Can I have *this* piece? Can I?" I pretended to ignore her. "Yiini!" I still pretended to ignore her.

But suddenly I noticed that her pant legs were wet, so, in an attempt to distract her attention, I said in my best imitation of a throaty "disgust" voice: "Aaq! You've peed in your pants! Aaq!" I repeated the exclamation several times, although I felt no real revulsion. When I stopped, Chubby Maata said: "Say it again." I repeated it.

Then she began to ask again whether she could have the bit of bannock, and again I bent my head to my writing. "Yiini!" she said. "I'm going out!" And she and Kaati went out with the bannock. I saw out of the corner of my eye that the other children present—Miika, her little brother Saali, and Rosi—were watching me, expecting a response from me in answer to Chubby Maata's "notice of impending theft"; but I gave none. Chubby Maata was perfectly cheerful throughout this conversation and didn't seem at all upset when I "scolded" her about her wet pants.

We have already watched Chubby Maata learning to respond playfully to my playful aggression. Now she is beginning to be able to counter my rejecting behavior and my "scolds" without freezing (as she did in Episode 31) and without taking even playful vengeance (as she did in Episode 33). In addition, Chubby Maata makes use of her knowledge of several adult "rules" to try to persuade me to gratify her very unadult and improper demand for bannock. She demonstrates virtuous restraint—"I won't take *this* one"—and instead asks for only a very tiny piece, trying to convince me that the piece is insignificant and worthless. Moreover, she makes her request on behalf of someone else, not for herself, and she asks for the piece instead of merely helping herself to it. The fact that she does her best to get my permission and gives me every opportunity to tell her to put the fragment back also demonstrates that she knows she shouldn't ask for *any* bannock, no matter who is to receive it and how insignificant the piece. She invites me to be her monitor, her conscience.[29]

Her request takes the form of a game that older children and adults often played with me, testing my willingness to part with some coveted possession. They would call my attention playfully to their intended "theft" of the object: "Watch, Yiini, I'm stealing it!" I would pretend to be alarmed, exclaiming in "fear" and pretending to grab the threatened object protectively, whereupon the "thief" would put the object back and we would both laugh. But because Chubby Maata doesn't use the cue "Watch—I'm stealing" and because, in my Protestant fashion, I have her tagged as an "insatiable child" whose proclivities in that direction ought to be curbed, it doesn't occur to me to respond playfully.

Because I don't play, Chubby Maata expects—indeed, pushes—me to grant or refuse her request in serious mode, but I am unwilling to move in either direction. I was afraid that acquiescence would set a troublesome precedent for future demands, whereas refusal would establish a confrontational relationship, a Qallunaaq-style parent-child relationship, which I fell into all too often. I hoped that if I ignored her request, she would find it fruitless and desist by herself. Perhaps I was also curious to see what she would do.

But it is *my* strategies, both distraction and silence, that are fruitless. By the time I attempt to deflect Chubby Maata's attention, she is single-mindedly focused on her goal, the state that Inuit disapprovingly label *uirit-*. She makes fun of my distracting device or at least plays with it: "Say it again." And then she returns to her request. The result is that she gets the bannock.

Chubby Maata's reaction to my not very serious scold is interesting. Whether she recognizes its bogus nature and carries on my play, or does not recognize it but converts the criticism into play herself, her strategy is a major achievement. We have already seen that one of the most approved ways of dealing with conflict is to play with it, and one of the highest terms of praise for a mature Inuk is that he or she "doesn't take it seriously." It appears that the seeds of this attitude are already sown.

There can be other dimensions in such requests for repetition, too. We know that children in our own culture also play with difficult issues like learning to be simultaneously blamer and blamed, and I have already suggested that when Chubby Maata tried to maneuver me into refusing her request, she was asking me to be her external conscience. The same may have been true when she told me to "say it again." In her efforts to incorporate both goodness and badness into her self-image, Chubby Maata does not invent playfellows to take the brunt of the badness and the criticism, as Fraiberg's Stevie does (1959:141–145). Chubby Maata plays with the identities of real people and the moral qualities of those identities, distancing herself sometimes from the blamed person and sometimes from the blamer.[30]

At the same time, remember that when Chubby Maata says something untoward, Liila asks her to "say it again—louder" or to expand on what she has said (Episodes 1, 30A) so that Chubby Maata's inappropriate words will enter the public arena, where both others and Chubby Maata herself can hear them with a critical ear. And when Chubby Maata does something inappropriate like pulling Rosi's hair (Episode 1), Liila tells her to "do it again—harder" so that Chubby Maata will discover the unpleasant consequences of her act. So it seems possible that Chubby Maata, playfully imitating what Liila does, may be engineering a monitor for *me*, mocking my scold and repeating it so that *I* can hear its inappropriateness.

We'll see later that Chubby Maata also echoes me when I praise her. In these instances it sounds very much as though she is distancing herself a bit from both praise and blame—setting them in an arena between us to be bounced back and forth, accepted or returned to me—playing with people's opinions of her as a way of "hearing" and learning to deal with them.

As time goes on, Chubby Maata's interactions become more elaborate, more inventive, and more independent of adult dramas and interrogations. At the same time, she continues to dramatize the problems that adults have presented her with, as we shall see in the two longer and more complicated encounters that follow. Both of the interactions happened during visits that Chubby Maata made to me by herself—her second and third such visits.[31] Before we look at these episodes, I will frame them with a few orienting remarks and a short dramatic prologue.

As I mentioned in Chapter 1, it was not usual for Qipisa children of any age to visit (*pulaaq-*) other households, as adults did. After children outgrew their caretakers, they most often ran in packs, sometimes in pairs. When they came into a house—unless it was the home of very close kin with whom they felt comfortable, not *ilira-* —they clustered by the door, watched silently for a few minutes, replied briefly to questions, and then ducked outdoors to play or ran on to another house. If they felt more at ease, they might settle down for a while to play with some child of the house or accept a cup of tea if it was offered, but only in the coziest and most intimate of settings—at home or in a household that was almost home—would they initiate conversation with older persons (including teenagers) or volunteer information.[32]

When visiting me, once they felt at ease, children tended to behave as they did in the homes where they felt most familiar. They came in, stretched themselves out on the sleeping platform, looked at my magazines or other interesting objects, asked for paper and pencils with which to draw pictures, and chattered volubly among themselves and to me, passing on all the current news and their opinions about it, asking questions and teaching me words. Whenever footsteps were heard outside or if the outer porch door opened, my young visitors—even teenage ones—would hastily hide whatever they had been doing or looking at, sit up abruptly, and silently watch the inner door until it opened.[33] If the newcomer was someone of whom they were *ilira-*, one of the children would whisper, "Let's go out," and the whole flock would rise up and fly away; otherwise, they would relax and resume their interrupted pursuits.

Very few children visited me by themselves. The independent, four-year-old Miika did so occasionally, and so did Liila's fourteen-year-old sister, Liuna, and ten-year-old brother, Juda. But Chubby Maata was the youngest child who came alone, and the only one of her age who did so. She, more than other children, also treated me as a mother or caretaker. Episode 35 is a good example of that treatment. Nevertheless, it is clear that the roles I played for Chubby Maata shifted back and forth during the course of her visits.

Prologue to Episode 35 (February 5)

Episode 35, Chubby Maata's solo visit to me on a February afternoon, was preceded in the morning by two small encounters which might be relevant to the afternoon visit.

In the first encounter, Chubby Maata and Kaati came into my qammaq together, both backpacking large dolls in their parkas. Kaati announced, and Chubby Maata echoed, "I've acquired an offspring (*qitungngaq*)." Addressing Kaati, I said, "Is it your darling little daughter?" Kaati replied, "(It's) my baby—isn't it?" She turned to Chubby Maata for confirmation. Chubby Maata said, "Yes; my baby." Then Kaati, with a smile, said to me—as she almost always did when she came in these days, "I've come to fetch bannock." I rudely replied, "Don't be always fetching." Kaati said, "I haven't eaten bannock today." I smiled, but my tone was defensive as well as amused: "Not so! You ate bannock just a little while ago." (Liuna had served her tea with bannock in my qammaq just an hour earlier.) Kaati said, "Eeee!" dropping her tongue out and smiling as if to say, good-naturedly, "Aren't I silly to have forgotten!" I smiled too. Chubby Maata said, "*I* didn't fetch." Her tone seemed to me halfway between statement and question, as if she were asking for confirmation. I said, approvingly, "Ee (that's right)." The girls went out, seeming to be in very good humor.

Some time later, I encountered the girls again, outdoors. They still had their dolls with them, but now the dolls were "walking" from Kaati's house to Chubby Maata's. When Chubby Maata saw me, she walked her doll over to where I stood and made it "bite" my leg. I unfortunately didn't record my response to this "attack," but I'm sure it was pacific, and I imagine it was amused and playful.

This doll play—together with Chubby Maata's virtuous remark about not having "fetched"—seems to tell us something about how these two little girls saw themselves on that day. The second encounter also contains a message about how Chubby Maata saw me.

Mothers they were, certainly—grown-up and caring for children who were themselves growing up. When the girls first came to visit in the morning, their babies were small enough to be carried, but by noon those little ones had begun to walk. Chubby Maata's "not fetching"—which she took care to point out to me—was also mature behavior. At the same time, those mothers were them-selves babies, still called so by their doting caretakers. Not so long ago they too had been carried daily in the parkas of mothers and babysitters, and even now they were given a lift on a pair of shoulders from time to time (see Episode 27). It would be strange if the children didn't identify with the dolls that they were putting through the paces of the same life stages they were themselves going through.

The doll play, then, shows us that Chubby Maata and Kaati just now feel like both grown-ups and babies. We shall see presently that Chubby Maata shows me the same mixture of selves in her next two visits. She has played "grown-up" to me before—even explicitly identified with me in Episode 1—and I have suggested the possibility that such demonstrations of adultness and bigness, like the games in which she playfully aggresses against me, might, at moments of need, strengthen her image of herself as a child who is growing up and growing strong, one who can hold her own in interactions with the scary Qallunaaq. In this case I wonder whether it might be partly the morning's games that made it possible for the little girl to visit the Qallunaaq alone and converse freely, as older people did.

It seems to me that the playfully aggressive act of Chubby Maata's walking doll could also have had a strengthening effect, although the meaning of the act is not necessarily simple. The doll could have been retaliating on Chubby Maata's behalf for my most immediate crime: the refusal of bannock a few hours earlier. More broadly, she could also have been retaliating against—and identifying with—the aggressor that is one of Chubby Maata's images of me. In other words, the aggressive Chubby Maata may derive her energy from Yiini-the-aggressor, but the person she is aggressing against may be the "mother" of the doll that bit me, that is, "mother" to herself, Chubby Maata: again Yiini, a bad mother, who not only refuses bannock but also scolds and has other scary potentials as a Qallunaaq. At the same time, Yiini is a mother who is good enough to be safe to attack, even good enough to trust as mother to a baby Chubby Maata. Indeed, it's also possible that the doll is *ugiat*-ing me: expressing affection in her attack, a kiss in her bite. We'll see these complicated mothers and Chubby Maata's complicated feelings about them again in Chubby Maata's next two visits.

In short, Chubby Maata and Kaati in their doll play and, I think, later in their play with me are acting out their own lives, as I imagine children everywhere do. They are playing all the roles that their lives contain, past, present, and future—practicing the roles, and perhaps garnering strength to live the lives.

Now let's watch Chubby Maata's matinee performance on the day of the doll play. Though I didn't manage to record all of the abundant conversation that occurred during this visit, I include the event for comparison with the visit that follows it (Episode 36). Both dramas give us vivid glimpses of Chubby Maata's complex state of being: the mixture of adult and baby, the mixture also of hostility and trusting affection, and the internal dialogue concerning the placement of goodness and badness in her world. Most of the events in the first visit, there in embryonic form, are elaborated in the second, but if the two dramas are juxtaposed, I think we can also see some significant differences—differences that show us the direction in which Chubby Maata is moving.

Episode 35 (February 5)

Chubby Maata came in and went without hesitation to the sleeping platform, where she sat down. Once settled, she announced (of course, in Inuktitut, her only language): "Miika's household has a maniki." Puzzled, I asked, "What?" She repeated the word several times before I finally understood and said, "Ohhh! A monkey! Is it alive?" "Yes," she said.

Then she said she had to pee, and she attended to it all by herself, taking the toilet can out of the box where I kept it, pulling down her heavy pants, and squatting precariously over the can, which was far too big for her to sit on. But when she got up, she came over to me and said, "Pull my pants up," holding onto my arms with touching trustfulness as I tugged the trousers up to her waist.

She sat down again close beside me on the sleeping platform and looked at the torn plastic sheeting on my plywood floor. The tape that had attached two sheets of plastic together had come off. "Are you going to sew it?" she wanted to know. I said, "It can't be sewn." "Will you tape it?" "I have no tape," I said. Chubby Maata said, "*We* have lots." It was exactly what an adult would have said in offering help. I said, "Ee," meaning "I hear you and take note"—an appropriate reply to such an offer.

Then she said, "I've come to learn," and began to recite: "A, B, C, D . . . " But after D or E she got tangled and said instead, in very clear English, "Tell me what you think of me"—the final sentence of the English alphabet song. She must have heard it from one of the older children who had learned it in Pangnirtung. I invited her to repeat after me, "A, B, C, D . . . ," but she couldn't get much farther with me than she did by herself.

I don't remember what followed. My next note says that after some time, Chubby Maata, standing in front of me but at a little distance, said, "Hold me." It was the first time she had ever made that request of me, and I was touched. I held out my arms to her, and she came and sat between my legs, facing outward, as children of her age did with their caretakers, leaning back against me and resting her arms on my thighs. Her body felt very relaxed, and I felt cozily protective and happy. But sitting in that way, she suddenly said, "You're bad." Feeling amused and curious about the contrast between this hostile-sounding pronouncement and her trusting behavior, I asked, "Why (on earth)?"[34] Chubby Maata replied, "You're good." "Are *you* good?" I asked. Chubby Maata raised her brows: "Yes." That was the end of that exchange.

There was a lot more talk, which I didn't record. Chubby Maata asked for tea only once and accepted my word when I said there was none.

Later that day, when the teenage Maata came to visit me, I told her what Chubby Maata had said about the monkey in Miika's house. Maata made no reply, but I heard her afterward, outdoors, repeating the story to Liila. Liila asked Chubby Maata, "Did you say that to Yiini?" Her voice was pleasantly questioning. Chubby Maata must have wrinkled her nose, denying it, because then her mother said, in the same light and pleasant tone, "Did Yiini lie?" I couldn't see Chubby Maata's reply, of course. But three days later, when I was watching Liila scrape a sealskin, she asked me, "Did Chubby Maata tell you the other day that Miika's household had a monkey?" When I confirmed that she had, and a live monkey to boot, Liila smilingly told me, "We tell little children that there's a monkey. She believed it." I asked whether that was done to scare the children, and Liila confirmed that it was.

Episode 36 (February 7)

Two days after the visit just described, Chubby Maata came to visit by herself again. This time I recorded everything that happened.

Chubby Maata's first act was to sit down on the sleeping platform and shake her pigtailed head to show me that she was wearing Rosi's beaded braid decorations. I duly admired them. "Rosi's," said Chubby Maata. I said, "Ee." I also asked her whether she had seen the new puppies, born that morning to Muuki, the dog in Miika's household. She raised her brows but didn't elaborate.

Then she said, "I'm not fetching." Bannock, she meant, as usual. I said, "Atau (hurray)!" Chubby Maata echoed: "Atau!" I said again, "Atau!"

Next, bending her head over my lap, she tried to press down the clip on my writing board and said, "I usually do this." I think she had succeeded in moving the clip before, but this time she couldn't make it budge. I tried to help her press, putting my hand over hers, but I only hurt her hand. She grimaced and gave up.

Instead, she waved her hand around and said, "Don't take these things with you when you leave—OK?" The question—"ai?" in Inuktitut—was said in the suggestive, saccharine-persuasive tone that adults used toward her when trying to influence her behavior. It was also the tone that adults used when playing with me the same game that I think Chubby Maata was imitating: "You're going to give me this when you leave, *aren't* you?" I don't remember whether I said yes, no, or just laughed.

Then she noticed my torn flooring, as she had done before, and again asked, "Are you going to sew it?" I said, "Ee." Chubby Maata made a throaty "disgust" noise—"Aa-aq!"—and said in that tone, "Just look at that awful thing!" She sounded amusingly like her grandmother. (It was the tone I used to her four days later, when she wet her pants [Episode 34].)

She picked up my eraser: "What's this?" I said, "An eraser." She started to erase the notes I was taking. "Not those," I said.

She picked up one of the note slips on my writing board and asked, "Are you writing to yourself?" I said I was. She pretended to read, in a whisper I could hardly hear: "To Yiini and . . ." She was imitating the conventional opening of a letter in Inuktitut, the equivalent of "Dear Yiini."

I made a comical gesture with my mouth, and Chubby Maata immediately tried to imitate it: "Like this?" I said, "Ee," even though she had not done it right. I repeated it several times, and each time she watched me intently and tried to copy what I did: "Like this?" Each time I said, "Ee," but she kept on trying and telling me to do it again so that she could watch. She did a pretty good job of copying, and it got better as she went on. But I got tired of that game and stopped making the face.

Then, finally, Chubby Maata said, in a hardly audible whisper: "Tea? When it gets hot?" She tested the kettle with her hand and found it cold. I think I refrained from comment, but I might have said, "There isn't any."

Chubby Maata turned her attention to the seal-oil lamp and started to reach for the wick-trimming stick, which, three weeks earlier, I had forbidden her to use (Episode 31). In midreach she suddenly stopped, withdrew her hand quickly, turned, and smiled at me. I said, unnecessarily, "No!" Chubby Maata echoed, "No!" and then playfully ran her fingernail down my cheek—not hard enough to scratch—and began to play with my face and glasses.

I rescued my glasses, whereupon she put her hand on the end of my pencil, impeding me as I wrote these notes on her behavior. When I said, "No!" she playfully bent her head to mine, so that our foreheads touched; she was practically in my lap. Then she threw herself into my arms and said, smiling, "I consider you my mother."

I hugged her: "Really?" She wrinkled her nose, smiling, and said, "Shall I tie your tie?" She was referring to the shoelace in the neck of my heavy turtleneck sweater, which I used as a draft-protecting drawstring. She began to twist the laces together, leaning on me comfortably as she did so. And as she twisted, she whispered, "I don't like you." I echoed, "You don't like me?" Chubby Maata wrinkled her nose, denying dislike, smiled, and whispered, "I'm a horrid little evil spirit (tunraq)." "What?" I asked, wanting to be sure I had heard correctly. "*I* am," said Chubby Maata. Then, still whispering, she said: "Are we going to go to *our* house? My mother is at our house." I smiled.

She began to hum then and to sing fragments of a hymn—"Jiisusi maliklugu (Follow, follow Jesus)"—and as she sang and hummed, she twisted and twisted the shoelace at my neck. "You won't be able to undo it," she said, smiling. As she worked at the lace, she also whispered, "I saw the puppies." And then she began to play with my sleeve, turning the cuff back.

At this point, Juda came in. Chubby Maata, still standing between my legs, turned, saw him, and went back to playing with my cuff. Juda smiled to see her and sat down. Then we heard adult steps outside. Chubby Maata quickly sat down, sedate and still, on the sleeping platform by my leg, but when her father entered, she resumed her cuff play. Jaani smiled and said, "She's visiting, the sweetheart." I said, "I find her a very fine visitor." Jaani made no comment but only asked to borrow my lantern and left. Chubby Maata continued to play with my sleeve, but soon Juda went out, and Chubby Maata followed as soon as he was gone.

I said, in English, "Bye-bye." Chubby Maata, in the doorway, turned and waved in Qallunaaq style: "Bye-bye."

Chubby Maata's solo interactions with me are very much determined by the continued emotional force of issues already familiar to us—issues concerning mothers and babies, goodness and badness, hostility and affection—and all of these are thoroughly tied up with the issue that seems to be most in the forefront of her mind: how to get bannock. Let's look at the ways in which these issues are reflected in Chubby Maata's relationship with me. How far has she come in her ability to manage them, psychologically and socially? And how is she using me to help her grow through the problems that exercise her?

At the beginning of Episode 35, the first of these two solo visits, I am not sure who I was for Chubby Maata. The news that she offers me about the monkey in Miika's house is, I suspect, a little scary for her. (Liila told me afterward, remember, that children are told about monkeys to scare them.) Although Chubby Maata doesn't sound frightened, she may be excited and a little nervous about the idea of the strange animal. She may associate it with the new puppies that are expected to appear any day now in Miika's house. New puppies, like monkeys, are both exciting and scary, because children are warned that if they go too close, the mother of the pups may bite. Indeed, Chubby Maata may have been told the monkey story in order to keep her out of the qammaq where Muuki is about to whelp. Perhaps telling me about the monkey makes the idea of that animal—and of the puppies?—less scary. I see no evidence that Chubby Maata is trying to scare *me* this time. She may be trying to impress me with her exciting information or share it with me in adult fashion.

The next act that I recorded is clearly that of a grown-up girl: she has to pee, and she attends to the whole process by herself—until the final moment, when her stiff and heavy trousers defeat her. Then, when her limits are reached, she reverts in a most matter-of-factly trusting way to her baby self. And when I have pulled up her pants, as a good mother would, she sits down close by me, again as if I were her mother—but what she says sounds like *her* mother: "Are you going to sew (your torn flooring)?" She not only notices that something is not as it should be in the house; she has ideas about how to fix it, ideas that, although unfeasible, are not far-fetched. Even the final offer of repair material—"We have lots"—accurately imitates what an adult would say. She is "helping" me as much as she can.

In the next scene, Chubby Maata is still a big girl, a schoolchild this time, who already knows quite a lot, and she is telling me pretty clearly, I think, that she wants to be admired for knowing it—whether or not she knows what the English phrase "Tell me what you think of me" means. But again her limits are soon reached. And the next action I recorded—though I think it didn't follow immediately—is a trusting baby one. "Hold me," she says, inviting me to play mother, and playing baby to my mother. Does she feel safer being a baby after she has demonstrated, up to a point, that she *can* be a big girl? Or, on the contrary, does she want the reassurance of being recognized as a *babykuluk* after her attempt to be an admirable big girl runs into obstacles?

Interestingly, it is when she is most relaxed and confiding that she says, "You're bad." Why does she do this? Let's examine some possibilities.

We have seen that "You're bad" or "I don't like you" ("I consider you bad") has been for some time Chubby Maata's standard defense against her fear (*kappia*-) of me. A few days after this visit, she and Kaati (at Kaati's initiative) will retaliate again in this way when I refuse to give them the bannock they ask for.[35] Concerning this particular visit, however, my notes contain no other evidence that Chubby Maata fears me, nor did I record any conflict of interest that might have provoked her condemnation.

We know, though, that Chubby Maata has been learning that "You're bad"—and "You're good," too—are dangerous things to say in general. She could be testing, then, experimenting, playing with disliking, as we have seen her do before (Episode 18, Chapter 5). She may feel safer doing so with me than with many other adults because, unlike other adults, I don't interrogate her about whether she likes people, considers them good. Even her feelings about *me* are, for the moment, not under discussion; the adults seem to have given up trying to make her *ilira*- me; and I, amused and charmed by the games she plays with her ambivalences and transitions, try to avoid rattling her. So she may wonder what will happen if she says this dangerous word to me, in the absence of more critical adults.

Yet it would be surprising if the strong suggestions Chubby Maata has been given about the advisability of *ilira*-ing me hadn't left a residue of unease.[36] So another possibility is that Chubby Maata, experimenting with a dangerous word, is also experimenting with a dangerous *feeling* and trying to order her relationship with *me*. Though she seems to feel safe at the moment, it may be that she has scared herself, going just a little too far in trusting me and in laying herself open to my affection for her. She may need now to create a little distance between us for reassurance and put herself in a dominant position. Her "You're bad!" may be the verbal equivalent of the bite her doll gave me that morning—but there is the same possibility of double meanings, affectionate as well as hostile: saying the opposite in good Inuit fashion.[37]

Why does Chubby Maata reverse herself when I ask her *why* I am not good? For one thing, she may be rattled by the open-endedness of my question, may take it as a sign that her negative pronouncement is disapproved of.[38] On the other hand, her mother has suggested to her good reasons for disliking me, not considering me good (Episode 29), which Chubby Maata could draw on here if she chose to, but she does not choose to. Is there a part of her that likes me? Her confiding behavior says that there is, and my question may make her aware of that side of her feeling.

A possibility that I have already suggested, and for which we see more evidence in her next visit, is that Chubby Maata may be playing with me, using me—a "mother" who is not a mother, whom she does not need and fear to lose—as a surrogate on whom to practice integrating the good and bad qualities of her real mother. She is also, I think, playing or experimenting with her own good and bad qualities, as we saw her do in Episode 18. At this moment, she claims that she is good, but in her next visit, we see her claim badness.

In Episode 36, two days later, which I recorded more fully, we see variations and elaborations of the same themes. As the events unfold, they show us several developments in Chubby Maata's journey out of babyhood.

Chubby Maata is very pleased with herself when she comes in. I expect that her big sister's hair decorations had been admired by her mother and perhaps by her father before she came to show them to me. She is not interested in telling me about the new puppies, in answer to my question, but instead assures me—as she had done two days earlier—that she is not fetching. She is pointing out to me, and perhaps to herself, that she would *like* to fetch and is controlling that wish. (She will return to this problem at the end of the visit, with a little less control.) Now when I praise her, she echoes me, turning the praise-saying into a game. Is she also talking to herself aloud in my voice, the better to hear what is said?

In pressing the clip on my clipboard, Chubby Maata is again demonstrating that she is grown up, as she did when she said, "I can reach to here" (Episode 20). She fails, but the composure with which she fails strikes me as even more adult than the strength to press a stiff clip. And she goes on to *play* with me in the manner of her elders. The game of "Why don't you give to me?" expresses

Chubby Maata's own wishes, too, and both she and Kaati will play it with me persistently from now until I leave at the end of March. In her attitude toward my possessions and in the way she expresses that attitude, Chubby Maata is already very mature—though her elders consider that she is too young to play that game, and when they hear her, they tell her to stop (Episode 38). I suspect they think she can't be trusted to know the difference between playful and serious behavior and to set appropriate limits. Their discomfort may be increased, too, by the fact that she is expressing their wishes together with her own. In any case, I give Chubby Maata no reason to expect a windfall when I leave.

Chubby Maata continues in the same adult mode, both serious and playful, when she interrogates me again about my torn flooring. And this time she may be playing, subtly, with hostility. Her expression of mock disgust—said in a deep voice, locked in the throat by a tucked-in chin and tight-curled tongue— was one that adults used frequently when trying to persuade a child (or an anthropologist) to avoid some filthy or otherwise undesirable object or act. Chubby Maata's grandmother Arnaqjuaq used it more than most, and Chubby Maata had heard her use it to *me* when Arnaqjuaq was trying to persuade me to throw away my old balaclava, a wool cap with a "hole" in it, which Chubby Maata liked to play with and "break" (the verb is Chubby Maata's). Here Chubby Maata is criticizing my house or my housekeeping.[39] Perhaps she is telling me that my goods aren't worth having anyway—or even that *I* am no good because I won't give away my possessions. And in this she may be echoing conversations of her elders, to which I was not privy.

But now her attention is diverted. She picks up an interesting and unfamiliar object, my eraser, asks what it is, and experiments with its use. Sometimes, when she asks one of her parents or me what things are, she is playing a game, one that is more than likely to elicit affectionate remarks from her parents about what a darling—or mindless (*silait-*)—little baby she is. This time, however, since she doesn't fire questions at me in rapid succession, hardly waiting for answers, it sounds much more like a big girl's serious request for information. Again I discourage her interest in my possession, but she is not fazed. It is still the big girl who asks the next question, a perceptive one: "Are you writing to yourself?" I am reminded of the visit two days earlier, in which, after her grown-up remarks about my flooring, she played schoolchild. This time she pretends to read, imitating the only purposeful form of writing that she knows: a letter. She uses the same hardly audible voice in which people read aloud to themselves and in which she sometimes talks to herself. She has elaborated her

question and my answer, playing a game with herself and perhaps also identifying with the adult writer. She goes on to copy me in another way, too, imitating
my facial gesture, and is persistent in her efforts to improve her copy. Perhaps,
in learning to make a tunraq face, she is strengthening herself, enlarging her
repertoire of means for identifying with, and defending herself against, scary
people, as she did in learning "*nya*-nya" some weeks earlier (Episode 24). Or
perhaps she is honing her ability to retaliate against bad people, as she did in
Episode 33, when I refused to give her bannock. But we'll see presently that she
is beginning to find other uses, too, for the role of tunraq.

Now, finally, Chubby Maata can contain her wish for tea no longer. But *adult*
visitors are usually offered tea, and she has been very adult. Moreover, her
request is made with exemplary restraint: with a realistic sense of contingencies
("if it gets hot?") and a good deal of *ilira*—although not quite enough to
prevent her from making the request in the first place.

When tea does not materialize, she accepts the fact with mature equanimity
and turns—pragmatically, or merely by association?—to the lamp that's used
for heating water. Perhaps if she trims the flame, the tea will heat? But again an
earlier prohibition (Episode 31) is fresh in her mind, and she stops herself, with a
smile, self-conscious or conciliatory, to the prohibitor. My repetition of the
interdiction was completely unnecessary, and I would not have repeated it if I
had seen in time that Chubby Maata was withdrawing on her own initiative.
Again she echoes my judgment on her behavior, and again she seems to be
talking to herself through me. Is she taking possession of my scolding, reinforcing her own acted-out prohibition? Or is she mockingly turning it back to me?
(She will do this again, four days later [Episode 34].) Chubby Maata doesn't like
my intervention; she shows it in the mildest and most playful way by running
her fingernail down my cheek—not hard enough to hurt me. (Her mother
would have criticized this play, calling it *ugiat*-ing.) Then even that gently
hostile act seems to her too aggressive; she controls it further by converting it
into almost-neutral play with my face and glasses. The play is not completely
nonaggressive, however; it is still necessary for me to rescue my glasses. When I
do so, Chubby Maata switches to another form of playful, almost-concealed
aggression: impeding my writing. When I forbid this, her response is again
playful.

She doesn't echo my prohibition this time, doesn't incorporate the scolding
or return it to me; she disarms me with the affectionate behavior of a baby to her
mother. Indeed, she explicitly pretends to *be* my child, as if to say, "Don't hurt
me, I'm your darling little baby." It is a strategy she often uses when her real

mother criticizes her or, as we have seen, when she is asked an awkward question, a strategy that allows her to evade responsibility for her misbehavior, since babies, by definition, are not responsible.

There may be maturity in this strategy, too, however: the blend of controlled hostility and affection, which we saw moving toward more control and affection and less open hostility when Chubby Maata stopped scratching my cheek and began to play with my face, moves even farther in the same direction here, when she first bends her forehead to mine and then throws herself into my arms, the arms of a surrogate mother.

But I am not her mother for long. When I ask her if she really considers me so, she smilingly denies it and offers to tie the laces at my neck—an act whose motives may be as tangled as my laces after Chubby Maata's ministrations. Is she helping me and at the same time demonstrating and practicing her developing skill in tying? She has done that on other occasions. Or is she mischievously knotting me up, so that I'll never get the laces undone? She will claim that aim presently. She might even be playfully strangling me.[40] All of these motives could be involved. The sequence and combination of her actions are pretty clear evidence of a tangle: leaning against me cozily, whispering that she doesn't like me, then—still in a whisper—denying dislike and taking the evil qualities unto herself. All the motives that draw Chubby Maata in different directions— grown-up and baby, affectionate and hostile—are pulling and twisting her at once, as she twists and twists my laces.

I imagine that Chubby Maata frightened herself a little here, as I think she did in Episode 35, when she pretended I was her mother, and she may have been even more alarmed when I cross-examined her on that claim. She doesn't *really* want me to be her mother, any more than she wants Maata to adopt her (Episode 9) or wants to swap fathers with Saali (Episode 11). She may also be playing again with the complexly good and bad qualities of mothers—those bad qualities including, this time, my own recent prohibitions; playing, too, a little farther on, with her own goodness and badness, as she has done before.

Chubby Maata tries out two "solutions" to her dilemmas. First, she pretends—with a certain diffidence (is it *ilira-*?)—that she is an evil spirit, a move that allows her both to explain her antisocial actions and feelings and to take responsibility for them in a playful mode that is halfway to serious. More, it puts her back in a potentially dominant position over me, one from which she can scare me if necessary. But she doesn't try to scare me; she suggests—again with diffidence—that we go home to her real mother, where she will presumably be safe, from bad mothers and even from evil spirits. This retreat to babyhood is her other solution. Her whisper tells us, I think, that she knows she has gotten herself into a tight spot. Perhaps, for the moment, she has reached the limits of her ability to play with goodness and badness, with affection and hostility, and with pretend mothers who might turn real.

Nevertheless, when I don't respond to her suggestion that we go to her real mother, she goes on playing, and her behavior continues to reflect a mixture of feelings as she sings and hums a pious hymn and continues to twist the lace at my neck, impishly announcing that I won't be able to undo it. First of all, the hymn, though it may be just coincidence (it is probably the only one that Chubby Maata knows), seems extraordinarily appropriate to the circumstances: "Follow Him, follow Him, Jesus, follow Him; over there, over here, I will never fear (*kappia-*)."[41] Indeed, if I won't take her to her all-succoring mother, perhaps Jesus will rescue her.

But is it still the little tunraq who is humming so comfortably and tangling up my laces? Liila would again have said that Chubby Maata was *ugiat*-ing: killing or, in the human case, attacking, without weapons, as dogs do, out of an access of affection. And remembering the little girl cozily leaning against me, happily humming and choking me, I wonder whether I was indeed seeing one of the childhood origins of that adult blend of tenderness and aggression.

Is it possible that Chubby Maata herself has *ugiat*-ing in mind? As she twists my laces, she returns to the subject of the new puppies. She has gone to visit the puppies but (I heard from Rosi) has been warned to keep her distance, because the puppies' mother is "scary" (*iqsi-*, a strong word that, like *kappia-*, refers to physical danger). Chubby Maata knows that bitches with newborn litters may protect (*sirnaaq-*) them by attacking children who come too close; she may also have been told that bitches sometimes kill (*ugiat-*) their own pups to protect them from intruders. Yes, indeed, mothers can be very scary.

So Chubby Maata's return to the subject of the new puppies could be either a baby confidence and a request for reassurance or a grown-up attempt at conversation or both. The whisper is a clue to the presence of dangerous feelings, though she seems to find it safer now to express nervousness about those puppies than it was at the beginning of the visit.

The play with my cuff is repetitive, even a little perseverative, and perhaps calming. Certainly it is safer than the aggressively toned twisting at my neck, the tangling that I "won't be able to undo." I sense in my little companion an emotionally neutral (perhaps a bit tentative?) connection with me, now, neither hostile nor affectionate, neither *kappia-* nor *ilira-*—a retreat from tension. It is as though Chubby Maata has reached a momentary equilibrium in her feelings or is taking a rest from the intense and troubling ones.

At this point, Chubby Maata is also able to be appropriately sensitive to entering visitors. Her response to adult footsteps shows us that she has learned a thing or two about the behavior that is expected of her when visiting and that, in general, she has begun to feel *ilira-* where it is called for. We have seen that *ilira-* behavior occasionally appears even with me, although most of the time Chubby Maata continues to treat me, in the absence of critical adults, in a rather special way which she knows the adults toward whom she feels *ilira-* would not approve of were they to see it. Her doting father is charmed by her "equilibrated" visiting behavior—babylike in its un-*ilira-* quality but at the same time maturely quiet—and does not criticize.

When Chubby Maata finally leaves, she leaves alone, not with her father, nor yet with her young uncle Juda, though the timing of her departure seems triggered by Juda's. She doesn't ask me to go with her either, as she did when she first thought of leaving. Her movement now is independent, autonomous, grown-up—a thread that has been strong throughout much of her visit and is perhaps stronger yet in this moment of equilibrium.

JOURNEY OUT OF BABYHOOD

It appears that Chubby Maata has an ongoing problem of how to incorporate me into her life. I am a puzzle, an anomaly even in a world in which other of her associates are still not fully categorized.[42] I am sometimes motherlike but not kin and not responsible for her care; a Qallunaaq and a relatively new entrant into her world but no longer a stranger; occasionally scary but nowhere near as scary as strange Qallunaat; sometimes even a playfellow. In my benign modes—good mother, admirer, playfellow—I provide tea with milk and bannock with butter and jam; I help and hold, enter into play and conversation. When I am bad, however, I withhold tea and bannock, prohibit play, and occasionally scold. Bad *mother*? The incident of the doll play suggests this role, as do occasional ambiguous references to mothers and hostile-affectionate baby behavior. But often and overtly, it is my Qallunaaq origins that are drawn on as a perceived source of badness; as an insulting epithet, a tool in expressing hostility; and possibly also, on occasion, as a means of keeping the good separate from the bad: mother is good, Qallunaaq is bad.

All this complexity—enhanced by Liila's warnings—certainly creates for

Chubby Maata some uncertainty about what to expect and, as we have seen, arouses uncomfortable ambivalence: dislike and liking, fear and attraction. At the same time, my presence creates opportunities for Chubby Maata. Both because I interrogate and curb much less than other adults do outside her home and because she is not firmly bonded to me—she doesn't really need me, emotionally or socially—she is much less *ilira-* of me than of other nonfamily adults, and so she has a certain freedom of action with me that she doesn't have with others. She has discovered that when other adults are absent, she can practice and play with roles and express dangerous likes and dislikes, by and large without fear that she will be asked awkward questions about them. And this freedom of action gives *us* a golden opportunity to watch her mind at work. So what do we learn from Episodes 35 and 36 about Chubby Maata's journey out of babyhood? And how does she use me in that progress?

The first thing that strikes the eye is how grown-up Chubby Maata's self-presentation is during much of both visits. It is a relaxed, un-*ilira-* performance that Liila (unlike me) would certainly not consider appropriate, let alone adult. Chubby Maata repeatedly demonstrates and dramatizes her knowledge of the world and the skills, both social and physical, that she has acquired, and she tries to acquire new ones. She is playing with and practicing the behavior of her elders. Nonetheless, in the first visit, when she reaches the limit of her abilities, she reverts easily to babyhood: she asks that her pants be pulled up; she asks to be held.

These two reversions are not alike, however; nor are their consequences. After asking me to help her with her trousers—a request for practical assistance—she returns without difficulty to adult conversation about my flooring, and the tone of her talk is helpful. This comfortable seesawing between more and less grown-up selves strikes a snag after Chubby Maata's second baby gesture. This gesture, a request for intimate contact, might or might not have had a playful or experimental element in it, but it certainly contained a good measure of the serious—I read it at the time as wholly and innocently serious— and so I think it might have frightened a "baby" who was no longer quite a baby. It could have frightened her in more than one way. If Chubby Maata was not quite certain that she wanted her mother to hold her tightly, not quite sure that her mother would hold her securely if she wanted it, or not quite sure how free she was to come and go at her own will, she might fear that, like Maata, I might hold on too tightly and steal her from her real mother. I have suggested that, in making the two contrary pronouncements, "You're bad" and "You're good," Chubby Maata might have been, among other things, experimenting with the dangerous qualities of mothers—or merely with the dangerous business of disliking and liking in general: how close is it safe to come? She might also have been employing a little hostility to create a safe distance between us two dangerously connected individuals. In any case, I think it's clear that badness and goodness are problematic for Chubby Maata and also that she senses danger in the cozy, baby attachment—to me and to her own mother—that a large part of her still wants to have.[43]

At the beginning of the second visit, Chubby Maata again dramatizes how grown-up she can be. The Baby of this visit is different, however. She is not a *real* baby, she is an actress, and her performance has manipulative purposes. She does not appear on stage until I have twice frustrated Chubby Maata, the first time by inadvertently failing to recognize her mature attempt at self-control (when she refrains from touching the wick-trimmer) and the second time by blocking her vengeful interferences with my glasses, face, and pencil—gestures that in their playfulness were also mature. I have pushed Chubby Maata back into babyness; she assumes the role of the "darling baby" in an attempt to conciliate an aggressor and avert incipient conflict. Of course, to be successful, a darling baby has to have an opposite number, a mother to wrap around her little finger, hence the declaration "I consider you my mother." But in so claiming, Chubby Maata has again inadvertently created a dangerous connection, and again she retreats, denying my motherness and asserting, this time, not that I am bad but that she dislikes me. At the same time, her smile gives witness that she is still playing the darling baby, she maintains the term (-*gi*-) that connects her with me,[44] and she whispers, as though uneasy (*ilira-?*) about what she is saying. Then, when I question her dislike of me, she denies that, too, and transfers badness from me to the little tunraq—herself—though she continues to twist my laces in a slightly perilous way. She seems again torn between affection and hostility and perhaps aware at some level that whatever she says is dissonant with some part of her rather complicated feelings. There may also be a grain of awareness that disliking *me* makes *her* bad from the point of view of her elders and that a show of weakness is more productive than a display of strength—the plot that we saw limned in Chapter 5.

This is a more mature plot than that of Episode 35, in which Chubby Maata first asserts flatly that I'm bad, then equally flatly reverses her judgment, says that I'm good, and agrees that she is good, too. But both versions sound as though Chubby Maata were on the way to acquiring a complex image of mothers, even though she still can't label both the good and the bad person "mother" and (in Episode 36) wants to be taken home to the safe shelter of her good—real—mother.

The incident of the wick-trimming stick and the little tunraq of Episode 36 also give us a glimpse of a complex Chubby Maata in embryonic form—a Chubby Maata who can take some responsibility for her actions and recognize that she is not perfectly darling (-*kuluk*). (Compare also Episode 18 in Chapter 5.) When Chubby Maata withdraws her hand from the trimmer and smiles at me, I think we are finally seeing *ilira-,* the fear of criticism, in the making. Conscience as well.[45] Both phenomena seem to be fertilized by Chubby Maata's ambivalence about my uncomfortably tangled nature—ambivalence that makes it dangerous to label me bad. In taking the tunraq identity upon herself, Chubby Maata creates a locus for badness that preserves the all-goodness of both her mothers and at the same time takes a step toward seeing *herself* as a complex person who can both appeal for love and claim unworthiness. If Klein's argument (1975b)—that destructive anger is the origin of protective love—applies in Inuit contexts, it may be that affection (*nallik-*) is actually being created in this situation. At the same time, perhaps there is still a possibility that the little evil spirit may frighten me, hurt me, and so make herself feel just a little stronger.

So the tension between affection and hostility in Chubby Maata's relationship with me pushes her forward toward adulthood, even while it pulls her back into babyhood. She is moving closer to recognizing that she lives in a complicated world in which goodness and badness, liking and disliking, are found in one and the same person, whether that person is a mother, an other, or herself. Drawing on mature skills as well as baby ones, she experiments with behaviors that simultaneously express ambivalent feelings and further her fundamentally incompatible aims. And in her playfully controlled actions, we can see another sort of growth: the ability to *perform* and, conversely, to mask real aspects of herself.[46]

Chubby Maata dramatizes both positive and negative feelings, simultaneously concealing and displaying the negative in the positive. Moreover, in her performances, real emotions and false but useful ones are already intricately blended. It is clear that Chubby Maata *feels* both affection and hostility toward me. It is equally clear that she is *using* those feelings to serve her purposes. She needs hostility to defend herself against my bad behavior, whether that of "mother" or "Qallunaaq"; she needs it also to defend herself against her own dangerous liking for me in my benign manifestations. When she evicts me from

the role of mother and reverts to the position she has held for several months—
that she doesn't like me—she does it partly for reasons of safety. The trouble is
that, as we know, dislike isn't altogether safe, either. How can she stay in my
good graces if she feels that way? She has been told repeatedly that hostility does
not lead to offers of tea and other good things. Moreover, she does like me. So
she tries to conciliate, to disarm and soothe me, by expressing affection, performing it as a *babykuluk* would do. In this baby performance we can see
foreshadowed the outlines of adult Inuit conflict management: conciliation,
and the suppression of hostility in serious mode while expressing it in aggressive
play and under the cover of nurturant concern (*nallik-*).

Liila would have been particularly pleased by one other feature of Chubby
Maata's behavior during her second visit: the whispers. Here we have a strong
indication that at long last, as a result of the tension between hostility and
affection or attraction, Chubby Maata is beginning, now and again, to show
not only toward others but toward me something that looks like *ilira-*. These
whispers give me a dramatic sense of the unease that underlies adult *ilira-*
feelings.

A SHARE OF THE GOODIES: PRACTICING PERSUASION

Chubby Maata demonstrates in her relationship with me that the problems of
managing attachment that have been presented to her by her elders are working
in her, even though her goals and strategies are not always the same as theirs.

The management of ambivalent feelings is not the only issue that concerns
Chubby Maata, however. A major problem in the last weeks of my stay in her
camp—a problem she shared with nearly everyone else—was how to acquire a
share of the goodies that I was certain to leave behind. Visiting me, men and
children alike[47] often joked, "Watch, Yiini, I'm going to steal ————" or
"You're going to give me ———— as a remembrance, aren't you?" Occasionally
people even said, "I'm going to kill you so I can have ————." Chubby Maata
and her small peers participated in these "theft" games—never more charmingly than one day just before I left. On that occasion, Chubby Maata and
Miika were talking to each other playfully in my qammaq. Their game of turn-
taking was modeled on an adult way of developing a joking narrative.

Episode 37 (March 24)

Said Miika to Chubby Maata, "When she leaves, she'll leave her things. Her
boots."

"And her pack," said Chubby Maata.

"And her parka."

"And her sleeping bag."

"And her sweater."

"And these things, too." Chubby Maata waved at the food on my side platform.

"Let's steal," said Miika, grinning at me impishly.

"Yes, let's," said Chubby Maata.

This play, however, was initiated by Miika, who was a year and eight months older than Chubby Maata. To conclude this portrait of Chubby Maata's three-year-old mind, I want to describe two versions of her own ways of addressing the problem of Yiini's Possessions. The first incident (Episode 38) occurred at the beginning of March, the second (Episode 39) at the end of the month, on the same day as the game we've just looked at (Episode 37). The first of Chubby Maata's two attempts to acquire my goods failed, and it is an interesting case because it shows us that the right way to go about getting what you want when you are adult is the wrong way when you are three. The second attempt was much more sophisticated. It was also undertaken when Chubby Maata and I were alone together. And it succeeded—or so Chubby Maata thought. Whether or not it really succeeded, it is of interest because it shows us how very much Chubby Maata has learned about the principles and the logic of adult relationships in her world. Almost all the lessons I have described in this book are reflected in the strategies that Chubby Maata uses in the second episode to get a piece of bannock. But first the failure.

Episode 38 (March 2)

Chubby Maata came in alone to visit me, sat down on the sleeping platform, waved her hands toward the two side platforms where I kept foodstuffs, cooking equipment, and various other things, and said, "When you leave, I'm going to acquire those things."

Chubby Maata knew her games quite well, but she didn't reckon with her audience. Unfortunately for her, her grandfather Mitaqtuq was also there, drinking a cup of tea. He didn't say, "Oh, really?" smile, or ignore her, as I might have done. He said, "What things?" His back had been turned to Chubby Maata when she waved. I replied for her: "Those things," pointing to the food platform. Mitaqtuq, in a mildly disapproving voice, said to his granddaughter, "She (meaning Chubby Maata) is ignorant (*qauyimangngit-*)." But Chubby Maata, in the saccharine-persuasive voice that she had often heard from adults addressing her, blithely continued: "Leave! Do leave!"

This time her grandfather's tone was sharper: "She's ignorant!" Chubby Maata seemed to pay no attention. She picked up a small box of matches that lay beside her on the sleeping platform and tucked them under her shirt, smiling at me: "I'm going to take these."

Mitaqtuq said: "No. Put them down. You'll burn yourself." I too said, "No!" But it was unnecessary; Chubby Maata had already put the matches down, in response to her grandfather's prohibition.

Mitaqtuq himself was one of the most frequent players of the games he forbade his granddaughter to play with me; but then, his age, his gender, his reputation as a joker, and perhaps also my special relationship with his family gave him license.[48] Chubby Maata's imitation of her elders' game was fairly accurate. An adult or older child would have focused on one specific item at a time, rather than encompassing with a sweep of the arm everything I owned, and would have discreetly referred to my *eventual* departure, instead of trying to rush the event. But the plot was right, and the voice was perfection itself. How was Chubby Maata to know that the bald and brutal questions that *she* was asked in play—"Can I have *you*? Right now?"—were out of place here? She did not realize that it was inappropriate for children to initiate such games with adults, especially with outsiders. Children, as we know, should show *ilira-* restraint with these people.

Moreover, as I have mentioned before in connection with *ugiat*-ing, children were not always trusted to keep "antisocial" actions safely within the bounds of play. Here too, I think, Mitaqtuq genuinely feared that Chubby Maata might cause a dangerous fire if she had matches in her possession.

Let's look now at Chubby Maata's inventiveness on a later occasion when she and I were alone together and she had a much freer rein.

Episode 39 (March 24)

Chubby Maata came in, opening my damp-swollen door by her own efforts without asking for help.[49] Sitting down on the sleeping platform, as usual, she announced, "I'm not going to fetch." Bannock, she meant. I said, "Hurray!" Perhaps accidentally, she pulled slightly awry the caribou hide that she was sitting on and remarked, "I broke it." Then she patted two of the hides and said, "This is your mattress and that is . . . " (I missed the end of that sentence.)

Chubby Maata gave a little bounce and smiled at me, a gesture that was characteristic of her in her baby mode, but she didn't take possession of it; she said, "*Kaati* does this."

She touched the tea kettle, which I had hung over the seal-oil lamp to heat just before she came in. "It's not hot," she observed. I said, "Ee," agreeing with her. She repeated her action several times, saying each time, "I'm not burned."

She sang a little song about somebody stabbing or being stabbed (*kapi-*); I wasn't sure which, but I thought that she might have been singing about the doctor or nurse in Pangnirtung, who gave children shots.

I think it was right after the song that she remarked, "Because you're not a Qallunaaq, are you?" I said, "Ee (that's right)." Chubby Maata continued, "You're not Yiini." "Who am I, then?" I asked. "Kiuna," said Chubby Maata, inventing a name. It belonged to no one she knew, and I don't believe it was a name at all, but it rhymed with the name of her young aunt Liuna.

After a bit, she said, "I've just come to fetch bannock." I pretended not to hear her. Chubby Maata then engaged in the following activities.

Using a chanting voice reminiscent of the one that her grandmother Arnaq-juaq had used in playing "BAAAD" with her (Episode 16), Chubby Maata said, "Give me ———." I imagine it was bannock she asked for, though I missed the word.

Then, still in a "play" voice—was it the same chant?—she said, "Give me bannock and I'll give *you* something." The word she used, *payuk-,* though her baby tongue tripped over it, was the word that adults used when they took or sent people a gift of food.[50] She went on: "I'm not going to payuk- you anymore."

I asked, wickedly, "Have you ever payuk-ed me?" "Ee," said Chubby Maata. I pressed her: "What (did you give me)?" Chubby Maata said: "Candy and ——— and ———." She named several items, which I failed to record; all were inventions. She repeated these promises and threats several times, always in a playfully exaggerated voice, but she was no longer using the chanting tone that recalled accusations of badness. Once, when she was threatening not to *payuk-* me, she said, "Because I'm going to kill you." Her voice was cheerful or playful.

Then Chubby Maata hid her face in her hands and "cried" in a mock-crying voice: "My faaather—my faaather—because I miss (*unga-*) him." (Jaani, to-gether with most of the other men and older boys, had been away for some time, unable to come home from Pangnirtung because of dangerous, thawing ice in the sound.) Chubby Maata repeated her mournful plaint several times, and in the intervals between wails, she said, in an exaggeratedly slow, distinct, and rhythmical voice that sounded cheerful, even playful, "Give me bannock!"

After several repetitions of the father theme, she shifted to "Mother!" but the crying was still mock. And, as before, after she had "cried" a bit, she demanded in a cheerful voice, "Bannock!"

At some point, Chubby Maata also made various vocal noises, all of them shrill and some of them so piercing that I told her to stop or she'd kill me. But all the noises were cheerful.

Indeed, Chubby Maata's manner throughout her visit was either cheerful or playful, but she grew more and more single-mindedly focused on her goal, and her "arguments" escalated from "I'll reward you if you'll give me bannock" to "I'll retaliate if you don't give it" to "I'm unhappy, I'm unga-, I *need* it" to—finally—an appeal to the all-succoring mother. Every time I tried to change the subject, she returned to it, and her *direct* demands—"Give me bannock!"—increased in frequency until in the end they supplanted the dramas altogether. Nevertheless, her playfully exaggerated tone of voice never faltered.

At that point, the tea that I was heating began to steam noisily, so I said, "Let's us two have tea." Immediately, Chubby Maata said, "Me, too." And her voice at last resumed the tone of an ordinary, conversational request.

I wanted, incorrigibly and foolishly, to make it clear to her that I was *offering* the tea, that she wasn't winning her game, so I remarked, "Yes, I just said, 'Let's us two have tea.'" She repeated: "Me, too." I gave up, then, saying, "Ee," and gave her tea, accompanied, as always—she knew it would be—by a small piece of bannock.

Chubby Maata took the bread cheerfully and bit into it. Then she said, in the voice of everyday commentary, "It's not buttered." I put butter on the remaining half.

That wasn't the end of the play, however. When Chubby Maata had finished eating and drinking, she announced, "(This is) our cup; I'm going to take it home," and she got up to leave. But instead of carrying the cup away with her, she said with a smile, "Close your eyes." She squeezed her own eyes shut to show me how. I obeyed, and Chubby Maata surreptitiously, silently, put the cup down on the side platform, where it belonged.

As she left—again opening the door without help—she said, smiling, "I'm going to steal the things in your porch." I said, "No," in an unconcerned voice. She repeated her threat and left, asking if she should shut the door tighter. I said yes. She lingered in the porch for a moment and then went out.

At the beginning of this visit, Chubby Maata again demonstrates her physical, social, and cognitive maturity: she opens a difficult door without help, announces her intention to not ask for bannock, and tells me that she knows who uses the caribou hides on my platform and how. She continues in the same vein when she distances herself from her baby behavior, observing and commenting on her "destruction" of the hide she is sitting on and attributing to Kaati the baby bounce and smile that was more characteristic of herself in baby mode than of Kaati.

Chubby Maata's baby self peeps through when she tests the tea kettle. Her wish for bannock (which she knows comes with tea) is very strong, but at the same time she assures me—and herself?—that she is aware of the danger of touching hot objects. I have the impression here that controls in the process of being internalized still need an audience.

The little song that follows and then the questions that follow the song seem to be commentaries on danger, too, as well as ways of dealing with that danger.[51] Small children often assumed that Qallunaaq women were nurses who might give them shots, and adults rang changes on this fear, sometimes reinforcing it, sometimes reassuring and comforting. Chubby Maata, as we know, has also been given other reasons to fear Qallunaat in general and Yiini in particular: we adopt children, we scold, and we aren't like her. So when Chubby Maata suggests that I'm not a Qallunaaq, she is probably assuring herself on various counts that I'm not scary—and, of course, if I'm not a Qallunaaq, then I can't be Yiini. Or even the other way around: if I'm not Yiini, then I'm not a Qallunaaq. In either case, in changing my identity, Chubby Maata pulls my sting so that I can't make her feel *ilira-*. All the more so if the name she invents for me is associated in her mind with that of Liuna, the teenage aunt with whom she is most comfortable.[52]

Now, after making me a safer antagonist, Chubby Maata introduces the primary purpose of her visit: the acquisition of bannock. And her strategies, which combine the naive directness of a baby with the playfulness of an adult, show us how very much she has learned—as well as a few things she has not learned—about the rules that govern interpersonal relations in her world.

Chubby Maata begins with a direct and matter-of-fact statement: "I've just come to fetch bannock." Like many of Chubby Maata's direct requests, this one doesn't work, whereupon Chubby Maata, as often before, resorts to play. (Compare the scene in Episode 1, in which Chubby Maata tries to oust Rosi from her position between Liila's knees.)

The chanting voice in which Chubby Maata chooses to express her wish may be borrowed from one or more of several people. It is the voice of "*piungngit-tuuq* (he, she, or it is BAAAD)!" Arnaqjuaq used it powerfully to criticize

Chubby Maata, her parents, and her genitals (Episode 16). Mitaqtuq and Juda use the same voice with the same verbal content to criticize the weather. And perhaps most relevantly—though I'm not absolutely sure that Chubby Maata was present—Rosi had used the tone two days earlier, changing the words. She used it first—in conjunction with a comic posture and facial expression—to ask, item after item, for everything in my qammaq: "Give me, please, ——— because I don't have ———." Then, when no gifts were forthcoming, she used it to insult me: "May your horrid hair get sopping wet; may your glasses get broken; may your note slips be thrown away . . . "[53] Chubby Maata, whether or not she heard Rosi, has chosen a voice that is both playful and powerful, a most appropriate medium through which to express a real demand. Perhaps even without defining herself as playing, she has understood the forcefulness of that mode of acting and is using it to twist my arm. Perhaps she is also telling me indirectly that I am bad because I don't give her the bannock she wants. But this playful voice works no better than the serious demand.

What if she offers reciprocity—a bribe made by an equal to an equal? Will that help her to achieve her goal? No.

What about the threat of withholding reciprocity? Now Chubby Maata takes a dominant role: she will punish me. The level of pressure is maintained, even escalated, while at the same time, maintaining the playful tone of the attempted extortion, Chubby Maata demonstrates that she is in control of her behavior and can temper her request. Alas, this works no better.

I try to turn the tables by asking, in my Protestant fashion, if Chubby Maata has "earned" the bannock. Is it true that she has given me things in the past? Chubby Maata pretends that she has and, in answer to my probe, invents specific items. This doesn't work, either. Chubby Maata repeats her promises and threats and even escalates her warnings dramatically—"I'm going to kill you"—but consistently, persistently, she maintains the playful tenor of the interaction.

Eventually, defeated in her grown-up "equal" and "dominant" roles, Chubby Maata attempts to exercise the power of weakness. She resorts to playing the unhappy baby and tries to elicit nurturant (nallik-) behavior, first from an unspecified adult, then specifically from a mother. She knows that childish distress is often attributed to unga- feelings and that such feelings are tenderly treated. She tries several styles of crying, but all of them sound happy. The fact that Chubby Maata is playing, and not seriously unga-, is exposed not only by her unreal tears but also by the interruptions in her performance of sorrow—intervals in which she reverts to a rhythmically exaggerated and naively, charmingly, explicit statement of the motive behind all this drama: "Give me bannock!"

When none of her dramatic scenes work, Chubby Maata finally, gradually, returns *almost* to her starting point, a rhythmic, repetitive, single-minded statement of her wish. However, once having adopted a playful mode of expression, she never drops it until it is clear that the wish has been granted. On the other hand, once Chubby Maata has overcome the opposition, she need not resort to play to make further requests. Her wish for butter is expressed with appropriate indirection and in an ordinary conversational tone.

We see now that Chubby Maata has learned the following principles with which to influence behavior and acquire what she needs or wants: first, you have to give in order to get; second, if you don't give, you won't get—and worse, you could be attacked; third, the deprived and woeful should be given to, and weakness may therefore be more powerful than strength; fourth, mother is the most reliable giver; and finally, requests should not be made directly, but if you do make them, a playful strategy is more likely than a serious one to be efficacious—sooner or later—in overcoming resistance. All of these principles will serve Chubby Maata well in adult life.

In her last actions, Chubby Maata reverts again to play, shifting the focus of the "I want ———" game from bannock to my other material possessions, which are still unobtainable. But not only does she playfully pretend to steal the wished-for objects, she equally playfully demonstrates—again for a potentially critical audience—that in reality she will *not* steal. She can fool me into imagining and fearing that she will steal, but she knows the truth, or creates and discovers it in demonstrating it: the fact is, she has moral principles and can act morally without being told to do so, even when she is out of sight. It sounds as though she is tempted in the porch, but if so, she overcomes the temptation. She even offers to help me—and incidentally ensures that she endures temptation in solitude, without a strengthening audience—by shutting my door tightly, tightly, against the cold breezes and against my view of her. "Look, mother, how grown-up I am."[54]

Epilogue: Episode 40 (March 26)

Two days later I left. As I waited for the plane to come, Chubby Maata said to me, "You're not going to go on the plane."

"Why (on earth)?" I asked.

In a mild version of the dramatic, throaty voice in which adults warn children about dangers, real and imaginary, Chubby Maata said, "Horrid old doctors!"

I said, "Because you don't want me to go?"

Chubby Maata raised her brows in agreement.

Conclusion: Mazes of Meaning

I am tempted to leave my readers as I left Chubby Maata on that March day a long time ago: abruptly, and with her words in their ears. A "conclusion" to a study of process is a contradiction in terms. There is no end, no totality, no final resolution to Chubby Maata's growing, and I can't recount how she continued growing or what she is like as an adult because I don't know. On the analytic plane, many aspects of the dramas remain untouched, and it would be a daunting task to pick up even a few of the questions I have dropped along the way. On the broadest scholarly level, too, there are so many different discussions that might be pursued in an afterword that I—standing, by choice, at the edge of the swirl—am at a loss to choose among them.

What is play, for example, and what does it do for social communities?[1]

What of emotions? How are they born, shaped, given meaning? What work do they do in social life? And what do small children understand of their own emotions and those of others?[2]

What is culture? Is anything left of it if we fully recognize the individuality and variety within its boundaries?[3] What does it mean to "share" a value, an attitude, a feeling? And just how individual *are* individuals, anyway?

How do children *experience* their worlds? What roles do they play in their socialization? What do small children understand of social situations?[4] Through what processes do they learn what to say, do, and feel, and what to value (Schieffelin 1979)? What experiences support—and change—those patterns of thinking, feeling, and valuing?[5] What can we learn from investigating such matters "interpretively"?[6]

What are the origins and the psychodynamics of affiliation and attachment? How are these human qualities—prerequisite for social life everywhere—emotionally shaped and played out in different cultural worlds? Are there, for example, culturally variable scenarios for the relations among attachment, trust (and mistrust), reliance on others, and self-reliance (Bowlby 1979)?

How should narrative be interpreted?[7]

How is meaning generated?

How can we take account of the roles that observers and authors play in creating, interpreting, and presenting data? What constitutes "data"? Can we speak of "truth" at all in a postmodern, deconstructed world?

All these issues, broad and broader, are under scholarly examination at this moment, and I think Chubby Maata has a little something to contribute to all of them.[8]

Moreover, as if this were not enough, debates tend to shift, questions move in and out of salience, and new ones arise all the time.[9] So instead of placing boundaries around the "relevance" of Chubby Maata, I would like to leave readers, whoever they may be, free to pursue whatever they find of interest in my "home movies" of her three-year-old life.

Nevertheless, I promised when we set out on our journey with Chubby Maata that she would show us something beyond herself, something about the kinds of generalization that a study of one individual can generate. So before we leave our little girl to continue her growing, undisturbed by anthropologists, I return briefly to that question.[10]

FROM ONE CHILD TO CULTURE

I think Chubby Maata and the adults who play with her so dramatically have given us ample evidence that examining closely the intentions, motives, understandings, and misunderstandings that are the currency of those dramas can teach us a great deal about how one child is growing, socially, emotionally, and cognitively; how she is negotiating the problems that confront her. Of course, we can't generalize about the particular problems that each child of Qipisa has to deal with or the specific understandings that each acquires, because, obviously, the details of experience—the child's family environment and daily experience in the "serious" realm; the particular structures of the dramatic sequences enacted with each child; the adults' motives for enacting a certain drama with a certain child at a certain moment in a certain way; the child's accumulated potentials for understanding the adults' words and actions; and the abilities of the adults to understand the child's responses—all these vary in each case. A complex knowledge of one child's vicissitudes can, however, suggest questions about the experience of other children that might not otherwise occur to us. Chubby Maata could be compared with Kaati, Saali, Rosi, and others to produce a densely textured picture of similarities and differences among Qipisa children—not merely in behavior and in the substance of attitudes but also in the structure of understandings and motivations, the thought-and-feeling processes that support visible and audible behaviors and attitudes. We know, when we think about it, that behavior and mental life are not likely to be related in a one-to-one way; similar inner processes may result in a range of emotional and cognitive outcomes, while similar outcomes may be underlaid by a variety of motivations. Nevertheless, in both private and scholarly life, I think we too often *attend* to action and *assume* motive, thought, and feeling. Chubby Maata and her peers may give us pause and help us to make more realistically complex our ideas about the operation of individuality in culture.[11] At the same time, they may give us a richer sense of the multilayered ramifications of culture in personal lives.

Chubby Maata has other lessons to teach us, too, both about the psychological dynamics of culture and about how children become cultural persons. These are two sides of the same coin.

First, remember that, alerted by recurrent questions in the dramas and interrogations directed at Chubby Maata, we outside observers have discovered that these events can also be analyzed in terms of themes or issues: "Are you a baby?"; "Who do you belong to?"; "Who does *this* belong to?"; "Who do you like?" We know that dramas built around these questions teach Chubby Maata to notice, and eventually to manage, her babyness; to know where home is; to recognize her friends and relatives, and to treat them properly. These are fundamental human issues, which almost certainly have to be addressed by children everywhere. Nevertheless, there are good ethnographic grounds for supposing that the "same" issues may take very different shapes in different cultural environments, be incorporated differently into everyday life, and give rise to different problems.[12] In a word, we must suspect that they participate in different plots in different worlds. The securities and dangers, pleasures and discomforts, that attend being a baby as well as belonging, loving, and being loved are not everywhere the same; they may even be elaborated in variant ways within Qipisa. Again, close attention to Chubby Maata's situation can suggest comparative questions that would not occur to us if we didn't have in-depth understanding of one case.

It was Chubby Maata who showed me that there are recurrent plots in everyday life—that, indeed, life is lived in plots, though we are more often conscious of their presence in books than at home.[13] I discovered them, as she did, in the process of tracking key questions, tones of voice, gestures, and other messages from one interaction to another.[14] Seeing her pulled and pushed in various directions by powerful dramas that enacted the probable consequences of words and actions, I discovered, as she did, that issues and their associated feelings developed, combined, and conflicted in various ways. And standing back a little farther, I found in those interlocking messages the plots we have looked at: complex, tangled, contradictory, even dangerous.

The plots that engage Chubby Maata are, of course, not created entirely through the medium of challenging questions and playful dramas. The dramas grow out of and enact everyday life, and children have everyday experiences that support and confirm the messages contained in the dramas. At the same time, the dramas are a vital force in maintaining those everyday plots; indeed, they recreate them cognitively and emotionally in every new generation. By presenting issues, usually emotionally dangerous ones, in exaggerated and personally relevant form, by blowing up the alternatives monstrously—not "Would you like to come visit me?" but "Would you like to come live with me?"; not "Look, Saali's wearing the shirt you gave him" but "He's stolen your shirt!"; not merely "Your mother's hurt her finger" but "She's going to die!"; not "May I admire your penis?" but "Shall the puppy bite it off?"—the dramas make the plots visible and salient to children. More than that, by presenting the issues in such emotionally forceful ways, they help to create the thoughts, feelings, and motives that support the culturally appropriate plots. And they create the child's sense of "being-in-the-world," the nature of his or her experience of the world.

From a child's point of view, the plots are "out there," facts of culture which she or he has to find and learn to deal with, in playfully dramatic interactions and in all other encounters. Because children are initially unable to distinguish playful statements and questions from serious ones, they experience through these emotionally powerful dramas, in intensified and vivid form, the power of others to control their lives, to act on them in dangerous ways.

At the same time, and paradoxically, because the dramas present children with questions and not answers, because they allow them to make what they perceive to be their own decisions, they enable each child to experience him- or herself as responsible for his or her own fate. In other words, exactly because, unbeknown to themselves, children are manipulated as "objects" in these dramas, they can experience themselves as efficacious actors, as "subjects," helping to create the plots of their lives. The plots, the perils, enter Chubby Maata's life very directly as dilemmas, problems of how to *act*. Chubby Maata wants safe and satisfying relationships and possessions, and in order to get them, she must make decisions, sometimes very difficult ones, about how to behave. In making choices, she activates the plots, imbues them with personal meaning, and thus makes them real. We may say that she *creates* personal variants of the plots that govern her parents' lives, and in so doing, she is both creating herself and being created. In her actions, culture and person actively create each other.

Adults, too, certainly reaffirm their own emotional commitment to their worlds and so both recreate culture and renew themselves as they dramatize, manage, and sometimes negotiate the issues in their own lives through their charged interactions with children.[15] The emotional involvement of adults in the dramas may intensify the involvement of the children as well, and heighten the children's sense that the play is serious and real. And I suspect that it is because adults have profound reasons of their own for enjoying the play that the dramas endure from generation to generation. So I think we can begin to see some of the ways in which the world of Qipisa—and perhaps other worlds, too—come to be cognitively structured, emotionally experienced, and reproduced by those who have grown up in them.

Further, watching Chubby Maata thread her way through mazes of intentions, motives, understandings and misunderstandings, questions and counter-questions, plots and subplots, we see with new eyes how richly tangled are the structures that people in interaction create. It can also make us aware of the labyrinth of potential and shifting meanings that children have to trace out repeatedly, and repeatedly try to make *temporary* sense of, by selecting links; by codifying perceptions; by forming, testing, and revising hypotheses about relationships and about consequences of action; and so on. I suspect that Chubby Maata's journey has much in common with the processes we all go through as we struggle to create meaning.

At the same time, following Chubby Maata's steps can increase our sense of the potentials for diversity in the understandings that individuals within one society may build. (I stress the *potentials* and not the *fact* of diversity, for reasons I come to presently.)

My first attempts to understand Inuit dramas moved me some distance in this direction.[16] When I saw mothers playfully teaching their babies—who should grow up pacific—to enjoy biting and throwing stones at them, I was reminded that the motives underlying values, attitudes, and behaviors are not always straightforward and simple (Briggs 1978). People may behave generously because they fear their stingy inclinations or may act with fierce independence because they fear being dependent. They may reject others because they love them or treat them with warm concern because they fear them—or because they enjoy and fear their own aggressive impulses. So I learned to look beneath the *substance* of culture—"values," "attitudes," and "behaviors"—to find how these surface phenomena are generated and *experienced,* to find the emotional resonances and motives that underlie them. (See, for example, Briggs 1975, 1982.)

But taking dramas out of the distinctive contexts in which they occurred, as I did at first, and assigning meanings to the words and gestures of the drama according to my own logic and sense of likelihood, instead of observing the child's reactions to the messages and the adult's responses to these reactions, allowed me to slip easily into the assumption that all children understood the messages in the same way: in the way *I* analyzed them. I am sure, now, that this was an illusion.[17] Looking at the dramas played with Chubby Maata, retaining all the details of the interactions in those contexts, led me to a more complicated notion of the nature of "sharedness" in society, a notion that Wallace (1961) pointed us toward a long time ago and that postmodernists and deconstructionists have lately rediscovered with a new twist (or twists). I suddenly saw the possibilities for individual variation with respect to all the variables I had previously distinguished: the overt substance of values and behaviors, their underlying meanings, and the processes by which they are acquired and maintained. Perhaps the values of some of these variables may be shared to some extent by some individuals some of the time, but the nature and extent of this sharing must remain open questions. Not only may individuals differ among themselves, but also any one individual may differ from himself or herself at different points in time.[18]

Thus one little girl has introduced me to a view of culture—Inuit culture, and perhaps culture in general—that is far more complex than the one I held before I met her. Led by Chubby Maata, I have come to share with other scholars of the 1990s an interest in the processes through which culture may be organized and created in the minds and bodies of those who participate in it. As I said in the Introduction, I see culture now as a collection of materials that are available for selection[19]—that is, available for being invested with affect, hence meaning. And I think that one of the ways in which this emotional investment may be brought about is by creating a sense of problem, a personally relevant and even dangerous problem, that focuses first attention and then efforts to solve or cope with the problem. In other words, ties among the elements of culture—elements in themselves disparate—are created by affectively motivated resonances which build plots around problems. I wonder, indeed, whether it is the problematic elements in culture that keep it active, alive in the awareness of its carriers and flexible, responsive to change.[20]

I see Inuit culture experienced by one three-year-old—and, by extrapolation, other Inuit—as a mosaic of dilemmas which echo, cross-cut, confirm, and negate one another; dilemmas that are never totally resolved but have to be juggled and rearranged time after time. The fact that the Inuit adults I know are continually watchful, constantly testing the responses of others, argues that a habit of living with dilemmas—continually constructed and reconstructed as experience changes—carries over into adulthood and lasts a lifetime.

In addition to giving us a richer and more complex picture of the psychological structure of values, attitudes, and behaviors and of the possibilities for individual diversity at various levels of analysis, Chubby Maata has shown us how *actively* emotions, values, and attitudes as well as behavior are negotiated in the learning of them, through question and answer, response and counter-response. And since anything that is negotiated may be renegotiated, I think we can also see clearly now the possibilities for flux and change in any individual's understandings of his or her world. In Chubby Maata's world, patterns of resonance among phrases, questions, tones of voice, and so on shift continually as each new repetition of a question modifies, even kaleidoscopes, the lessons contained in previous dramas and creates new lessons. It is, then, impossible for a child to acquire a "total" and fixed set of understandings. There is no total culture.

The impossibility of an observer's acquiring a total and fixed set of understandings follows as a matter of course. When one opens one's eyes to the multifaceted and untidy interrelationships that characterize everyday life, there are always new angles from which the data can be analyzed. One question leads to another—for anthropologists as well as for Chubby Maata—because there is no totality and no permanence to the meaning-structures she is building.[21]

Appendix 1: Additional Episodes and Unabridged Episodes

CHAPTER 3

Episode A1 (October 29)

(The section in bold type is Episode 5).

Liila and Chubby Maata came to visit me. The first order of business was refreshment: tea for Liila, water and bannock for Chubby Maata. While Chubby Maata was eating, Liila took her daughter's piece of bannock from her, put it in her own mouth, and pretended to swallow it. Chubby Maata was not distressed; she smiled and remarked that the bread was "gone"—whereupon Liila took part of it out of her mouth and gave it back to her daughter. (I wondered whether perhaps Chubby Maata knew all along that the bread wasn't gone.)

At some point while she was eating, Chubby Maata said something about the milk on my side platform. I didn't hear the beginning of this exchange but tuned in when Liila said, "Take it home." Chubby Maata smiled self-consciously and ducked her head sideways toward her mother in a gesture that also looked self-conscious. Liila repeated several times, "Take it home." Chubby Maata continued to smile and wrinkled her nose: "No." "Why (not)?" asked her mother. Chubby Maata said, "Because I'm scary (*kappia-*)."[1] Puzzled by her misconstructed word, I said, "What?" Chubby Maata didn't answer. (More self-consciousness?) Liila again told her several times to take the milk home, but Chubby Maata consistently refused.

Chubby Maata chattered steadily, asking her mother questions, the subject of which escaped me. Among other things, Chubby Maata presented Liila with a list of names, all of which Liila rejected ("no," "no," "no"), one after the other. I wonder now, looking at what happened next, whether Chubby Maata was asking her mother what her names were, though I never otherwise heard her (or any other child) do this. Another more likely possibility is that she was asking who did something or other. In any case, Liila finally said, in an affectionate but protesting tone, "That darling little one is pretending to ask a lot of questions!" Chubby Maata persisted nevertheless, until Liila said, "You." Chubby Maata repeated, questioning, "You?" Liila: "You."

At this point, I lost some of the interaction. When I began paying attention again, Chubby Maata was standing in front of her mother, sucking a lollipop. Liila beamed at her and held out her arms, saying something in a tender (*aqaq*-ing) tone. Chubby Maata smiled her broad baby smile at her and came to her. Liila *aqaq*-ed her daughter, held her close, and snuffed her face long and hard. Then she said to her, "Who are you?" "What?" queried Chubby Maata. "Who are you?" her mother asked again. "Chubby Maata," said the little girl. "Who else?" "Malvina" (her other English name). "Who else?" "Kaati," said Chubby Maata. (I think she was naming her friend, not herself, this time.) "Who else?" "Luisa." (The name belonged to Liila's sister.) "Who else?" "Rosi" (her own sister). "Who else?" "Chubby Maata Malvina." "Who else?" "Rosi."

Liila did not succeed in eliciting any of Chubby Maata's Inuit names. Instead, she began to recite words for her daughter to imitate: " . . . baby—not baby—baby—not baby . . . " Instead of repeating the words, Chubby Maata smiled her broad baby smile at her mother, a *qaqa*-ing smile. Liila said something in a tender *niviuq*-ing voice about Chubby Maata's being a sweet little (-*kuluk*) baby and then said, "Say 'ungaa.'" Chubby Maata said, "Ungaaa," in a more or less matter-of-fact voice, not imitating the sound of a cry, but with her baby smile. Liila *aqaq*-ed and snuffed her. Chubby Maata interrupted her by pointing to the skylight and asking in a conversational voice, "What's that out there?" Her mother, also in a conversational voice, replied, "Sila." (The word means weather, outdoors, the world.)

The last game of the visit was initiated by Chubby Maata, who began to ask her mother: "Who's at our house? Rosi?" "No." "My father?" "No." "Luukasi?" (naming the two-year-old adopted son of her paternal grandparents). Her list was longer, but I didn't record the other names she mentioned. In the middle of Chubby Maata's interrogation, Liila heard Rosi crying outside, and she and Chubby Maata went out to investigate.

Episode A2 (October 29)
(The section in bold type is Episode 4.)

A couple of hours after Episode 5, Chubby Maata came back, this time with her father, Jaani. Jaani sat down on the sleeping platform, and Chubby Maata sat between her father's knees with his arms around her. Pointing to one of my seal-oil lamps (a *qulliq*), Chubby Maata asked her father, "What's that?" She knew full well what the answer was. Jaani said: "A qulliq. Because you're charmingly lacking in understanding (*silait . . . kuluk . . .*)?"[2] His voice was affectionate, *niviuq*-ing. I didn't see her response, if indeed she made one.

Jaani then asked, "Are you a baby?" Chubby Maata wrinkled her nose. Jaani's arms were still around her, and his voice was tender. "Say 'ungaa,'" he said. Chubby Maata wrinkled her nose.

A little later, Jaani poured a cup of tea for his daughter and asked her, "Are you going to put milk in it?" Chubby Maata smiled self-consciously. He asked again, "Are you going to put milk in it?" She smiled again and said, "I don't own it." He said something in a reassuring tone of voice—I didn't catch the words—and put milk in her tea. She accepted it.

Episode A3 (November 29)
(The section in bold type is Episode 2.)

Liila came in with Chubby Maata and started to trim my lamp wick. Chubby Maata, watching her mother, asked in a conversational voice, "Do those bite?" Liila replied in an abstracted voice, "Mmm." Not understanding what Chubby Maata was referring to, I asked, "What?" She repeated her question: "Do they bite?" She was looking at the white, fuzzy catkins, material for lamp wicks, which were drying beside the lamp.[3] I said, "Ee (yes)." Chubby Maata didn't seem distressed; she played with the oily scrap of cardboard on which I rested the wick-trimmer. Liila warned her off several times—"It's all sooty!"—but to no avail.

A few minutes later Chubby Maata began to say to her mother, "Let's go home." I asked her, "Because you're going to do what?" Chubby Maata replied, "Because I'm going to suck a bottle—at our house." I questioned

further: "Because you're a baby?" Chubby Maata raised her brows, then beamed her shining baby smile, clapped her hands, and turning to her mother, said, "I *am* a babykuluk, *aren't* I?" Liila smiled: "Mmm." "Come, then," Chubby Maata urged, "Let's go home!" Liila got up and they left.

CHAPTER 4

Episode A4 (January 14)

The newly married Maata and I were visiting in Tiimi's and Rota's house. Their daughter, Miika, who was not quite five, was also at home. Maata, sitting on the side platform, said to Miika, a child she was particularly fond of, "Who are you?" Miika said, "Ukaliq." It was her Inuktitut name, the name of the deceased wife of her great-grandfather Natsiq. Maata hugged her and said: "Have you been a baby for a long, long time (*babytuqaaluuvit*)? Are you very very baby (*babypaaluuvit*)?[4] Ki-i-ss (me)." Maata drew out the word in a playful way, but not in the crooning tone that was usually used by adults when they invited small children to snuff them. She said to Miika: "Like this. This is how you'll kiss someday (she used a remote-future verb form). Give me your tongue." And she kissed Miika, a long, deep French (and very un-Inuit) kiss, while Tiimi, Rota, and I watched with some fascination. Tiimi said, "Is that how *you* kiss?" I didn't record Maata's answer. Miika's face, both during the kiss and afterward, was expressionless.

Tiimi then said to me: "Come sit on my knees. Want a baby? I'll give you one." I expect I laughed and said, "No!"—my usual response to sexual joking. (An interrogation followed concerning my difficulties with a flirtatious visitor from Pangnirtung.)

CHAPTER 5

Episode A5 (November 17)

Saali, not quite three years old, came with his uncle Paulusi to pay a visit in Chubby Maata's house. As visitors do on entering, they stood politely by the door. Liila smiled at Saali and said: "What a nice little visitor! Shall we acquire him?" Saali wrinkled his nose: "No." But Jaani smilingly elaborated his wife's overture, offering Saali in exchange for himself one goody after another: baking powder, jam, crackers . . . At each offer, Saali glared and raised his arm in a threat gesture.

Then Liila and Jaani turned to Chubby Maata and, in the dramatic tone of excited anticipation that was used with small children, asked *her:* "Shall we acquire him?" Chubby Maata beamed and ran to Saali. I had the impression that she was delighted at the idea of having a resident playmate. But Saali again raised his arm in a threat gesture and batted and kicked at Chubby Maata. And when Chubby Maata tried to pull him into the room, he shrieked. His eyes all this time were wide and staring, and his face was stiff and frightened-looking.

Jaani came and picked up Saali bodily, brought him kicking and yelling into the room, and put him down. Everybody present laughed or smiled in amusement at Saali's loud resistance.

Jaani offered other goodies: a stapler ("Listen!"—crack—"It's a toy gun!") and, finally, a camera. But again, each time, Saali glared and raised his arm in the threat gesture.

Then Jaani said to Saali, in a "persuasive" voice, "Let me touch your penis." Saali didn't move. Jaani turned down the pressure lantern so that it was nearly dark and approached Saali with his hand held out toward Saali's crotch (which was clothed). Saali made a loud protesting noise, a wordless cry characteristic of Inuit children.

Chubby Maata brought a can of something out of the cupboard, probably intending to eat its contents. Liila said to her: "Yes, let's buy him for that. A little boy . . . he has a darling little penis. Shall we buy him? Take that can to his mother." Saali made a protest noise again and went to sit on his uncle's knees. (Paulusi was by then sitting on the couch at the far end of the room, opposite the door.)

Jaani followed Saali and continued to poke his finger into Saali's open fly. At one point I thought Saali's expression was slightly dreamy.

Next, Jaani picked up a dead seal fetus, which was lying on the floor with a string around its neck, a small basket attached to the string.[5] Chubby Maata and Rosi had been playing with the fetus. Jaani brought it toward Saali's penis and said, "It's going to bite your penis!" Saali watched with a stiff, frightened face.

Liila's grown brother Juupi came in and began to poke *his* finger into Saali's fly, while Jaani retreated to the other end of the room and began to fix the camera. Juupi asked, "Shall I bite it?" and then pretended the fetus would bite or eat Saali's penis. Saali protested. Juupi began twisting the string of the fetus and the basket around Saali's boot and then pretended to pull the boots off. Saali again protested. Next, Juupi began pulling Saali off his uncle's lap, telling him when he protested that it was Chubby Maata who was doing it.[6] Sometimes, indeed, he told Chubby Maata to do it, and she obeyed. Saali protested each time and climbed back up. All these protests took the same form: Saali cried out wordlessly, raised his hand in a threat gesture—though he never struck out—and withdrew his legs from the attacker. His face was stiff and wide-eyed in fear. Juupi, laughing, continued his pulling game as Saali's protests escalated in volume.

Just once, Saali laughed, very briefly, as Juupi pulled him off Paulusi's lap; and then Juupi said, "*Now* he's beginning to just smile!" But Saali reverted to protests, and the game continued. Once Juupi asked Saali, "Are you getting ilira-?" I didn't see Saali's answer. Paulusi sat passively, neither helping nor hindering the proceedings.

Now Liila's sixteen-year-old brother, Pitaruusi, came in and sat down in the middle of the couch, between Liila and Saali, who was at this point sitting beside Paulusi rather than on his lap. Pitaruusi pretended to pull down Saali's pants in back. He also "attacked" Saali's penis; I'm not sure whether he said "let me bite" or "see" or "touch it." In any case, Saali shrieked and slid hastily down from the couch. Pitaruusi put him back up beside Paulusi and said in an exaggerated, saccharine, soothing tone, "Because we two will go snowmobiling tomorrow, shall we?" Then he added in a more ordinary, conversational voice, "Because you lack understanding (you're *silait*-)?" Saali didn't respond.

The next person to come in was Arnaqjuaq, and with her came Papi. Rosi and Chubby Maata both ran to hug the puppy, but when Papi approached Saali, Saali cowered, batting and kicking at the friendly little dog. Jaani, seconded by Arnaqjuaq, told Rosi to take Papi over to Saali so that Papi could play with Saali's penis. And to Saali he said, "He bites." Rosi obeyed. Saali stared, his face stiff, and as Papi approached, he cried and swatted at the puppy. One of the men asked him: "Because you're afraid (*iqsi*-) he'll hurt you? Are you afraid?" Saali's stiff expression didn't change, but he said to Paulusi, "Remove him." Paulusi neither moved nor took protective action. Instead, he replied, in a "don't be silly" voice, "I can't remove him." Just once, as Papi wagged his tail and lapped at him in friendly fashion, Saali smiled.

But one of the men told Chubby Maata to put her hand into Saali's pants and touch his penis; and when she obeyed, Saali—who had never touched any of his adult tormenters—struck her, hard, and burst into tears, together with Chubby Maata. She retreated to her bottle, which stood on the couch beside her mother, and sucked quietly.

When Saali stopped crying, Jaani lay down on the floor and scratched the surface surreptitiously, pretending that the sound was made by an evil spirit: "There's a tunraq down there." Saali, his face stiff again, looked down toward the floor. Arnaqjuaq, who was watching all this with a very amused expression, said to Chubby Maata in a matter-of-fact voice, "Stop sucking (your bottle); play with the fetus." Chubby Maata did play with it briefly but then took up her bottle again, whereupon Juupi exclaimed loudly, in the throaty voice of exaggerated disgust: "Aaaq! She's sucking a bottle!" And Chubby Maata burst into tears again.

Finally, Paulusi got up to leave and for a moment stood by the door. To my surprise, Saali didn't immediately follow him. One of the men—Jaani or Juupi—noticed this and said to him: "Paulusi's leaving! Are you going to stay here? *Do* stay here! Won't you?"—this last in the saccharine voice of seductive persuasion. But Saali uttered a cry of protest and immediately went and stood close by Paulusi. Paulusi appeared to ignore him, but they left together. Till the very last moment, Jaani pretended to pull Saali back into the house, saying, "There's somebody who has a darling little penis out there!" Juupi, turning to me, smiled broadly and said, "But that one sitting over there has a darling little vulva, doesn't she?" Arnaqjuaq laughed, and so did I. Juupi went on: "Are we two going to *qitik-* (play tag)? So I can goose you."[7] Arnaqjuaq and I laughed again.

Arnaqjuaq went home soon after Paulusi and Saali, and I followed her after a few minutes. While I was visiting her, Saali's mother came in without Saali. Arnaqjuaq asked her if Saali was asleep, and she said yes. He must have gone to sleep as soon as he got home. But I noticed the next day in church that he approached with happy confidence his tormentors of the previous evening. And when I asked Arnaqjuaq later if they had been trying to make Saali feel *ilira-,* she first looked puzzled, then laughed and said: "No! They were happy! People are so delighted by his penis because he's the only boy in the family; even his mother treats him like that—loving (*nallik-*ing) him." I said, "Saali seemed not *at all* happy." Arnaqjuaq laughed again. "Yes, whenever he's played with, he feels completely miserable. He's like that. He's very possessive of his penis."

Episode A6 (March 3)
(The section in bold type is Episode 11.)

I was visiting again in Tiimi's house, together with a number of other people, including Arnaqjuaq. A few minutes after I entered, Chubby Maata came in and went straight to her grandmother, who was sitting on one of the side platforms in the inner half of the qammaq. Rota, in an amused voice, commented to the world at large, "She's unstoppable, she goes straight to her goal (*katsungait-*), as usual." Then she added, this time speaking to Chubby Maata, "I'm going to shoot your father." Chubby Maata looked at Rota with a

blank face. Rota, with an amused smile, asked, "Do you like (*piugi-*) him?" Chubby Maata wrinkled her nose. Rota double-checked: "You don't like him?" Chubby Maata raised her brows, confirming that she didn't like him, whereupon Rota turned to Saali, who was standing near her, and exclaimed in mock surprise: "You don't like him! Saali! Here's a potential father for you! She doesn't like her father!" Saali seemed to ignore these remarks. Chubby Maata's face was watchful. No further games were played with her while I visited. Instead, the focus of play shifted, first to Saali, then to me.

Saali was eating raisins or currants out of a paper bag when I went in. I asked, "What's that you're eating?" He happily replied, "Berries." (Small children used the word for raisins, too.) Then after a pause, he added, "They're all gone." I said, in mock surprise, "All gone?!" and I put out my hand playfully toward the bag to feel its contents. Saali, noting the coldness of my hand as it brushed his, said, "Because you're cold?" Then he added hastily, "Yes, they're all gone" and he put his hand on the telltale bulge in the bag, to prevent my feeling it. I ignored him, and he went on eating.

A few minutes later, Mitaqtuq came in and held out his hand to Saali, saying, "Give *me* some." Saali refused. Mitaqtuq then made as if to grab the bearskin that was thawing by the stove and said in a mock-threat voice, "I'm going to have *that!*" Saali yelled, "NO!" and kicked at Mitaqtuq, who said in a voice that spoke both reproof and matter-of-fact logic, "Because you didn't give me (any raisins)." Saali at once got up and took a handful of raisins to Mitaqtuq, but as he approached, Mitaqtuq said, "I don't want that kind of thing." Saali hesitated, and Arnaqjuaq confirmed, "Yes, he doesn't want them." Saali turned back to his seat then. Arnaqjuaq said to him in a low and confidential voice as he passed her: "Just me alone, yes? I helped to give birth to you."[8] Saali raised his brows in agreement, but whether he actually gave Arnaqjuaq the raisins he had intended for Mitaqtuq, I don't know.

A few minutes later, Rota said to me, "Are you going to marry Paulusi?" I responded, "Why on earth?!" "Because he shot a bear. That's his bear." I said, "Ee!" pretending admiration. Saali said, "*I'm* going to shoot a bear." Arnaqjuaq *aqaq*-ed him with tender amusement—"Ait!"—and slapped her hand affectionately in his direction.

CHAPTER 6

Episode A7 (October 23)

Luisa brought Kaati in to "school" this morning, but Kaati didn't want to stay. She blinked her eyes rejectingly[9] and turned away toward Luisa, who took her out. A little later, however, she came back by herself, and the other children asked her if she wanted to participate. She did briefly sit and draw, but then she got up and went out. As she left, Chubby Maata said to her, "Because you're afraid (*kappia-*)?" I didn't see Kaati's answer. Rosi said, "*I'm* not kappia-; you're the only one."[10]

Episode A8 (November 10)

(The section in bold type is Episode 22.)

Chubby Maata, visiting me with her mother, announced that she was a teacher (using the word that adults use for "missionary" rather than "school-teacher") and taught me words, reciting them in a serious voice with great clarity and distinctness so that I could repeat them after her: "qu-lliq (lamp)"; "i-quu-si-ssaq (toilet paper)," mispronounced in her baby speech; "su-kaq (sugar)"; "pani-kaq (cup)"; "i-ku-mait (matches); because they *are* matches, mother?" Liila assured her that they were.

Chubby Maata recited other words for me to learn, too, which I failed to record, and then began to ask her mother a series of property questions: "Is this *our* qulliq?" Liila raised her brows: "Yes." "Is *that* our qulliq?" (I had two.) Liila wrinkled her nose: "No." "Does it belong to Kaati's household?" Liila raised her brows. "Whose is *this* one? Ours?" Liila raised her brows. But after two or three more repetitions, she said, "Stop asking questions," and Chubby Maata obeyed. Her questions had not sounded gamelike; they were asked unsmilingly and without patterned rhythm.

Episode A9 (January 29)

Chubby Maata came in, sat down relaxedly on my sleeping platform, and began a conversation peppered with requests for tea and bannock. I told her that there was none, and she accepted my refusals equably enough. Then she began a game that adults and older children often play with unsuspecting peers or juniors. The initiator of the game calls the name of another person or makes some remark, and if that other person says, "Hai (eh)?" meaning "What did you say?" the game player replies, "She (or he) said 'Hai.'" That's all there is to the game, but the unexpected reply to the innocent question "Hai?"—the blocking of the normal passage of information—amuses all parties. The exchange can be repeated a number of times before it is dropped, especially when children do it to each other. Chubby Maata had to teach me to say "hai (eh)?" instead of "suvaa (what)?" in response to her opening "Yiini," but then I played it successfully until she tried to initiate a switch in roles. The dialogue went like this:

Chubby Maata: "Yiini."

Yiini: "Suvaa (what)?"

Chubby Maata: "Yiini."

Yiini: "Suvaa?"

Chubby Maata: "Yiini."

Yiini: "Suvaa?" (This sequence was repeated several more times.)

Chubby Maata: "Say 'hai (eh)?'"

Yiini: "Hai?"

Chubby Maata: "She said 'hai.' Yiini."

Yiini: "Hai?"

Chubby Maata: "She said 'hai.' Yiini. Say 'Chubby Maata.'"

Yiini: "Chubby Maata."

Chubby Maata: "She said 'hai.'" (She should have said "hai?" leaving *me* to say "She said 'hai.'")

Tangling up the lines—had she wanted to keep the punch line for herself?—Chubby Maata brought the game to a halt. I said, "I'm going out"; she cheerfully followed me.

I wonder now whether Chubby Maata was innocently blocking the flow of conversation the way I had—not innocently—blocked her requests for tea. The game certainly had the effect of putting control of the communication back into her hands.

Episode A10 *(February 13)*

Kaati and Chubby Maata came in early in the morning while I was putting on my boots. As they started to open the door, I heard them say to each other in cheerful voices, "Maybe she's pretending to sleep (*siningnguaq-*)," and then, as they saw me through the open door, "No, she's not pretending to be asleep!"

Kaati, almost as soon as she entered, said in the same cheerful voice, "I'm not fetching—bread." Alerted by the wordbase "fetch," which in Inuktitut precedes the negative form, I said, "No! . . ." and simultaneously Chubby Maata said, "*I'm* not fetching!" While she was speaking I continued my speech to Kaati: " . . . Don't be always fetching!" Then I said approvingly to Chubby Maata: "Yes, good for you, you're not fetching (*aisingngittukuluuvutit*)!" She smiled. After I had expressed my approval of Chubby Maata's restraint, I repeated my criticism to Kaati in a disapproving tone: "Don't be always fetching! It's not good (*piungngit-*)!" The two of them left then, but as Kaati moved toward the door, she turned the tables on me with smiling eyes: "Yiini is not good (*piungngit-*)." And I heard them say to each other again in the outer porch, as they retreated, "Yiini is not good." "Ee."

Episode A11 *(February 16)*

A fragment of a note tells me that Chubby Maata came to visit me with her father's two-year-old (adopted) brother, Luukasi, in tow. "Yiini," she said, "I've come to learn." But this subject was not pursued.

She turned her attention to my can of butter: "We have this kind. We've just finished it." (That is, "it's all gone.") This was a strong hint, to which I was not receptive.

Then she looked at my torn floor covering and, with an impish expression and hand poised to tear, she asked: "Shall I tear it? Shall I?" She repeated the question several times, but I don't know what I replied. She didn't tear it.

Finally, she arrived at what I am sure was the primary purpose of her visit: "Are there any candies?" I said, "Yes." "Where? In the porch?" "No." "In here?" "No." "Because they're all gone?" "Yes." "Who finished them? Kaati?" "Yes." Chubby Maata grimaced—a tunraq face of mock aggression, copied from her elders. Then she said to the uncomprehending Luukasi, "You too?"—inviting him to grimace, too. But Luukasi only smiled.

They turned and started out, but they were a little slow in getting through the doorway, and I, feeling chilly and impatient, said, "Quick—shut the door, please!" Chubby Maata, in response, deliberately, though briefly, held the door *open*.

Episode A12 *(February 27)*

I went to visit in Chubby Maata's house and found the whole family at home. Jaani was dyeing a seal net, Liila was frying eggs, and the two girls were walking around the room, doing what, I don't know. When I sat down on the couch, Chubby Maata climbed up beside me, drinking a baby bottle full of juice. When she finished her bottle, she began to play with the shoelace in the neck of my sweater: "Shall I tie it?" she asked. I said, "Yes." She leaned against me, smiled very cozily at me, and said, "Matiiusi is going to make you cry—while you're asleep." She repeated this threat a number of times, in the later repetitions changing the name of my assailant to Piita and then, more playfully, to Iita. (Piita was a young man visiting from Pangnirtung who had arrived in Qipisa that evening; he was a relative stranger to Chubby Maata. Matiiusi, too, her father's teenage brother, had recently returned to camp after an extended absence.)

Episode A13 *(March 3)*

When I went into Chubby Maata's house in midafternoon, I found Liila sitting on the couch, smoking a cigarette, while Chubby Maata stood in the bedroom door, whining: "(Give me) a suck! Come on!" Her mother ignored her. I thought perhaps Liila was trying to wean her.[11] I said sympathetically, "What's the matter (*suuviit*)?" Chubby Maata went on crying, and Liila went on smoking.

After a few minutes, Chubby Maata, all by herself, stopped crying, picked up a pair of scissors, and began to snip at pictures of Elvis Presley, which were taped to the wall above the couch. And she started to sing a song, with words that she made up as she went along. The only words I understood were "My mother doesn't want me to suck."

After a little while, Liila said to her daughter, "Would you like to suck from me?" "Yes!" said Chubby Maata, and she came and sucked peacefully for a few minutes at Liila's dry breast. Liila said in a tender, *aqaq*-ing tone, "Baby."

Jaani came home while Chubby Maata was nursing and "kissed" first her leg with gentle bites and then her face with a snuff. Chubby Maata sucked on. But after a little while, Liila withdrew her breast, saying in an impatient voice, "There's no milk in it." Chubby Maata protested: "That's not so, it has milk!" But Liila said, in the same impatient voice, "I'm too hot!" and pushed her daughter off.

Chubby Maata began to whine again, but in a less urgent tone this time: "Give me something to drink (*niuqaq-*). Come on!" Liila explained to me that the milk supply was low, and I assured her that I had lots. So then Liila poured a cup of tea for her daughter, put milk in it, and gave her a piece of bannock with jam on it. Chubby Maata finished this snack and then asked for a bottle, which Liila gave her.

She climbed onto the couch with her bottle and leaned against me, front to front. I put my arms around her, and she began to play with my face, idly and gently, as she drank. Liila and Jaani, meanwhile, were eating frozen meat, squatting by the carcass on the floor near the door. (Liila had offered frozen meat to Chubby Maata, too, but she didn't want any.)

Liila, seeing that Chubby Maata was playing with my face, cautioned her, "Don't hurt (*a'a-*) her!" Chubby Maata was by no means hurting me, though she distorted my features by pulling, twisting, and poking. Liila nevertheless turned a worried eye now and then on her daughter's play and once exclaimed in a slightly alarmed voice, "Yes, indeed, she's beginning to really attack (*ugiat-*) her!" I said, "No, no, she's not ugiat-ing." But Liila, not reassured, continued to issue her warning from time to time: "Don't hurt her!"

After a while, Chubby Maata lay down in my lap, my arms still around her, and continued to drink from her bottle and to play with the nipple, squirting the milk in drops at her face, pushing the nipple in, and so on. Once she broke wind and smiled at me, impishly: "You farted!" I smiled back: "*You* (did)." Chubby Maata wrinkled her nose with a smile, denying responsibility. I queried, "Who was it, then?" Chubby Maata said sweetly, "Me."

She tired of her bottle before it was finished and got up to go to Kaati's house. But it was already dusk, and Liila said in a loud, warning voice: "No! Tunrait will get you! It's dark!" Chubby Maata still wanted to go. Her mother said in the same voice of exaggerated warning: "Kaati will hurt (*a'a-*) you!" I was startled by that threat; perhaps Chubby Maata was, too.[12] It worked. She came back.

Episode A14 (March 7)

The Qallunaaq game officer from Pangnirtung, accompanied by two Pangnirtung Inuit, had come to Qipisa on an official visit, and all three men were staying in Jaani's house. Shortly after they arrived, I went in to visit and found the house full of Qipisa residents who had come, as I had, to greet—or just to see—the new arrivals. Jaani, Liila, and their two daughters were also at home, Chubby Maata sitting on or between her mother's knees, her expression solemn and her eyes wide, while Rosi, as silent and still as her sister, stood near her mother. Arnaqjuaq, ignoring Rosi, said to Chubby Maata, "Are you afraid of the strangers (*aallasi-*)?" I saw no response. Arnaqjuaq asked again, "Because you feel ilira-?" Chubby Maata wrinkled her nose: "No." "Because you feel shy (*kangngu-*)?" Another wrinkle of the nose. "Do you *not* feel ilira-?" Chubby Maata raised her brows: she did not feel *ilira-*.

Arnaqjuaq dropped the subject, but a few minutes later she asked Chubby Maata, "Shall Jakupi (naming one of the Inuit visitors) be your father?" If Chubby Maata answered, I didn't see it. Her grandmother may have asked once more but then, receiving no answer, desisted.

My attention was diverted at this point, but a surprisingly short time later it was recalled by a loud and happy commotion. Chubby Maata and Kaati were running from one end of the room to the other, one trying to capture a doll that the other was carrying, and both of them yelling cheerfully: "She doesn't belong to you! You can't have her!" They seemed not to hear Liila's and Luisa's repeated instructions to stop being wild (*uimak-*).

It looked to me very much as though the two children were acting out—and triumphantly winning out over—the threat that the game officer might adopt a little girl.[13] Interestingly, Rosi, who was not subject to any interrogations, remained very subdued during my visit, which was more than an hour long, and stayed close by her mother.

Episode A15 (March 11)

Three days after the game officer's company arrived, they left. The next morning, while I was drinking my breakfast tea, Chubby Maata came to visit me by herself. Sitting down comfortably on the sleeping platform, she noticed a piece of chewed gum, which some visitor had left near the qulliq. "That's our gum, isn't it?" she said; "I'm going to have it." She picked it up and began to chew it. (I paid no more attention, but after she'd gone, I noticed it still lay by the lamp.)

I got up to scrape the night's frost off the inside of my overhead window, and when I sat down again Chubby Maata moved closer and closer to me until she was leaning on my leg. She pointed to various items on the side platforms and said, "Our qulliq, our qulliq, our qulliq, our qulliq." None of the items she pointed to were lamps; nevertheless, I said—probably without much interest—"Ee (yes)."

Then she said, pointing to a burnt match, which I had neglected to throw away, "Give me that match." When I gave it to her, she played with it. First she wound an imaginary thread round and round the match head and pretended to snap off the head with the thread—a trick that her elders played. Then she drew faint lines of soot on my white duffel sock and on the leg of her pants. When I protested, she drew invisibly on the dark tip of my sealskin boots instead. I again protested (I can't imagine why): "Eeee!" whereupon she returned to my sock, very gently ran the match over its top, and said, "It can't be seen." And a minute later: "It's all gone," meaning the soot on the match.

At some point while Chubby Maata was playing with the match, I asked her, out of curiosity, "Do you like (*piugi-*) the game officer?" She wrinkled her nose. I pressed: "You *don't* like him?" She raised her brows. I asked, "Why?"—that uncomfortably challenging question. Chubby Maata lowered her chin to her chest and sat perfectly still. I repeated the question several times. Chubby Maata was as if cast in stone; but finally, still without moving or looking at me, she said in a subdued and expressionless voice, "I don't like him." In pity and remorse, I let the matter rest.

Chubby Maata began to throw the match at me. I took it and put it in the trash can. Then she turned her attention to four tiny china squirrels, which someone had given me. She wanted to know whose they were and where I had gotten them. I told her and, at her request, gave them to her to play with. When I handed them to her, she said: "May I have them? I'm going to have them." And she tucked them into the front of her shirt. I think she also said, "I'm going to take them home."

To distract her from the project of taking them home, I said jokingly, "Are those (hidden squirrels) your breasts?" "Yes," said Chubby Maata. "Have a suck." I complied, bending my head to the "breast" she held toward me. She urged me to do it again—and again; and I did, several times. Eventually, however, I got bored and only made a perfunctory sucking noise without bending my head, whereupon she insisted that I "come here." But when, for variety, I pretended to bite the "breast," she withdrew and looked at me with reproach: I had overstepped. I stopped "nursing" then, and Chubby Maata stopped asking me to. She played with the squirrels for a few more minutes by herself and then handed them back to me: "Here, Yiini."

Next, Chubby Maata asked for tea. I gave her some but pointed out to her that the bread was frozen. "Never mind," she said; she would accept tea without bannock. But when she got the tea, she wanted bannock and tried to cut it herself, using the backside of the knife blade. I said loudly in a warning voice: "No! Because you'll cut yourself!" She echoed me with her baby pronunciation: "Because you'll cut yousef!" I heard it as mildly mocking, but she put the knife down. Then she said: "I really want bread. I'll go home and fetch some and leave the tea here, all right?" I said, "All right." In a few minutes she came back with bannock and said, "(I want it with) butter on it." I obliged.

While Chubby Maata was drinking her tea, she spilled a little and asked for a rag to wipe it up with. While wiping, she noticed a small brown streak on the floor, where I had stamped out a rag that had caught fire four days earlier and had nearly burned down my qammaq while I was next door visiting the newly arrived game officer. My observant little visitor asked, "Was that (spot) on fire?" I said yes. She ate her bannock, finished her tea, and left.

Episode A16 (March 14)

Seeing me approaching my qammaq, Chubby Maata waited politely outside for me to enter before she went in. Once inside, she noticed, as she had before, that the plastic covering on my floor was torn, and she asked if children had broken it. I probably said no, since in fact the damage had not been caused by children. In response, Chubby Maata pulled my balaclava off and said in a tone of pleased satisfaction, "I've broken it completely."

Episode A17 (March 22)

Rosi, visiting me with eight-year-old Miali and perhaps other younger children but no adults or teenagers, began to ask for everything in sight. She spoke in a chant that was reminiscent of the voice used in "PiungngitTUUQ (you're BAAD)!" and her expressionless face, widened eyes, and bowed legs belonged to a comic posture called *qaviiq-*. "Please give me ——— because I have none," said she, over and over again. She asked for some things that were not visible, too. When I challenged her, "Because there is some?" she said, "Yes"; and when I asked, "Where?" she said, "Hidden." Miali stood silently by, unsmiling.

At the same time, Rosi, in the same chanting voice, showered insults—or were they threats?—on me: "May your horrid hair get soaked; may your glasses get broken; may your note slips be thrown away . . ." At some point, probably when I tired of this performance, I said, "Go (out and) play." To this, Rosi replied: "*You* can't play—no wonder, (you're) an old woman, a man, a Qallunaaq."[14]

Appendix 2: Episodes in Chronological Order

Date	Episode	Date	Episode
October 1	7, 10	January 8	30B
7	3	9	9
8	20	10	32
10	16	14	A4
23	A7	17	31
29	4 (=A2), 5 (=A1)	27	15
November 6	21	29	33, A9
10	22 (=A8)	February 5	35
17	A5	7	36
20	18, 23A, 25	11	34
22	23B	13	A10
24	26A, 26B	16	A11
25 or 26	26C	27	A12
26	1	March 2	38
28	14	3	11 (=A6), A13
29	2 (=A3)	4	13, 17
December 1	12	7	A14
13	19	11	A15
17	24	14	A16
20	27	22	A17
21	8, 28	24	37, 39
30	6, 29	26	40
January 5	30A		

Appendix 3: Glossary

Inuktitut is a polysynthetic language. This means that, in general, an Inuktitut verb translates as an English sentence. Reading from left to right, a verb has a base (root), which is modified by the postbases (suffixes) that follow it. An example, a bit extreme, perhaps, is a comical tongue-twister that people played with during a certain period in Qipisa: *tiiliurutitaaqtuminiuniraqtauyumaangngilanga.* This word divides and translates as follows:

> tii-liu-ruti-taaq-tuminiu-niraq-tau-yumaa-ngngi-langa

> tea-make-er-acquire-formerly-say-(passive)-(distant-future-want)-not-I

In other words, translating from right to left: I will never want it to be said of me that I once acquired a teakettle. (The base is *tii-* [tea]).[1]

To spare Western readers the visual complexities of Inuktitut and focus their minds on the wordbases, which are important for the discussion, I have usually lopped off the postbases and given just the base, or the base plus one or two relevant postbases, followed by a hyphen: *niviuq-, ilira-, uqangnguaq-* (= *uqa(+)ngnguaq-*). Occasionally it is a postbase that is of interest. In such cases, I precede, or precede and follow, the postbase with a hyphen: *-kuluk, -ruluk, -vik-*.

Word forms that are neither preceded nor followed by a hyphen may be nouns, exclamations, or verbs that, in truncated form, become complete words in baby talk. Thus, for example, Chubby Maata may demand, "Amaamak (suck)!" That is her complete utterance, even though the proper adult form would be "Amaamallanga (let me suck)!"

To avoid confusion about whether a word form is nominal or verbal, I translate verbs as though they had infinitive forms—"to worry," "to play"—although there is no infinitive form in Inuktitut.

Words are rendered as they are spoken in the Qipisa dialect. Hence, some words and bases that appear in *Never in Anger* (Briggs 1970) look a bit different here: *naklik* is here *nallik-; iqhi* is here *iqsi-*. In addition, the Inuktitut word for "white person," which I anglicized from *qaplunaaq* to *kapluna* in *Never in Anger,* appears here in its proper Baffin Island form as *Qallunaaq.*

With a few exceptions, noted below, I transcribe Inuktitut words phonemically, following conventions commonly used for rendering Canadian Inuktitut in Latin letters:

a is pronounced as in "ah," or, when short and unstressed, like the **u** in "but."

i is pronounced as in "in" or like the **e** in "me" or, in the vicinity of uvular consonants, like the **e** in "hem." It is never pronounced like the **i** in "high." Occasionally, being afraid that readers would be too strongly tempted to pronounce **i** as in English, I have unphonemically transcribed a long **i** as **ee** instead of as **ii** (see "double letters," below).

o. See **u.**

u is pronounced as in English "ooh," except in the vicinity of uvular consonants, in which case it is like the **o** in "hoe" or the **aw** in "haw." In proper names I follow the Canadian Inuit practice of transcribing the sound "o" as **o.**

g is a velar fricative, not a stop as it is in English.

j. See **y.**

k is a velar stop, as in English "king."

q is a uvular stop, which has no equivalent in English; it's a little like an Arabic glottal **q** but not quite so far back in the throat.

ng is pronounced as in "hung," never as in "hungry."

r is uvular, as in French.

y is more fricative than in English, almost like **j,** although it is not a stop. Because Canadian Inuit tend to use **j** when writing their names in Latin letters, I, too, have used **j** in proper names. An exception is my own name, Yiini, which

I continue to write with **y** because it will be familiar in that form to readers of *Never in Anger* (1970) and my other publications.

' represents a glottal stop.

Double letters (**mm, aa, ngng,** and so on) represent long consonants or vowels, which are phonemically different from short consonants and vowels. The last vowel in a word may also be lengthened interrogatively; and vowels in chants, croons, or exclamations—*kuuniik, aaaahai, aaakuluk, aaaiiit, unaaaluk*—may be prolonged for expressive emphasis. These lengthenings are not phonemic. In this glossary, I have indicated the possibility of expressive lengthening by inserting an extra vowel in parentheses: *aa(a)hai, ee(e)*.

ks and **qs** are pronounced more or less like **ksh.**

ll is pronounced more or less like **tl.**

All other sounds are pronounced more or less as in English.

Inuktitut words appear in italics in the text, with two exceptions. When a word is used in a direct quote, with or without an English translation in parentheses, I refrain from italicizing it, in order not to visually interrupt the flow of the sentence; however, when the Inuktitut word is inserted parenthetically into a quote, as a translation of an English word in the sentence, I do italicize it. Thus "Babykuluuviit?" and "Do you feel ilira-?" but "Don't hurt (*a'a*) her!" The second exception is four Inuktitut words that are not central to the discussion but that appear frequently in the text. These are italicized only on their first occurrence: Qallunaaq (white person); qammaq (wood-framed tent); qulliq (seal-oil lamp); tunraq (evil spirit).

I have derived the definitions that follow in various ways. Most I have deduced from spoken contexts, drawing also on my previous knowledge of the Utkuhikhalik dialect; others come from definitions I requested in Qipisa in Inuktitut; still others I have checked with bilingual Canadian Inuit women friends whose native dialects vary, and often I have expanded or modified my original understanding of these words on the basis of what these women have told me. I mention these facts because definitions derived from listening to conversation and from asking for definitions tend to be qualitatively different (see Briggs 1995a for a discussion of this point), but in only two cases do I specify my sources—in one case (*ilira-*) because I draw on a published work (Brody 1975) and in the other case (*sillu-*) because the variations in the definitions are relevant to a point I make in Chapter 6.

aa(a)hai!: an exclamation that contradicts, indicating disbelief of what has just been said; something like "yes, you did too!"

aa(a)kuluk!: another tender exclamation, which means something like "dear little one." See *-kuluk.*

aallasi-: to fear strangers.

aa(a)q!: an exclamation of disgust, as when smelling something bad.

ai?: "isn't that so?" or "won't you?"—a question that asks for agreement. Sometimes, when used in speaking to small children, it is uttered in a voice that I dub "saccharine-persuasive."

aippatuakuluga: "my sweet little other (wife), the only one I have."

aisiq-: to fetch (something).

> *aisingngittukuluuvutit:* "you're not fetching, good for you" (or "how nice!").

a(a)i(i)t!: a tender and untranslatable exclamation, which can sound either like a cross between a croon and a groan or like a sudden, sharp, even shrill cry. I once saw a newborn infant jump, startled, and cry, as if slapped by the sound; but a week or two later, she smiled at the same sound. A person uttering this sound is *niviuq*-ing or *aqaq*-ing (see below).

aittui-: to pass on or distribute something; often said of germs, but also of more desirable things.

aiyai!: an exclamation indicating fear or a startle; sometimes a warning, like the English "look out!"

amaamak(-): This word form can be either a noun, referring to a woman's breast, or a verb, meaning to nurse at the breast or to suck a baby bottle. In baby talk it is used in its verbal senses as a complete word, without verbal postbases.

anaanak: mother.

anniq-: to injure; to be injured.

anniruk!: "hurt her!"

aqaq-: to speak, sing, or chant tenderly to a small child, using repetitive phrases or tunes which create and express an affectionate bond between an adult or adolescent and a small child or baby.

ataatak: father.

ataataksaq: adoptive father; literally, "father-material" or "potential father."

atau!: an excited exclamation of approval, like "hurray!" or "good for you!"

atiq: name; name-soul.

a'a-: to feel or to cause injury or pain (baby talk).

a'aa(a)!: an exclamation of pain, like "ouch!" or "that hurts!"

angu(uuu) putu(uuu): a Qipisa rendition of the eider duck's mating call. I didn't check what meaning, if any, the speaker gave to the cry; he was chanting to his small son to put him to sleep. But it happens that the word for "male" or "man" is *angut* and the word for "hole" is *putu*.

babuga: bubble gum (the English word said with an Inuktitut accent).

baby: a tender, *aqaq*-ing word, borrowed from English.

> *babykuluk:* "darling little baby," an *aqaq*-ing word.
>
> *babykuluuvi(i)t?:* "are you a darling little baby?" (*aqaq*-ing).
>
> *babypaaluuvi(i)t?:* literally, "are you very very baby?" Another *aqaq*-ing word, which, freely translated, means something like "are you our treasured little baby?"
>
> *babytuqaaluuvi(i)t?:* literally, something like "have you been a baby for a long long time?" An *aqaq*-ing word.
>
> *babyummigavi(i)t?:* "are you a baby, too?"
>
> *babyugavit:* "because you're a baby."
>
> *babyuvit?:* "are you a baby?"

ee: "yes"; also "oh, I see."

> *eeelaaq!:* "yes, indeed!"

eeee: sometimes a protesting noise, meaning something like "don't do that!" It could also express a neutral "I hear you" or an amused "oh, really?!"

haa!: a playful exclamation of surprise, which means something like "well, what do you know about that!"

hai?: "what did you say?" A request for repetition of something unheard.

haló: the English word "hello." Adults speaking to children sometimes used this word as a name for me, in order to remind the children that I was a scary Qallunaaq.

hatuq-: to give a gift in gratitude; to be grateful.

hee(e)?: "what was that you said?" Uttered either in asking for a repetition of something unheard or in pressuring the person addressed—child or anthropologist—to agree with the speaker.

ih!: an exclamation of surprise, like "oops!" in English, said when catching oneself in a mistake.

ikumait: matches.

ilira-: to fear or to arouse the fear of being unkindly treated; to respect, with overtones of fear. There is no exactly comparable concept in English. Hugh Brody (1975:158–159) captures essential dimensions of the meaning when he defines *ilira-* as "the feeling of nervous awe that comes from being at an irreversible disadvantage, a situation in which one cannot modify or control the actions of another; . . . one is (also) *ilira* of a person whose actions cannot be predicted, nor understood." *Ilira-* and *kappia-* feelings are discussed and contrasted in Brody (ibid.), in Briggs 1970:345–347, and in Chapter 6 of this book.

> *iliranaq-:* to arouse *ilira-* feelings.

ilisaiyuq or *ilisayuq:* to learn. A word used in north Baffin for Euro-Canadian-style schooling (Stairs 1992:122).

inusuttut: young persons; teenagers, not fully adult.

iq!: an exclamation of alarm or sudden surprise.

iqqaitigigaviuk?: "does she remind you of someone (or something)?"

iqsi-: to fear or to arouse the fear of physical injury; perhaps a stronger word than *kappia-* (see below).

iquusissaq: Chubby Maata's pronunciation of *iquutissaq:* toilet paper.

isuma: refers to all functions that we think of as cerebral—mind, thought, memory, reason, sense, ideas, will.

isummaksaiyuq or *isummaksayuq:* to teach; literally, to cause thought to increase. A word used in north Baffin to distinguish Inuit learning processes from Euro-Canadian formal education (Stairs 1992:122).

kamiksaq: material out of which boots are to be made.

kangngu-: to feel or cause to feel a wish to avoid observation or self-display; physical modesty.

kapi-: to puncture; to spear; to give a (medical) shot.

kappia-: to fear or to arouse fear of physical injury; also a "lowest common denominator" word for fear—thus, when I didn't understand a word for a specific kind of fear, people would substitute the word *kappia-* in explanation.

> *kappianaq-:* to arouse fear (in general) or fear of physical injury.
>
> *kappianaqtunga:* "I'm scary" (what Chubby Maata says by mistake, meaning *kappiasuktunga*), in Episode A1 (see Appendix 1, n. 1).
>
> *kappiasuktunga:* "I'm scared."

katsungngait-: to go to one's destination or pursue one's goal energetically, overcoming all obstacles; to be unstoppable. Always in my hearing said as a criticism, it implied lack of consideration for others.

kinauvi(i)t?: "who are you?" A question that was often addressed to small children in an attempt to elicit their names, both the names by which they were addressed and those that were not ordinarily used but that were part of their spiritual essence: the "name-souls" of other Inuit, usually deceased or elderly. For an excellent discussion of Inuit naming practices and beliefs, see Nuttall 1992. Nuttall is writing about West Greenland, but much of his description is applicable also to Qipisa.

kuinat-: disgusting, revolting, tickly. Said of both objects and live creatures, such as worms, bees, flies, and lemmings, that make people shudder with distaste or revulsion. The exclamation "kuinat!" means both "how disgusting!" and "it tickles!"

-kuluk: a tender diminutive, something like "darling little."

kunik-: to kiss or snuff. An old-style Inuit kiss was a deep intake of breath with the nose pressed against the skin of the person kissed. The word form can be used without verbal endings, in a tender, crooning voice: *ku-u-(u)-ni-i-(i)-k.* People often use this voice to invite or urge small children to kiss babies and also to invite babies and small children to present their faces to be kissed.

-lauq-: "was" or "were" in the recent past; also used as a polite way of making a request: "please."

malik-: to follow, literally or figuratively.
  maliklugu: "follow him."
maniki: monkey, an English loan word.
matu: door.
minaqsi-: to give a special treat to someone special.
mitaq-: to joke.
  mitaqtunga: "I'm joking."
-miut: people, as in *Qipisamiut,* "people of Qipisa."

nallik-, nalligi-: to feel or to arouse concern for another's welfare, physical or emotional; to feel pity or protective, nurturant affection. Nowadays this word covers also the Western notion of romantic love, but I do not use it in that sense in this book. *-gi-* is a postbase that creates a link or relationship between people: *nalligiviuk?* means "do you love him?" For a more complex discussion of the meanings of *nallik-,* see Briggs 1995a.
  nallingnaq: lovable; pitiable; "she/he makes one feel protective."
ningngat-: to be angry.
  ningngassaari-: to make someone angry; to provoke, goad.
niuqaq(-): as a noun, a drink, often tea; but by children often used as a verb, without verbal endings, to mean "give me something to drink."

niurruaq (pl. *niurruat*): visitors from outside the camp. A bugaboo for small
  children.

niviuq-: to communicate tenderly with a small child or baby. I can discover no
  very clear line between *niviuq*-ing and *aqaq*-ing, though *aqaqs* are perhaps
  more structured.

panikaq: cup.

paniksaq: adopted daughter; literally, "daughter-material" or "potential daughter."

paqlatsiti-:[2] to celebrate (a first catch, a birthday, or whatever) by throwing
  goods into the air, for camp members to scramble and grab for.

payuk-: to take or send a bit of food from one's own house to the house of
  someone else in the same camp or community.

pingigaq-: to worry.

pingnguaq-: to play, pretend.

  pingnguaqtunga: "I'm playing" or "I'm pretending."

piqatau-: to participate.

piti-: to share, to give some of (something).

pitsialaurisi: "please behave well."

piu-: good.

  piugi-: to consider (someone or something) good; to like (someone or
    something). In the mouths of adults or older children, *piugi-* may also
    refer to sexual attraction, but I think not in the conversations quoted
    in this book.

    piugingngit-: to consider (someone or something) bad; to dis-
      like.

    piugiviuk?: "do you like her/him/it?"

  piungngit-: bad.

    piungngittuaralaaraaluk: a (probably) playful-affectionate scolding
      word, difficult to translate literally; perhaps something like
      "cussed little bad one." For more extended discussion of this
      word, see Chapter 6, n. 28.

    piungngitTUUQ!: "really VERY BAAD!" A playful word, said in an
      exaggeratedly emphatic voice, with the accent on the final sylla-
      ble, where it doesn't normally belong.

  piusaq-: to consider good.

    piusarunnangnginnavit?: because you're unable to like (or consider)
      good?

pivik-: to take or mean something seriously. Often said as a criticism of someone's inability to take a joke.

pulaaq-: to visit other households within the camp.

qaitqu-: to ask or wish that something or someone be brought (to the speaker).

> *qaitquyara:* "I told (someone) to bring it/him/her"; or "I wanted him/her to come."

qammaq (pl. *qammat*): In Qipisa (unlike Chantrey Inlet), this word refers to a wood-framed, wood-floored winter tent insulated with a thick layer of heather laid between two sheets of canvas.

Qallunaaq (pl. *Qallunaat*): a white person or people.

qaqa-: to "show off," display oneself in order to get affectionate attention—behavior characteristic of a small child.

qaqquallanga: "let me crack between my teeth" or "crunch" (something hard).

qauyima-: to know, be aware, understand.

> *qauyimangngit-:* to be ignorant, unaware, lacking in understanding.

qaviiq-: to assume a comic posture and perform comic gestures, to burlesque. The posture assumed and the gestures were always the same: bowed legs, cheeks sucked in, index finger of one hand extended and rotated in the palm of the other hand. I could not find out what, if any, meaning the posture and gestures had.

qia-: to cry.

> *qiaguirit!:* "stop crying!"
>
> *qialirit!:* "cry!"
>
> *qiangngillutit!:* "don't cry!"
>
> *qiasarait-:* to cry easily. The word is chanted in this form, without the pronominal ending, as a criticism. The chant-voice used is an imitation of the English-speaking child's taunt "NYA-nya nya-NYA-nya."

qimaktau-: to be left behind. A fear of both children and adults, being left behind is an emotionally charged situation, which has powerful connotations of abandonment. Among other things, adults speak of "being left behind" by loved ones who have died.

Qipisamiut: people of Qipisa.

qitik-: Several Inuit have told me that this word means to play games (in general). However, when Qipisa young people spoke of *qitik*-ing, the referent was always a game of tag in which (I was told) the goal was to catch and lick the shoulder of another player, thereby earning the right to "goose" the person caught.

qitungngaq (pl. *qitungngait*): offspring of human or animal.

qulliq: a flat-bottomed, half-moon-shaped, soapstone lamp with a wick of crushed plant fibers, something like cotton, along the flat edge. The lamp was fueled by seal oil and was used for cooking as well as heating and lighting the qammaq.

qumiu-: to save something (such as food) for someone.

quqvik: a can (or any container) used as a toilet.

quyana!: "never mind!" or "who cares!"

quyannamik: "thank you."

-rit: the second-person singular "intransitive" imperative pronoun: "you" (as subject).

-ruk: the second-person singular "transitive" imperative pronoun: "you (as subject) or her/him/it" (as object).

-ruluk: a diminutive with negative connotations, something like "horrid little."

sila: world; weather; wisdom; understanding.

    silait-: lacking in wisdom and understanding.

    silaittukuluugavi(i)t?: a tender but critical expression, something like "have you, darling little one, no understanding?"

    silatuu-: wise, great in understanding.

sillu-: A bilingual Inuit woman from the Baffin area defined this word for me in English as to withdraw or be in a state of withdrawal in order to conceal injured feelings and to protect feelings from being further injured; "feeling slighted" (Rachel Qitsualik Tinsley, personal communication 1996). One Qipisa person, when asked to define the word in Inuktitut, associated it with feeling *kappia-*; another person, with feeling *ilira-*. See Chapter 6, n. 4.

sinik-: to sleep.

    siningnguaq-: to pretend to sleep.

sirnaaq-: to overprotect. See the Introduction, n. 4, and Chapter 5, n. 24, for more extended discussion.

sukaq: sugar (an English loan word).

suli: still.

summan?: why?

surat-: to break (an object that can fall to pieces or be disassembled); Chubby Maata uses the word to mean "tear."

suvaa?: "what (did you say)?"

su(u)vi(i)t?: "what (on earth) are you doing?"

> *suyuruluuvitli?:* literally, "in what horrid little (ways) are you behaving, then?"; more loosely, "what sort of behavior is that, then?" or "what on earth are you doing?"

talee: three (the English word spelled the way Qipisamiut pronounced it).

tuni-: to give or hand to (someone). This is the most general term for giving.
> *tuniuqai-:* to distribute, give to everyone who is present.

tunraq (pl. *tunrait*): originally, a shaman's helping spirit. Tunrait were dangerously powerful but were evil only if a shaman did not effectively control them or use them to good ends. Now, under Christian influence, they are considered to be simply evil spirits.

tuyuuq-: to send a gift to someone at a distance.

uatsiaru!: "after a while!"; "just a minute!"; "wait a little!" Children hear this very often from their caretakers.

ugiat-: to attack and injure in an access of affection (if the attacker is human). A bitch who kills her pups to protect them from an outsider's attack is said to *ugiat-*. Also, to kill without weapons, as an animal does.

uiksaq: a betrothed man; literally, "husband-material" or "potential husband."

uimak-: to run around noisily and wildly; to be confused or cause confusion.
> *uimanaq!:* an exclamation of protest against a situation that is causing confusion—especially against noisy children.

uirit-: to be single-mindedly set on one's goal; persistent; stubborn.

unaa(a)luk!: "that bad one!"

unakuluk!: "that darling little one!"

unga-: to feel dependent attachment or longing; to wish or arouse the wish to be with another person; quintessentially, the love of small children for their parents. For a more complex discussion of the meanings of *unga-*, see Briggs 1995a.

ungaa: the sound of an infant's cry.
> *ungaalirit:* "say 'ungaa.'"

uqangnguaq-: to talk nonsense; to pretend-talk; to joke.
> *uqangnguaqtunga:* "I'm joking"; "I'm just pretending."

uqu(u)quu(u): a baby-talk word that refers to game food; to an animal, live or dead, that is used for food; or occasionally, in playful extension, to wildlife of any sort, including insects.

Utkuhikhalingmiut: people of Utkuhikhalik (Chantrey Inlet, central Arctic). (This word is written in the Utkuhikhalingmiut dialect.)

-vik-: time or place, as in *sini'vik,* a time or place to sleep.

Yiini: Jean, the anthropologist.

> *Yiiningaasit!:* "Yiini, as usual!"
>
> *Yiiningnguarit:* "pretend to be Yiini."
>
> *Yiiniralaaraaluk:* (probably) a play word, which, like *piungngit-tuaralaaraaluk* (see above), was, in its origin, a tender or playful scold, which Kaati may have heard directed at herself. Roughly, "that cussed little Yiini!" See Chapter 6, n. 28, for further discussion.

Notes

PEOPLE

1. See the pronunciation guide in Glossary (Appendix 3) for the use of "j" and "y" in proper names.

INTRODUCTION

1. Although the events I describe are history (see Chapter 1, n. 1), I use present as well as past tenses in the book. When I was socialized as an anthropologist, it was our custom to write in the present tense (of course, with appropriate disclaimers) even when the situation one was describing had changed, and I participated (of course, with appropriate disclaimers) in that tradition. Now, however, that convention no longer serves. Our dissatisfaction with it stems partly from the recognition that societies, never really static in the past, are now transforming themselves with breathtaking rapidity. Under such circumstances, speaking of traditions as though they were unchanging lifts a society out of time and "freezes" it and those who belong to it into a way of life that they no longer identify with. On the other hand, speaking of those traditions in the past tense gives the impression that they are dead. We are on the horns of a dilemma.

   Some of the practices and ways of thinking that I describe in this book are still active today while others are not, so neither tense works well. I have settled on the following compromise. I describe in the past tense my experiences in the camp and the events that I observed—as one would do in ordinary conversation. I also use past tense for generalizations that are based on those past experiences, even though I know that some of the general statements continue to apply, in whole or in part, to some or many individuals almost everywhere that Inuit live. I hope that this use of the past tense will encourage readers who know, or will come to know, Inuit to keep their eyes and ears open, to think about the origins of the behavior they see and hear, and not to jump prematurely to the conclusion that people think, feel, and act today exactly as they used to do.

Nevertheless, I use present tense for analysis of the events described. My aim is to set off a more abstract, "experience-distant" level of analysis from the events themselves and from more "experience-near" thoughts about what might have motivated those events (Geertz 1983). At the same time, I hope the present tense will make situations more immediate and so enable readers to share a little in the world of Chubby Maata.

Both this Introduction and the Conclusion draw heavily on a paper that was developed out of the book manuscript (Briggs 1991b, 1992b). I return those thoughts now to their original context because they summarize well some of the issues that are dealt with in the book at greater length and with more evidence.

2. The protagonist of Hughes's *Eskimo Boyhood* (1974) is not Inuit but Siberian Yupik; nevertheless, many of the childrearing practices that Hughes describes are strongly cognate with Inuit ones.

3. This "leader" was an old man who was father (biological or adoptive), grandfather, great-grandfather, or father-in-law of all but one of the other men in the camp. I put "leader" in quotation marks because, outside of his own household, his leadership was exercised in very limited contexts—mainly when the camp moved—and his juniors were free to follow or not. Even so, most of the younger men did choose to follow most of the time.

4. It must be said, nevertheless, that in Inuit societies there were many exceptions to this benign picture. Stepchildren, children adopted in midchildhood, orphans, and children who had been absent for a long period in hospital, quite often experienced searing rejection. Bonds formed in infancy were critical to the fate of a child, and if these were lacking or if they were threatened by the possibility that a child might die—a real and much feared possibility in remote camps—then affection could be withdrawn or never offered. Sometimes, too, if a child had been very ill or was a favorite whom the parents feared to lose, parents might treat her or him in a way that overtly resembled rejection— and that I am sure was difficult for the child—although the behavior was called "over-protection" (*sirnaaq-*) and adults perceived it to be motivated by intense affection. A child who was *sirnaaq-*ed might be attacked, treated harshly, fed and clothed poorly, and scolded constantly. I was given four justifications for this treatment. First, *sirnaaq-*ing children makes them strong and independent, enabling them to take care of themselves and not have to rely on the help of others. Second, if somebody wants to hurt a child's father but does not dare to attack him directly, they might hurt his favorite child instead, if they could identify that child. *Sirnaaq-*ing the child conceals the father's affection and keeps the child safe. Third, if parents have been accustomed to expressing affection toward a child, the child will be greatly missed if it dies; a *sirnaaq-*ed child will be missed

less. Finally, in *sirnaaq*-ing a beloved child, the parents are testing themselves "to see if we can do it." Because the natural inclination of parents is to express affection, they find it hard to rein themselves in. The extent to which these rationales may cover other unrecognized and disapproved feelings, such as hostility, is not at issue here. Discussions of Inuit ambivalence about attachment can be found in Briggs 1978, 1995a, and 1995b. In Qipisa, I have known three children who were adopted after infancy and who seemed to be less loved than others, and two whose young mother, an unhappy outsider, seemed to be unusually tried by her children's presence, but there were no children who were *sirnaaq*-ed in this special way. See Chapter 5, n. 24, for further discussion of *sirnaaq*-ing.

5. See Briggs 1979a for a fuller discussion of Inuit attitudes toward "playful" and "serious" behavior.

6. Because people—adults and children—never completely understand and purely cherish one another, and because children can misunderstand even the most benign motives, I think all socializers everywhere in the world play with fire, and we are all burnt in one way or another; but to defend that view would require another volume. Or more than one.

7. I discuss questions of evidence more fully below.

8. The presence of adult agendas and the intermingling of messages for adults and children are illustrated especially clearly by Episode 9 in Chapter 4 and Episodes A4 and A5 in Appendix 1. Even when a message was intended primarily for a child, it certainly resonated powerfully for adults who had been educated in the same way, and I argue that it reinforced their own socially valued behavior. See, for example, Briggs 1994.

9. Compare Bateson's discussion, in "A Theory of Play and Fantasy," of the metamessages that signal play and his wonderful definition of play: "These actions, in which we now engage, do not denote what would be denoted by those actions which these actions denote" (1972:180).

10. See also Morrow 1990:142–143 concerning the difficulty of eliciting from Yupik firm definitions of "groups" and their "boundaries" and "simple facts," such as the name of a ceremony or the number of villages that participated in it. For Inuit, and perhaps for Yupik too, kinship is another domain in which students encounter bewildering indeterminacy. Important bonds, albeit labeled with kin terms, were (and are) very often idiosyncratically constructed, based not on biology but on a person's name and on the emotional relationship between the individuals concerned. Hence, they are, from our point of view, fictive and unpredictable. Even worse, people tend to have more than one Inuit name, and—when speaking Inuktitut—they don't reliably use the same one all the time.

11. Because the concepts of behavior and action are used differently in different disciplinary discourses, I want to clarify my own usage. In this book, "behavior" (sometimes used in the plural) is an all-inclusive term which refers to words as well as to deeds and is not restricted to superficial, mindless aspects of those phenomena, as it is when behaviorists use it. "Action," when used in the singular, is also all-inclusive, synonymous with "behavior," but the plural form, "actions," is narrower; it generally signals a contrast between verbal behavior and other physical acts, as in the phrase "questions and actions."

12. At the Hebrew University of Jerusalem in 1980–1981, Don Handelman and I taught a

seminar on play, in which we analyzed some of my Inuit dramas. A good deal of my later thinking stems from those stimulating discussions. I owe a sizable debt to Handelman's insights.

13. The operation of unconscious knowledge in social and psychological life has been discussed from a variety of perspectives, in wide-ranging contexts, for different audiences, and to different ends. I first encountered the idea—two varieties of it—in a collection of Whorf's (1956) writings. In a fascinating letter to the psychologist Dr. English, written in 1927, Whorf asks for a label for a kind of "connection" that he has noticed between ideas, one different from "association" (1956:35–39); and in a paper on grammatical categories, originally published in *Language* in 1945, Whorf describes the marking of "covert categories" (1956:87–101). Sapir (1958:544–559) goes further. No anthropologist-psychologist-linguist has argued more charmingly and persuasively than he in support of the idea that the patterns governing most social behavior are unconscious and that, indeed, human life would be unmanageable if it were conducted entirely at a verbal level. Polanyi, too, in various writings but perhaps most fully in *The Tacit Dimension* (1967), has shown us how indispensable is "tacit knowledge" to the conduct of social and intellectual life. I am sure many others have made similar points in their own ways, in various contexts, and for different audiences, as the wheel turns. (Freud is too well known to require citation.)

14. For an explicit contribution to the debate about emotions, see Briggs 1995a.

15. I recognize that this style of analysis is not to everyone's taste. This point was once vividly made for me by a scholar who came to anthropology from biology. Following a seminar that I had given on Chubby Maata, this man remarked that my analysis reminded him of the pile of empty crawfish shells on his plate at dinner the previous evening—four times as big as the full shells and just as useless. I was amused, but the remark also made me realize that, once one has skinned the cat, there is more than one way to go about trying to understand what the cat is all about. The way chosen depends on one's goals. If one wants to find the design of the skeleton, one carves off all the flesh and throws it away. If, on the other hand, one is interested in the physiology of the cat, one observes with care every detail of the flesh and all the connections among the organs. If it is the biochemistry of the cat that is of interest, observation will be even more detailed, but the anatomical structure may vanish from sight. And so on. My interest in Chubby Maata is, metaphorically, a mix of the physiological and biochemical—with a dash of photography for love. I bequeath the skeleton to my critic.

16. Qipisamiut, like other Inuit and many other peoples, too, had a repertoire of dramatic voices for communicating with small children. The Qipisa voices were so distinct from one another that (unlike Inuit) I gave them labels: saccharine persuasion, protective caution, threatening warning, disgust, alarm, excited anticipation, and a few others. Inuit themselves label the tender, crooning, or excited tones of affection *aqaq*- and *niviuq*-. I had originally intended to analyze the relationships between verbal messages, on one hand, and messages conveyed in these tones of voice or by another repertoire of conventional gestures, on the other hand. This intention was defeated by the wish to finish this book in my lifetime. Nevertheless, I would like to alert readers to the fact that the different channels as often contradicted as supported one another, not only because ambivalent feelings might be simultaneously expressed but also because Inuit made a

practice of "saying things backward," as one Inuit friend put it. The webs of meaning so created for unwary children must have been—and may still be—tangled indeed and must complicate considerably the picture I draw in this book.

17. There are cultures in which people appear to be interested only in the surface of behavior, not in its underlying causes and motivations. Joanne Prindiville, speaking of the Indonesian Minankabau, said that when she tried to excuse an inappropriate action by pleading that she had not intended to offend, people replied simply, "You did it"; you committed the act (personal communication). Fajans (1985) tells us that the Bainang of Papua New Guinea "deemphasize concepts of interior states" (392), are "reluctant to speculate about motivations . . . and feelings[,]either of themselves or others, . . . [and] do not offer interpretations of the meanings of . . . behavior and events . . . in these terms" (367). They prefer to attribute causation to outside agents. Personal emotions—as distinct from socially constructed sentiments—are recognized, but they are feared: they "invade" the social order and cause madness (392). Such ethnographic cases raise a knotty question: in analyzing how such societies work, is it appropriate for outside observers to introduce a foreign concern with motivation? And if the answer is yes, how should it be used? Can motives be given explanatory weight? We need not concern ourselves with this issue here, since Inuit do take note of motives and consider inner states important. Nevertheless, I think we should keep in mind that the principles governing analysis and the kinds of evidence used might have to be adapted to particular cultural environments.

CHAPTER 1: CHUBBY MAATA'S WORLD

1. Although I have specified the place where these events took place, I have suppressed the exact year in order to protect identities. I spent a total of about two years with Qipisamiut during five widely spaced field trips during the decade 1970–1980.

2. See Glossary (Appendix 3) for a possible meaning of this cry.

3. In the days before baby bottles, Inuit children usually nursed until the next baby was born, which might be as long as three years. For an account of the weaning of a three-year-old in a central Arctic camp, see Briggs 1970:157–162. After bottles were introduced, children often continued to suck on demand until they were four or even older, though little by little they were made self-conscious about this behavior and stopped of their own accord.

4. I can think of no better word than "moo" to bring this voice to life. It was a deep voice with exaggerated undulations and expressed disapproval or, in the mouths of children, wordless protest and rejection. (The protests of Inuit children were most often wordless.) I have heard the same voice in other parts of the Arctic as well. For other illustrations of its use, see Briggs 1970.

5. The postbase -vik- that Liuna used means both "time" and "place."

6. In Inuktitut conversation, the superordinate clause in a causal sentence is often omitted. The content of the missing clause is usually obvious, but its omission forces hearers to listen actively and to infer content from circumstances.

7. On Baffin Island, bannock used to be made by putting the oil or fat in the dough and hanging the dough in a dry frying pan over the seal-oil lamp. When stoves replaced lamps for heating and cooking, the dry-cooking method was retained, either on top of the stove

in a frying pan or in the oven in a baking pan. In all these cases, the bannock tasted like baked bread. In the central Arctic, on the other hand, the oil or fat was placed not in the dough but in the frying pan, and the resulting bannock had a sweet, fatty taste—a little like a doughnut—which Qipisa people and I too liked very much.

8. The one dreadful exception is described in Episode A15 in Appendix 1.

9. A more complicated picture will emerge in Chapter 6, but I didn't perceive the complexities at first.

10. This is Episode A7 in Appendix 1. Qipisa people, like other Inuit, often answered questions with silent gestures; children almost always did so when they were ill at ease. A wrinkled nose meant "No" and raised eyebrows or widened eyes meant "Yes." In my presence, Chubby Maata and her peers rarely answered questions with words, so in this book I repeatedly say, "I didn't *see* (an answer)." And when I write, "She wrinkled her nose, 'No,'" or "she raised her brows, 'Yes,'" I mean that the negation or affirmation was in the gesture; it was not accompanied by a word.

CHAPTER 2: "BECAUSE YOU'RE A BABY"

1. Both "Because you're a baby" and "Are you a baby?" are single words in Inuktitut: *babyugavit* and *babyuviit,* respectively. I explain in the Glossary (Appendix 3) how Inuktitut words are structured.

2. The Inuit conventions for answering negative questions are the opposite of English ones. A "Yes" in response to "You don't want (tea)?" means, "You are right, I don't want (tea)." Similarly, a "No" means "You're mistaken, I do want (tea)."

3. This statement is, of course, an oversimplification. As I said in the Introduction, I assume that intentions and motives move in and out of various levels of awareness and that meanings shift depending on circumstances and experience. I therefore remind readers to keep open throughout the possibility that any particular act may be motivated simultaneously or sequentially in several ways, only a few of which—or even none—may be deliberately intended or conceived and understood in words.

   Here and throughout the book, when I use the word "unconscious," I am not making assertions, based on evidence, about the psychodynamic processes involved in a particular action. My intention is to suggest that actors might not have been able to give verbal shape either to their motives or to the meanings that a particular act had for them.

4. In addition to babyness, a number of other themes weave into and out of Episode 1 and resonate with other dramas. These potentially provide more clues to important issues in Chubby Maata's life. It would be illuminating to follow these threads separately to see where each leads and how it develops and then to consider how the themes might combine; I do some of this in later chapters. I do not, however, aim for complete analysis of any drama, because I don't think there is a single, definitive whole to be constructed. I assume that the perceptions of the actors (including the audiences) are various at any given moment of the drama and continually change retroactively, both within the period of play and afterward, as further experiences accumulate. One could suggest at most a few of the ways in which some of the threads might combine for some of the actors some of the time. My own, even more limited aim is to understand as best I can a fragment of what happens to *one* actor, Chubby Maata. So in order to reduce dizziness, both mine and my

readers', I restrict this first analysis to just two dimensions of the drama: the subject of babyness and the operation of play. Other scholars may wish to explore other themes and trace their possible connections with other dramas and interrogations.

5. I am reminded here of an incident I described in *Never in Anger*, in which Inuttiaq, teaching Saarak the syllabary, mischievously inserted words that Saarak couldn't possibly pronounce (1970:81–82). Other imitation games with Saarak are described on pp. 114–115. On the charm of a baby's unaware or foolish (*silait-*) behavior, see also Chapter 3 in this book.

6. In Chapter 6 we will find Chubby Maata carrying this adult role further, asking *me* to imitate *her*.

7. Here I am assuming that children give up *roles* as units, rather than relinquishing separate behaviors one at a time, an assumption that may not always or generally be correct. But adults mark undesirable behaviors as belonging to identities—"baby," "child," "boy"—which argues that behavior changes may indeed be governed sometimes by a conception of "role." For more on the subject of identities and roles, see in Chapter 2 the summary section entitled "The Fate of Babyness II."

8. This technique of correcting or criticizing by means of questioning *can* be acquired very early, though. See Chapter 3, n. 5, for an example of its use by another three-year-old in the camp.

9. In these interactions, are the children also learning to feel a little ambivalent or mistrustful of caretakers? We shall return to these related issues in Chapter 5.

10. See, for example, Episode A13, March 3, in Appendix 1.

11. The Inuit concept of *ilira-* does not translate easily into English. The feelings that constitute this complicated emotion and attitudes toward it are outlined in Chapter 6. The ways in which *ilira-* feelings, together with the unavailability of alliances, work to create moral behavior are also discussed at some length in Chapter 5.

12. This situation is reminiscent of the one described in *Never in Anger* (1970:149–151), in which Saarak is taught first to display herself to an admiring audience and then to hide modestly from that same audience. Here, too, the change is effected by a shift in the value attached to a baby game: "Laah! Let me kiss you!"

13. This discussion is the subject of Chapter 6.

14. Of course, the dichotomy is not really so tidy. Chubby Maata was simultaneously companion and toy for Liila when the latter dictated gestures and words for her to imitate. But for Chubby Maata it was companionship that was salient then, and now she can't perceive her mother's play at all, since she has not yet reached the point of being able to see her own role as toy.

15. I also heard adults use imperative forms when speaking to children in serious mode, but I did not record the polite *-lauq-* used in play mode.

16. See Chapter 2, n. 3.

CHAPTER 3: "*ARE* YOU A BABY?"

1. The complex associations that Inuit make between affection and aggression and, in particular, between two culturally patterned, physically aggressive ways of arousing and expressing affection, *ugiat-* and *sirnaaq-*, are more fully discussed in Briggs 1975, 1978, and 1982. See also the Introduction, n. 4, and Chapter 5 of this book.

2. The Utkuhikhalingmiut are the people I wrote about in *Never in Anger* (1970). In that book, where their name occurs frequently and I feared that English-speaking readers might stumble over it, I abbreviated it to "Utku." But in this book, where the Utku are named only four times, I have chosen to use their full name, as I also sometimes call the Qipisa people by their Inuktitut name: Qipisamiut.

3. Other instances of adult "baby" behavior are described in Chapter 4, Episode 9, in the section "Shall I Nurse?"

4. The *silait*-ness of small children is also useful to adults, as it justifies casting children as characters, all unwitting, in the adults' own interpersonal or intrapersonal plots. As we go on, we will see signs of these plots in some of the supposedly child-centered dramas, but systematic discussion of adult agendas is beyond the scope of this book.

5. When I speak of "rights," I am thinking of Saali, a little boy just a few weeks older than Chubby Maata, who one day was strenuously trying to reclaim his orange-soda-filled baby bottle from his four-and-a-half-year-old sister, Miika, who was drinking it all up. "Because she's a baby?" he yelled. His mother returned the bottle to him. We will meet Saali in Chapter 4.

6. The full incident is Episode A3 in Appendix 1.

7. The old Inuit way of kissing was to press the nose against a person's skin and inhale.

8. The full incident is Episode A2 in Appendix 1.

9. The full Inuktitut word is *silaittukuluugaviit.*

10. I use the clumsy expression "stage of development" because Qipisamiut, like many other Inuit, didn't arbitrarily link the acquisition of skills with chronological ages, as we do.

11. It is interesting that two hours prior to the exchange between Jaani and Chubby Maata that I recorded in Episode 4, Liila, visiting me with Chubby Maata, had protested in an affectionate voice that Chubby Maata was asking too many questions, but she had not explicitly associated her "criticism" with Chubby Maata's babyness, she had not called her *silait-,* and she had referred to Chubby Maata's questioning as "play": "This sweet little one is pretending to ask a lot of questions." Under these circumstances, Chubby Maata had gone right on asking questions and cheerfully said "ungaa" on request, apparently oblivious to any serious threat in her mother's comment; her baby identity was secure. But Episode 5, another fragment of this same encounter between Chubby Maata and Liila, shows us that Chubby Maata hovers on the edge of babyhood. (The entire exchange is described in Episode A1 in Appendix 1.)

12. At the first stage of understanding—certainly before language is acquired, but even after that time—I think tone must always be dominant. A lovely example of giving precedence to tone comes from an Utkuhikhalingmiut child. The child's grandfather used to *aqaq-* her when she was two by crooning, always in the same voice, "What a lovable little one; did you mistakenly think you weren't lovable?" But when she was a bit older—three or four—he began to croon different words to the same tune: "What a greedy little thing . . . " The old man was criticizing his granddaughter's demanding behavior, but for a long time that fact didn't register with her. She continued to hear the affection in the tone and not the criticism in the words. Her interpretation came to light one day when I refused to make bannock for her, and she shouted at me, "You *have* to make bannock for me because I'm greedy!"

13. The full incident is Episode A1 in Appendix 1.

14. The full incident is described in Chapter 6, Episode 29.

15. The role of young teenage socializers in the education of small children would be an interesting subject to investigate. Although girls in their early or middle teens were often given babies to "adopt" and care for under the watchful eye of the girls' mothers, adults didn't always trust teenagers to have an appropriate sense of behavioral limits. It was thought that the nurturant, *nallik-* feelings of the young people were still imperfectly developed, and indeed, I observed this to be true. When enacting "dramas" with small children they didn't always stop when the children became distressed; they didn't have adult tolerance for children's irritating behavior; and they had a tendency to confront misbehaving children directly instead of imaginatively distracting their attention. Adults chided them when they overstepped too far. Nevertheless, Liuna's action in Episode 8 makes me wonder whether younger socializers may sometimes have been of service to their elders—just as dramas were of service—in providing a context in which it was acceptable to take unacceptable but effective action. In this case, for instance, I am not sure that Liila or Arnaqjuaq would have physically overridden the children's protests and put them to bed willy-nilly. Nor am I sure that the children would have accepted such an action from mother or grandmother. But when Liuna did it, it worked. (At least in the short run. After lying in bed for a while and talking with Liuna, Rosi got up again and watched her parents playing cards. Liila *aqaq-*ed and snuffed her, played cards with her, and only once remarked in a discontented voice, "Rosi won't go to sleep; she slept too long today." She was still up when I left at 11:30.)

16. See the full version of Episode 5 in Appendix 1 (Episode A1). Another example can be found in Episode 28 in Chapter 6.

17. In fact, Chubby Maata did not always use denial as an adult would. One day, when she had just been heard shouting at her playfellow Kaati, her grandfather Mitaqtuq tested her to see if she would admit to being angry. When she did admit it, he laughed slightly and said, "Because you're a baby, yes?" When I asked what he meant, he explained, "If she were older, she would have denied it." We'll return to the question of "backwards" messages shortly.

18. See, for example, Episode 18 in Chapter 5.

19. Adults would intend the tone to be dominant also in the other "backwards" way of expressing affection that we have met, namely, the *ugiat-*ing attacks that we saw in Episode 1. In the case of *ugiat-*ing, however, it must have been harder for a small child to give the tone of voice its appropriate weight, because the attacks could be painful. I have seen children alternate between tears and laughter, as they wondered whether the blow they had received was hostile or affectionate.

20. Compare Episode 9: "Ih! I almost agreed."

CHAPTER 4: "WANT TO COME LIVE WITH ME?"

1. In the following description of the adult world of Qipisa, I omit some details of relationship that don't figure in my story, and I am deliberately vague on certain other points in order to protect the identity of the characters.

2. It was not uncommon for Inuit who had suffered the loss of a person important to them to

fill the gap through adoption, real or symbolic. Sometimes a small child who had lost his or her mother was "adopted" by the surviving father. But sometimes the adoption was for benefit of an adult who had lost or never had a spouse. And whether it was the child or the adopting adult or both who had suffered the loss, an exceptionally strong and tender bond (*unga-*) often developed between the two, as happened, for example, with Natsiq and Nivi after Nivi's mother died. For other examples, see Briggs 1970:162–164.

I don't believe that Miika continued to sleep with her grandfather much beyond the age of four. Before Miika was born, Natsiq had had a similar relationship with another granddaughter, Nivi's daughter Miali, who, like Miika, was named for Ukaliq. When Miali was an infant, Nivi took her to her grandfather's tent every night when he was ready to go to bed. The baby slept beside him until he fell asleep, and Nivi reclaimed her before her own household went to bed. The little girl continued to sleep with Natsiq until she was about four. Then Miika was born, and the new infant granddaughter took the place of the four-year-old.

3. Names—especially Inuit names but also sometimes Qallunaaq names (Nuttall 1992:90–93)—were and are an important source of bonds between individuals in Inuit society. One such bond, often a strong one, was created between people who shared one name. While I have no evidence that Maata felt a special identification with her small "same-name," it is a possibility. See Chapter 6, n. 18, for discussion of some other Inuit ideas about names.

4. Some Qipisa child had picked up from Pangnirtung children this English formula—"One, two, three, GO!"—for starting a race, and it was in wide use in Qipisa at the time this incident occurred. It was always said in English, although none of the children spoke that language.

5. Saali was not, biologically speaking, Chubby Maata's mother's brother. The kin term that Chubby Maata used was determined not by genealogy but by Saali's name, as Saali may have been named for one of Chubby Maata's uncles. Alternatively, he may have just happened to have the same name as one of the uncles. Yet again, Chubby Maata may have been given the name of someone who had once called someone of Saali's name "mother's brother." The possibilities are numerous.

Because a person may have several mother's brothers or other kin of a single category, diminutives like "darling little" (-*kuluk*) or "horrid little" (-*ruluk*)—neither one necessarily to be understood as emotional expressions in this context—were often attached to the kin terms to distinguish between individuals.

6. Compare Briggs 1970:148–149.

7. There is other evidence, too, that Maata's newly married state influenced her play with small children. See Episode A4 in Appendix 1.

8. See the Introduction, n. 16.

9. The judgment that testing is going on is based on several kinds of evidence. The most direct evidence is that adults sometimes stated explicitly, in conversation with a friend or in answer to my questions about motives, that this is what they were doing. Once I heard a teenager comfort a friend with whom she had been playing in this way by saying, "I was only testing you." Sometimes, too, adults, observing a child's refusal to be drawn by one of these playful questions, remarked with satisfaction, "She/he knows." Finally, as I have

said, when a child could no longer be drawn into a particular drama, adults stopped enacting that drama with that child.

10. The value of weakness is discussed in Chapter 5.

11. I owe this point to Dr. Inge Lynge (personal communication 1989).

12. Compare Briggs 1970:172–173.

13. On other occasions, too, Juupi introduces adult sexuality into a game ostensibly played with a child. One example occurs later in this sequence, as we have seen, and yet another is found in Episode A5 in Appendix 1.

14. I write "good progress" in quotation marks because I was the only person who saw my relationship with Chubby Maata in such simplistic terms. The development of that relationship, including Liila's role in it, is the subject of Chapter 6.

   When I checked the dates on which I had recorded changes in Chubby Maata's behavior toward me, for the purpose of writing Chapter 6, I discovered that in an earlier published account of this sequence of dramas (1991b, 1992b) I had inadvertently hastened the development of our relationship by a month or so and simplified it considerably. (A lesson in the virtue of compulsive record checking!) In early January, Chubby Maata had not "completely lost her fear" of me (Briggs 1991b:126, 1992b:35); on the contrary, she was still teetering back and forth very noticeably between fear (*ilira-*) and dislike (*piugingngit-*), and a more relaxed and trusting attitude; and Liila, driven, I am sure, by a mixture of feelings herself, was trying to modulate her daughter's treatment of me. All of these matters are discussed more fully in Chapter 6.

15. Boys were by no means free of fear, however. One young man was so alarmed on one occasion when I was playing the role of evil spirit that he became convinced that I had stolen his soul. Ten years later he still would not speak to me.

16. See the preceding note.

17. Remember that in Episode 1 Liila explained and condoned Rosi's attack on Chubby Maata by saying, "She's ugiat-ing you because you're a baby."

18. This distinction was pointed out to me by Vicky Steinitz (personal communication).

19. In English we express this conflict by setting "I want to" against "I ought."

20. Of course, the way I divide up "issues" and "themes" and the conceptual labels I attach to them influence the interrelations I see and the plots I construct. If I decide to talk about *three* issues—attachment, belonging, and possession—then it makes sense to say (as I shall, presently) "People are possessed, like objects," or "Fear of being possessed makes attachment problematic." If I didn't distinguish among these three issues, I wouldn't be able to make the "association" between people and objects or to see possession as "related to" attachment. Perhaps these concepts do some violence to Inuit experience—even to experience in general, which can rarely be so neatly classified in the living of it. Nevertheless, I think that, rough and ready as they are, they allow me to see, through a glass darkly, something meaningful to Inuit. And if I am aware of the effects of labeling on perception, I open the door to other (more Inuit?) ways of seeing.

21. When Qipisa people adopted children in infancy, the adopted children tended to be very much loved—perhaps even more so than if they had not been adopted. Nevertheless, I never saw a child respond positively to a playful offer of adoption like the one dramatized in this sequence. Indeed, such dramas were designed to discourage any desire to be

adopted. Maata was much loved by her adoptive family; nevertheless, one may well ask how her own history of adoption influences her understanding of this drama. The answer is not necessarily simple.

22. Interrogations directed toward children who were already adopted taught them to be aware of that fact and to identify correctly their various "parents." Thus, when Kaati's biological father—who was, by adoption, her sociological brother—came to the camp to visit, Arnaqjuaq and Mitaqtuq asked her, "Who is he to you?" "Where's your big brother?" "Who's your daddy?" And when baby Aita was brought to visit in her natal home, Liila, her biological mother, would coo at (*aqaq-*) her, "Who made *you*?"

23. In Chapter 5 we'll encounter another powerful drama (Episode 16) which may resonate for Chubby Maata with the open-ended question of whom she likes. There the question is reversed: who likes Chubby Maata? And the implicit—though superficial—answer is: nobody. In Episode 16, Arnaqjuaq merely suggests the existence of a united audience, but in the present drama, the judges are right there, and memories of such experiences may well enrich Chubby Maata's sense of the reality of troops in array when that reality is only hinted at; at the same time, questions of liking vibrate with the opposite possibility of disliking. We'll return to matters of liking and disliking in Chapter 5.

24. A fourth danger is that the right to belong, even the right to exist, may be contingent on the wish of someone to possess one, so *not* being loved could be even more dangerous than being loved. We will find hints of this dilemma in Chapter 5, but I don't see it in the present sequence of dramas.

25. See, for example, Episode 29 in Chapter 6 and Episodes A1 and A2 in Appendix 1.

26. I am not sure that Chubby Maata is capable of empathy yet, but resonances she certainly experiences.

27. There is evidence that the connection between mother and home often lasted well beyond babyhood. Much older children, too—up to age ten or twelve in my observations—came to fetch their mothers when the latter were out visiting. "Mother, come home," they pleaded. When mother asked whether anything was wrong, the answer was no, and if she asked why she should come, the answer might be a self-conscious smile and a repetition of the demand: "Come home!" Mother might "moo" at the child, "Always following mother!" but after a few minutes, if she couldn't distract the petitioner, she often gave in and went home. I judge, therefore, that the child wanted her not because something had happened at home that required her attention but simply because home was not home without her. I have also seen husbands go out to seek company or even follow their wives on a visit "because," they said, "it's lonely at home when my wife is out." I have already pointed out the association between wife and mother.

28. There are actually two perils, here and in other instances of wild, *silait-* behavior. One danger is being physically injured, the other is being laughed at. But I think that Chubby Maata is only beginning to perceive the second danger and that in Episodes 1 and 9 she is oblivious to it.

29. This subject is discussed at greater length in Chapter 5.

30. When adults engaged in "wild" behavior with one another, it was always defined as "play"; it was always in public, in the presence of an amused audience; and often, though not always, it was in contexts that were bounded by labels. There is, for example, a word

qitik-, which two Inuit women familiar with Baffin Island dialects (one is from Pangnirtung) have defined for me as "playing games." When Qipisa young people used the word, they were referring to a sort of tag that they played outdoors on dark nights. They told me that the goal of the game was to "lick the shoulder" of another player, and Juupi told me that anyone who was caught in this way could be "goosed." (See Episode A5 in Appendix 1.) It is possible that Juupi, describing the game in this way, was playing a sexual game with me, as young men often did. But it is equally possible that the game—which was certainly wild—*was* sexually toned. Another labeled context for wild behavior was the celebration *paqlatsiti-* (they all fall in disarray), which was held for birthdays and for "first achievements" of children, when old and young alike scrambled and shoved to catch the rain of goodies that the celebrating parent tossed out to the waiting camp. Apart from these named events, wild behavior occurred among teenagers, who often expressed affection in *ugiat-*ing ways: hitting, biting, pinching, kicking, and ripping one another's clothes. Older men, too, occasionally pursued young girls—including prepubescent children—with loud cries of excitement, threatening to goose them (Briggs 1975:180).

The "victims" of these events sometimes had mixed feelings about their experiences. Small children, tripped over and pushed aside in the chaos of *paqlatsiti-* celebrations, cried and were ignored by their excited elders. I once heard girls of eight or nine, in private conversation among themselves, "counting coup": "I've been goosed five times and kissed eight times . . . " But they—together with older girls and young women—also expressed fear of being goosed, and they avoided houses where these events might occur, saying that they felt *ilira-*.

31. Readers interested in the social functions of behavior that playfully inverts the values of "serious" life have a rich literature to explore. Two scholars whose work drew me as early as the 1970s are Babcock (1978) and Handelman (all the papers in *Models and Mirrors* [1990], some of which go back two decades and are reworked into a larger theoretical framework in the 1990 collection). Many other works can be found in the bibliography of *Models and Mirrors*.

CHAPTER 5: "WHO DO YOU LIKE?"

1. The form *piugi-* is composed of two elements: a base (or root), *piu-*, "good," and a postbase (or suffix), *-gi-*, "to be in relationship with." Thus a literal translation is "(to) consider good" or "(to) be in a good relationship with." It is often appropriate and less clumsy to translate *piugi-* as "(to) like (somebody)" and its opposite, *piugingngit-*, as "(to) dislike (somebody)." Sometimes, however, I translate literally, in order to clarify Inuit ways of thinking about relationship and attachment.

Piu-, "good," can also occur with the postbase *-saq-*, in which case it refers to the act of liking or considering good in general, without designating a particular relationship. Thus *Piusarunnangnginnavit?* means "Because you're unable to like (or consider good)?"

Finally, *piu-* can occur with a pronoun in the absence of any other postbase. In such cases, it refers to a quality of the person or object designated by the pronoun: *Piuvit?* ("Are you good?").

Readers will notice that my translations of *piu-* and its various postbases focus sometimes on the emotion of liking, sometimes on the attitude of considering good, and sometimes on the action of treating well. This range of meaning reflects the close associations that Inuit—like many other peoples—make among thought, feeling, and action. Other linguistic evidence supports the interpretation that "wanting" is very much akin to "doing." Just one example: the postbase *-tqu-* means both to wish (that something would happen) and to tell (someone to do something). Thus the word *qaitquyara* means both "I want her (or him) to come" and "I order him (or her) to come."

Some critics have wondered whether Chubby Maata was being taught to moderate her feelings or only her behavior. There is no doubt in my mind—and I hope to convince readers—that, in these emotionally intense interactions, she is learning *both*. I think Inuit take for granted, as I do, that it is emotions that govern behavior. The lessons about *piugi*-ing are only one case in point.

2. It should be remembered, here and throughout, that the dramas are not necessarily presented chronologically, and statements that seem sequential may not necessarily be so. Except in cases where one drama follows another immediately or almost immediately (as do Episodes 26A and B, and Episodes A1 and A2), a chronological ordering of statements would be meaningless, because the dramas presented in this book are only a small sample of those that Chubby Maata experienced every day.

3. Clinging is not the only possible defense against fear of loss. Another route to salvation— one that lifts one clear of the entire quagmire of contradictory feelings about liking—is to voluntarily let go. Adults did this when they *sirnaaq*-ed a favorite child or one who had been ill (see the Introduction, n. 4). And I suspect that anxiety about loss was one of the motives that urged Inuit toward outgrowing *unga-* feelings and made them embarrassed to feel *unga-* when they grew older. But *unga-* feelings were rarely overcome. This tension is not clearly in focus yet for Chubby Maata, but it is there, in the background, waiting to be discovered. Compare also Klein's observations (1975b:321–322) concerning the weakening of attachment and the push toward emotional and physical independence that may arise out of a fear of losing a loved person.

4. See the diagram of a qammaq on page 27.

5. The word that Rota used was *ataataksaq,* which translates, literally, as "father-material" or "father-potential." The postbase *-ksaq* (material or potential for [something]) designates adoptive relationships, among others. An *uiksaq* (potential husband) is a man who is betrothed, and *kamiksaq* (boot material) is just that: material destined to be made into boots; but a *paniksaq* is an adopted daughter and an *ataataksaq* is an adoptive father. Rota was suggesting that Jaani be substituted for—or perhaps added to—Saali's own father.

6. The interrogations directed to Saali and me also contained lessons in the proper appreciation and treatment of one's fellows, but I omit them here for fear of moving the discussion too far afield. The full sequence, as it was played, is described in Episode A6 in Appendix 1.

7. As mentioned in Chapter 2, *ilira-* is a complicated concept from the point of view of an English-speaker; it denotes a complex blend of emotions. See the last section of Chapter 5 and also Chapter 6 for more extended discussions of what it means, how it works, and attitudes toward it.

8. There may have been social reasons for Rota to feel a somewhat unusual degree of distance from most households of the camp. She had been adopted as a baby by her grandmother,

and when her grandmother, some years later, married Natsiq, Rota accompanied her to Qipisa as a half-grown child. Although the other three children in Natsiq's household were also adopted, they were all Natsiq's grandchildren and had been incorporated into his household long before Rota arrived. Moreover, their biological parents also had close ties with the community and sometimes lived in the camp, so Rota may have experienced them as more integral members of both household and community than she was while they were growing up. When she was grown, Natsiq arranged a marriage between her and one of her adoptive brothers, but in the meantime, Rota's grandmother (adoptive mother) had died, leaving Rota with only one genealogical relative in the camp: a younger brother who had been adopted at birth by Jaani's parents, Aana and Iqaluk.

Rota spoke of Qipisa as her home and seemed to have warm and easy relationships with her adoptive siblings as well as with Nivi, Natsiq's youngest and dearest daughter, who served as surrogate mother to all the adoptive children in his household. I have no reason to think Rota was unhappy in Qipisa. Nevertheless, it may be that her origin as an "outsider" and her more distant kin relationship with other households contributed to the rarity and brevity of her visits and the formality of her visiting behavior.

9. Again the kin term that Chubby Maata used was based on a "name relationship": the relationship that had existed between a previous holder of Chubby Maata's name and Iqaluk or some earlier holder of his name. As mentioned in Chapter 4, n. 5, suffixes attached to kin terms don't usually have their everyday meanings. Nevertheless, it is quite possible that Chubby Maata doesn't know this. If she understands -*ruluk* in its ordinary sense of "horrid little," even when it is part of a kin term, this may help to explain her dislike of Iqaluk.

10. Phyllis Morrow, in her paper on "symbolic actions [and] indirect expressions" in Alaskan Yupik (Eskimo) society (1990:141–158), tells us that one of the ways in which Yupik "defused the intensity" of confrontation when an offense had been committed was to revenge themselves not against the offender personally but against an object that symbolically represented the offender (148–149). (Her example, the smashing of a man's kayak, is taken from Fienup-Riordan 1988:48.)

Inuit also had (and may still have) a preference for indirection in many contexts. A case in point is one of the rationales that I was given for *sirnaaq*-ing a child—pretending that a most-favored child was least favored: if someone had a grievance against a father but feared to attack a strong man directly, he might injure or kill his favorite child instead. (See Introduction, n. 4). The logic is not the same as that of the Yupik discussed by Morrow, and Iqaluk's behavior is the inverse of *sirnaaq*-ing (the father is attacked instead of the child); nevertheless, the wish to avoid a breakdown of social relations seems common to all three cases.

11. "Dear little mother's sister" is again a "name term."

12. A few of the Qipisa children had lived for periods of time in Pangnirtung, where there were more Euro-Canadian influences, and children's chants and ritual formulae occasionally found their way back to the camp. Chubby Maata had heard Liila taunt or, rather, criticize *her* in the same tone, using the same word(s)—it is one word in Inuktitut—"qiasarait-": she cries easily.

13. It may be worth noting, nevertheless, that Arnaqjuaq does from time to time have

reservations about her son-in-law's character, so at another level she may mean it when she says that he is bad.

14. I remind readers, nevertheless, that, while Inuit in Chubby Maata's world and elsewhere valued protective concern (*nallik-*) very highly indeed, they were ambivalent about the sort of protective action, *sirnaaq*-ing, that created alliances. In Episodes 1 and 9, we saw glimmers of the difficulties that surrounded alliances, and the subject will be discussed again in the last section of this chapter. Nonetheless, adults often tested—and, I think, in the process, engendered—*nallik-* feelings in children by playfully inciting the children to *sirnaaq-* a "threatened" person. (For a central Arctic example, see Briggs 1970:173.) This is another of the many situations in which dramas taught proper feelings by inciting improper, or only partly proper, behavior.

15. I remind readers that motivations may vary from person to person and from instance to instance. In this case, the conclusions that I draw from evidence internal to the drama are supported by suggestions made to me by Inuit with whom I have discussed this incident and others like it, by Arnaqjuaq's own ways of thinking about these dramas, and by the warmth of Arnaqjuaq's everyday relationship with Chubby Maata. But her motivations are not necessarily those of other actors engaged with other children in other situations. (I have elaborated on these points in the Introduction.) I do not see deliberately hurtful intent in this interaction or, indeed, in most of Arnaqjuaq's social behavior; nevertheless, dramas do have the potential to incorporate such motives. Even Chubby Maata, beloved as she is, will certainly encounter some tangled motives from time to time; and when the intent, conscious or not, is to harm—or when Chubby Maata misunderstands motives that are not, in origin, dark—a drama may create complicated vulnerabilities.

16. As Minnie Aodla Freeman (personal communication 1996) put it, speaking of the "BAAAD" game, "It's dangerous to think you're perfectly good."

17. I owe this insight to another Inuit friend, Rebecca Qitsualik (personal communication 1965).

18. "Little mother" is a name term.

19. For an example of such an incident, see Episode A5 in Appendix 1. This incident, in which both Chubby Maata and Arnaqjuaq played large roles, occurred about six weeks after Episode 16. Though it is not yet in Chubby Maata's repertoire of associations at the moment we are analyzing, it soon will be, and she may already have experienced others like it. Episode A5 was played in celebration of Saali's maleness, but I saw no evidence that Chubby Maata recognized that motive.

20. Freudians will no doubt raise a triumphant "Ah ha!" at this point, while feminist theorists equally loudly cry, "Shame!" Bear in mind, however, that Qipisa was a hunting camp. Chubby Maata had often seen animals butchered and had had bits of meat cut for her to eat from raw carcasses laid out in full view. My view, here as elsewhere, is that we need to be guided by the ethnography in every case and not make the *assumption* that associations will vindicate Freudian theory.

21. When I outline the contradictory directives contained in these Inuit plots, people often ask whether this isn't a case of Bateson's "double bind" (1972:201–227). It is not. A defining characteristic of the double bind is that there is no right answer, a person "can't win" (201). Chubby Maata and her peers could and did win—as I hope I show—by

keeping their eyes, ears, and minds open and exercising the intelligence that was developed through these dramas and interrogations. Those who are nevertheless inclined to be critical of the rigors that Inuit imposed on small children might consider whether there are not tangled lessons to be learned about social life in our own world. How, if at all, do *we* help children to untangle the coil?

For other variants of the argument concerning the construction of morality, see Briggs 1979a, 1979b, 1982, and 1990. Ambivalences and dilemmas concerning attachment are discussed and summarized in a different way in Briggs 1995b.

Further insight into the ways that Inuit have interrelated autonomy and dependence in "voluntary mutuality" without introducing social hierarchy can be found in Phyllis Morrow's perceptive paper on how and why Yupik persons and American legal functionaries misunderstand each others' behavior (1996:405–423; the term quoted is first mentioned on 414). The worldview and social relationships of Yupiit (Siberian Eskimos) are remarkably similar to those of Canadian Inuit, geographically distinct though they be.

22. The distinction made in Inuktitut between the baby's natural, dependent, *unga-* attachment to mother and the more mature, protective love, *nallik-*, bears some resemblance to the distinction that Melanie Klein (1975b:306–343) makes between the baby's first love for the good, satisfying mother and the later, more complicated love born of the baby's conflicting emotions toward a mother who turns out to be not always satisfying. Klein tells us that the baby wishes to destroy or injure the ungratifying mother, but then, fearing to lose her—because she is still loved and needed—baby feels guilty and wishes to protect mother against those destructive impulses: "Even in the small child one can observe a concern for the loved one which is not . . . merely a sign of dependence upon a friendly and helpful person" (311). Winnicott (1965:73–81) adds that in order for this concern to develop in the normal way, it is necessary for mother to give baby the opportunity to make amends, that is, she must express pleasure in her baby. I don't have data that would enable us to determine whether unconscious guilt and a desire to make reparation for fantasized injury underlie *nallik-* feelings, but the dramas certainly do enact loss of a loved one and provide children with the opportunity to protect that loved one and so learn to love maturely. See also Chapter 6, n. 27.

23. In this gender-sensitive age, someone reading this is sure to ask whether this was a typically feminine response or whether the same was true of men. The answer is that men were even more careful than women to avoid escalating conflict, whether by argument or by physical attack. Had they not done so, people would have been terrified, because men are naturally strong. Even in the song duels that were used long ago in various Inuit societies to resolve or dissolve conflict, direct rebuttals of the always humorous accusations were not allowed (Eckert and Newmark 1980:192). See below, n. 25.

24. Compare this rationale for letting children fight their own battles with the one more familiar to us: children—boys in particular—should learn to "stand up for themselves."

Readers who recall the discussion of "overprotection" (*sirnaaq-*) in the Introduction, n. 4, may be puzzled here, because in that note I presented only one side of this complex concept: protective behavior that took the form of "neglecting" much-loved children, treating them as Cinderellas (or Ash Lads—I borrow from Norwegian folklore so as to encompass both genders). One of the motives for this kind of backhanded protectiveness was to make a child strong and self-reliant, independent of outside help; and, as far as I know, the strategy was understood and accepted.

Another, more everyday, kind of protectiveness took the form familiar to us of fighting a child's interpersonal battles for him. This *sirnaaq*-ing, too, was thought to increase the child's strength, but in an undesirable way: feeling invulnerable in interpersonal relations might encourage aggression. So this kind of *sirnaaq*-ing was bad.

Both varieties of *sirnaaq*- and attitudes toward them show us that standing alone, without allies, was an ideal (I deliberately don't say "the" ideal) posture. In Inuit theory, isolation fostered both lifesaving strength and a socially useful sense of weakness. To be sure, an outside observer might wonder about the interpersonal consequences of Cinderella treatment. While the relatively mild experience of losing a fight could have made children feel accommodating toward people who in general treated them benignly, being consistently treated as a Cinderella or Ash Lad might have persuaded children that there was nothing to be gained by being obliging. In any case, both of these constructions of overprotection, taken together, give us a vivid glimpse of the ambivalence toward attachment, which was (and may sometimes still be) one of the most striking strains in Inuit emotional dynamics. This ambivalence—which owed much to dramas like those explored in this book—is most fully explicated in Briggs 1978. Manifestations of this tension in modern Inuit society are described in Briggs 1995b.

25. In various Inuit societies in the old days, serious conflicts were often handled through song duels, whose effectiveness depended on their being ambiguous. The duels were formal performances in which two offended parties, in the presence of the camp and in the context of festivities, took turns at singing insulting songs. The songs purported to be good-humored and playful and could easily be confused with the friendly songs—equally insulting—that joking partners sang at each other in similar social contexts. Moreover, the songs never named the person at whom they were directed (Eckert and Newmark 1980). Even when the well-being of the camp required that a wrongdoer be identified, the exposé was never formulated as a matter of individual against individual; either a spokesman for the camp would make the accusation in the presence of the camp (Muckpah 1979) or the shaman—again in the presence of the camp as a whole—would elicit a confession from the wrongdoer.

    For interesting analyses of the functions of ambiguity in Eskimo (both Inuit and Yupik) life, see Eckert and Newmark 1980:191–211 and Morrow 1990:141–158.

26. See above, n. 25.

27. See above, n. 25.

28. Of course, the world is not a perfect place. For an example of what can happen when balance is shaken, see Briggs 1995b.

29. Here and in Chapter 6 I draw on D. W. Winnicott's concept of "transitional object" (1971). I owe to Simon Grolnick (personal communication 1990) the suggestion that play might be a Winnicott-ian transitional object for Inuit, enabling them to experiment with reality while at the same time maintaining some distance from it. For elaboration of the argument that Inuit play makes emotionally difficult lessons easier to learn, see Briggs 1990.

30. Speaking of children in our own society, Selma Fraiberg makes this point vividly in *The Magic Years* (1959:133–168).

31. Children in our own culture also play with issues that concern them. The therapeutic use of play in the treatment of troubled children is well known, and Fraiberg, in her charming account of "normal" child development, gives us delightful examples of playful strategies invented by American children for dealing with the difficult matter of constructing a conscience (1959:141–145). One of these devices is the invention of an imaginary friend as a scapegoat. Chubby Maata does not invent invisible playfellows, but we shall see that in changing her own moral value and that of others, she can be quite imaginative.

    In general, there is a great deal of resonance between what Fraiberg tells us about the feelings and behavior of American two- and three-year-olds confronted with problematic issues and the behavior I have observed among Inuit children. It would be interesting to compare the emotional and behavioral processes of moral development in American children with those of Inuit children, considering that parental strategies differ considerably in the two cultures and that opportunities and contexts for play also differ across cultures.

32. This is, of course, a name term.

CHAPTER 6: "I LIKE YOU, I DON'T LIKE YOU"

1. See Chapter 1 for more on the subject of "school."

2. The same parents who assured their children that it was not necessary to *ilira-* me told *me* that the reason children were obstreperous in my qammaq was that I did not evoke *ilira-* and that I should make efforts to do so. People's unease about *ilira-*, their ambivalence, may be one of the reasons why that emotion is so often taught through dramas, where people can claim they are "only joking." For a complementary perspective on the meaning of *ilira-*, see Brody 1975:157–161, 205–206.

3. I have seen children, too, taught to kill in response to *kappia-* fears. See below, n. 9.

4. Definitions given me for a third "fear" word, *sillu-*, demonstrate the closeness between *kappia-* and *ilira-* and perhaps also illuminate the feeling of *ilira-*. One young Qipisa woman defined *sillu-* as "feeling very *kappia-* of a person," whereas another defined it as "feeling like crying because of *ilira-* feelings." A third woman, bilingual and from a different community, told me in English that in her understanding, the word refers to a state of withdrawal for the sake of concealing and protecting injured feelings, "feeling slighted" (Rachel Qitsualik Tinsley, personal communication 1996).

    Evidence for a causal relationship between *kappia-* and *ilira-* is provided by the remark of a young mother observing her four-year-old son's "fear" of me: "It's all right if he *kappia-*s you, it will make him *ilira-* you."

5. Unfortunately, I don't remember whether the games began when they entered the qammaq or later. Nor do I know whether the second followed immediately after the first or only after an interval.

6. The entire incident is Episode A8 in Appendix 1.

7. Here and elsewhere, I underscore that Chubby Maata's beam was a *baby* beam, because

this rapturous smile was always read as baby behavior. Older children—even children four years old like Rosi—and adults did not beam. I did so occasionally when I was excited by some unexpected and happy event, and adults seeing my expression laughed and teased me about my childish display, calling it *qaqa-* (seeking affectionate attention).

8. Remember that "No" in answer to a negative question in Inuktitut means "You're wrong" (see Chapter 2, n. 2). The convention is the opposite of the English one.

9. A common game that adults and older children played with little ones was to frighten them with threads or hairs, which they pretended were alive and moving. "Iq!" the adult would say, pretending to be afraid. "It's alive! Kuinat (disgusting, or tickly)!" Or "It bites!" Of course, when children recoiled, or when their eyes grew big and their faces still with fear, their tormentors comforted and reassured them that they were only joking. But, later, adults used this game—the fear it engendered—to quiet children or distract them from undesirable activities.

The wordbase *kuinat-* and the exclamation *kuinat!* referred most frequently to substances that are unpleasant to touch, such as slime, body products, insects, worms, and small animals like lemmings, but it also referred to the sensation of being tickled. It is possible that Inuit perceived all such kinds of touch as disagreeable in the same way; I do not know.

Kuinat-, in the context of a game, seems a mild, non-life-threatening fear, but the games fed a very real, life-long revulsion toward small *live* creatures, both insects and mammals—a revulsion that, in the case of lemmings, bees, and flies, often grew into a strong fear which adults experienced as both *kuinat-* and *kappia-*. Adults of all ages and both sexes conducted lemming hunts with fervid excitement, and women screamed and flailed with fear in the presence of bees or houseflies. Even tiny children were taught to kill what they feared. I once saw Natsiq—himself very *kappia-* and *kuinat-* of lemmings—hand a stick to his two-year-old great-grandson, who was crying with fear (*kappia-*) of a baby bird. Said he: "If you fear it, kill it." So it may be that children playing *kuinat-* games were fueled by pretty scary associations.

10. The full incident is Episode A7 in Appendix 1. See also Chapter 1, page 35.

11. To explore the dynamics of adult *ugiat*-ing is outside the scope of this book, but watching Chubby Maata in incidents like this one makes me wonder whether that aggressive expression of tenderness has childhood roots in ambivalence about attachment. At the same time, Chubby Maata may not yet be mature enough to identify emotionally with other creatures. Compare Fraiberg's anecdote about the caterpillar-squashing four-year-old (1959:190–191).

12. This was mentioned in Chapter 4, in the section "Who Do You Like?"

13. Notice the similarities between Chubby Maata's behavior in this game and in Episode 9 (Chapter 3), which occurred a few weeks later. In both cases, she seems to have a weather eye turned to the rules of the game: here, "Is that how it's done?" "Have you stopped playing?" and in Episode 9, "Ih! I almost agreed." And in both cases, after the frightening drama is over, Chubby Maata starts a game of running to the door and back.

14. Remember that main clauses in Inuktitut sentences are often omitted.

15. Compare her movement in Episode 1 from *being* a baby to *performing* a baby.

16. The answer "Ukaliq" was correct because Chubby Maata was named for an old lady

named Ukaliq, who had died some time before Chubby Maata was born. But there were several other Ukaliqs in the camp who had also been named for that old lady, and one of them was a little girl about eight years old. The fact that "Lia," the next name that Chubby Maata proposed, was the eight-year-old Ukaliq's sister raises the possibility that the Ukaliq Chubby Maata had in mind was the little girl and not the old lady. Although Chubby Maata had certainly been told that she was named for the old Ukaliq, she may not have had that fact firmly in mind.

17. See nn. 8 and 19 concerning the formulation of questions.

18. So far, I have only hinted at the importance of personal names in Inuit social life; the subject is too complex to expound in detail in this book. Nevertheless, to understand what I mean in saying that certain adults "are" Chubby Maata, the reader will need the following explanation.

   Inuit in general believed that a personal name (*atiq*) was a kind of "soul," which carried with it various characteristics of the previous name-holder: physical, mental, or moral traits, skills, and abilities. How these beliefs were incorporated into social life varied from one group to another, and individuals, too, could use or ignore dimensions of these beliefs to suit their purposes. (For interesting information about how individuals use name-relationships in a modern West Greenlandic community, see Nuttall 1992: 63–93.)

   It would be a mistake to consider the identity between persons as physical reincarnation, since, at least in some groups, a baby could be given a name while the previous holder was still alive, and it was also possible for several babies to be named for the same person and for a single baby to be named for more than one person. In a social sense, however, namesakes did embody the persons they were named for. In addition to their genealogical kin, children acquired the relationships—including the affective bonds and often rights and obligations—that had belonged to the previous name-holder, and, as we have seen, people were often addressed by terms appropriate to one or more of their names. A mother might call one of her daughters "brother" (Inuit names were not gender-specific) and another daughter "grandmother," while her husband called the same daughters "cousin" and "aunt." (I expose only the tip of this terminological iceberg here.) Sometimes children were brought up in a quite literal way as though they were their "names." A most dramatic case was described by Washburne and Anauta (1940), Anauta, a Labrador Inuk, having been named for, and brought up as, her grandfather. Most important in the present context, though, is that aspects of a child's behavior were sometimes thought to derive from her or his name; and contrariwise, attempts might be made to influence childish behavior by reminding the offender that she was an adult and not a child at all.

   See Chapter 4, n. 3, concerning bonds between people who share a name.

19. There is a logic behind the formulation of questions in Inuktitut, as in other languages. This logic has to do with the wish to avoid confrontation, demandingness, and invasion of another's mental space, as two Inuit friends from different parts of the Arctic have—in almost identical words—confirmed (Minnie Aodla Freeman and Rachel Qitsualik Tinsley, personal communications 1996). Especially in adult conversation, Inuit tend to avoid open-ended questions. "Closed" questions, though in a sense "directed," allow the

person interrogated to answer with a simple, unelaborated (and occasionally, perhaps, false) yes, no, or maybe, thus keeping most of the contents of his or her mind private. Open questions like "Why?" are heard as both intrusive and critical.

Inuit, talking with adults, also tend to ask questions negatively—a gloomy-sounding practice to a Qallunaaq ear. My Inuit friends tell me, however, that to an Inuit ear, positively phrased questions, like open-ended ones, generally have a confrontational, invasive sound, whereas negative questions are more circumspect. I would add that when disagreement or rejection is expected in answer, a negative question has the potential to override the unpleasantness of a disappointment and reaffirm the social bond. This is because, contrary to the English convention, agreement with the content of a negative query—"Aren't you going?"—is signaled by a "Yes (you're right, I'm not going)." Compare, in English, the tone of "Are you busy?" with "May I come in?" The former is the equivalent of the negative Inuktitut question, which allows the busy person to agree—a bonding act—without offending, whereas the latter question may require a possibly hurtful rejection, which risks cutting the link between the two parties.

But in speaking with a child, the questioner's aim may be (as we know) to make the child think. In such circumstances, questioners may phrase the directive question in a way that forces the person addressed to counter the assumption or the wish that is built into the question—in other words, to make a thoughtful effort to answer. In Episode 28, Chubby Maata has claimed that she does not *ilira-* Yiini. If this is true, she might be expected to like Yiini. Nevertheless, her mother's second probe—"Because you dislike her?"—invites Chubby Maata to agree that she *dis*likes me. I wonder whether her mother's startling non sequitur is pointing out a contradiction in Chubby Maata's feelings and suggesting that Chubby Maata think about it. Another possibility is that she is reminding Chubby Maata that she usually claims to dislike me, trying to derail her from her inappropriate non-*ilira-* stance and nudge her toward the easy answer, agreement with her mother's suggestion.

20. Note, too, that this engagement between tunrait, one small and bold, one big and cannibalistic, occurs four days after the Evil Spirit game (Episode 24), in which Chubby Maata experimented with a new fear-denying response: "*nya*-nya . . . "

21. In my notes, there are no further instances of Liila asking Chubby Maata directly if she *kappia-*s me; the question is now always, "Do you *ilira-* Yiini?"

22. The first two paragraphs of this episode appear in Chapter 3 as Episode 6.

23. In Inuktitut, what Liila asked was "Iqqaitigigaviuk?" Literally, this means "Because she is a reminder to you (of something or someone)?" Because the connection between this question and the previous one—"Because you don't resemble her?"—was unclear to me, I asked Liila what she meant. Liila explained: "When someone doesn't resemble another person, we say 'he is a reminder of someone or something else.'" Consultation with other Inuit friends and friends of friends produced the interpretation that Liila's question was intended to remind Chubby Maata that I was a Qallunaaq (unlike Chubby Maata) and that she had had some not very pleasant experiences with Qallunaat. My consultants agreed that Liila was trying to engender *ilira-* feelings in her daughter so that she would behave with appropriate restraint.

24. Compare Episodes A1 and A2 in Appendix 1. Both of these incidents, which occurred

two months earlier, demonstrate the efficacy of Liila's property-awareness training. Further evidence that Chubby Maata had already learned a good deal about the importance of ownership is that on November 10 (Episode A8), when she was visiting me with her mother, she interrogated Liila in a most earnest manner about the ownership of objects in my qammaq: "Is this *our* lamp?" "Yes." "Is *that* one our lamp?" "No." "Does it belong to Kaati's household?" "Yes."

25. Compare this exchange with the much less friendly one that took place a little more than a month earlier on the same subject (Episode 14).

26. "Fetching" was a named activity like "visiting," "eating," and "sleeping." It was almost always children who "fetched," and often the fetching was legitimate; running errands for their elders was one of the jobs of children. "Go fetch milk from Yiini" or "Fetch a cigarette from Rota." But sometimes small children took it upon themselves to fetch what *they* wanted from a neighbor—especially from Yiini. I would hear outside my qammaq "Let's fetch"; then the qammaq door would creak open and two or more small persons would appear in the doorway: "We've come to fetch." "[Fetch] what?" "Bannock." In such cases, fetching was rude, and adults discouraged it.

Another way that children had of trying to acquire things they wanted, especially food, was to "wait." This, too, was a named activity; it was as rude as "fetching" but so inconspicuous to the untrained eye that I was not at first aware of it. I learned about it one day in March when Saali came in with a boy of seven who was visiting in Qipisa. I broke off writing up notes to converse with them a little. When I resumed writing, Saali said, "Let's go out," but the other replied very quietly, "Wait awhile." This exchange was repeated several times at intervals; then Saali asked, "What is it you want to get?" "I don't want anything," said his companion. Saali eventually departed alone, while the seven-year-old continued to sit for some time in perfect silence on the edge of my sleeping platform. I was impressed with his mature visiting behavior—until a couple of older children came in. They took one look at my demure little visitor; then one of them mooed: "He's waiting. He wants too much." My visitor left without a word. Later, his mother told me that the boy's father had jokingly told his son that I would give him a piece of candy, but never a word did the boy say; he just waited. Chubby Maata, Rosi, and Kaati knew about the waiting strategy, too, but they didn't know enough to be silent. On the one day that they tried it with me, they came in, sat down, and one of them—I didn't record which—announced, "I'm waiting."

27. My fieldnotes show that I first began to pay close attention to the to-ings and fro-ings of Inuit children vis-à-vis adults in 1970, when I noticed what I labeled "approach-avoidance games." There were many of these, and of course they were variously motivated. One particularly vivid example, designed to teach a little girl to feel *ilira*- in households that were not hers, is briefly analyzed from different angles in Briggs 1975:179 and 1994:177.

We have seen that many of the dramas that challenge Chubby Maata, too, are likely to make her feel somewhat ambivalent about approaching others. And later, when I encountered psychoanalytically oriented studies of child development (especially Fraiberg 1959; Klein 1975a, 1975b; Mahler et al. 1975; Winnicott 1965, 1971; and a series of seminars presented by D. M. A. Freeman to a psychoanalytic-anthropological colloquium [see

Freeman 1985, 1986]), I became aware of fundamental "developmental tasks" that, in our own children, give rise to seesawing behavior. Among such tasks, which I think we might usefully look for across cultures, are moving out of the first close relationship with a caretaker and entering on a "separate" existence; and learning to deal with an imperfectly gratifying world and with one's own positive and negative feelings (in Klein's terms, love and hate [1975a, 1975b]) toward the imperfect people who populate that world.

It may be that a sense of these issues has guided me throughout as I described the vicissitudes of Chubby Maata's journey out of babyhood, but I am particularly aware of this influence now, as I begin to discuss Chubby Maata's efforts to locate Goodness and Badness. I caution readers, however, to look for differences as well as seductive similarities when they compare the situation and the responses of our little Inuit girl with what psychoanalysts see in our own children. Familiar-looking behavior is suggestive, but it does not allow us to *assume* that familiar motives and feelings underlie it. Psychodynamics can be approached only by close observation, and my data do not permit systematic comparisons between worlds.

28. In translating Kaati's Inuktitut sentence—*Yiiniralaaraaluk piungngittuaralaaraaluk, Qallunaaq*—I rely heavily on her disgruntled, scolding tone of voice. The first two words mean something like "cussed little Yiini, bad little one." Inuit friends have suggested to me that Kaati is imitating affectionate, playfully scolding words that she has heard parents or siblings address to herself, a favorite child—words like *silaittukuluk* that mean she is bad and lovable at the same time.

29. Perhaps if I had been an Inuk, I would have experienced Chubby Maata as *my* conscience too, here and on other occasions when she and Kaati asked and I refused. An Inuit friend, Minnie Freeman (personal communication 1996) has reminded me that the rules worked both ways. True, the children shouldn't have asked; but since they *did* ask, it was incumbent on me to give.

30. But see Episode 36, in which Chubby Maata seems to "explain" her "dislike" of me by labeling herself a "tunraq."

31. Unfortunately, I took only scattered notes on Chubby Maata's first solo visit, which occurred on January 29. The text of those notes can be found in Episode A9 in Appendix 1.

32. I don't recall seeing any child display toward any adult other than me the sort of uneasy "bravado" exemplified by Chubby Maata's declamatory "toilet paper!" (Episode 29).

33. Compare the instructions Liila gave her daughters in order to calm them at the end of Episode 1 and again gave Chubby Maata in Episode 28 when the door opened.

34. In Inuktitut the word "why (*summan*)?" has a challenging quality and implies criticism. See above, n. 19.

35. For the full text of this encounter see Episode A10 in Appendix 1. Compare also, in this chapter, Kaati's reaction to my refusal to provide her with pictures to copy.

36. Both ease and unease were strikingly demonstrated on one of Chubby Maata's solo visits a month later, when I uncharacteristically asked her about her feelings toward another Qallunaaq, a game officer, who had been staying for a few days in her home. On that occasion, she was stricken, and the contrast with her usual manner made me realize how trusting her "normal" behavior was with me. See Episode A14 in Appendix 1 for an

illustration of Chubby Maata's feelings about the game officer and Episode A15 for the full account of her reaction to my questioning.

37. Among adults, saying the opposite *both* marks the unexpressed sentiment, displaying it in larger form than would be the case in an ordinary, straightforward statement, *and*— often, I think—expresses both sides of an ambivalence. When a child does it, innocent of the rules of adult speech, it may *only* express ambivalence.

38. Compare her jittery reaction to the interrogation about *piugi*-ing in Episode 9.

39. On two other later occasions, aggression was even more evident in Chubby Maata's associations to my torn flooring, though it was always playfully enacted. Visiting me on February 16 (Episode A11 in Appendix 1), she several times asked my permission to "break" it, her expression impish and her hand poised over the tear; and on March 14 (Episode A16 in Appendix 1), she first asked me whether children had broken the flooring, then pulled my balaclava off my head and said in a tone that I heard as pleased satisfaction, "I broke it completely." (*Surat-*, the word that she used in both cases, was incorrect from an adult point of view; correctly used, it refers to objects, like machines, which can be taken apart.)

40. Strong physical threats were not foreign to Chubby Maata's repertoire. Some days later, while Chubby Maata was playing with the laces at my neck, she smiled at me cozily and said (naming first her father's teenage brother, who often played with her, and then a visitor to the camp, whom she feared), "Matiiusi (or Piita) is going to make you cry while you're asleep." (See Episode A12 in Appendix 1.) And in one of her later games (Episode 39), she threatened to kill me if I didn't give her bannock.

41. Rather than using the original English words, I translate here the Inuktitut version of the hymn, which Chubby Maata was singing.

42. I am not sure that Inuit ever do "fully categorize" people. See again Morrow's remarks (1990:145)—I mention them in the Introduction—on the importance of indeterminacy in Inuit life. But perhaps our own categories are not as stable, bounded, and unidimensional as we like to think they are, either.

43. See above, n. 27.

44. See Chapter 5, n. 1, concerning the semantics of *piu-* and *piugi-*.

45. Fraiberg (1959:242) reserves the term "conscience" for a "system of built-in controls" that operates in the absence as well as in the presence of an authority, and she says that in North American children a true conscience is not usually seen until the age of four or five. Before that, an impulse will be controlled only when a potentially disapproving adult is in the room, and "guilt" will be experienced only when a "crime" has been discovered (138–139). Chubby Maata seems to be somewhere between these two "stages." She gives every sign of wishing for an audience to support her moral actions; on the other hand, we have seen her consistently resist when either mother or father tempts her to break the rule that she has learned. Whether she does this because an independent conscience tells her the rule must not be broken or because she sees through the seductive suggestion to the certainty that the tempter will disapprove if she takes the bait, I don't know. I suspect that the distinction between these two alternatives is more theoretical than practical, both in her world and in ours.

46. Compare the ability to "play baby," which Chubby Maata demonstrated in Episode 1.

47. Concerning the age and gender of those who played this game, see below, n. 48.

48. Most of the small, and not so small, children of both sexes played "When you leave . . . " and "Watch, I'm stealing . . . " with me. But I believe that the adults who did so were all male. Most were young bachelors who had "joking relationships" with me. Mitaqtuq was not young, but he was known and liked for the ease with which he joked. As I was a protegée of Mitaqtuq's family, it was Mitaqtuq who repaired my leaks and my lamp and made sure that my fuel can was full and my larder supplied with meat; he looked in, nearly every day, to be sure I was all right. And in company he often made me his stooge, his voice, as he dictated comically insulting and usually pointed lines for me to say to him and to others. Interestingly, though women of all ages joked with me and played other kinds of games with me, they did not, as far as I remember, enact dramas about acquiring my possessions. I have no idea why not.

    On the other hand, many adults of both sexes played these games with small children. Compare "Why don't you die so I can have it?" (Briggs 1979b). The interrogator in this drama was Arnaqjuaq, but the child was not Chubby Maata.

49. Episode 39 happened on the same day as Episode 37; unfortunately, I don't know which occurred first.

50. The gifting vocabulary in Inuktitut is rich and highly specific. Some examples, taken from various Canadian dialects: *tuni-*, give or hand to someone (the most general term); *tuniuqai-*, distribute, give to everyone; *piti-*, share, give some of; *tuyuuq-*, send as a gift to someone at a distance; *payuk-*, take or send a bit of food from one's own house to the house of someone else in the same camp or community; *hatuq-*, give a present in gratitude; *qumiu-*, save something (such as food) for someone; *minaqsi-*, give a special treat to someone special; *paqlatsiti-*, distribute by throwing goods into the air, so that camp members can scramble and grab for them (a way of celebrating a first catch or, in the years of Chubby Maata's youth, a birthday); *aittui-*, pass on something (said of germs but also of other more desirable things).

51. There have been other occasions, too, when Chubby Maata has made up songs about distressing events. See Episode A13 in Appendix 1. And remember that when she can't get into her house, she doesn't yell or cry; she chants (Chapter 1).

52. Compare Chubby Maata's invention of the name "Tiini" in Episode 1.

53. This interaction is Episode A17 in Appendix 1.

54. See above, n. 45. Both when she *pretends* to steal and tells me *not to watch* her restitution of my cup and when, invisible in my porch, she refrains from stealing, Chubby Maata gives us another kind of evidence that her moral behavior both does and does not require an audience. In playing with morality, Chubby Maata practices independent self-control. Play again seems to be a learning arena, "transitional" in Winnicott's (1971) sense.

CONCLUSION

1. Studies of play in recent years have multiplied like the sorcerer's broom; it is impossible to decide whom to cite. Scholars—Handelman (1990) and Babcock (1978)—whose insights started me thinking about the relationships between play and social order are cited in Chapter 4, n. 31.

2. Seminal contributions made by psychologists to the study of *children's* understanding of emotions and other mental phenomena include, among others, Dunn 1988, Harris 1989, Saarni and Harris 1989, and Wellman 1990. Like studies of play, cross-cultural studies of emotion have so proliferated in recent years that to list a few authors is to offend many. Relatively few of these, however, have focused on the *socialization* of affect. I therefore offend fewer, perhaps, if I mention one early symposium on the subject, which was published as a special issue of *Ethos* (Harkness and Kilbride 1983). Within that symposium, Lutz's brief discussion (1983:246–262) of the Ifaluk emotion of *metagu* is particularly interesting, partly because of its useful theoretical framework and partly because *metagu,* its cultural role as a "socializing emotion," and the means used to engrain it in children are both similar to and very different from the Inuit emotion of *ilira-* and the strategies we have seen employed to make Chubby Maata feel it. For other observations on the socialization of Ifaluk emotions, see Lutz 1988.

3. Not to mention the increasing permeability of those boundaries.

4. "Naturalistic" data on the development of social understanding in young American children can be found in the serendipitous studies that Dunn (1988) made of the conversations and social interactions of one- to three-year-olds and in a collection of essays edited by Bretherton (1984) on the symbolic play of infants and preschool children. Like Fraiberg's (1959) account of psychological issues in early childhood, these studies compare interestingly with Chubby Maata's behavior.

5. A number of recent studies of language socialization in different cultures point out that in learning what to say and how, when, and to whom to say it, children are also learning what to value and how to manage emotions. Crago 1988 has given us an Inuit example. Among works dealing with other cultures, contributions by Schieffelin (1979 and 1990), Ochs (1988), and the other authors (Eisenberg, Miller, and Clancy) represented in part 3 of Schieffelin and Ochs (1986) stand out.

6. Corsaro and Miller (1992) and the authors represented in their volume make a strong case for "interpretive" approaches to socialization, approaches that show children as active agents in negotiating their worlds. Wentworth (1980), from a sociological perspective, also argues that we should attend to the interactive processes involved in socialization.

7. Mishler (1995) has plotted for us a useful typology of the ways in which narrative researchers currently formulate their problem and the dimensions they consider in their analyses, while Nelson's collection (1989) illustrates an interesting variety of approaches to the interpretation of a small child's solitary monologues. My favorite account of a child's personal use of narrative is Peggy Miller's story about how her young son molded and remolded Peter Rabbit to his shifting purposes (Miller et al. 1993).

8. I venture to suggest that, in a small way, Chubby Maata's experiences may even address the malaise of our world, our time: the subterranean seepings of uncertainty; the unsettling of stabilities, large and small; the problems of finding ways to belong. I think she shows us that, under some circumstances, social and psychological worlds can be very solidly built on tangles, doubts, ambiguities, and ambivalences. Contrariwise, she reminds us that even in a simple world a sense of belonging may be psychologically complex, and may have to be negotiated.

9. To take just one domestic example: as scholarly discourses change, I have been amazed at

the variety of uses that *Never in Anger* (Briggs 1970) has (and has not) been put to and the changing shapes that praise and criticism have taken.

10. Again, as in the Introduction, the following discussion draws heavily on the paper in which I first formulated these ideas (1991b, 1992b).

11. In a different context, Eleanor Duckworth (1987), following Piaget, has vividly described individual learning processes among North American children: the very different routes by which children may learn to solve the problems with which they are presented in school—unbeknown to their teachers, who assume that everyone learns (or fails to learn) in the same way.

12. I think this supposition follows naturally from the abundance of knowledge we have about cultural variations not only in social structure and worldviews but also in the quality of interpersonal relations and in what is currently called the "construction of self."

13. To be sure, clinically oriented writers like Berne (1964), Laing (1969), Szasz (1961), Bateson (1972:201–227, 228–243), and other more recent therapists have pointed out the "game playing" in human relationships, too, but when they delineate plots, it is primarily to direct attention to destructive ways in which individuals manipulate others.

14. No doubt there are many other repetitive messages, too, in other communicative modalities: facial expressions, touches, smells, and so on.

15. This point—underdeveloped in this book—has much in common with anthropological analyses of the social functions of ritual, another enormous domain of study. Wentworth (1980:88), also speaking of "the (ritual of) socializing activity," makes the point that the act of enforcing social rules in teaching them to children reaffirms the adults' own commitment to those rules. (Wentworth is citing Berger and Luckmann 1966:58–61, but I don't think that is what these authors are saying on the pages cited; the point is really Wentworth's.)

16. The noncontextual mode of analysis that I used is described in the Introduction.

17. Of course, an observer's "logic and sense of likelihood" influence the way in which she or he interprets *one* child's interactions, too, but in the latter case, the availability of detail, strictly attended to, reins in galloping hypotheses at every turn.

18. For example, the "same" value may be psychodynamically different and may play different roles in the psychic economies of different individuals, or for the same individual at different points in the life cycle or even at different moments in the day, because it is associated with different tangles of experience. "Honesty" means something different to me on a day when I have been robbed than it meant when I learned "Thou shalt not steal" in Sunday school, and it means something different when I am afraid of being caught in a lie to an anonymous bureaucrat than it means when I am lied to by someone I love and trust. On all these occasions, the value I place on honesty is underlaid and supported by different emotions, associations, beliefs, and motives, and it gives rise to different behavioral tendencies.

19. It occurs to me that this is a rather Inuit way of looking at the world. The Inuit I knew in camps also tended to see objects—including people—not as static, preformed entities but as raw materials with multiple potentials (Briggs 1991a). Morrow 1990 makes much the same point about Yupik Eskimos.

20. To say that perceived problems produce a ferment conducive to self-awareness and change is by no means an original point on either personal or cultural levels. However, we sometimes argue (I have done so myself [1997]) that cultural awareness derives from a threat to the culture. From this perspective, change itself is the problem.

21. Even the dramas that I present in this book have many more riches to offer. They contain more themes and almost certainly more plots, are interconnected in more ways, and raise more questions than I have been able to delve into here. Perhaps in another lifetime—or somebody else's lifetime . . .

APPENDIX 1: ADDITIONAL EPISODES AND UNABRIDGED EPISODES

1. *Kappia-* is a fear of physical injury—a fear that Liila is trying to replace with the social fear *ilira-* (see Chapter 6), which would have been appropriate in this situation. Chubby Maata doesn't yet talk spontaneously about feeling *ilira-,* although she answers yes-or-no questions about whether she feels it. In her not-quite-three-year-old fashion, she also misconstrues the word she uses here, so that instead of saying she *feels* kappia- (*kappiasuktunga*), she says she *causes* the fear, is scary (*kappianaqtunga*).

2. The full Inuktitut word is *silaittukuluugaviit.*

3. For an explanation of Chubby Maata's unease, see Chapter 6, n. 9. Catkins were dried, then rolled between the palms to separate the fluff from the solid seed pod and to consolidate the fluff. The pod was removed and the packed fluff was spread in a low line along the straight edge of the half-moon-shaped qulliq. The qulliq was filled with enough oil so that the bottom edge of the fluff was submerged. When the fluff—the wick—had absorbed enough oil to saturate it, it was lit. It made a long, straight line of flame along the flat side of the qulliq.

4. I have translated literally here. Maata is *aqaq*-ing Miika; she means that Miika is a treasured baby. Miika is perhaps a little too old to be addressed this way—and much too young to be French-kissed.

5. This was not the only time I saw a seal fetus used as a toy, but of course it didn't happen very frequently, as pregnant seals were not often shot.

6. Compare Juupi's surreptitious attacks on Chubby Maata in Episode 9.

7. See Chapter 4, n. 30.

8. Arnaqjuaq meant that she had been his mother's midwife. Special kin terms were used by midwives and the children they helped to bring into the world.

9. All the Inuit children I knew had two ways of saying no without uttering a word. One, as we've seen, was to wrinkle the nose. The other, stronger and more hostile in appearance, was to blink the eyes. Adults, too, wrinkled their noses, but they did not blink their eyes.

10. This incident is also described in Chapter 1, page 35.

11. The word *amaamak-,* which Chubby Maata used, refers equally to sucking from a baby bottle and nursing from the breast.

12. We know that children were often—indeed, Chubby Maata had just been—cautioned not to injure (*aʼa-, ugiat-*) others. We also know that children often experienced mildly painful *ugiat*-ing attacks, which were always interpreted as playful and affectionately motivated, and that adults sometimes playfully feinted injury to a child or, more often, to

someone a child loved (see Chapter 5). Nevertheless, I had never before heard threat of injury used to deter a person from approaching another; nor did I ever hear such a threat again.

13. Compare Episodes 9 and 24 for other uses of running to the door and back.

14. This incident is referred to in Chapter 6, page 200.

APPENDIX 3: GLOSSARY

1. It is also possible to treat *tiiliuruti-* (teakettle) as a compound base, composed of the simple base, *tii-* (tea), followed by two postbases, *-liu(q)-* (make) and *-ruti-* (instrument for).

2. When preceded or followed by "i," the cluster "ts" may be phonemically "tt" or it may be moving in that direction as the dialect shifts toward geminate consonant clusters. For the moment, I choose to represent this cluster as "ts" because that is what it sounds like to the untutored ear.

References

Addams, Charles. 1954. *Homebodies.* New York: Simon and Schuster.

Ajurnarmat. 1979. Special Issue: International Year of the Child. Eskimo Point, N.W.T., Canada: Inuit Cultural Institute.

Anoee, Martina Pihujui. 1979. "Remembered Childhood." In: *Ajurnarmat,* Special Issue: International Year of the Child. Eskimo Point, N.W.T., Canada: Inuit Cultural Institute.

Arnheim, Rudolf. 1969. *Visual Thinking.* Berkeley: University of California Press.

Babcock, Barbara A. 1978. *The Reversible World: Symbolic Inversion in Art and Society.* Ithaca: Cornell University Press.

Bateson, Gregory. 1972. *Steps to an Ecology of Mind.* New York: Ballantine.

Berger, Peter L., and Thomas Luckmann. 1966. *The Social Construction of Reality.* New York: Doubleday.

Berne, Eric. 1964. *Games People Play.* New York: Grove Press.

Bowlby, John. 1979. *The Making and Breaking of Affectional Bonds.* London: Tavistock.

Bretherton, Inge (ed.). 1984. *Symbolic Play: The Development of Social Understanding.* New York: Academic Press.

Briggs, Jean L. 1970. *Never in Anger: Portrait of an Eskimo Family.* Cambridge: Harvard University Press.

———. 1974. "Eskimo Family Life." In: R. Prince and D. Barrier (eds.), *Configurations.* Toronto: Lexington Books, D. C. Heath, pp. 71–77.

———. 1975. "The Origins of Nonviolence: Aggression in Two Canadian Eskimo Groups." In: Warner Muensterberger (ed.), *The Psychoanalytic Study of Society,* vol. 6. New York: International Universities Press, pp. 134–203.

———. 1978. "The Origins of Nonviolence: Inuit Management of Aggression (Canadian Arctic)." In: Ashley Montagu (ed.), *Learning Non-Aggression.* New York: Oxford University Press, pp. 54–93.

———. 1979a. *Aspects of Inuit Value Socialization.* Ottawa: Mercury Series, National Museum of Man.

———. 1979b. "The Creation of Value in Canadian Inuit Society." *International Social Science Journal* 31:393–403.

———. 1982. "Living Dangerously: The Contradictory Foundations of Value in Canadian Inuit Society." In: E. Leacock and R. Lee (eds.), *Politics and History in Band Societies.* New York: Cambridge University Press, pp. 109–130.

———. 1983. "Le modèle traditionnel d'éducation chez les Inuit." *Recherches amérindiennes au Québec* 13(1):13–25.

———. 1990. "Playwork as a Tool in the Socialization of an Inuit Child." *Arctic Medical Research* 49:34–38.

———. 1991a. "Expecting the Unexpected: Canadian Inuit Training for an Experimental Lifestyle." *Ethos* 19:259–287.

———. 1991b. "Mazes of Meaning: The Exploration of Individuality in Culture and of Culture Through Individual Constructs." In: L. Bryce Boyer and Ruth Boyer (eds.), *The Psychoanalytic Study of Society,* vol. 16. Hillsdale, N.J.: Analytic Press, pp. 111–153.

———. 1992a. "Lines, Cycles, and Transformations: Temporal Perspectives on Inuit Action." In: S. Wallman (ed.), *Contemporary Futures,* A.S.A. Monograph no. 30. London: Routledge, pp. 83–108.

———. 1992b. "Mazes of Meaning: How a Child and a Culture Create Each Other." In: W. A. Corsaro and P. J. Miller (eds.), *Interpretive Approaches to Children's Socialization.* San Francisco: Jossey-Bass, pp. 25–49.

———. 1994. "'Why Don't You Kill Your Baby Brother?': The Dynamics of Peace in Canadian Inuit Camps." In: L. E. Sponsel and T. A. Gregor (eds.), *Nonviolence and Peace: Anthropological Insights.* Boulder, Colo.: Lynne Rienner, pp. 155–181.

———. 1995a. "The Study of Inuit Emotions: Lessons from a Personal Retrospective." In: J. A. Russell et al. (eds.), *Everyday Conceptions of Emotion.* Dordrecht, The Netherlands: Kluwer, pp. 203–220.

———. 1995b. "Vicissitudes of Attachment: Nurturance and Dependence in Canadian Inuit Family Relationships, Old and New." *Arctic Medical Research* 54(suppl. 1):24–32.

———. 1997. "From Trait to Emblem and Back: Living and Representing Culture in Everyday Inuit Life." *Arctic Anthropology* 34(1):227–235.

Brody, Hugh. 1975. *The People's Land.* Harmondsworth: Penguin.

Chance, Norman A. 1966. *The Eskimo of North Alaska.* New York: Holt, Rinehart, and Winston.

Clancy, Patricia M. 1986. "The Acquisition of Communicative Style in Japanese." In: Bambi B. Schieffelin and Elinor Ochs (eds.), *Language Socialization Across Cultures.* Cambridge: Cambridge University Press, pp. 213–250.

Corsaro, William A., and Peggy J. Miller (eds.). 1992. *Interpretive Approaches to Children's Socialization*. San Francisco: Jossey-Bass.

Crago, Martha Borgmann. 1988. "Cultural Context in Communicative Interaction of Inuit Children." Ph.D. diss., McGill University, School of Human Communication Disorders.

Dewey, John. 1965. *"The Influence of Darwin on Philosophy" and Other Essays in Contemporary Thought*. Bloomington: Indiana University Press.

Duckworth, Eleanor. 1987. *"The Having of Wonderful Ideas" and Other Essays on Teaching and Learning*. New York: Teachers College Press.

Dunn, Judy. 1988. *The Beginnings of Social Understanding*. Cambridge: Harvard University Press.

Eckert, Penelope, and Russell Newmark. 1980. "Central Eskimo Song Duels: A Contextual Analysis of Ritual Ambiguity." *Ethnology* 19(2):191–211.

Edwards, Betty. 1979. *Drawing on the Right Side of the Brain*. Los Angeles: J. P. Tarcher.

Eisenberg, Ann R. 1986. In: Bambi B. Schieffelin and Elinor Ochs (eds.), *Language Socialization Across Cultures*. Cambridge: Cambridge University Press, pp. 182–198.

Fajans, Jane. 1985. "The Person in Social Context: The Social Character of Baining 'Psychology.'" In: Geoffrey M. White and John Kirkpatrick (eds.), *Person, Self, and Experience: Exploring Pacific Ethnopsychologies*. Berkeley: University of California Press, pp. 367–397.

Fienup-Riordan, Ann. 1988. "Eye of the Dance: Spiritual Life of the Bering Sea Eskimo." In: William W. Fitzhugh and Aron Crowell (eds.), *Crossroads of Continents: Cultures of Siberia and Alaska*. Washington: Smithsonian Institution Press, pp. 256–270.

Fraiberg, Selma H. 1959. *The Magic Years*. New York: Charles Scribner's Sons.

Freeman, Daniel M. A. 1985 and 1986. "Normal Child Development from a Psychoanalytic Perspective." Taped seminars presented at "Childrearing Across Cultures," sessions at the Interdisciplinary Colloquium on Psychoanalytic Theory and Methods in Anthropological Fieldwork, American Psychoanalytic Association, New York, December.

Freeman, Minnie Aodla. 1978. *Life Among the Qallunaat*. Edmonton: Hurtig.

Freud, Anna. 1966. *The Ego and the Mechanisms of Defense*. New York: International Universities Press.

Freud, Sigmund. 1951. *The Psychopathology of Everyday Life*. New York: Mentor Books, New American Library.

Geertz, C. 1983. "From the Native's Point of View: On the Nature of Anthropological Understanding." In: Geertz, *Local Knowledge*. New York: Basic Books, pp. 55–70.

Goffman, Erving. 1959. *The Presentation of Self in Everyday Life*. New York: Doubleday Anchor.

Hall, Edward T. 1959. *The Silent Language*. New York: Doubleday.

———. 1969. *The Hidden Dimension*. New York: Doubleday Anchor.

Handelman, Don. 1990. *Models and Mirrors: Towards an Anthropology of Public Events*. Cambridge: Cambridge University Press.

Harkness, Sara, and Philip L. Kilbride (eds.). 1983. Special Issue: The Socialization of Affect. *Ethos* 11(4).

Harris, Paul L. 1989. *Children and Emotion: The Development of Psychological Understanding*. Oxford: Blackwell.

Honigmann, John J., and Honigmann, Irma. 1959. "Notes on Great Whale River Ethos." *Anthropologica* 1:106–121.

———. 1965. *Eskimo Townsmen.* Ottawa: Canadian Research Centre for Anthropology, University of Ottawa.

———. 1970. *Arctic Townsmen.* Ottawa: Canadian Research Centre for Anthropology, St. Paul University.

Hughes, Charles C. 1974. *Eskimo Boyhood.* Lexington: University Press of Kentucky.

Klein, Melanie. 1975a. *"Envy and Gratitude" and Other Works, 1946–1963.* London: Hogarth Press.

———. 1975b. *"Love, Guilt, and Reparation" and Other Works, 1921–1945.* London: Hogarth Press.

Laing, R. D. 1969. *Self and Others.* 2nd ed. Harmondsworth: Penguin.

Laing, R. D., and A. Esterson. 1964. *Sanity, Madness, and the Family.* Harmondsworth: Penguin.

Lutz, Catherine. 1983. "Parental Goals, Ethnopsychology, and the Development of Emotional Meaning." *Ethos* 11:246–262.

———. 1988. *Unnatural Emotions.* Chicago: University of Chicago Press.

Mahler, Margaret S., Fred Pine, and Anni Bergman. 1975. *The Psychological Birth of the Human Infant: Symbiosis and Individuation.* New York: Basic Books.

Miller, Peggy J. 1986. "Teasing as Language Socialization and Verbal Play in a White Working-Class Community." In: Bambi B. Schieffelin and Elinor Ochs (eds.), *Language Socialization Across Cultures.* Cambridge: Cambridge University Press, pp. 199–212.

Miller, Peggy J., et al. 1993. "Troubles in the Garden and How They Get Resolved: A Young Child's Transformation of His Favorite Story." In: Charles A. Nelson (ed.), *Memory and Affect in Development,* Minnesota Symposia on Child Psychology, vol. 26. Hillsdale, N.J.: Lawrence Erlbaum, pp. 87–114.

Mishler, Elliot G. 1995. "Models of Narrative Analysis: A Typology." *Journal of Narrative and Life History* 5(2):87–123.

Morrow, Phyllis. 1990. "Symbolic Actions, Indirect Expressions: Limits to Interpretations of Yupik Society." *Etudes/Inuit/Studies* 14(1–2):141–158.

———. 1996. "Yupik Eskimo Agents and American Legal Agencies: Perspectives on Compliance and Resistance." *Journal of the Royal Anthropological Institute,* n.s., 2(3):405–423.

Muckpah, James. 1979. "Remembered Childhood." In: *Ajurnarmat,* Special Issue: International Year of the Child. Eskimo Point, N.W.T., Canada: Inuit Cultural Institute.

Nelson, Katherine (ed.). 1989. *Narratives from the Crib.* Cambridge: Harvard University Press.

Nuttall, Mark. 1992. *Arctic Homeland: Kinship, Community, and Development in Northwest Greenland.* Toronto: University of Toronto Press.

Ochs, Elinor. 1988. *Culture and Language Development: Language Acquisition and Language Socialization in a Samoan Village.* Cambridge: Cambridge University Press.

Polanyi, Michael. 1967. *The Tacit Dimension.* London: Routledge and Kegan Paul.

Saarni, Carolyn, and Paul L. Harris (eds.). 1989. *Children's Understanding of Emotion.* Cambridge: Cambridge University Press.

Sapir, Edward. 1958. "The Unconscious Patterning of Behavior in Society." In: Sapir, *Selected*

Writings of Edward Sapir. Edited by David G. Mandelbaum. Berkeley: University of California Press, pp. 544–559.

Schieffelin, Bambi B. 1979. "How Kaluli Children Learn What to Say, What to Do, and How to Feel." Ph.D. diss., Columbia University.

———. 1990. *The Give and Take of Everyday Life: Language Socialization of Kaluli Children.* Cambridge: Cambridge University Press.

Schieffelin, Bambi B., and Elinor Ochs (eds.). 1986. *Language Socialization Across Cultures.* Cambridge: Cambridge University Press.

Stairs, Arlene. 1992. "Self-Image, World-Image: Speculations on Identity from Experiences with Inuit." *Ethos* 20:116–126.

Szasz, Thomas S. 1961. *The Myth of Mental Illness: Foundations of a Theory of Personal Conduct.* New York: Dell.

Wallace, Anthony F. C. 1961. *Culture and Personality.* New York: Random House.

Washburne, Heluiz, and Anauta. 1940. *Land of the Good Shadows: The Life Story of Anauta, an Eskimo Woman.* New York: John Day.

Wellman, Henry M. 1990. *The Child's Theory of Mind.* Cambridge: Bradford Books, MIT Press.

Wentworth, William M. 1980. *Context and Understanding: An Inquiry into Socialization Theory.* New York: Elsevier.

Whorf, Benjamin Lee. 1956. *Language, Thought, and Reality: Selected Writings of Benjamin Lee Whorf.* Edited by John B. Carroll. Cambridge: Technology Press of MIT; New York: John Wiley and Sons; London: Chapman and Hall.

Winnicott, D. W. 1965. *The Maturational Processes and the Facilitating Environment.* New York: International Universities Press.

———. 1971. *Playing and Reality.* London: Tavistock.